Also in the Variorum Collected Studies Series:

DONALD R. KELLEY *(Reprint)*
History, Law and the Human Sciences
Medieval and Renaissance Perspectives

RICHARD KAY
Councils and Clerical Culture in the Medieval West

BRIAN TIERNEY
Rights, Laws and the Infallibility in Medieval Thought

BRIAN TIERNEY
Church Law and Constitutional Thought in the Middle Ages

ROBERT FEENSTRA
Legal Scholarship and Doctrines of Private Law, 13th–18th Centuries

KATHERINE FISCHER DREW
Law and Society in Early Medieval Europe

CARY J. NEDERMAN
Medieval Aristotelianism and its Limits
Classical Traditions in Moral and Political Philosophy,
12th–15th Centuries

STEPHAN KUTTNER *(Reprint)*
The History of Ideas and Doctrines of Canon Law in the Middle Ages

CHARLES B. SCHMITT (Ed. Charles Webster)
Reappraisals in Renaissance Thought

GABRIEL NUCHELMANS (Ed. E.P. Bos)
Studies on the History of Logic and Semantics

LEWIS W. SPITZ
The Reformation: Education and History

LEWIS W. SPITZ
Luther and German Humanism

VARIORUM COLLECTED STUDIES SERIES

The Writing of History and the Study of Law

Professor Donald R. Kelley

Donald R. Kelley

The Writing of History and the Study of Law

VARIORUM
1997

Published by VARIORUM
Ashgate Publishing Limited
Gower House, Croft Road,
Aldershot, Hampshire GU11 3HR
Great Britain

Ashgate Publishing Company
Old Post Road,
Brookfield, Vermont 05036
USA

ISBN 0-86078-639-0

British Library CIP Data

Kelley, Donald R. (Donald Reed), 1931– .
The Writing of History and the Study of Law.
(Variorum Collected Studies Series; CS576).
1. Historiography. 2. History–Study and teaching.
3. Law–History.
I. Title.
907

US Library of Congress CIP Data

The Writing of History and the Study of Law / Donald R. Kelley.
p. cm. – (Variorum Collected Studies Series; CS576).
1. Law–Philosophy. 2. Law–Study and teaching.
3. Historiography. I. Kelley, Donald R., 1931– .
II. Series: Collected Studies; CS576.
K230. K42W75 1997 97–7874
340'.1–dc20 CIP

The paper used in this publication meets the minimum requirements of the American National Standard for Information Sciences – Permanance of Paper for Printed Library Materials, ANSI Z39.48–1984. ∞ TM

Printed by Galliard (Printers) Ltd., Great Yarmouth, Norfolk, Great Britain.

COLLECTED STUDIES SERIES C576

CONTENTS

PART TWO: MODERN HISTORY

PART THREE: HISTORY AND THE LAW

This volume contains x + 348 pages

INTRODUCTION

This second selection of articles continues the exploration of some of the same terrain covered in my *History, Law and the Human Sciences* (Variorum, 1981), likewise taking the study of history as a starting point; extending explorations into adjacent fields of legal, political, and social thought; and confronting some of the larger questions of the modern human sciences. In the earlier volume Renaissance humanism occupied a central position, though modified by my growing appreciation of medieval carry-overs and of later aspects of the tradition of European scholarship, while the essays in this volume are the result of the centrifugal force of curiosity leading me increasingly away from historical scholarship narrowly conceived to larger issues of intellectual, cultural, and political history.

From the beginning my interests have focussed on phenomena of intellectual continuity and revival – and in a general sense (to invoke a much used and abused term) 'historicism'. For me, however, this is a historicism neither of the 'new' nor of the pejoratively labelled 'old' variety, but rather that associated with the retrospective interpretation of historical testimony and evidence, texts and records, which now goes by the name (another much used and abused term) of hermeneutics. How humanity, and not only intellectual humanity, has viewed, judged, employed, exploited, criticized, and/or rejected the putative 'Past', as it can be understood from particular points of view and inferred from largely written records and residues, and also how it has theorized about these activities – these have been the main questions underlying these essays.

There are many ways of construing a bygone past: as myth, as revered tradition, as cultural heritage, as national genealogy, as human burden, as a structured process whose patterns can be made intelligible, as 'one damn thing after another', etc., etc. Personally, I do not believe in a single hypostasized Past – which is to say that I accept all the above (except, perhaps, for the 'structured process') as plausible points of view for plausible stories – for informed interpretations – determinable from the words of earlier actors and authors. These essays represent further mappings and soundings inquiring into the writing of history and its various cultural transformations and applications from the point of view of the modern human sciences, which aspire to give meaningful expression to the results of historical study.

The first paper is a broad survey of European historiography in the

Renaissance, while the next four treat ideological and confessional aspects of historical writing and controversy in the Protestant Reformation: history employed to enhance German culture through Tacitean and proto-national antiquities and myths; to legitimate the Lutheran party, in the commissioned work of Sleidan, through a broad study of the religious and political history of early modern Europe; to associate the Huguenot victims of Catholic tyranny with a Great Tradition of martyrs going back to the primitive church; and (in the case of the quondam Huguenot La Popelinière) to raise the study of history above such confessional controversy to the level of human wisdom. The last essay in this section suggests some of the larger effects of history as a way of reorganizing the arts and sciences reinstituted by the revival of learning.

The four essays of the next section consider historiography in the Romantic and Victorian periods: French Romantic history, in the wake of and in reaction to, the Revolution, reestablishing ties with old-regime legal traditions; German Romantic history rehabilitating myth and applying it likewise to the enhancement of the national heritage; a Scottish pioneer in the writing of intellectual history; and the 'very old' Marx (counterbalancing the 'very young Marx', emerging disillusioned from the legal tradition, considered in an essay in my previous volume), a sadder but wiser Marx discovering cultural anthropology and the larger context of historical development beyond the parochial economic model of 'middle Marx' (*Das Kapital*, etc.).

Essays eleven through fourteen (which are related to my book on *The Human Measure: Western Social Thought and the Legal Tradition* [Harvard, 1990]) take up the legal tradition and its interpretation in relation to social and cultural as well as historical thought: the intellectual significance of custom in its perennial struggles with natural law (the law of 'first' nature) and the written law of the modern State; the hermeneutical dimension of the Roman legal tradition and its modern continuations as a countervailing force to legislative sovereignty; the image of the lawyer as the ideal scholar and man of action; and the intellectual, juridical, and ideological continuity formed by the French *hommes de loi* before, during, and after the French Revolution.

History, though it affects to recapture a departed past, is a practice that is always carried on in the present; and in reviewing these essays I am always struck how very past, now, are the 'presents' in which they were originally written. In this present I hardly recognize their author, though I do recognize some of his errors and misjudgments. However, these flaws are part of an effort which still seems to me worthwhile and whose continuity and value I continue to sense and to learn and write about.

DONALD R. KELLEY

Rutgers University
December 1996

ACKNOWLEDGEMENTS

Grateful acknowledgement is made to the following persons, journals, institutions and publishers for their kind permission to reproduce the studies included in this volume: The University of Pennsylvania Press, Philadelphia, PA (for studies I and XI); Princeton University Press, Princeton, NJ (II); The University of Chicago Press, Chicago, IL (III); The American Historical Association, Washington, DC (V); Kluwer Academic Publishers, Dordrecht (VI); Wesleyan University, Middletown, CT (VII); Syracuse University Press, Syracuse, NY (VIII); Edoardo Tortarolo, Editor of *Storia della Storiografia*, Turin (IX); *The Journal of the History of Ideas*, New Brunswick, NJ (X); Cambridge University Press, Cambridge (XII); The Warburg Institute, London (XIII); The University of Rochester, Rochester, NY (XIV).

PUBLISHER'S NOTE

The articles in this volume, as in all others in the Collected Studies Series, have not been given a new, continuous pagination. In order to avoid confusion, and to facilitate their use where these same studies have been referred to elsewhere, the original pagination has been maintained wherever possible.

Each article has been given a Roman number in order of appearance, as listed in the Contents. This number is repeated on each page and is quoted in the index entries.

I

HUMANISM AND HISTORY

HISTORY EMERGING FROM HUMANISM IS ACTUALLY MY THEME, for as Eugenio Garin has observed, "The modern conception of history appeared on the terrain of humanist 'philology' at just the point where 'consciousness' of the 'novelty' of humanism arose."[1] The "Renaissance" itself reflected a new perspective and awareness of a "middle age" between antiquity and modernity, while humanism raised history to the level of a liberal art, that is, one of the *studia humanitatis*. History also had important links with the other four of these humanities. Along with "method" it represented one of the two parts of the art of grammar, and indeeed "historical sense" (*sensus historicus*) was equivalent to literal or grammatical as distinguished from figurative interpretation. With rhetoric history had even closer ties, since it was likewise devoted to concrete, causal, and didactic description (adding only the further criterion of truth); and as "philosophy teaching by example" it could also be seen as a branch of moral philosophy. History was of course normally contrasted with poetry; but there was a historical connection, since many Renaissance authors came to believe that history had originally emerged from poetic forms. In these and other ways the study of history illustrated and conformed to the "encyclopedic" aspirations of Renaissance humanism and especially of that scholarly aspect of humanism called philology.

This concept has become not only commonplace but perhaps also too commonplace, for in some ways it reflects the rhetorical hyperbole of humanists more than the historical circumstance that the much-deprecated "middle age" before the fourteenth century revival had its own sense of "history" both as a form of thought and as a literary genre. Medieval authors carefully distinguished between annals, chronicles, and history; had their own ideas of historical truth, which they distinguished from prophecy as well as from fable and poetry; and developed their own methods of investigation, authentication, and criticism. They also had sophisticated notions of "tradition" and of cultural change (for example, under the guise of "reformation," "renovation," the "translation of Empire and of learning," of periodization, and even of anachronism). Nor were they in a sense unaware of the "humanist" values of historical study.

"History," wrote Henry of Huntingdon in the twelfth century, "is the major mark of distinction between rational beings and brutes."[2]

* * *

Yet it remains true that no authors before the fourteenth century displayed the self-conscious literary posturing and critical nostalgia characteristic of Petrarch, who is as seminal a figure in the humanist conception of history, as of philology in general. "Among the many subjects that interested me I dwelt especially upon antiquity," he wrote, "for our own age has always repelled me, so that, had it not been for the love of those dear to me, I should have been born in any other period than our own. In order to forget my own time, I have continually striven to place my self in spirit in other ages."[3] And so indeed he did in his famous letters to Cicero, Quintilian, Varro, Livy, and Homer (not to mention Cola di Rienzo). This feigned correspondence is filled with a curious combination of excitement (at contact with their manuscript remains) and melancholy (at the destruction wrought by time to their reputations as well as to their works). How "mangled and mutilated" was the copy of Quintilian's *Institutes of Oratory* that came into Petrarch's hands! "I recognize therein the hand of time—the destroyer of all things," he lamented, from "the land of the living . . . on the very first day of our becoming acquainted"—that is, his discovery of the manuscript—which, to show the vividness of Petrarch's sense of history, was "on the 7th of December, in the 1350th year of him whom thy master [Augustus] preferred to persecute rather than to profess."[4] And to Livy he wrote: "I should wish (if it were permitted from on high) either that I had been born in thine age or thou in ours. . . . As I read I seem to be living in the midst of [Scipio, Brutus, Cato, Nero, and others] not with the thievish company of today, among whom I was born under an evil star." Cicero was his chosen model, though Petrarch deplored the activism that had distracted Cicero from his literary pursuits. It was indeed Petrarch's discovery of Cicero's letters to Atticus that had inspired his imaginary correspondence with the ancients—symbolizing in his own very personal way one of the tasks of humanism from that time on.

Behind this sentimental pose Petrarch was in fact capable of impressive historical criticism, perhaps best illustrated in his exposure of a forged Austrian donation, allegedly made by Caesar to the Habsburgs but filled with a variety of ludicrous anachronisms, including ignorance of Caesar's style (always third person, for example) and of the Roman calendar.[5] To historical writing as such Petrarch's contributions were marginal, but again he showed an almost unprecedented sense of the special demands of historical study, which he set apart not only from mere chronicle but also from disputatious scholasticism, which he abhorred in any case. As he remarked in the preface to his *De viris illustribus,* "I am neither the peacemaker among conflicting historians nor the collector of every minute fact; but rather, I am the copier of those whose verisimilitude or greater authority demands that they be given great credence."[6] He registered his particular approval of Cicero's "first law of history," which was to tell the truth and, what is more, the whole truth, although he added that for didactic purposes his Lives of the ancients were highly selective and artful. Other exhibitions of Petrarch's historical skills include his *Rerum memorandum libri IV,* his epic poem *Africa,* and his critical notes on the text of Livy. What Petrarch accomplished for history in general was to establish Latin antiquity as a cultural and political ideal and to make it an object of historical study rather than the living but sadly degenerate tradition it had been for Dante: "What is all history but the praise of Rome?"[7]

On such grounds Petrarch created not only a scholarly tradition but also a legend—as the first (*il primo,* Leonardo Bruni called him) to open the way to a true understanding of history. Aside from Boccaccio, Coluccio Salutati was the first Petrarchist in this sense, and he continued to emphasize the central place of history in political as well as ethical terms. Than history, he wrote, "nothing is more elegant, . . . nothing more capable of moving while delighting the spirit."[8] This refrain was continued by Bruni, who was Salutati's successor as Florentine chancellor as well as champion of good letters, which he expanded by his pioneering study of Greek authors. "First among such studies I place history," he declared, ". . . for it is our duty to understand the origins of our own history and its development, and the achievements of Peoples and Kings." The aim of such study, he added, was both to enlarge political foresight and to draw moral examples. "Thus," he concluded, "history renders us both wiser and more moderate."[9]

Bruni established the model of humanist historiography in his *Historia florentini populi,* which occupied him from at least 1416 until his death in 1444. If his literary inspiration came from Livy and Thucydides, his perspective was more immediately fashioned in the crucible of recent Florentine experience, especially the long conflict with Milan and the attendant "crisis" of the early fifteenth century, which reinforced his republican commitments and led him beyond the largely moral preoccupations of Petrarch to the social and political concerns associated with what has been called "civic humanism." Following Salutati (who had made his own discovery of Cicero's familiar letters), Bruni praised Cicero precisely as one who illustrated the ideal of a life at once active and contemplative. Bruni also embraced the Ciceronian view of history as a repository of lessons (*plena exemplorum historia*) to be memorialized and imitated or avoided. As he wrote in the preface to his masterwork: "History . . . involves at the same time a long continuous narrative, causal explanation of each particular event, and appropriately placed judgments on certain issues."[10] The public good and great deeds of the Florentine past had hitherto been neglected, Bruni continued; "I have decided, therefore, to write the known history of this city, not only for my own time but for earlier ages as far as they can be studied." In Livian style, then, he began *ab urbe condita* ("from the founding of the city"), except that he displayed a characteristic humanistic impatience with such "fables" as those of Trojan origins and Carolingian restoration. According to Bruni, Florence had been an Etruscan settlement and later a military colony under Sulla—a thesis that satisfied the demands both of historical criticism and of republican ideology.

Having disposed of the crucial problem of origins, Bruni went on to describe the loss of both civil liberty and classical literature, as Cicero's republic was replaced by Caesar's empire and as the empire itself collapsed under pressures of invading barbarians and usurping popes. His sources included classical authors and medieval chroniclers such as Orosius, Paul the Deacon, and especially Bruni's Florentine predecessors, the brothers Villani and Goro Dati; but in keeping with his theory of translation, that Ciceronian Latin provided the most complete expression of reality, he transmuted and in a way homogenized his uneven and disparate authorities in a classicist-rhetorical solvent.[11] In keeping with Ciceronian convention, too, he devoted particular attention to individual psychology, often presenting his interpretation of motives and policies through the ancient devices of orations or dialogues. Yet throughout this fusion of classical form and medieval substance his theme remained the rise of Florence to greatness, which is to say republican liberty and humanist culture—and of course military success.

Medieval darkness descended on the Roman–Florentine tradition with the fall of the western empire in 476, and there were no glimmers of light until after the defeat of the Lombards in 774. "From the time when the liberty of the Italian people was recovered," Bruni wrote in his biography of Petrarch (referring to this event), "the cities of Tuscany and elsewhere began to revive, and to take up classical studies, and somewhat to refine the coarse style," especially from the time of Dante. It was in this social and political context that Petrarch, through his recovery of Cicero, could become "the first . . . to restore to light the ancient elegance of style, which was lost and dead."[12] It was in this context, too, that Bruni expanded Petrarchan self-understanding to include the political ideals and historical perspective of civic humanism. Florentine "liberty" and "virtue" (*virtus*, in a sense not far removed from Machiavellian *virtù*) did not survive the century, but Brunian history, as the chief teacher of prudence, practical wisdom, was preserved in the tradition of humanist historiography from Bruni to Machiavelli and beyond.

In terms of both the art of history and what has been called "the myth of Florence"[13] Bruni's work was an inspiration to later generations. Among practitioners of Brunian history were two of his successors in the chancery, Poggio Bracciolini and Bartolomeo della Scala, and various vernacular historians, including Francesco Guicciardini and Scipione Ammirato as well as Machiavelli. Poggio was a great humanist scholar in his own right; and his *Historiae florentini populi,* a continuation of Bruni's but narrower in scope, was a relatively minor work, assembled in the last years of his life (1455–59). While Bruni modeled his book on Livy, Poggio chose rather to follow the lead of Sallust; and his concern was largely with military and diplomatic affairs from the mid-fourteenth century. He also devoted considerable attention to psychological factors, especially anger and the drive for power, and likewise emphasized the didactic value of his work. Less successful was the *Historia florentinorum* of Scala, who began again with origins but who had not even reached the fourteenth century before his death in 1497. Other products of the Florentine school included a history of the First Crusade by Benedetto Accolti, another Florentine chancellor (1458–64); a history of Pisa by Giannozzo Manetti; several works by Matteo Palmieri; a history of the Italian wars and another on ancient Rome by Bernardo Rucellai; and others. But none of these works before the time of Machiavelli and Guicciardini surpassed, and few equaled, the standard set by Bruni.

* * *

In the course of the fifteenth century this new style of historiography—erudite, eloquent, elitist—attracted a growing number of practitioners outside of Florence. It also attracted a growing audience through the new art of printing, which (providentially, to the humanists' way of thinking) appeared just in time to carry their cultural message.[14] Among the most distinguished were two historians of Venice, Bernardo Giustiniani (1408–1489) and Marcantonio Coccio (known as Sabellico, ca. 1436–1506), who during the 1480s both wrote histories of the Serenissima, again *ab urbe condita* in a Livian and Brunian fashion, though without the same critical ability. Giustiniani had the characteristic humanist fascination with origins but remained satisfied with the old Trojan theory combined with the view, taken by Sabellico as well, that the *prisci Veneti* came from Gaul. Yet in political terms he regarded Venice as heir of the Roman Empire; and indeed he described Venetian history as a synthesis of those two concepts which Florentines assumed to be opposed—*imperium* and *libertas*—a balance maintained by an ancient and continuous tradition of nobility and institutional order. Sabellico, a student of Pomponio Leto and an admirer of Flavio Biondo, was more successful, and indeed his history had virtually official status. Florence's longtime rival Milan also found a number of scholars to celebrate its ancient splendors and modern successes, including Bernardino Corio's *Patria historia* (1509), a humanist effort despite its vernacular form; and so did the Kingdom of Naples, whose most notable historians were Giovanni Pontano and Lorenzo Valla. This fashion in historiography was followed with varying degrees of fidelity and success by several of the smaller Italian states, including Genoa, Siena, Mantua, and Ferrara.

The proliferation and publication of such books and their classical models in the late fifteenth century testify to the popularity of humanist historical writing but only indirectly to the increasing depth and breadth of historical studies in general. For it was the work not of official historiographers, publicists, or local antiquarians but of a few unconventional scholars eager, in the spirit of Petrarch, to explore new areas or to apply new methods. The vision of history that was emerging a century after Petrarch's death was transformed by several factors: discoveries of classical manuscripts by Poggio and others and consequent new influences, such as those of Tacitus and Polybius; accumulating labors in archaeology, topography, and related fields, such as the history of language, literature, art, law, and institutions; the central place given to history by educators like Guarino and Vittorino da Feltre; and especially the techniques of historical, "grammatical," and conjectural criticism that lay at the roots of the great western tradition of "philology" and historical science.[15] The continuity of this tradition is neatly illustrated by a manuscript of Livy, which was successively examined and emended by Petrarch and Lorenzo Valla, whose criticisms, declarations, and general perspective provided a model for generations of scholars concerned with historical reconstruction and expression.[16]

From several angles Lorenzo Valla appears to be the dominant figure of fifteenth-century historical studies, although his contribution to historiography was modest and flawed. Valla led assaults on the past from various directions, his efforts including critical notes on the New Testament as well as on Livy, analyses of the texts of classical Roman law (the "fathers of jurisprudence," Petrarch had called these authors), translations of Herodotus and Thucydides, and especially his writings on the Latin language, representing the main thrust of his attempt to restore *Romanitas*—ancient civilization as a whole—again exhibiting the Petrarchan combination of aesthetic and historical motives, of *elegantia* and *philologia*. Valla's basic ideological theme was that, through Latin language and civil law, the Romanist tradition he represented still ruled: although political power had vanished, "yet we reign still, by this more splendid sovereignty, in a great part of the world."[17] Of course the barbarians continued to threaten, and Valla provided both a defense against the enemies of good letters and an implicit justification for historical scholarship in his *Disputationes dialecticae,* which was a humanist critique of degenerate Aristotelian philosophy. In general the effect of Valla's argument was to reject the inhuman categories of scholasticism (predicaments, transcendentals, and the rest) in favor of those of ordinary language (*usus hominum*), that is to say the "historical sense" of grammar and the "elegance" of rhetoric, which was his own "profession."

It was essentially this train of thought that led Valla to contradict Aristotle's commonly accepted judgment that history was inferior to—that is, less philosophical than—poetry. "History is more robust than poetry," Valla wrote, "because it is more truthful. It is oriented not toward abstraction but toward concrete truth, . . . teaching by example"; and he repeated the maxim of Cicero that "without history one remains always a child."[18] Valla's own most famous and most exemplary contribution to historical truth was surely his declamation against the Donation of Constantine, which was at once a critique of a particular canonist forgery (made on historical and philological as well as legal grounds) and a general attack on papal tradition—"not only against the dead," as he put it, "but the living also . . . and the authorities."[19] The only "authority" to Valla was that of "antiquity" as a whole, and even that only as interpreted by philological experts. What gives Valla a central place in the history of history in general is not his somewhat commonplace *Historiarum Ferdinandi regis Aragoniae libri tres* or even his polemical exchanges with Bartolomeo Facio about the nature of history, but rather his efforts at textual criticism, most notably his historical notes on the New Testament, his philological study of Roman law, and his critique of ecclesiastical tradition, which had a powerful impact on Protestant scholarship and perspective.

The major figure in humanist historiography before Guicciardini was surely Flavio Biondo (1392–1463), who to a remarkable degree combined the best qualities of Bruni and Valla with Livian narrative and Varronian erudition. Inclining toward the latter was his *Roma instaurata* (1443–46), devoted to the topography of ancient Rome and to the monuments of the Christian city as well; his *Italia illustrata* (1448–53), a geographical and historical survey of the fourteen regions of the peninsula based on extensive travel and observation; and his *Roma triumphans* (1452–59), a ground-breaking study of ancient institutions dedicated to his fellow historian Aeneas Silvius Piccolomini and including a short essay on legal history, *De militia et jurisprudentia*. In discussing the body of the city, he explained, one should not neglect its soul, that is to say its system of laws—like history itself a comprehensive reflection of human, or national, wisdom.[20] But Biondo's major work was his magisterial *Historiarum ab inclinatio romanorum imperii decades,* perhaps the most influential view of postclassical and medieval European history before its most famous descendant, the perhaps derivatively entitled *Decline and Fall of the Roman Empire* by Edward Gibbon, who likewise found his inspiration among the Roman ruins.

Biondo's book purported to survey the entire sweep of medieval European history—that *medium aevum* which Petrarch had perceived and the next century named—starting with the invasion of Rome by the Goths in 410.[21] He began, in other words, with that crisis of late antiquity which had inspired Augustine's *City of God* and the historiographical supplement by Orosius; and while Biondo could attain neither the depths of Augustine's insights nor the breadth of Orosius's geographical vision, he did pursue in unprecedented detail Bruni's theme of the collapse and revival of the Roman tradition. The work divides into four "decades" of books, the first reaching to the beginning of the Carolingian Empire, the second to 1410 (thousandth anniversary of the sack of Rome), the third to 1439, and the last, containing only two books, to 1441, the sections on his own century having been composed first. Neither focus nor subject is consistent, but the overall theme is clear: the replacement of the declining pagan *respublica* by the emergent *orbis christianus,* and of the caesars by Christ as *imperator;* and it is reflected in his system of dating, which changes significantly from *ab inclinatione imperii* to *anno Domini.* His horizons are Europewide, and he has a more coherent view of Italy as a community of cities, but his remarks about areas outside are scattered and increasingly infrequent, especially concerning his own age. To some extent this restriction may have been the result of his gloomy view of *praesens tempus,* especially after the outbreak of the Great Schism in 1378, but partly it was his inability to master the depressing pattern of interstate conflict in the fifteenth century and the wars that dominated his narrative.

Yet Biondo made an impressive effort to utilize an extraordinary range of sources (more than fifty), including not only familiar medieval chronicles but also writings (especially letters) of Dante and Petrarch, papal privileges and registers, canon law and of course archaeological and epigraphic material; and he tried to discuss cultural as well as political and military affairs. He tried also, however fitfully and awkwardly, to achieve a Ciceronian style; and perhaps most importantly he displayed a political point of view that gave direction as well as distinctiveness to his narrative. He had positive things to say about the new urban growth of northern Italy as well as the ancient empire. The principal civilizing mission he followed, however, was neither Bruni's civic humanism nor the imperialism of Bruni's Milanese and Venetian counterparts; rather, like Valla in his last years, it was that of the Roman church and so, unfashionably, of medieval tradition.

There were other medievalists who owed less to the humanist movement. One was Bartolomeo Sacchi (Platina), although his *Lives of the Popes,* extending to the pontificate of Paul II, was ostensibly aimed at "urging men to prudence, fortitude, modesty, and all the other human virtues."[22] The book was filled with enough scandalous revelations to be even more influential in the next century, through the Protestant adaptation of Robert Barnes as well as the edition and continuation by Onufrio Panvinio. Another genre was the universal world chronicle, which originated with Eusebius and Jerome and which also received new life in the hands of Protestants in the sixteenth century. Fifteenth-century collections having at least some connection with humanism included the world chronicle of St. Antonino of Florence, the *Enneades* of Sabellico, and to some extent the German chronicle of Hartmann Schedel, all of which had recourse to the old Augustinian (and Orosian) pattern of six ages and Four World Monarchies. Perhaps the most popular of all such attempts to write history not *ab urbe* but *ab orbe condito* was the *Supplementum chronicarum* of Jacopo Filippo of Bergamo, though among Protestants the *Chronicon carionis* was most authoritative, especially after receiving the humanist and Lutheran endorsement of Philipp Melanchthon.[23]

One of the most famous products of the Roman tradition, though it belongs to the category of contemporary history or memoirs, was the *Commentarii* of Biondo's friend Aeneas Silvius Piccolomini, humanist, diplomat, and (during the period covered by this work, 1458–64) Pope Pius II.[24] Aeneas Silvius was contentious, a bit vain and eccentric in a fashion not unlike that of Petrarch, with whom he also shared the humanist obsession with fame as a literary form of immortality. Drawing on a lifetime of travel and diplomatic experience, Pius II dealt with a variety of political matters, ranging from the Italian scene to France and the empire to the problem of the crusade; but the papacy remained the most constant focus, his own omnivorous interests the basis of selection, and a vivid and highly personal style the mode of discourse. Humanist attitudes were displayed prominently in this work and others, notably his abridgment of Biondo's *Decades,* his history of Bohemia and of Emperor Frederick III, and a famous letter on Germany that established an important link between Italian and northern humanism.

Related to, though not fully integrated with, humanist historiography was the work of "antiquarians," who went beyond the literary sources and methods of the Brunian school. Their motto was perhaps best expressed in the verse of Poliziano about

> the wonderful faith of history reborn,
> the wonderful second dawning of Rome.[25]

Ciriaco d'Ancona was one of the first to practice the art of *antiquitates* in order "not only to raise from the depths monuments which have been destroyed, but also to bring the names of cities back into the light."[26] Epigraphy had been born in the age of Petrarch, perhaps most notably with the commentary by his sometime friend Cola di Rienzo on the Capitoline inscription of the ancient *lex regia;* and it was developed further by Biondo and his sixteenth-century disciples, including Alessandro d'Alessandro, Carlo Sigonio, Onufrio Panvinio, and Fulvio Orsini. Numismatics was another embryonic humanist discipline, studied in a literary fashion by Guillaume Budé and more technically by Enea Vico, who unearthed coins of formerly unknown Roman emperors. In the period of the Counter-Reformation, Christian antiquity likewise was subjected to archaeological study according to the attitudes and methods of humanism.[27]

Most significant in the convergence of conventional history and antiquities was the study of Roman law, especially pursued through the examination of the famous Florentine manuscript of Justinian's Digest by such "grammarians" as Angelo Poliziano, Alessandro d'Alessandro, Lodovico Bolognini, Pietro Crinito, Budé, and Antonio Agustín.[28] The central figure in the emergence of "legal humanism" was Andrea Alciato, whose disciples at the University of Bourges formed a school (the so-called *mos gallicus iuris docendi*) on the basis of his literary and historical approach. Commentaries by Alciato, Budé, Ulrich Zasius, and others on the Digest title *De origine iuris* led to more systematic investigation of legal history, including eventually the whole European legal tradition arising and diverging from Roman law as well as pre-Justinianian law going back to the Twelve Tables. The reconstruction of legal antiquity was carried on by a distinguished line of humanist scholars, including Johann Oldendorp, Carlo Sigonio, Bishop Jean du Tillet, François Baudouin, and especially Jacques Cujas. It should be added that analogous humanist assaults were directed at canon and feudal law, the sources of which were also incorporated into historiography, thus helping to give it a social and cultural dimension that it "classically" lacked.

* * *

Like the classicist movement itself, the new-style historiography emerged relatively late in Germany, and it was informed by competitive and often invidious motives. The first scholar to address the subject was Peter Luder, self-styled *poeta et historiographus* who taught at Heidelberg in 1456; and about the same time the effects of humanism could be seen in the old chronicle tradition, notably in Sigismund's work on Augsburg, fabulous and uncritical as it was. Perhaps most important for a critical view of German history and certainly for the rehabilitation of German culture was the contemporaneous discovery of Tacitus's *Germania*, which was passed on to German humanism by Aeneas Silvius, whose own book of that title was also seminal.[29] Tacitus had emphasized the indigenous, unmixed character of the Germans, the purity of their morals and economic relations, and the liberal and democratic nature of their political institutions; and these perceptions provided the ideological base for German historiography as well as a vehicle for critical scholarship and for the exposure of legends, such as that of Trojan origins. Important in another way was Biondo's *Italia illustrata*, both as a model of historical-topographical writing and as a challenge to German national sentiment. In response to it Conrad Celtis and some of his colleagues labored to produce a *Germania illustrata* to justify and to magnify their own tradition. "Let us be ashamed, noble gentlemen," he declared, "that certain modern historians (who, publishing new *Decades*, boast that they have equalled the ancient Roman Empire) should speak of our most famous leaders merely as 'the barbarians' . . . in order to . . . disparage the reputation of us Germans."[30]

Contemporaneously, Jacob Wimpheling lamented that the Germans had not joined the Romans, Venetians, English, French, and other peoples in producing a national history, and in 1505 he published the first humanist history of Germany. Wimpheling's *Epitome rerum germanicarum usque ad nostra tempora* was so dominated by Celtis's counsel that it might seem to be closer to Bruni's *Laudatio Florentinae urbis* than to his history of Florence, except for its adherence to chronological order. He cast Germanic origins back to Homeric times, thus declaring them to antedate Rome herself. He went on to celebrate notable events and personalities, including Ariovistus, "first king of the Germans," various victories over foreign kings, and the fortunes of the German empire from Charlemagne; and he ended with a survey of German cultural triumphs, especially the invention of printing.[31] More critical, certainly more in line with Italian models, were the pioneering books of Albert Krantz on the Saxons and the Wends, which also took up the problem of Germanic origins, dismissing again Trojan "fables," though retaining others.[32] Influenced by Biondo and Aeneas Silvius, he also published studies of Scandanavian history. Very soon, of course, German humanist historiography was swept up in the maelstrom of the Reformation, although historical writing in humanist style continued to flourish, most notably in Johann Aventine's writings on Bavarian history and Beatus Rhenanus's *Rerum germanicarum libri tres* (1531), which was fully abreast of modern scholarship and critical methods.[33] While celebrating German antiquity and some of its myths—"the German people have always lived in total liberty," he declared proudly—he rejected the popular forgery of Annius of Viterbo that would push it back to the offspring of Noah.

In France the new historiography also arrived rather late, and it was even more closely associated with the old chronicle tradition, powerfully represented in the fifteenth century by Thomas Basin, Georges Chastellain, Philippe de Comines (or Commynes), and the ongoing *Grandes chroniques* of Saint-Denis. The mythico-historical link between French and classical culture was suggested in the famous formula, the "translation of learning" (the *translatio studii*) accompanying the *translatio imperii* of Charlemagne as king of the "French," which the Saint-Denis chronicles cited almost verbatim from Chrétien de Troyes: "in the city of Athens philosophy formerly resided, and in Greece the glory of chivalry. Then from Greece it passed from Rome, from Rome to France. God grant that it be kept there to the glory of His name, which lives and rules throughout eternity."[35] This general theme, and even such supporting anecdotes as the founding of the University of Paris by Charlemagne, were retained by humanist authors, though they displayed skepticism about grosser legends, such as that of Trojan origins.

Of the new history in France the first example was Robert Gaguin, a former member of the circle of Guillaume Fichet, who had been responsible for the introduction of printing into France in 1470 and who had enjoyed a long career as diplomat and scholar.[36] Like Wimpheling a decade later, Gaguin lamented his countrymen's neglect of their history and proposed to remedy the situation through his own *Compendium super francorum gestis* of 1495, prefaced by a letter by Erasmus (his first published work) likening Gaguin to Livy. In fact, Gaguin's book was a hastily assembled narrative derived mostly from the chronicles of Saint-Denis, though he dropped some of the fables (such as Charlemagne's crusade), made use of some documentary sources (such as the Pragmatic Sanction of Bourges), and of course trumpeted the basic national message, which was that neither the kings nor the culture of France was in any way inferior to Rome's. In fact his effort was already being superseded by an Italian scholar who had come to France in 1483 and had begun work on French antiquities much in the spirit of Biondo, his principal model and (though often unacknowledged) source.

Paolo Emilio, often regarded as the first official historiographer of France, in any case received official support for the project of composing a national history; and his *De rebus gestis francorum,* like Gaguin's work, was often cited as a legal authority.[37] Though basically a narrative history in Italian style, this book of "Paul-Emile" was based on extensive ethnographic, philological, and topographical investigations, venturing into the comparative study of institutions, discussion of social and religious customs, and other monographic subjects. It was the judgment of Erasmus that Paolo Emilio's work was distinguished more by its eloquence than by its accuracy, and yet it certainly marked an advance over Gaguin's book in terms both of form and of content and especially of the "scissors-and-paste" method characteristic of so many Renaissance historians (not including Biondo). Paolo Emilio's work exhibited both a wider range and a more critical use of sources; and it at least tried to present a synthesis of its materials rather than a mere assemblage of uneven sources followed singly and eclectically. Both books were popular during the sixteenth century, enjoying many editions and French translations, but it was Paolo Emilio's book that became the model and major authority and indeed furnished the official image of the French monarchy for generations. It was also the nucleus of the great tradition of vernacular historiography down to the nineteenth century.

In England Paolo Emilio's counterpart was also an Italian émigré and a still more distinguished humanist. Polydore Vergil, before arriving in England in 1502, had already shown his attachment to a historical point of view with the publication of his *De rerum inventoribus* (1499), a kind of historical encyclopedia, which also set down his conception of history.[38] For Vergil, Moses was the "inventor" of history, but the discipline itself was a wholly human enterprise, concerning the actions and deeds of men and the causes and effects thereof (*consilia, causae, dictae, factae, casus et exitus*). By 1502 he had finished the first books of his *Anglica historia* and dedicated it to Henry VII.[39] Vergil built upon a chronicle tradition as rich as the French and was perhaps more strongly affected by it than he thought, in terms not only of chronology but also of such monkish subjects as droughts, floods, harvests, and miracles. Aside from such habits, Vergil was a worthy graduate of the humanist school, priding himself on his eloquent Latin and including orations in classical style. He took a skeptical view of the problem of English origins, especially the Trojan and Arthurian legends, and indulged in numerous critical asides not only on his sources and moral lessons but also on such degenerate institutions as English universities, monasteries, and the profession of common law. The work began with a discussion of geographical context, proceeded by devoting one book to each king, and fell into large divisions of pre- and post-Conquest. Before the complete version was published in the year of Vergil's death (1555) it had become, like Paolo Emilio's, the principal authority for English history during the sixteenth century, though it also provoked some hostile reactions.

From the late fifteenth century the new Latinate historiography was Europewide, extending from Sicily and Scandinavia and from the Iberian peninsula to Russia.[40] Many contributors were ecclesiastical authors who had only superficial contacts with humanism; others enrolled very deliberately in this school, such as Juan Margarit y Pau, who devoted himself to pre-Visigothic history under the direct influence of Bruni, Biondo, and Aeneas Silvius; and Albert Krantz, who did the same for Scandinavia and Russia. Some were Italians who undertook to write of other nations, among them Antonio Bonfini and Filippo Buonaccorsi (Callimachus Experiens), who composed histories of Hungary and Poland. Humanist historians were outspoken in their contempt for medieval antecedents—the "new history," Vergil called it scornfully—and so for example Biondo could reject Geoffrey of Monmouth as outdoing "the dreams of the drunken or the feverish." Admittedly, however, such criticism was often undertaken on grounds not so much of historical truth as of the rhetorical device of critical rejection (the *topos anasceua*) or some ideological consideration such as national honor or antiquity (and so, for example, Krantz could reject the notion of Trojan origins for Swabia while accepting it for France), and the humanists were quite capable of introducing their own mythical constructs.

In general the achievement of humanist historiography down to the sixteenth century was twofold. First it was to Latinize, if not classicize, the medieval past by dissolving, as it were, its uneven and "barbaric" sources in a solvent of Neociceronian, Neolivian, or Neotacitean prose, by giving it some coherence and continuity through establishment or imputation of causal relationships, through literary devices such as orations and dialogues, and through extracting moral and political lessons from this reconstructed past. Second, it proclaimed and sometimes practiced an ideal of truth and scholarly standards—*fides et eruditio* was Erasmus's formula and *certissima philosophia* that of Alciato—which placed historical writing on a basis of secular learning rather than theological convention and random chronology.[41] These accomplishments were made, it should be further noted, in the first age of print culture; and from this circumstance arose other consequences of major significance for the study of history: the development of new methods and research tools, the beginning of cooperative scholarship and a public domain of historiography that could expand in qualitative as well as quantitative terms, the proliferation of new specializations and so-called "auxiliary sciences," the unprecedented flourishing of history as a form of popular entertainment and propaganda, and (for good or ill) the formulation of common issues to investigate and to debate.

* * *

The study of history was always shaped by contemporary political and social pressure, and never as extensively as in the early sixteenth century. As the historical perspective of Bruni had been fashioned in the "crisis of the early Italian Renaissance," so that of his intellectual descendants Machiavelli and Guicciardini was in many ways the product of the crisis—or rather the calamity—of Italy occurring in the wake of the wars set off by the French invasions of 1494 and 1498.[42] The historiographical practice, largely vernacular, of the members of this generation of '94 was directed not so much to problems of cultural provenance and pedigree but rather to the particular political predicament facing the Italian states, and especially Florence, from the last quarter of the fifteenth century. The "causes" of the Italian wars were discussed by Rucellai, Comines, and others before Guicciardini's exhaustive treatment; but of course there were many more issues attendant on this ancient question—problems of counsel, formation of policy, marshaling support, social control, constitutional management, diplomatic relations with other states, and in general a whole constellation of topics tied to what has been called the "vision of politics on the eve of the Reformation." Such was the context not only of the "calamity of Italy" but also of a new phase of humanist historiography emerging from the old tradition of so-called civic humanism.

Of this particular calamity and general crisis Niccolò Machiavelli was the most significant intellectual product, observer, and interpreter—as of what we might call the vision of history in this same period he was a pioneering and seminal exponent. The other primary source of his historical work was the classical tradition, and indeed he carried further the dual enterprise that Bruni had begun a century earlier. In *Il principe* and the *Arte della guerra* Machiavelli endorsed the humanist recommendation that history should occupy a central place in education, especially that of a prince, though his arguments were political and military rather than moral and philosophical. In his *Discorsi sopra la prima deca di Tito Livio* he tried more comprehensively to ransack ancient history and modern experience for political lessons. "Whoever considers the past and the present will readily observe that all cities and all peoples are and ever have been animated by the same desires and the same passions; so that it is easy, by diligent study of the past, to foresee what is likely to happen in the future in any republic, and to apply those remedies that were used by the ancients, or . . . to devise new ones from the similarity of the events."[43] This idea was the starting point for Machiavelli's famous "new route," which was to do for statecraft what had been done for so many other fields, that is, give it a firm historical foundation. In fact, by taking Roman history as a model or experience Machiavelli was only continuing more purposefully what Dante and Petrarch had begun, except that his aim was not to "praise" but rather to criticize and learn from Rome.

In 1520 Machiavelli seized the opportunity to write the history of his own city for the ruling Medici family. In the subsequent *Historie Fiorentine* he set himself directly in the tradition of Bruni and Poggio, though he began by complaining that, despite their exact treatment of foreign affairs, "upon the subject of civil discord and internal strifes they had been entirely silent, or had written far too briefly concerning them."[44] So it was that Machiavelli turned to the "most remarkable" subject of political dissensions and their consequences for Florentine social life and constitutional order. Following Biondo, he began with the descent of Germanic tribes into the Roman Empire and then, following Bruni, took up specifically Florentine origins; and he ended with the death of Lorenzo de' Medici in 1492 just on the threshhold of another and no less destructive wave of "barbarian" invasions. Like Bruni, Machiavelli prized above all the republican liberty of Florence; but like Biondo he was forced in his narrative to trace the decline of that liberty, especially through the interfering policies of the popes, the rise of factions, and the ruin of the nobility (hence civic capacity for self-defense) and more fundamental class conflict. Like Bruni, too, Machiavelli celebrated the superiority of republican excellence (*virtù;* Latin *virtus*), but experience along with a broader view of history had taught that republican government was the most unstable of all. This was the basic lesson of Florentine and Roman history—and the political predicament underlying Machiavelli's advice for the Prince.

We must not make a caricature of Machiavelli's view of history. He was quite aware that predictions, like policies, were never infallible and that, as he remarked in the *Discorsi,* "we never know the whole truth about the past." Yet he could find no better guide, and he did his utmost to formulate a systematic interpretation of historical change. In the history of Florence it was expressed in various general comments (not unlike those of Bruni or Comines) on political psychology, patterns of social conflict and factionalism, the conditions of political *virtù,* and trajectory of political *fortuna*. In the *Discorsi* it took the more general form of a commentary on the famous (but newly revived) Polybian theory of constitutional cycles (*anacyclosis*), in which "monarchy becomes tyranny; aristocracy degenerates into oligarchy; and the popular government lapses readily into licentiousness," all because of the weakness of human nature, especially in social groups, and an endless alteration of generations. "Such is the circle which all republics are destined to run through," Machiavelli concluded.[45] "Tend to run through," we should perhaps amend, for such unqualified naturalism really does justice neither to Machiavelli's social psychology nor certainly to his concrete appreciation of the historical process.

Guicciardini, Machiavelli's younger and politically more eminent friend, shared many of his assumptions and views. "Past events throw light upon the future," Guicciardini opined in his *Ricordi,* "because the world has always been the same as it now is. . . . Things accordingly repeat themselves, but under changed names and colors, so that it is not everyone who can recognize them."[46] Yet Guicciardini, too—though deeply disillusioned by the calamity that had victimized him and Machiavelli as well as their city—had a subtler conception of historical change and indeed criticized his colleague for his tendency to jump to conclusions. Guicciardini tried twice to write the history of Florence, but even more than Machiavelli he was a man of the generation of '94; and his masterwork, the *Storia d'Italia,* started just where Machiavelli's history ended—with the "calamity of Italy," following the death of Lorenzo de' Medici, which for Machiavelli likewise marked the beginning of Italy's ruin. Like Gibbon's, Guicciardini's theme, though cast "within living memory," was epic—"rich for its variety and extent, and full of appalling disasters, for Italy has suffered for many years every kind of calamity that may vex mortals either through the just wrath of God or through the impious and wicked actions of their fellow men."[47] It was also carried out with unprecedented breadth of vision and depth of research, especially in archival sources, including those of the Giucciardini family.

With astonishing control of massive detail and multiple story lines, Guicciardini's narrative described and analyzed the first four years of the Italian wars starting in 1494, showing the policies and ambitions of the barbarians and his countrymen's weakness and progressive loss of mastery. In this pioneering effort of national synthesis Guicciardini provided a broad range of political analyses, character sketches, and descriptions of negotiations and actions, making full use of humanist forms and conventions, including orations. Although he did not scruple to invoke supernatural signs and events to enhance the drama of the Italian calamity, his focus was always human psychology and interaction. Yet like Machiavelli he well realized that the way of the fox had in the last extremity always to yield to the way of the lion, and as he remarked about the events of the spring of 1494: "More important than the speeches of the ambassador and the replies they received were the preparations by land and sea which were being made everywhere." Violence and injustice were the real protagonists of Guicciardini's story from this point, and the lessons he drew from his observations and investigations were even more pessimistic than Machiavelli's. It is perhaps because of this lack of idealism, combined with his acumen and mastery of detailed narrative in humanist form, that Guicciardini has been judged by some as the greatest historian between Tacitus and Gibbon.[48]

Machiavelli and Guiccardini set a style—or rather, in the tradition of Thucydides, Polybius, and Tacitus, they revived a style—of analytical, political narrative that has been continuallly practiced since the sixteenth century, beginning with their own Florentine epigones, including Francesco Vettori, Filippo Nerli, Bernardo Segni, Jacopo Nardi, Benedetto Varchi, Donato Gianotti, Scipione Annunciato, and other interpreters of Florentine history in the postrepublican period. It was a form that, still under the influence of humanism, was practiced variously around Guicciardini's time by Johann Sleidan in Germany, Jacques-Auguste de Thou in France, and William Camden in England, to mention only the most distinguished. The connections between history and political science were also reinforced by other scholars, for instance by Machiavelli's likeminded French contemporary Claude de Seyssel, another product of '94.[49] Seyssel also followed a humanist impulse and believed that of all ancient literature "history is the most profitable," and one result was a series of translations of historians, including Thucydides (based on Valla's Latin version), along with his own history of Louis XII and, most famously, his *Monarchie de France,* a sort of French counterpart to Machiavelli's *Principe* with even more historical parallels, from Venetian as well as Roman history. Like Machiavelli and Guicciardini, Seyssel thought that the first aim of historical study was "to understand causes and effects," which has always been the premise of political narrative.

* * *

In the sixteenth century the "new learning" implied religious heresy as much as humanist learning; and this implication suggests another crisis—or rather "calamity"—which, though hardly noticed by Italian political historians, had even more lasting consequences. The Protestant Reformation, which orthodox critics preferred to regard as the Lutheran "scandal" and which even Machiavelli saw only as a "pretext" for monkish troublemaking, produced even more unsettling shifts of perspective, since it called into question almost the whole of Christian tradition. Under Lutheran influence history was again viewed not *ab urbe* but *ab orbe condito*, according to the old Augustinian scheme and the "four world monarchies" (Medes, Persians, Greeks, and Romans), ending with the "translation of the empire to the Germans." In his preface to Robert Barnes's (evangelical version of Platina's) *Vitae romanorum pontificum* Luther acknowledged the didactic value of historical studies, but it was Philipp Melanchthon who most effectively introduced the humanist conception into Protestant doctrine, especially in his preface to the very popular *Chronica carionis*.[50] "Without history," Melanchthon was fond of quoting from Cicero, "one remains forever a child"; and this conviction became a major premise in his educational reforms of the universities of Protestant Germany. In other Protestant confessions, including Calvinism, history was increasingly prized not only to celebrate the pedigree of "true religion," for instance in martyrologies, but also as a weapon in the endless doctrinal controversies of that age.[51]

The first great exponent of Lutheran historiography was Johann Sleidan, author of an enormously popular textbook of universal history, *De quatuor summis imperiis* (Englished a century later as *The Key to History*), and of the official history of the Lutheran Reformation. Educated as a humanist, Sleidan admired and indeed translated into Latin works of Froissart, Comines, and Seyssel; and he carried their style of political analysis into his own major work, which he privately referred to as a "history of the restored church." Epic in theme, European in scope, annalistic in method, and based on extraordinary archival researches, Sleidan's *De statu religionis et republicae Carlo Quinti Caesari commentarii* carried the dual stories of political conflict and the expansion of evangelical religion from 1517 to his death in 1556. He tried to preserve classical forms, though they were often overwhelmed by documentation and by his efforts to discuss social and ideological factors beyond the narrower focus of political historians like Guicciardini, whom he in some ways resembles. Lutheran partisanship did not prevent Sleidan from maintaining a frankness and a fidelity to Cicero's "first law of history" that many critics found excessive, and he was forced to compose an "apology" for his history, in which he proclaimed his devotion both to *vera religio* and to *vera historia*. "If mine is not true history," he wrote, "then there is no such thing as a credible political history (I except sacred histories)."[52]

In a longer perspective Lutheranism entailed a general critique of Christian tradition, like humanism beginning with an idealized antiquity, which in this case was to say the "primitive church"; and it envisaged a wholly spiritual heritage, as contrasted with the corrupt "human traditions" of the Roman church. Yet for this very reason Protestant historians were licensed to discuss human history, including that of the church, in purely secular terms. What is more, they were able to subject it to the severest sort of historical criticism, Valla himself becoming a particularly useful model. So it was that Protestant historiography, in theory as well as practice, was able to advance the cause of humanist scholarship, though not without building up its own heroic legends, as in the fabricated intellectual hagiography of Matthias Flacius Illyricus called *Catalogus testium veritatis*. Most impressive is the monumental *Centuries* assembled by Flacius and his Magdeburg colleagues, which grouped together and discussed central topics of ecclesiastical history—persecutions, doctrines, ceremonies, miracles, and politics, among others—according to commonplaces corresponding to the *loci communes* of the reformed logic of Melanchthon and other humanists and similar to the historical method being developed contemporaneously by Jean Bodin.[53] On the other side of what one historian has called the "confessional iron curtain" the great response was the equally monumental compilation by Cesare Baronio, the *Annales ecclesiastici*, which massively reasserted Catholic tradition, and did so neither *ab orbe* nor *ab urbe* but *ab Incarnatione*.

The great classic of ecclesiastical history was surely Paolo Sarpi's *Istoria del Concilio Tridentino* (1619), the "Iliad of our times" as he regarded it. Sarpi enjoyed a classical education before joining the Servites and tried to unite sacred history with humanist form.[54] As a Venetian (and critic of the Interdict of 1606) Sarpi sympathized with many goals of evangelical reformers, criticizing indulgences and indeed, in his *History of Benefices*, the corrupting effects of ecclesiastical property in general; and he admired and followed Sleidan in his writing on the sixteenth century. Supporting "reformation," he lamented the "deformation" endorsed by the Council of Trent, which "brought about the greatest corruption of the Church since the name of 'Christian' was first heard." Among more theological protests Sarpi ridiculed the Tridentine fathers for claiming the authority of the Holy Ghost for the Vulgate version when this endorsement was explicitly denied by the translator himself, St. Jerome. In dramatic and often ironic or humorous fashion he depicted the dramatic battles of the Tridentine fathers as well as the political and religious "causes" of the council, yet with the utmost respect for the virtues of historical accuracy (though this was denied and denounced voluminously by his nemesis Sforza Pallavicino). Many details he included against his own sense of relevance on the grounds that "some sharp mind will perhaps discover in [them] something important which I was not aware of."

While being used as a weapon of controversy in this age of confessional strife, history continued to be celebrated in classical style, especially through an increasingly popular sixteenth-century genre called the "art of history" (*ars historica,* analogous to the Horatian *ars poetica*), which originated in letters, educational treatises, and prefaces to historical works. In these works the emphasis was on the writing of history and its essential properties, which included elegance and form as well as truth and utility, causal analysis, and explanation in terms of times, places, circumstances, and persons.[55] These arguments were developed by a number of authors in the fifteenth century, including Guarino, Valla, Bartolomeo della Fonte, and Giovanni Pontano, before being discussed in a series of systematic treatises in the middle and later sixteenth century, beginning with Sperone Speroni in 1542 and especially with Francesco Robortello in 1548. The central issue was still whether Aristotle was right when he judged poetry to be more philosophical than history, though increasingly important was the Polybian criterion (*norma Polybiana,* in the words of Uberto Foglietta) of objective truth as well as "pragmatic" value. Valla had long before upheld the superiority of history over philosophy on these grounds, but sixteenth-century authors went further. In his contribution to the *ars historica,* for example, Francesco Patrizi argued that if the task of the philosopher was to understand causes, that of the historian was to understand both causes and effects, so he had a better grasp of the truth (*cognizione del vero*).[56] For Patrizi history was an autonomous, if a rather eclectic science.

The humanist "art of history" persisted into the seventeenth century, asking the same old questions: Is history an art or a science? What are its divisions, its standards and rules, its uses? In Italy the literary tradition was maintained, as it was in Spain. The commonplace character of this genre, unchanging into the nineteenth century and with recognizable descendants even today, can be seen in the treatise of Luis Cabrera de Córdoba devoted to "the understanding and writing of history." "I have described the importance of history and of the good historian," he writes, "the qualities he must have and those of authentic and complete history [*perfecta historia*] and how they may be acquired."[57] In the work of German methodologists such as Gerardus Vossius and Bartolomäus Keckermann the tendency was to rearrange the materials of history according to Ramist, or at least Ramoid bifurcating logic and so to shift the emphasis from the writing to the reading of history, though it must be added that "history" for these writers suggested empirical knowledge (*cognito singularium* in Keckermann's phrase) rather than understanding in temporal perspective.

In France the shift of emphasis to historical knowledge (rather than the narrative art) was even more conscpicuous, and it was much reinforced by a fruitful marriage between history and law. The "methods" of history of François Baudouin and especially Jean Bodin tried to bring together a number of classical, Christian, and modern concepts and practices—the pragmatic political history associated with Polybius and (for Bodin) Machiavelli, the universal perspective of Augustinian (and Lutheran) *historia sacra*, the developments of modern techniques of historical criticism and authentication, and especially the accommodation of geographic, institutional, and social factors associated with "legal science."[58] With Bodin and disciples like Pierre Droit de Gaillard and Henri de La Popelinière history achieved not only recognition as a science but a position "above all sciences" as the source of all human disciplines; thus it was joined to the investigation of human culture as a whole and was not merely the "new route" taken by Bodin, and Machiavelli before him, toward political science. For these authors, moreover, history implied the human rather than the physical aspect of creation—*res civiles* rather than *res naturales*, according to the distinction made in Baudouin's method of history, and civil rather than natural history in the more famous Baconian formula.[59]

More significant for the study of history than this rhetoric and theorizing were the scholarly developments of the later sixteenth century made possible by the mutual reinforcement of the humanist impulse and the new art of printing, which itself, according to Budé, was "the restitution and perpetuation of antiquity."[60] Among the most conspicuous results were the publication and correction of classical (and, increasingly, medieval) authors and collections of sources, not to speak of bibliographical aids such as Conrad Gesner's *Bibliotheca universalis* (1545), which included a topically arranged listing of histories "in general," followed by chroniclers, historiographers, antiquarians, and contributors to the genre *de viris illustribus*. Through a sort of transvaluation of classicism, philological investigations were also undertaken into the sources of medieval history; and among the fruits of this were Simon Schard's *Illustration of Ancient Germany*, concerning Tacitus and later commentaries (including works of Wimpheling, Conrad Peutinger, Celtis, and Aeneas Sylvius), and Pierre Pithou's *Annals and Histories of France*, containing works from the eighth century through the tenth. Although they were fascinated with printing, sixteenth-century scholars did not turn away from the treasures of manuscript culture. Baudouin called attention to the riches that the Vatican archives must hold for the historian, while Jean du Tillet began the systematic ransacking of the royal archives to enhance the "defense and illustration" of France already being carried on in literary ways. A work of the next century by Baldassare Bonifacio celebrated and offered a brief historical survey of the archivist tradition in general.[61]

The late sixteenth and seventeenth centuries were the heroic age, too, of modern "criticism," of that *ars critica* which aimed not only to "emend" texts through reason and erudition in the fashion of Poliziano and Budé but to bring about the "restitution" of antiquity as a whole. Among the giants of this enterprise were Isaac Casaubon, whose translation of Polybius was a major contribution to the "royal science" of politics as well as to historiography; Justus Lipsius, "professor of history and jurisprudence" at Leiden; and especially Joseph Justus Scaliger, whose great *Opus de emendatione temporum* laid the foundation for the modern science of chronology.[62] These men and their colleagues established on a solid footing the scholarly tradition culminating in the work of Mabillon, Muratori, and the *Monumenta Germaniae Historica*. If the driving force of this tradition was religious conviction, its substance continued to be the product of the humanist impulse—that science of philology whose fruits are not only too numerous to mention but also too various to be comprehended from one point of view.

* * *

In the sixteenth and seventeenth centuries latinate historiography continued to flourish in all parts of Europe, as did its vernacular imitations; and among its most renowned practitioners were medieval historians like Juan de Mariana, William Camden, and George Buchanan as well as writers with a more universal reach like Paolo Giovio and Jacques-Auguste de Thou, just to mention a few whose fame survived them. De Thou was surely the most admired and remained a model of eloquence and impartiality through the Enlightenment, gaining praise from both Voltaire and Gibbon and chosen by Dr. Johnson as a text worthy of translation despite the heroic scale of his analysis (almost five thousand folios for sixty-one years). De Thou's *Historia sui temporis* began in 1546 and covered the period of the religious wars and the aftermath in extraordinary detail and international depth in a Polybian and Tacitean style, chronologically arranged and ornamented with biographical sketches (in effect obituary notices) of notable figures.[63] The embarrassing frankness with which he treated sensitive partisan issues brought him under the threat of censorship and led him to write an apology for objective and nonpartisan narrative that included religious as well as political matters and which did not ignore the terrible evils of the age. There were other distinguished historians of de Thou's generation in France—La Popelinière, Jean de Serres, Bernard du Haillan, Nicolas Vignier, and François Belleforest among them—but none of these vernacular historians, and probably no other European historian writing in Latin, matched the influence of de Thou down to the nineteenth century.

National historians continued to follow the Livian model, especially those who were supported as court historians—royal historiographers—beginning with Paolo Emilio and a series of vernacular historians including du Haillan, de Serres, and François Eudes de Mézeray, founders of a sort of guild of the "artisans of glory," devoted to the ideological interests of the monarchy.[64] There were also other more specialized efforts to plumb the remote past—antiquarianism in the style of Biondo but aimed at resurrecting "barbarian" antiquity. The pioneering *collections pour servir à l'histoire* published by du Tillet, Pithou, Schard, and others provided not only a scholarly basis for a fuller narrative but also an ideological arsenal for works of historical interpretation, perhaps most notably in François Hotman's notorious *Francogallia,* which sought to celebrate and in a sense to ressurect the "ancient constitution of France" as his Protestant colleagues had harkened back to the ideal of the primitive church. Although Hotman opposed a supposedly purifying Germanism to a supposedly corrupt Romanism in his interpretation of the course of French history, and although he was moved by partisan (religious as well as political) motives, he was still adhering to the humanist program: back to the sources![65]

Historical studies gained breadth as well as depth and political acumen during the sixteenth century, as illustrated by the penetration of historical notions into other disciplines. A central concern originating in the humanist program was language itself, and the infiltration of historical attitudes into this field was one of the conditions for the advance of the science of philology in this period. Insights into the history of the Latin language were provided in Valla's *Elegantiae,* in Erasmus's *De copia verborum,* and Pietro Crinito's *De honesta disciplina,* among other works written in the tradition of Varro; and indeed the famous quarrels over "Ciceronianism" and the "corrupt" Latin of medieval authors presupposed a historical view of linguistic change.[66] The same interests carried over into studies of the vernaculars and inspired such efforts as those of Etienne Pasquier and Claude de Fauchet in literary history. Another incipient but recognizable genre was legal history, which emerged especially from commentaries on the Digest title "On the Origin of Civil Law." Here the pioneering work of Aymar de Rivail's *Historia juris civilis* established the pattern of Roman history by joining the primary sources of law with the Polybian cycle of change (*anacyclosis*): the *leges regiae* of the monarchical period, the *senatusconsulta* of the aristocratic period, and the *plebiscita* of the popular period before the establishment of the empire; and his *Historia juris pontificii* provided a similar survey of canon law.[67] Valentinus Foster and others continued this investigation into the medieval and modern periods. More generally, the impact of jurisprudence was to widen the vision of history to include institutional and social materials and to extend it geographically to reinforce humanist interests in universal history. "Historical studies must be placed upon a solid foundation of law, and jurisprudence must be joined in history" is the way that Baudouin expressed this enrichment of the conventional "art of history."[68] When combined also with a universal perspective, a Eusebian concern for religious matters, and a Polybian interest in pragmatic political explanation, history could become truly catholic—truly "integral and perfect."

Other areas were opened up to historical investigation and interpretation. Viewing the general progress of what he called "Design," Giorgio Vasari studied the accomplishments of Renaissance painters, sculptors, and architects and so laid the foundation of art history. Louis Le Roy, regius professor of Greek in Paris, offered sketches of the history both of philosophy and of political thought from ancient times in connection with his translations of Plato and Aristotle.[69] History itself was historicized in certain contributions to the *ars historica,* beginning with that of Bartolomeo della Fonte, including that of Bodin, and culminating in that of La Popeliniere, whose *Histoire des histoires, avec l'Idée de l'histoire accomplie* represents perhaps the most comprehensive of all humanist formulations of the "new history" of the Renaissance.[70] La Popelinière recognized a four-stage pattern in the development of historiography: first a period of "natural history," that is, oral tradition and myth; second a period of "poetic history" (anticipating the famous views of Vico); then "continuous history," including simple chronicles and annals; and finally a kind of civilized history, which added eloquence and an awareness of causation to the narration of facts—the level actually achieved by humanist historiography.

The fifth stage, envisioned by La Popelinière's *histoire accomplie,* had not yet been attained; but it was discussed by various scholars pursuing a broad cultural ideal, among them Le Roy, du Haillan, and Gaillard and of course La Popelinière himself, whose "design for a new history of the French" derived from the humanist view that "all the sciences, arts, and other human inventions originate in history," and that historians ought also to consider geography, forms of government, the crown and its various institutions and legal organization, social classes, and religion.[71] Perhaps the most serious and concrete contribution toward such a design of "perfect history" was undertaken by that "Montaigne" of history, Etienne Pasquier, whose *Recherches de la France* touched not only on legal and institutional antiquities, such as the history of universities, the Parlement, and the Gallican church, but also on art, literature, and even popular culture.[72] In this lifetime search for the "spirit" of French society and culture Pasquier was also joined by his colleague Claude de Fauchet and by Nicolas Vignier. To these scholars hardly anything was alien; and in many ways, in reach if not in grasp, they represent the fulfillment of the humanist conception of history, at least in a national context.

What this work suggests above all is that most grandiose aspect of the humanist legacy, which might be called the encyclopedic impulse. The humanist movement had begun in a sense as a celebration of the ancient *enkyklios paideia* with special emphasis on the humanities; and it was led in its mature stages to survey and to appreciate the totality of the arts and the sciences in a large historical perspective—a perspective that opened also on the future and perhaps favored the moderns over the ancients. Rudimentary examples include Polydore Vergil's *De rerum inventoribus,* which surveyed the origins and "inventors" of disciplines, and on the negative side Juan Luis Vives's *De causis corruptarum artium,* which offered skeptical critiques of the inadequacy of human disciplines, including the deceptions of history itself. More comprehensive was Christophe Milieu's *De scribenda universitatis rerum historia,* which discussed the universality of history in terms even more encyclopedic than those of Baudouin a decade later.[73] For Milieu *historia* encompassed nature but more importantly human culture, and this historical manifestation of humanity Milieu divided into three categories: *prudentia,* which included the practical or technical arts necessary for human sustenance; *principatus,* which referred to social and political organization (essentially, the history of the states); and most extensively *sapientia,* which classically meant wisdom ("the knowledge of things divine and human") but which came to imply both the "encyclopedia" of arts and sciences and "culture" in an anthropological sense (as later and more famously used by Vico), including literature (*literatura*) in a general sense including history itself.

Perhaps the most successful attempt to realize this ideal in historiographical terms was made by Le Roy, Budé's disciple and biographer. The encyclopedic vision that Budé had applied to philology, Le Roy transferred to universal history; and the result was what one scholar called "the first treatise devoted to the history of civilization."[74] Le Roy's *De la vicissitude ou variété des choses en l'univers*—"and," as the title continues, "the concurrence of arms and letters by the first and most illustrious nations of the world since civilization began until the present"—was a comparative study of world cultures, especially the "heroic ages," according to a pattern that was cyclical (the biological trajectory already applied by Seyssel to France and by Polydore Vergil to England) on a national level but progressive in universal terms (one of the central themes being the intellectual and technical superiority of the moderns to the ancients). Although he began by celebrating the achievements of philology—to which indeed he had devoted his own life—he laid stress on novelty, especially "the new seas, new types of men, manners, laws, and customs" of the modern age.

In the seventeenth century the "new Philosophy that cast all into doubt" concentrated much of its skepticism on the historical attitudes associated with the humanist tradition. For Bacon "history" continued to suggest little more than the data that, according to the empirical method, were to be shaped by reason, while Galileo, like Descartes, had only contempt for those "memory-experts" who, thinking as well as looking backward, were as remote as possible from philosophy.[75] In his own way Leibniz, too, tried to subsume historical by natural knowledge. "To judge history distinctly, one may compare it to the body of an animal," he wrote. "The parts of history correspond thus: chronology to bones, genealogy to nerves, hidden motives to invisible spirits, useful examples to juices, and the details of circumstances to the whole mass of human flesh."[76] In that conceptual war which Ernst Troeltsch found dominant in seventeenth-century thought, naturalism seemed in many ways to be victorious over historicism.

In other ways, however, humanist scholarship continued to prevail, most notably in the work of scholars like Selden, du Cange, and Mabillon, which represented the culmination of Renaissance "philology." For such critical minds history continued to be prized as a special and independent form of knowledge—indeed as science in its own right and even a vocation (a "profession," in the term applied by Milieu, La Popelinière, and others). As much as reason itself history was, for humanists more elaborately than for Henry of Huntingdon, a distinguishing feature of humanity. About "that fretful animal we call man," Daniel Heinsius, in his essay on the value of history, wrote that "he would be free from the limits of time and space. . . . He would gather into one focus the immeasurable great vastness of ages and generations. . . . History renders man contemporary with the universe."[77] It is one of the most important bequests made by humanism to the modern world.

NOTES

1. *Rinascimento* 1 (1950): 97, review of F. Simone, *La coscienza della rinascità negli umanisti francese* (Rome, 1949). In general see H. Baron, "Das

Erwachsen des historischen Denkens im Humanismus des Quattrocento," *Historisches Zeitschrift* 147 (1932): 5–20; A. Buck, *Das Geschichtsdenken der Renaissance* (Krefeld, 1957); P. Burke, *The Renaissance Sense of the Past* (London, 1969); W. K. Ferguson, *The Renaissance in Historical Thought* (Cambridge, MA, 1948); P. Joachimsen, *Geschichtsauffassung und Geschichtsschreibung in Deutschland unter dem Einfluss des Humanismus* (Leipzig, 1910); D. R. Kelley, *Foundations of Modern Historical Scholarship: Language, Law, and History in the French Renaissance* (New York, 1970); N. S. Struever, *The Language of History in the Renaissance* (Princeton, 1970); R. Weiss, *The Renaissance Discovery of Classical Antiquity* (Oxford, 1969). The most recent and most comprehensive survey is E. Cochrane, *Historians and Historiography in the Italian Renaissance* (Chicago, 1981), essential also for bibliography.

2. Henry of Huntingdon, *The Chronicle*, trans. T. Forester (London, 1853), xxvii. And see, among others, G. Ladner, "Die mittelalterliche Reform-Idee und ihr Verhältnis zur Idee der Renaissance," *Mitteilungen des Instituts für österreichische Geschichtsforschung* 40 (1952): 41–59; R. Renucci, *L'aventure de l'humanisme européen au Moyen-Âge* (Paris, 1953); M. Schulz, *Die Lehre von der historischen Methode bei den Geschichtsschreibern des Mittelalters* (Berlin, 1909); J. Spörl, *Grundformen hochmittelalterlichen Geschichtsanschauung* (Munich, 1935); W. J. Brandt, *The Shape of Medieval History* (New Haven, 1966); M. T. Clanchy, *From Memory to Written Record* (London, 1979); and J. Knape, *Historie in Mittelalter und früher Neuzeit* (Baden-Baden, 1984).
3. "Letter to Posterity," in *Petrarch, the First Modern Scholar and Man of Letters*, ed. J. H. Robinson and H. W. Rolfe (New York, 1898), 64. And see W. Handschin, *Petrarch als Gestalt der Historiographie* (Basel, 1964); E. Kessler, "Geschichtsdenken und Geschichtsschreibung bei Francesco Petrarca," *Archiv für Kulturgeschichte*, 51 (1969): 109–36; T. E. Mommsen, "Petrarch's Conception of the 'Dark Ages,' " *Medieval and Renaissance Studies*, ed. E. F. Rice, Jr. (Ithaca, 1959), 106–29; and P. de Nolhac, *Pétrarque et l'humanisme* (Paris, 2d ed. 1907; reprint, 1965).
4. *Letters to Classical Authors*, trans. M. Cosenza (Chicago, 1910), 84, 100ff.; and see G. Billanovich, "Petrarch and the Textual Tradition of Livy," *Journal of the Warburg and Courtauld Institutes* 14 (1951): 137–208.
5. E. H. Wilkins, *Petrarch's Eight Years in Milan* (Cambridge, MA, 1958), 226.
6. "Petrarch's Prefaces to *De viris illustribus*," trans. B. Kohl, *History and Theory* 13 (1974): 139.
7. Mommsen, "Petrarch's Conception," 122. Cf. H. J. Erasmus, *The Origins of Rome in Historiography from Petrarch to Perizonius* (Assen, 1962), and W. Rehm, *Der Untergang Roms im abendländischen Denken* (Leipzig, 1930).
8. "Letters in Defense of Liberal Studies," in *Humanism and Tyranny*, ed. E. Emerton (Cambridge, MA, 1925), 290–377; and see also B. L. Ullman, *The Humanism of Coluccio Salutati* (Padua, 1963).

9. *De studiis et litteris*, in *Leonardo Bruni Aretino. Humanistisch-philosophische Schriften mit einer Chronologie seiner Werke und Briefe*, ed. H. Baron (Leipzig and Berlin, 1928; reprint, Wiesbaden, 1969), 169.
10. *Humanism and Liberty*, ed. and trans. R. N. Watkins (Columbia, SC, 1978). On Bruni see H. Baron, *The Crisis of the Early Italian Renaissance*, 2 vols. in 1 (Princeton, rev. ed. 1966) and *From Petrarch to Leonardo Bruni* (Chicago, 1968); and B. L. Ullman, "Leonardo Bruni and Humanistic Historiography," in his *Studies in the Italian Renaissance* (Rome 2d ed., 1973); C. C. Bayley, *War and Society in Renaissance Florence* (Toronto, 1961); and more generally E. Cochrane, *Historians and Historiography;* E. Fueter, *Geschichte der neueren Historiographie* (Berlin, 3d ed. 1963); D. Hay, *Annalists and Historians* (London, 1977); and D. J. Wilcox, *The Development of Florentine Humanist Historiography in the Fifteenth Century* (Cambridge, MA, 1969); also J. E. Seigel, *Rhetoric and Philosophy in Renaissance Humanism* (Princeton, 1968); and F. Vegas, "La concezione della storia dell'umanesimo alla Controriforma," *Grande antologia filosofica*, ed. M. F. Sciacca, et al. (Milan, 1964), 10:1–59.
11. See L. Green, *Chronicle into History* (Cambridge, 1972).
12. "Vita di Petrarca," in *Leonardo Bruni Aretino*, ed. Baron, 64.
13. See Cochrane, *Historians and Historiography;* and Wilcox, *Development of Florentine Humanist Historiography.*
14. Besides Cochrane and Fueter, *Geschichte der neueren Historiographie*, see B. Reynolds, "Latin Historiography, A Survey 1400–1600," *Studies in the Renaissance* 2 (1955):7–66; and P. H. Labalme, *Bernardo Giustiniani: A Venetian of the Quattrocento* (Rome, 1969). J. W. Thompson, *A History of Historical Writing* (Chicago, 1942), discusses many minor writers but must be used with caution.
15. A. Grafton, *Joseph Scaliger; A Study in the History of Classical Scholarship* (Oxford, 1983); and W. H. Woodward, *Studies in Education During the Age of the Renaissance, 1400–1600* (Cambridge, 1906; reprinted New York, 1967); also P. Burke, "A Survey of the Popularity of Ancient Historians, 1450–1700," *History and Theory* 5 (1966): 135–52; and J. Jehasse, *La renaissance de la critique* (Saint-Etienne, 1976).
16. See above, note 4.
17. *Elegantiae latinae linguae*, preface, in *Opera omnia*, ed. E. Garin (Turin, 1962), 1:4; and see Kelley, *Foundations of Modern Historical Scholarship*, chap. 2, and E. Gaeta, *Lorenzo Valla: Filosofia e storia nell'umanesimo italiano* (Naples, 1955); also L. Janick, "Lorenzo Valla: The Primacy of Rhetoric and the De-Moralization of History," *History and Theory* 12 (1973): 389–404.
18. *De rebus a Ferdinando rege et maioribus eius gestis*, in *Opera omnia*, ed. Garin, 2:6.
19. *The Treatise of Lorenzo Valla on the Donation of Constantine*, ed. and trans. C. B. Coleman (New Haven, 1922), 21; and see J. Levine, "Reginald Pecock and Lorenzo Valla on the Donation of Constantine," *Studies in the Renaissance* 20 (1973): 118–43.

20. Flavio Biondo, *Scritti inediti e rari*, ed. B. Nogara (Rome, 1927), 138.
21. *Historiarum ab inclinatione Romanorum imperii decades* (Venice, 1483); and see D. Hay, "Flavio Biondo and the Middle Ages," *Proceedings of the British Academy* 45 (1959): 97–125; and F. Gilbert, "Biondo, Sabellico, and the Beginnings of Venetian Official Historiography," in *Florilegium Historiale: Essays Presented to Wallace K. Ferguson*, ed. J. G. Rowe and W. H. Stockdale (Toronto, 1971), 275–93; also L. Varga, *Das Schlagwort vom "Finsteren Mittelalter"* (Baden, 1932), and Ferguson, *Renaissance in Historical Thought*.
22. Bartolomeo Sacchi, *Historia de vitis pontificum romanorum*, ed. Onofrio Panvinio (Venice, 1562), fol. 1; Robert Barnes, *Vitae romanorum pontificum* (Basel, n.d.); and in general M. Miglio, *Storiografia pontificia del Quattrocento* (Bologna, 1975).
23. C. A. Patrides, *The Grand Design of God* (London, 1972).
24. *Memoirs of a Renaissance Pope: The Commentaries of Pius II*, trans. F. A. Gragg, ed. L. C. Gabel (New York, 1959).
25. Angelo Poliziano, *Opera omnia* (Basel, 1553), 621.
26. Besides Weiss, *Renaissance Discovery*, see C. Mitchell, "Archaeology and Romance in Renaissance Italy," *Italian Renaissance Studies*, ed. E. F. Jacob (London, 1960), 455–83; E. Mandowsky and C. Mitchell, *Pirro Ligorio's Roman Antiquities* (London, 1963); and F. Saxl, "The Classical Inscription in Renaissance Art and Politics," *Journal of the Warburg and Courtauld Institutes* 4 (1940–41):19–46.
27. S. Bertelli, *Ribelli, libertini e ortodossi nella storiografia barocca* (Florence, 1973).
28. Besides Kelley, *Foundations*, see D. Maffei, *Gli inizi dell'umanesimo giuridico* (Milan, 1956); H. E. Troje, *Graeca leguntur* (Cologne, 1971); and E. Viard, *André Alciat, 1492–1550* (Paris, 1926); also R. Metz, "La contribution de la France à l'étude du decret de Gratien," *Studia gratiana* 2 (1954):495–518. And see below, note 67.
29. E. C. Scherer, *Geschichte und Kirchengeschichte an den deutschen Universitäten* (Freiburg im Breisgau, 1927); F. L. Borchardt, *German Antiquity in Renaissance Myth* (Baltimore, 1971); H. Tiedemann, *Tacitus und das Nationalbewusstsein der deutschen Humanisten* (Berlin, 1913); E. L. Etter, *Tacitus in der Geistesgeschichte des 16. und 17. Jahrhunderts* (Basel, 1966); R. Buschmann, *Das Bewusstsein der deutschen Geschichte bei den deutschen Humanisten* (Göttingen, 1930); P. Joachimsen, "Tacitus im deutschen Humanismus," *Neue Jahrbücher für das klassische Altertum, Geschichte und deutschen Literatur* 17 (1911): 697–717; and K. Schellhase, *Tacitus in Renaissance Political Thought* (Chicago, 1976); also the fundamental collection in Simon Schardius, *Historicorum opus*, vol. 1, *Germaniae illustrationem continet* (Basel, 1574).
30. Cited by G. Strauss, *Sixteenth-Century Germany, Its Topography and Topographers* (Madison, WI, 1959), 21; see also L. W. Spitz, *Conrad Celtis: The German Arch-Humanist* (Cambridge, MA, 1957); and Joachimsen, *Geschichtsauffassung*.

31. Jacob Wimpheling, *Epitome rerum germanicarum* (Strasbourg, 1505).
32. Albert Krantz, *Saxonia* (Cologne, 1520), and *Wandalia* (Cologne, 1519). There is no critical study of this important historian.
33. Beatus Rhenanus, *Rerum germanicarum libri tres* (Basel, 1531), 3; and cf. idem, *In P. Cornelium, Tacitum Annotationes* (Lyons, 1542). Beatus also lacks a modern critical study.
34. See P. Archambault, *Seven French Chroniclers* (Syracuse, 1974); H. Baumann, *Die Geschichhtsschreiber Philippe de Commynes und die Wirkung seiner politischen Vorstellung in Frankreich um die Mitte des 16. Jahrhunderts* (Munich, 1982); and S. Kinser, introduction to *The Memoirs of Philippe de Commynes*, trans. I. Cazeaux (Columbia, SC, 1969); also J. Voss, *Das Mittelalter im historischen Denken Frankreichs* (Munich, 1973).
35. *Grans chroniques de France* (Paris, 1837), 4; and see G. Spiegel, *The Chronicle Tradition of Saint-Denis* (Leiden, 1978).
36. J. P. Bodmer, "Die französische Historiographie des Spätmittelalters und die Franken," *Archiv für Kulturgeschichte* 45 (1963):91–118.
37. C. Vivanti, "Paulus Aemilius condidit historias?" *Annales* 19 (1964):1117–24, and K. Davies, "Some Early Drafts of the *De Rebus Gestis Francorum* of Paulus Aemilius," *Medievalia et Humanistica* 12 (1958):99–110.
38. Polydore Vergil, *De rerum inventoribus* (Basel, 1536), 49.
39. D. Hay, *Polydore Vergil* (Oxford, 1952).
40. See above, notes 10 and 14.
41. See *Le lettere di Andrea Alciato giureconsulto*, ed. G. L. Barni (Florence, 1953), 222, and M. P. Gilmore, "*Fides et Eruditio:* Erasmus and the Study of History," *Teachers of History: Essays in Honor of Lawrence Bradford Packard*, ed. H. S. Hughes and M. P. Gilmore (Ithaca, 1954), 9–27; and A. Bonilla y San Martín, *Luis Vives y la filosofia del renascimiento* (Madrid, 1929), vol. 2.
42. See especially F. Gilbert, *Machiavelli and Guicciardini: Politics and History in Sixteenth-Century Florence* (Princeton, 1965), and R. von Albertini, *Das florentinische Staatsbewusstsein im Übergang von der Republik zum Prinzipat* (Bern, 1955). Cf. J. H. Hexter, *The Vision of Politics on the Eve of the Reformation* (New York, 1973), and E. Hassinger, *Empirisch-rationaler Historismus* (Munich, 1978).
43. Niccolò Macchiavelli, *The Discourses*, 3.43. For further bibliography here, as elsewhere, see Cochrane, *Historians and Historiography.*
44. Machiavelli, *History of Florence*, trans. W. Dunne (New York, 1901), intro. See also F. Gilbert, "Machiavelli's Istorie Fiorentine," in *Studies on Machiavelli*, ed. M. P. Gilmore (Florence, 1972), and his introduction to *History of Florence* (New York, 1960); M. Phillips, "Machiavelli, Guicciardini and the Tradition of Vernacular Historiography," *American Historical Review* 84 (1979): 86–105; and P. Bondella, *Machiavelli and the Art of Renaissance History* (Detroit, 1973).
45. *Discourses*, 1.2.
46. Francesco Guicciardini, *Ricordi*, trans. N. H. Thomson (New York, 1949), 71.

47. Francesco Guicciardini, *History of Italy,* trans. C. Grayson (New York, 1964), 85. And see M. Phillips, *Francesco Guicciardini: The Historian's Craft* (Toronto, 1977), and idem, "The Disenchanted Witness: Participation and Alienation in Florentine Historiography," *Journal of the History of Ideas* 44 (1983): 191–206; and V. Caprariis, *Francesco Guicciardini: Dalle politica alla storia* (Florence, 1950).
48. J. R. Hale, intro. to Guicciardini, *History of Italy,* vii.
49. Claude de Seyssel, *The Monarchy of France,* ed. D. R. Kelley and trans. J. H. Hexter (New Haven, 1981). Cf. "Exordium" to his translation of Justin, *Histoire* (Paris, 1559), trans. ibid., 163, and the edition of J. Poujol, *La Monarchie de France* (Paris, 1961).
50. *Chronica carionis* (Wittenberg, 1580), preface by Melanchthon (1558), and Luther, "Preface to Galaenus Capella's History," in *Works,* ed. and trans. L. Spitz (Philadelphia, 1960), 34:275. In general see E. Menke-Glückert, *Geschichtsschreibung der Reformation und Gegenreformation* (Leipzig, 1912); P. Fraenkel, *Testimonia Patrum: The Function of Patristic Argument in the Theology of Philipp Melanchthon* (Geneva, 1961); H. Brettschneider, *Melanchthon als Historiker* (Insterberg, 1880); J. M. Headley, *Luther's View of Church History* (New Haven, 1963); H. Lilje, *Luthers Geschichtsanschauung* (Zurich, 1932); E. Schäfer, *Luther als Kirchenhistoriker* (Gütersloh, 1897); and esp. A. G. Dickens and J. M. Tonkin, *The Reformation in Historical Thought* (Cambridge, MA, 1985).
51. See H. Berger, *Calvins Geschichtsauffassung* (Zurich, 1955); Bertelli, *Ribelli, libertini e ortodossi;* and P. Polman, *L'elément historique dans la controverse religieuse du XVIe siècle* (Gembloux, 1932); also P. Bietenholz, *History and Biography in the Works of Erasmus of Rotterdam* (Geneva, 1966).
52. Johann Sleidan, "Apology for His History," in *General History of the Reformation* (London, 1689); and see D. R. Kelley, "Johann Sleidan and the Origins of History as a Profession," *Journal of Modern History* 12 (1980):573–98; A. G. Dickens, "Johann Sleidan and Reformation History," in *Reformation, Conformity and Dissent,* ed. R. B. Knox (London, 1977), 17–43; and I. Vogelstein, *Johann Sleiden's Commentaries* (Lanham, MD, 1986).
53. See especially H. Scheible, *Die Entstehung der Magdeburger Zenturien* (Güttersloh, 1966); also C. K. Pullapilly, *Caesar Baronius, Counter-Reformation Historian* (South Bend, IN, 1975).
54. Paolo Sarpi, *History of Benefices and Selections from History of the Council of Trent,* trans. P. Burke (New York, 1967); and see W. Bouwsma, *Venice and the Defense of Republican Liberty* (Berkeley, 1968).
55. See G. Cotroneo, *I trattatisti dell'"Ars historica"* (Naples, 1971); R. Landfester, *Historia magistra vitae* (Geneva, 1972); and *Theoretiker humanistischer Geschichtsschreibung,* ed. and intro. E. Kessler (Munich, 1971), reproducing essential texts; also Giorgio Spini, "The Art of History in the Counter Reformation," in *The Late Italian Renaissance, 1525–1630,* ed. E. Cochrane (New York, 1970), 91–133; G. H. Nadel, "The Philosophy

of History before Historicism," in *Studies in the Philosophy of History,* ed. G. H. Nadel (New York, 1965), 49–73; F. Lamprecht, *Zur Theorie der humanistischen Geschichtsschreibung* (Winterthur, 1950); C. Trinkaus, "A Humanist's Image of Humanism: the Inaugural Orations of Bartolommeo della Fonte," *Studies in the Renaissance* 7 (1960):90–147; B. Reynolds, "Shifting Currents in Historical Criticism," *Journal of the History of Ideas* 14 (1953): 471–92; and D. R. Kelley, "Faces in Clio's Mirror," *Journal of Modern History* 47 (1975):679–90, and 54 (1982):320–26.

56. Francesco Patrizi, *Della historia dieci dialoghi* (Venice, 1560), 7, in Kessler, "Geschichtsdenken und Geschichtsschreibung"; and see P. M. Arcari, *Il pensiero politico di Francesco Patrizi da Cherso* (Rome, 1935).

57. Luis Cabrera de Córdoba, *De historia para entenderla y escribirla,* ed. S. M. Diaz (Madrid, 1948), intro. Cf. A. Seifert, *Cognitio historica. Die Geschichte als Namengaberin der frühneuzeitliche Empirie* (Berlin, 1976), chap. 5.

58. See Kelley, *Foundations;* J. H. Franklin, *Jean Bodin and the Sixteenth-Century Revolution in the Methodology of Law and History* (New York, 1963); J. L. Brown, *The Methodus . . . of Jean Bodin* (Washington, DC, 1939); A. Klempt, *Die Säkularisierung der universalhistorischen Auffassung* (Göttingen, 1960); *Jean Bodin: Verhandlungen der internationalen Bodin Tagung,* ed. H. Denzer (Munich, 1973); *La "République de Jean Bodin: Atti del convegno di Perugia* (Florence, 1981); *Jean Bodin: Actes du Colloque Interdisciplinaire,* 2 vols. (Angers, 1985). G. Huppert, *The Idea of Perfect History* (Urbana, IL, 1970). C. G. Dubois, *La conception de l'histoire en France au XVIe siècle* (Paris, 1977); also J. H. Preston, "Was There an Historical Revolution?" *Journal of the History of Ideas* 38 (1977):353–64; and see below.

59. François Baudouin, *De institutione historiae universae* (Strasbourg, 1561), l; M. Erbe, *François Bauduin (1520–1573)* (Gütersloh, 1978); and M. Turchetti, *Concordia o toleranza?* (Geneva, 1984).

60. Guillaume Budé, *De l'institution de prince* (Paris, 1547), 63; also in C. Bontems et al., *Le prince dans la France des XVIe et XVIIe siècles* (Paris, 1965).

61. Baldassare Bonifacio, *De archivis* (Venice, 1632), and in general see Kelley, *Foundations,* and above, note 29.

62. See Jehasse, *Renaissance de la critique;* Grafton, *Joseph Scaliger;* and V. A. Nordman, *Justus Lipsius als Geschichtsforscher und Geschichtslehrer* (Helsinki, 1932).

63. S. Kinser, *The Works of Jacques-Auguste de Thou* (The Hague, 1966). On the national traditions see F. S. Fussner, *The Historical Revolution* (New York, 1962); F. J. Levy, *Tudor Historical Thought* (San Marino, CA, 1967); A. B. Ferguson, *Clio Unbound* (Durham, NC, 1979); B. S. Alonso, *Historia de la historiografia española,* 3 vols. (Madrid, 1944–50); H. R. von Srbik, *Geist und Geschichte vom deutschen Humanismus bis zur Gegenwart,* 2 vols. (Munich, 1950–51); and more generally E. Breisach, *Historiography: Ancient, Medieval, and Modern* (Chicago, 1983), with further bibliography.

64. O. Ranum, *Artisans of Glory* (Chapel Hill, NC, 1980).

65. François Hotman, *Francogallia,* ed. R. E. Giesey, trans. J. H. M. Salmon (Cambridge, 1972); and D. R. Kelley, *François Hotman* (Princeton, 1973). Also see below, note 72.
66. See A. Bernardini and G. Righi, *Il concetto di philologia e di cultura classica* (Bari, 1953), and below.
67. E. von Moeller, *Aymer du Rivail, Der erste Rechtshistoriker* (Berlin, 1907), and D. R. Kelley, "The Rise of Legal History in the Renaissance," *History and Theory* 9 (1970): 174–94.
68. Baudouin, *De institutione,* 89.
69. Louis Le Roy, *De l'origine, antiquité, progrès, excellence, et l'utilité de l'art politique* (Paris, 1553); and idem, "L'origine, progrès et perfection de la philosophie . . . ," in *Le Phedon de Platon* (Paris, 1553); and see W. Gundersheimer, *The Life and Works of Louis Le Roy* (Geneva, 1966), and below, note 74.
70. Henri de La Popelinière, *Histoire des histoires, avec l'Idée de l'histoire accomplie* (Paris, 1599); and see D. R. Kelley, "History as a Calling: The Case of la Popelinière," in *Renaissance Studies in Honor of Hans Baron,* ed. A. Molho and J. Kirschner (Florence, 1971), 773–89; G. W. Sypher, "La Popelinière's *Histoire de France,*" *Journal of the History of Ideas* 24 (1963): 41–54; and M. Yardeni, "La conception de l'histoire dans l'oeuvre de La Popeliniere," *Revue d'histoire moderne et contemporaine* 11 (1964):109–26; also C. Vivanti, "Alle origine della idea di civilità, Le scoperte geografiche e gli scritti di La Popelinière," *Rivista storica italiana* 74 (1962):225–47.
71. Henri de La Popelinière, "Le dessein de l'histoire nouvelle des françois," in *Idée de l'histoire,* 401ff.; Le Roy, *Consideration sur l'histoire françois et universelle de ce temps* (Paris, 1568), and "Project ou dessein du royaume de France . . . ," in *Exhortation aux François pour vivre en concorde* (Paris, 1579). Cf. Nicolas Vignier, *Bibliothèque historiale* (Paris, 1582).
72. See D. Thickett, *Estienne Pasquier* (London, 1980); R. Bütler, *Nationales und universales Denken im Werke Etienne Pasquiers* (Basel, 1948); J. Espiner-Scott, *Claude Fauchet* and her supplementary thesis containing unpublished documents (Paris, 1938); also P. Ronzy, *Un humaniste italianisant, Papire Masson (1554–1611)* (Paris, 1924); and more generally H. Baron, "The *Querelle* of the Ancients and the Moderns as a Problem for Renaissance Scholarship," *Journal of the History of Ideas* 20 (1957): 3–22, and J. Schlobach, *Zyklentheorie und Epochenmetaphorik* (Munich, 1980).
73. See Kelley, *Foundations,* 129.
74. A. Le Franc, "Le traité 'De la vicissitude ou variétaté' des choses de Louis le Roy e sa veritable date," *Mélanges Lanson* (Paris, 1922), 115. Louis Le Roy, *De la vicissitude ou variété des choses en l'univers* (Paris, 1584), fol. 215, echoing themes appearing in his own *G. Budaei viri clarissimi vita* (Paris, 1540); see above note 69 and in general S. Kinser, "Ideas of Temporal Change and Cultural Process in France, 1470–1535," *Renaissance Studies in Honor of Hans Baron,* ed. Molho and Kirschner, 703–55.
75. See Seifert, *Cognitio historica;* L. F. Dean, "Francis Bacon's Theory of Civil

History Writing," *Literary History* 8 (1941): 161–83; and cf. Galileo, *Dialogue Concerning the Two Chief World Systems*, trans. S. Drake (Berkeley, 1953), 113.

76. Leibniz, cited in Thompson, *History of Historical Writing*, 2:100; and cf. E. Troeltsch, *Der Historismus and seine Probleme* (Tübingen, 1922), 104.

77. Daniel Heinsius *The Value of History*, trans. G. Robinson (Cambridge, MA, 1943), 10–11.

II

TACITUS NOSTER: THE *GERMANIA* IN THE RENAISSANCE AND REFORMATION

Populi Germaniae ueteris in summa libertate vixerunt.
Beatus Rhenanus (1531)

SCARCELY KNOWN before 1450, Tacitus was alive and well in the sixteenth century.[1] To suggest the extent and quality of his reception, especially in Germany, here is a bit of doggerel from a contemporary poem "In Praise of the Ancient Germans" ("Ein Lobspruch der alten Deutschen"). I do not think that my rendering is significantly less elegant than the original German jingle:

Good manners to the German
  count more than laws to Rome.
Not fraud, nor guile, nor usury
  find place in the German home.
Adultery and whoredom are
  unknown in the German's life.
He covets no man's woman but
  honors his proper wife.
He knows neither gold, nor profit,
  nor any such form of greed,
But takes the produce from the land
  and thus satisfies his need.
He never eats or drinks too much;
  he's modest in his dress.
When he say "no," he means it,
  and "yes" when he says "yes."
To self and friends, he's always true,
  and likewise to his mate.

[1] The essential work is now Ridé (1977), but retaining some value in a massive literature are Krapf (1979), Stackelberg (1960), Tiedemann (1913), Buschmann (1930), Etter (1966), Joachimsen (1910 and 1911), Strauss (1959), Schellhase (1976).

T.J. Luce and A. Woodman, eds., *Tacitus and the Tacitean Tradition* (Princeton, 1993), pp. 152–167, 185–200.

All his life he lives, you see,
  in a pure and simple state.[2]

It was in this stereotypical way that the *Germania* was read in the century after its recovery, and my purpose here is to trace briefly the formation of this image.

Almost alone among classical authors Tacitus was both ancient and modern. Gibbon was ready to "esteem the birth of Tacitus more truly noble than that of kings," and (as this collection suggests) his afterlife has been no less impressive. "The greatest of Roman historians" (as Ronald Syme called him), Tacitus was also, in his posthumous life, "the father of ancient Germanic studies" (in the words of Frank Borchardt).[3] Not only classicists, then, but also modern European historians have taken a professional and proprietary interest in his work and its later *fortuna*; and so to both ancients and moderns (and perhaps to postmoderns) he remains "our Tacitus"—*Tacitus noster*.

The most comprehensive study of Tacitus' *Germania* (before the seventeenth century) is the commentary of Andreas Althamer, published in 1529.[4] These *scholia* afford an ideal introduction to the story of the modern fortune of what is a foundational text in the history of modern historiography, mythology, and ethnography. Of the *Germania* Althamer

[2] *Ein Lobspruch*, cited in Ridé (1977: 2.953):

Bey den guten sitten mehr hand golten
  Und ghalten sein in grössern ehrn
Dann gut gesetz bey den Römern
  Kein wucher, auffsatz, trug, noch list
Bey jhn in brauch gewesen ist
  Ehebruch, unzucht, und hererey
Ist keim gelassen worden frey
  Ein yeder hat sein eynigs weyb
Geliebt, wie seinen eygen leyb
  Niemand seins nechsten gut hat bgert
Sie haben sich des ackers gnert
  Gar nichts gewest von yrkeim gelt
Damit verdorbet wird all welt
  Sie haben wahr gaben umb wahr
Eins umbs ander was notig war
  Kein furwitz braucht in tranck und speyss
Mit kleydung hieltens eine weyss
  Ihr Ja war Ja, Ihr Nein war nein
On alle gleyssnerey und scheyn
  In einfalt hand ihr zyt vertriben

[3] Borchardt (1971: 177).

[4] Althamer (1529: 2), "Exactissima vero haec est Germaniae descriptio." In Schardius (1574), which is the basic collection of sixteenth-century Tacitean scholarship.

wrote, "This is certainly the most accurate description of Germany"; and in those days most scholars would agree. Besides relying on the (now lost) account by Pliny, Tacitus had reported on what he had seen as well as what he had heard ("non tantum auribus, sed et oculis testis"). What is more, though a Roman, Tacitus displayed an extraordinary affection for Germany (*amor Germaniae*); and if Althamer was impressed with the accuracy of Tacitus' essay, he was no less conscious of the evidence and arguments it provided for his own life work, which was "to illustrate, to dignify, and to celebrate Germany" ("Germaniam illustrare, ornare, celebrare") and to memorialize its culture and traditions. In this campaign Althamer marched under two banners. He was both a humanist devoted to the study of history and a recent convert to the Lutheran faith, which likewise looked back to an idealized (Christian) antiquity; and Tacitus furnished inspiration and materials for both projects—for the scholarly resurrection of the German past and for the Protestant effort to purge the German nation of Romanist contamination so as to achieve what commentators on Tacitus celebrated as *Libertas Germaniae*.[5]

Tacitus was an Italian (*homo Italicus*), and he owed his modern rebirth in the early fifteenth century to Italian scholars. Yet by the early sixteenth century he had become, for German authors like Althamer, "our Tacitus," as he calls him ("Noster Tacitus, Cornelius noster").[6] He was the one who had first defined and given unity to German culture, and in his posthumous life he was the one who revealed to modern Germans their institutional, cultural, and ethnic ancestry. By analogy—and in invidious comparison—with conceptions of the Roman cultural heritage, modern Germanists ("periti Germaniae," Althamer called them) sought their own *majores* and looked at the barbarian society described by Tacitus as the first form taken by their fatherland: their motto was not "Roma communis patria" according to the famous civilian formula (*Digest* 50.1.3), but rather, in Althamer's paraphrase, "Germania communis patria."[7]

The story of the early discovery and "reception" of Tacitus' works has been told many times. The only manuscript containing the *Germania* was not discovered until the 1420s, when it was the object of unscrupulous and lustful pursuit by several scholars.[8] As Poggio Bracciolini wrote to his friend Niccolo Niccoli in 1427, "When the Cornelius Tacitus comes I shall keep it hidden with me for I know that whole song: 'Where did it come from and who brought it here? Who claims it for his own?' But do not

[5] Gebwiler (1519).

[6] Althamer (1529: 6).

[7] Althamer (1529: 71). And not the church but Germany became the common "Mother," as in Aventinus (1880: 1.307): "Das Teutschland, *vor zeiten* ein mutter und erneuerin, auch ein werkstatt aller volcken."

[8] Ridé (1977: 1.115ff.).

worry, not a word shall escape me."[9] Somehow, the manuscript passed from the monastery of Hersfeld to northern Europe, was made available to scholars north as well as south of the Alps, and became the basis for the first printed editions.

It was in the context not of humanist curiosity, however, but of ecclesiastical politics that the *Germania* first entered into the world of scholarly discussion. In an oration delivered before the Frankfurt Diet in 1454 Aeneas Sylvius Piccolomini, imperial counselor and ambassador of Italian humanism, flattered his German audience by recalling (with reference to Tacitus) the military prowess of the ancient *Germani*; and then he went on to exhort them to emulate these putative ancestors by fighting for a much grander cause—for a heavenly, not an earthly fatherland ("non pro terrena, sed pro celesti patria"), referring, of course, to the Crusade.[10] Four years later Aeneas Sylvius (then Pope Pius II) had an exchange with the chancellor of the Elector of Mainz, who, in the style of the *grauamina* literature of the conciliar period, protested papal abuses in Germany. The pope's response on behalf of the Roman church, "Mother of the German people," as he called it, added the new classical fuel provided by Tacitus—that is, the invidious contrast between the high character of ancient Germans and the corruption of their modern offspring. In 1471 Giovanni Antonio Campano (who offered corrections in the text of the *Germania*), urged the citizens of Regensburg to follow the manners of their ancestors (*uestigia maiorum*), although he really expected no such miracle.[11] Over the next generation the debate continued; and the upshot was an extraordinary *Kulturkampf* between Romanists and Germanists, which has persisted in various forms down to the present century.

In part this controversy was a variation on the Renaissance theme of Ancients-and-Moderns (a topos also reflected in Tacitus, incidentally), for the central issue was the alleged "barbarism" of the contemporary *Germani,* and the prime authority on both sides of the debate was Tacitus himself. The first German to refer to these ideas was probably Sigismund Meisterlin, whose *Schöne Chronik* (written about 1456) denounced the "fables" of Aeneas Sylvius; and during the fifteenth century Felix Fabri, Hartmann Schedel, Veit Arnpeck, and Johannes Trithemius referred to Tacitus' work.[12] After its publication in 1496, Pius' pioneering essay pub-

[9] Gordon (1974: 116), 25 September 1427.

[10] Aeneas Sylvius (1571: 678), *Oratio de Constantinopolitana clade et bello contra Turcos congregando* and (1034), *De Ritu. Situ. Moribus et Condicione theutonico descriptio* (1496). See also Schmidt (1962) and Strauss (1971: 35).

[11] Campano (1505), containing the text of *Oratio in conventu Ratisponensi dicta ad exhortandos principes Germanorum contra Turcos et [de] laudibus eorum.*

[12] Meisterlin (1522), translation (1456) of *Chronographia Augustensium* (1456). The reception of Tacitus in the fifteenth and sixteenth centuries is conveniently summarized in Tiedemann (1913: VIII–XXXV).

licized the *Germania* and the quarrel between the Romanists and the latter-day barbarians. Over the next generation it became crucial in provoking scholars, Germans and Italians alike, to a self-conscious and often emotional reexamination of the Germanic aspect of European civilization in the terms furnished by one of the oldest, and certainly the most comprehensive, of classical testimonies. In 1515 Jakob Wimpheling was still trying to refute the calumnies of Pius II and to counteract them with charges of Roman abuse and corruption. Three years later Franciscus Irenicus was carrying on the same good fight, the defensive war against charges of "barbarism"—a pejorative term that even the Italian Aeneas Sylvius (Irenicus recalled) had reserved for the enemies of Christendom.[13]

The publishing history of Tacitus' *Germania* is equally complicated. The *editio princeps* (which was also the *vulgata*) was published by Franciscus Puteolanus in Bologna in 1472 (and not, as so many scholars have said before and even after the researches of Jacques Perret, the derivative Venice edition, which must have been not "1470" but 1472 or later).[14] There were over a dozen editions published in Italy and Germany before Filippo Beroaldo's printing of the complete works in 1515. The first critical editions (by standards of those days) were those of Althamer's mentor Beatus Rhenanus (1519 and especially 1533 and 1544), printed with his seminal *Castigationes* and exploited in his great national history composed in the humanist manner, his *Rerum Germanicarum libri tres* of 1531. The high point came in 1574, when Simon Schardius published his great collection of Tacitus commentaries, including the work of Aeneas Sylvius, Althamer, Bebel, Wimpheling, Hutten, Gebwiler, Peutinger, and others.[15] It might also be well to recall that modern Tacitist scholarship (and scholasticism) coincided with the early stages both of the new "German art" of printing and of the "new learning" of the German Reformation. The first of these was a mighty support for the writing of—as the second was a major spur to the revising of—European history; and Tacitus was a central figure in both contexts.

Tacitist inspiration for research into the German past reinforced a drive already underway in medieval chronicles, such as those of Meisterlin and Hartmann Schedel. It was also joined to the humanist enthusiasm for history and national antiquities and to the cause of the Moderns in their quarrel with the Ancients. Whatever its past, "Germany today," declared Felix Fabri in his description of Swabia (c. 1488), "is not only equal to other nations but it surpasses self-promoting Greece, proud Rome, and quarrelsome France."[16] The case for the moderns was also presented by

[13] Irenicus (1518), with a preface by Pirckheimer; trans. in Strauss (1971: 72).
[14] See Perret (1949) and Robinson (1935).
[15] See n. 2, and Beatus Rhenanus (1519).
[16] Fabri (1605).

Trithemius' catalog of illustrious Germans (1495) and by contributions to the Italianate, but anti-Italian, genre called "Germania Illustrata," promoted by the German "arch-humanist," Conrad Celtis.[17] The heyday of the Italians had passed, according to Celtis, and now it was the Germans' turn. As Sebastian Franck summed it up in his *Geschichtsbibel* of 1531, the Germans were "a pious folk [*ein gottselig Volck*] versed in the techniques of painting, tapestry, engraving, sculpture, architecture, casting, writing, and other arts."[18]

The Tacitean themes on which German scholars performed their variations included not only comparisons between *Germania antiqua* and *Germania noua* but also the invidious contrast between Germany and Rome throughout the ages—although of course they inverted the terms of the discussion. As Sebastian Franck acknowledged, the Germans were "a people who, like the apes, want to imitate all the deeds and words of other nations"[19]—and indeed their anxiety to outdo the Italians at their own rhetorical games was apparent. A century earlier Lorenzo Valla had celebrated the cultural hegemony of Italy in these terms:

> We have lost Rome, we have lost authority, we have lost dominion, not by our own fault but by that of the times, yet we reign still, by this more splendid sovereignty [the Latin language] in a great part of the world. Ours is Italy, ours Gaul, ours Spain, Germany, Pannonia, Dalmatia, Illyricum, and many other lands. For wherever the Roman tongue holds sway, there is the Roman Empire.[20]

To these bold words introducing Valla's influential *Elegantiae latinae linguae*, Beatus Rhenanus offered, in his history of Germany almost a century later, a response and a virtual paraphrase and inversion of Italian claims: "Ours are the victories of the Goths, Vandals, and Franks. Ours the glory attached to the kingdoms that these peoples founded in the most illustrious provinces of the Romans, in Italy, and in the queen of cities, Rome herself."[21]

Beatus Aventinus' *Rerum Germanicarum libri tres*, which was published in 1531, was the locus classicus (or locus modernus) of the Germanist thesis, which conceived of national tradition in the broadest, indeed pan-German, terms—again in imitation of imperialist Romanism—including

[17] Spitz (1957).

[18] Franck (1538: fol. aVIb): "Es ist ein langmüttig, leutselig unnd, gegen anderen Nationen gehalten, ein Gottselig volck, das genen vil Nationen an sitten, Gott furcht, gutem gewissen heylthumb ist."

[19] Franck (1538: fol. bIIb).

[20] Valla (1962: 4), *Elegantiae Latinae linguae libri sex*, I, "Prae*atio."

[21] Aventinus (1886: 402): "Nostri enim sunt Gotthorum, Vandalorum Francorumque triumphi. Nobis gloriae sunt illorum imperia in clarissimis Romanorum prouinciis atque adeo Italia ac ipsa Roma regina urbium cunctarum constituta."

the entire linguistic, cultural, and ethnic community. In this effort he was of course not original. In the first place he was carrying on the arguments of humanists of an earlier generation, most notably Wimpheling, whose *Epithoma rerum Germanicarum usque ad nostra tempora* (1505) was written, he explained,

> in order that all Germans may discover in this summary the antiquities of Germany, read the biographies of the emperors, learn to know their merits, intelligence, campaigns, victories, inventions, nobility, fidelity, constancy, and love of truth of the Germans, and in order that this summary should encourage posterity, desiring to emulate, to try every day to add still grander achievements, thereby augmenting Germany by new merits.[22]

Beatus was also endorsing the premises underlying Luther's famous appeal in 1520 to the "German nation." But above all he was joining in the chorus of sixteenth-century Tacitists, such as the first translator of the *Germania*, Johann Eberlin von Günzburg, who likewise championed an early version of the *grossdeutsch—Germania Magna* being Eberlin's phrase, as *Gross-Teutschland* was that of Aventinus.[23]

In the humanist enterprises of literary figures such as Wimpheling, Celtis, Bebel, and Beatus Rhenanus, Tacitus became central to the canon of German literature and provided the agenda for further investigation. Not only political and military skill, according to Celtis, but also literary culture (*litterarum splendor*) had passed to the Germans; and it was to celebrate this national project that Celtis proposed his *Germania Illustrata*, designed to supplement and to supersede the *Italia Illustrata* of Flavio Biondo, whose historical and antiquarian studies of Roman history furnished a model for German humanist historians of the sixteenth century. "Our people does not lack for a past of glorious deeds," Bebel declared in his oration to Maximilian I in 1501; "we miss only the historians who should have recorded those deeds."[24] The Germans had no Homer or Herodotus, no Virgil or Livy; all they had, apparently, was "their"—which is to say, "our"—Tacitus.

What Tacitus provided, according to his modern "Germanist" disciples, was an "original image of Germany" ("prisca Germaniae imago") and its original manners ("prisci mores"), and beyond that a set of cultural topoi

[22] Wimpheling (1505), dedication to Thomas Wolf: "ut omnes Germaniae in hac Epitome antiquitates Germaniae uideant, uitam nostratium Imperatorum legant, Germanorumque laudes, ingenium, bella, triumphos, artium inuentionem, nobilitatem, fidem, constantiam et ueracitatem ediscant atque ut his breuibus ansam praebeamus studiosae posteritati, quo majora in dies student adjicere, et amplioribus rerum incrementis Germanorum laudes cumulare." Wimpheling (1501) sets down his historical method: "Primum uerisimilibus *conjecturis*, deinde *testibus maximis*, postremum vero historiis probatissimis."

[23] Ridé (1977: 2.652), Aventinus (1880: 4.2, 606), and Strauss (1963).

[24] Bebel (1501), in Schardius (1574: 95) and Strauss (1971: 64).

to be invoked and elaborated on by modern historians on what Tacitus called the Germans' "original rude simplicity" ("prisca illa et rudis simplicitas"). In his response to Aeneas Sylvius, Wimpheling rehearsed some of the Germanic virtues noted by Tacitus—*pudicitia, liberalitas, integritas, fides, libertas, constantia, fortitudo, ingenium,* and *nobilitas.*[25] There were of course less edifying national traits, such as the famous German tendency to drink "day and night" and to excess—"Trinken jha sauffen," noted Johann Eberlin von Günzburg in the margins of his translation of the *Germania*—but social virtues seemed to prevail.[26]

Most essential to the German self-image was Tacitus' belief that they were racially "unmixed" and autochthonous (*indigeni*—or as Albert Krantz put it, "in jhrem Lande geboren, ein einheimisch und eingesessen Volck").[27] The Germans, as commentators on Tacitus never tired of repeating, were simple in manners and free from usury, avarice, fraud, and trickery ("usuariam ueteres Germani non agitarunt, minimi auari, fraudulenti ac subdoli, sed simplices"); prone to war ("bellorum auidi"); and, above all, attached to freedom ("libertas Germaniae") and democratic government. They were superstitious and yet free from Roman idolatry—"Merk," Eberlin noted: "die Teutschen haben kein bilder der götter."[28] Their women were also treated justly, and marriage was honored—to the extent indeed that modern historians have spoken of a "German feminism" or a "Gothic feminism" derived from Tacitus' account.[29] The negative side of this image was the chauvinism and xenophobia that a selective reading of the *Germania* might encourage.

To these readings of the *Germania* there was also a political subtext; for as Tacitus remarked, German kings were elected, not hereditary, and ruled through counsel and consent. In the sixteenth century it was easy enough to argue (as indeed the French Huguenot historian and propagandist François Hotman argued in the first version of his *Francogallia*) that "our kings were of the same kind"—as also, he added, were those of the Germans, Danes, Poles, and Swedes.[30] In this connection it may also be noted that, while in their posthumous careers Tacitus and Machiavelli joined forces in their cynical realism, they also cooperated in the republican aspect of the "Machiavellian moment." In other words Renaissance "Tacitism" contributed not only to the sinister—"atheistic" and "tyrannical"—face of Machiavelli but also to the tradition that has been in recent years celebrated, exploited, and inflated under the label of "civic humanism."[31]

[25] Wimpheling (1505), in Schardius (1574: 349).
[26] Ridé (1977: 2.650).
[27] Krantz (1520: preface).
[28] Ridé (1977: 2.656).
[29] Costa (1977: 186) and Kliger (1952: 220).
[30] Hotman (1972: 221).
[31] Pocock (1975).

By the time that Althamer and Beatus Rhenanus were writing, of course, the debate between Romanists and Germanists was being swept into a larger controversy—that European phenomenon almost immediately christened, by friends and foes alike, The ("so-called") Reformation. Of course, this movement likewise had cultural, ethnic, and national as well as religious and political aspects; and in its workings Tacitus was once again posthumously complicit. Summing up the various commonplaces of Tacitism, Althamer celebrated this passage from Germanism to the evangelical faith of the Lutheran movement, which purged German tradition of idolatry and other popish evils and which promised to restore the good manners of the ancestors (*majores nostri*).[32]

Another Tacitean theme that appeared to be especially prophetic in the sixteenth century was the enduring distaste of the Germans for written law ("nulla legum disciplina" was Tacitus' phrase) and the fact that, again in Tacitus' words, "good manners are worth more [in Germany] than laws elsewhere."[33] This ancient topos (cited in the first line of the poem I quoted earlier) was altogether in keeping not only with Lutheran hatred of Judaic and canon law but also with German resistance to the burdens of Roman law. Echoing the *gravamina* of the previous century, the Estates of Wurttemberg in 1514 protested what they referred to as "the plague of lawyers who have been invading the courts of our land," and such complaints were also reflected in popular literature.[34] "Good lawyer, bad Christian" ("gut juristen, böse christen")—this old adage, cited by Luther against the Romanists, seemed to sum up the popular attitude toward written laws. Tacitus could be quoted in this connection, too, of course: "Corruptissima re publica plurimae leges."[35]

The defining trait around which all these virtues were gathered was the German love of liberty—"Populi Germaniae ueteris in summa libertate uixerunt" was the formula of Rhenanus—and this characteristic, too, had a religious as well as a social face.[36] "From all times the Saxons have been free," declared Ulrich von Hutten, "from all times invincible"—and the cause of Martin Luther would be no exception.[37] The "German liberty" celebrated by Beatus' teacher Hieronymus Gebwiler in 1519 converged with the "Christian liberty" proclaimed the next year by Luther, and the result was to transform the latter from a theological into a political

[32] Althamer (1536: fol. aaIIIa).

[33] *Ger.* 19: "plusque ibi boni mores ualent quam alibi bonae leges."

[34] Strauss (1971: 220), Luther (1967: 474), and Stintzing (1875).

[35] *Ann.* 3.27.

[36] Beatus Rhenanus (1551: 3).

[37] Hutten (1859–62: 1.389): "Wan die Sachsen seint alle zeit frey gewest, alle zeit unuberwindtlich." And cf. 1.385: "das *wir* unser Teutsch land der under allen nation in der gantzen welt die freyheit am meisten geburt." And see Holborn (1937).

concept—and ultimately into a justification for active resistance. The authority of Tacitus was invoked not only by German Lutherans but also by French Huguenots like the aforementioned François Hotman, whose *Francogallia* of 1573 was a celebration of the Germanic heritage (and attendant piety) of the French monarchy as well as an inflammatory contribution to the modern idea of political resistance. In this insidious way "our Tacitus" was posthumously conscripted into the tradition of modern revolutionary thought.

The Reformation was associated with another fundamental transformation, and this was the shift from the language of the Romanists to the language of the German *Volk*—and indeed to Gothic script and handwriting. As that herald of Lutheran protest, Ulrich von Hutten, proclaimed,

> Latein ich vor gschriben hab,
> das war ein yeden nit bekant.
> Yetzt schrey ich an das vaterlandt
> Teutsch nation in irer sprach.[38]

> Once I wrote in Latin
> And was listened to by none;
> Now I cry in German
> And am heard by everyone.

Tacitus himself, though very weak on German names, had encouraged this concern with the linguistic dimensions of culture, noting the importance of songs (*carmina*) for the ancient Germans. According to Althamer, the Germans did not commemorate their deeds or keep their laws through written records but rather through traditional songs (*cantilenae*) sung by *Magistrales,* or *Meistergesenge.* "Every folk and nation," wrote Aventinus, "has its own history in its language and mentality."[39] As Erasmus had "opened a window" on classical antiquity through his *Adagia,* so German scholars proposed to do for their own folk culture.[40] Another such contribution was Eberlin's translation of the *Germania* (1526), which celebrated "the origins, development, notable deeds, and misfortuntes of this most noble nation" ("diser woledlen Nation Anfang, furgang, Redliche Handelungen und zufällige schaden").[41]

This was in accord, too, with the Lutheran search for a revisionist alternative to the Romanist perspective on history. "It is an act of piety to study

[38] Ridé (1977: 2.606).

[39] Ridé (1977: 2.263); "denn ein jedes volck und nation hat ir besondere cronick nach sprach und weis."

[40] *Proverbia* (1508), subtitled "De laudibus atque philosophia Germanorum veterum."

[41] Ridé (1977: 2.645). Eberlin calls his translation (p. 647) "Ein zamengelesen buchlin von der Teutschen Nation gelengenheit, sitten und gebrauchen durch Cornelium Tacitum *vnd etliche andere* verzeichnet."

the achievements of one's own country" ("et pius est patriae facta referre labor"), Melanchthon remarked; and in an oration of 1558 he celebrated, in good neo-Tacitean style, "the virtue of the ancient Germans" ("De ueterum Germanorum uirtute").[42] In his reformation of a number of Lutheran universities, Melanchthon encouraged the introduction of courses in history, and in 1559 he published a new edition of Johann Cario's universal chronicle, adjusting it to Lutheran doctrine and advertising it with a preface constituting his contribution to the humanist genre known as *ars historica*.[43]

In general, however, what Tacitus inspired posthumously was not *historia*, as Andrea Alciato wrote in the preface to his annotations on Tacitus, but rather *eruditio*[44]—not narrative history but the more profound and perhaps mystical search for the founding fathers (*Vorfahrer, vorfordern*) and the difficult and myth-ridden questions of national spirit and origins. In his edition of the *Germania* Puteolanus had boasted that Tacitus treated not only deeds but also "the image, name, and nature" of the Germans.[45] What this required in the sixteenth century was to apply the techniques of philology, including the suspect but ever-popular methods of speculative etymology, to the study of German language, literature, law, place-names, and the like. One notable example of this was the treatise on *Various Proper Names and Primitive Etymologies Restored*, published in 1537 and at first attributed to Luther himself, though it was more probably by Spalatin or another scholar of Luther's circle.[46]

In the Renaissance the game of etymology (and the associated sport of what should be called eponymology) was beginning to acquire some linguistic rigor, but in fact doctrinal or national preference more often ruled; and (as Borchardt has said) historical "criticism" was often limited to the "topos of critical rejection" (*anasceua*).[47] The term "German," for exam-

[42] Melanchthon (1834–60: 11. col. 306, 317): "turbe est enim domestica ignorare"; also 3. col. 568, on Tacitus, "Nam absoluto libello, primum visus sum mihi integram quasi picturam Germaniae habere" and (col. 565) "veteris Germaniae imaginem aliquam"; 10. col. 874, "De veterum Germanorum virtute"; and (11.374, 383) orations on "Encomium Sueviae and "Encomium Franciae."

[43] Melanchthon (1834–60: 12. col. 705), preface to *Chronica Carionis*, and Brettschneider (1880).

[44] Alciato, *Encomium historiae*, published first as the preface to his *Annotationes in Cornelium Tacitum* (Milan, 1517).

[45] Puteolanus (c. 1475: Preface): "In rebus gestis non solum quid actum, sed quale; de eventu vero omnes causas explicat . . . hominum porro non solum gestas, sed quae fama, quod nomen, quae natura, quae vitae . . ." In the preface to Cuspian's chronicle (cited by Ridé, 2.715), Melanchthon says that history "ist doch nit notwendigers und nutzers, dann das man in historien erfahren sey und die selbigen wol wisse."

[46] Schardius (1574: 816), *Aliquot Nomina Propria Germanorum ad priscam etymologiam restituta*; also printed in editions of Luther's works.

[47] Borchardt (1971: 45).

ple, was associated with "Herman" (that is, Arminius, whom Tacitus had called the "liberator of Germany"), or "Heer-man" (lord-man), or "gar-man" (true man), and the term "Aleman" with "all-man" (*Allerley Mann, totus vir*).[48] Speculative soundings in the deep past were also attempted with the assistance of Renaissance mythology, especially in the work of Annius of Viterbo, who had drawn upon Tacitus' *Germania* in his ingenious fabrications. On the authority of (pseudo-)Berosus, one of Annius' forgeries, the "god Tuisto" mentioned by Tacitus was identified as a fourth son of Noah and the father of the nation called—through various etymological manipulations—Tuiscones, Teutonici, and Teutsch. These first Germans were also associated with the great-grandson of Noah, Ashkenaz, mentioned in Genesis, and with the king Askanios referred to in the *Iliad*. These Tacito-biblical-Homeric fabrications made their way, by way of Melanchthon and the *Chronica Carionis,* into the mainstream of modern German historiography—although critical scholars like Beatus Rhenanus began to cast doubt on the validity of these national myths, including that of Trojan origins.

In other ways, too, the reading of Tacitus promoted critical attitudes toward history. Humanist sensitivity to chronology and anachronism was heightened; and so Beatus Rhenanus, for example, distinguished between an ancient and a middle stage of national history—*prisca* and *media antiquitas,* which has been regarded as an early contribution to the concept "medieval." The reception of Tacitus also suggested the importance of chronological discrimination in the study of texts; that is, of asking, according to Beatus, "at what time that which you are reading was written, by whom and about what; then [to] compare the new texts with the old or vice versa, always keeping in mind the changes that have taken place."[49] As John D'Amico has pointed out, the quality of Beatus' textual criticism was especially impressive for that pioneering age—some fifty of his emendations of Tacitus still being accepted.[50] Beatus was one of those whose work, following Italian models, put German historiography on a firm critical basis.

If Tacitus was alive and well in Renaissance Italy and Reformation Germany, he was welcomed almost as enthusiastically in some circles in sixteenth-century France and England. Guillaume Budé was one of the first French scholars to read his work, and Budé's colleagues in the defense of the French monarchy were not slow to adapt the Tacitus of the *Germania* to their own ideological needs—which is to say the defense and illustration of

[48] E.g., Althamer (1529: 7–10), Beatus Rhenanus, (1542), Schardius (1574: 85), published the text of J. V. Willich's commentary on the *Germania.*

[49] Schaeffer (1976).

[50] D'Amico (1988).

the French or Frankish tradition described by Tacitus. Jean Du Tillet—archivist, antiquary, pioneering historian of the monarchy, and student of modern Tacitean scholarship—proclaimed with national pride and the usual invidious comparison of contemporary Italy, "the conformity of laws, customs, and manners, and speech of the Germans and the French."[51] The very name of the Franks signified freedom ("die freien Francken, hoc est liberi Franci," as Aventinus had written); and their history bore this out. According to Du Tillet "Tacitus confesses that the Romans fought the Germans many times without vanquishing them, and not only did they escape Roman domination but Rome was itself beaten and destroyed by them and their city captured and wasted. That is enough to show that France [*la France*] took its beginning from Germany and can have no more worthy origin."

This was the argument, too, of Hotman and other sixteenth-century French historians, Gallican as well as Protestant; and it was borrowed as well by English scholars, who wanted to claim similar distinctions for the Anglo-Saxon cousins of the Germans and Franks and their social and institutional arrangements.[52] To Milton, Tacitus was still "of all others the greatest enemy of tyrants."[53] The political implications of Tacitism were drawn out especially by those "constitutional antiquarians" who looked for traditions of liberty in the Hercynian forest where the ancient Germans frolicked, and found the roots of parliamentary government and even political democracy in the tribal customs described in Tacitus' *Germania*. These fanciful images made Tacitus' work, according to Samuel Kliger, the most important "Gothic" text in seventeenth-century England, contributing significantly to the Germanist myths of English history. According to Montesquieu (citing Tacitus), it was from the Germans, who were "certainly a free people," that "the English government have borrowed the idea of their political government."[54] This thesis, with its accompanying Hercynian topos—"This beautiful system was invented first in the woods," Montesquieu added—survived among English and American historians down to the present century.

Tacitus' authority was also invoked in the great debate over the origins of feudalism, which likewise raged between Romanists and Germanists. In France especially, scholars came to reject notions that feudal institutions were derived from Roman institutions such as the ancient clientele. By the sixteenth century the *communis opinio* (among historians if not jurists) was that the fief was a creation of the Carolingian Franks and that the

[51] Du Tillet (1607: 1.2), "De l'origine des François," and Kelley (1970: 229).

[52] Kliger (1952).

[53] Milton (1848: 1.128).

[54] Montesquieu (1989: 166).

attendant relationship of vassalage was traceable to the more ancient German tribes. Writing in the 1530s, Charles Dumoulin, greatest of French jurists, argued that the origins of vassalage (*vassalica clientela*) should be referred generally to the *comitatus* described by Tacitus; and most later historians, including scholars like Hotman and Spelman, agreed.[55] This dispute had been going on among civil lawyers since the thirteenth century, and Tacitus did not enter it until the early sixteenth century; yet his opinions—sustained by nationalist and confessional pride—have figured centrally in discussion between Romanists and Germanists down to the present century.

The posthumous life of Tacitus' *Germania* is not only considerably more extended chronologically but also more complex intellectually than these remarks have suggested. Early students tended to read Tacitus literally and to turn him into a canonical *auctor*. For others the lessons were subtler, and "our Tacitus" was represented not merely as a classical (or a modernist) text but as a profound commentator on the human condition in historical context. For this one concluding example must suffice, and it is both a powerful and an exasperating one.

Giambattista Vico qualifies as a Tacitist on various grounds, beginning with the fact that Tacitus was (with Plato, Bacon, and Grotius) one of his famous Four Authors. Vico admired Tacitus for describing man as he is, Plato for contemplating man as he should be (and Bacon for his scientific method and Grotius for his conception of human science). But Vico had a special admiration for the Tacitus of the *Germania*, which figures centrally and formatively in his *New Science*.

For Vico, Tacitus not only described man (and woman) as he (and she) is, but he suggested ways of seeing humanity as it had been before the written record of history became available—if not in a state of nature, then at least in a condition resembling the barbarism following the Flood. Tacitus was, Vico remarked, "most learned in the natural law of the gentes" ("the ius gentium naturale," which was another aspect of Vico's new science). Tacitus was in effect a critical witness of a primitive stage of civilization in which people, "ignorant of the causes of things, assigned everything to the gods and saw divine activity everywhere."[56] Thus (as Vico cites Tacitus again) "the ancient Germans spoke of hearing the sun pass at night from west to east and affirmed that they saw the gods." In Vico's own terms the old Germanic *carmina* mentioned by Tacitus reflected the "poetic wisdom" (*sapienza poetica*) of a preliterate society still under the spell of myth and nature worship. "Tacitus in his account of the customs of the ancient

[55] Kelley (1964: 225).

[56] Vico (1953: par. 375 [c. *Ger.*, 45], 470, 529, 643), Vico (1974), and Kelley (1976).

Germans," Vico recalled, "relates that they preserved in verse the beginnings of their history, and Lipsius in his notes on this passage says the same of the American Indians."

Many of the large generalizations formulated in Vico's *Scienza nuova* were suggested by the work of Tacitus and the massive scholarship it had accumulated. Thus, remarking on the German habit of collecting amber, Tacitus concluded that, because they were barbarians (*ut barbari*), they have never thought to ask what it is or how it was produced. Raising this insight to the level of anthropological generalization, Vico then characteristically went on to infer that "These rude and simple nations help us to a much better understanding of the gentile world with whom we are now concerned."[57]

Other Germanic customs, such as the aforementioned *comitatus* and the election of kings, permit us, Vico writes elsewhere, "to conjecture that the same custom must have prevailed among all the other first barbarous nations" ("primi popoli barbari"). So it was, too, with the practice of natural and hereditary (which were preferred over testamentary) successions of the Germans, which (Vico again added) "gives us reason to assume the same of all the first barbarous peoples." In one of Tacitus' famous aphorisms, "Good morality is more effective in Germany than good laws are elsewhere," and Vico again extended this insight into a "principle" of history. It was on the basis of such conjectures—and with the help of the same kind of etymological virtuosity ("goperisms," as some would call them) displayed by the early commentators on the *Germania*—that Vico erected his *Principia* of history, the *New Science*.

Of course Vico's philosophy of history was worked out principally in terms of the Homeric poems; but the work of, and the scholarship on, Tacitus furnished a sort of *ricorso* of Greek history—a parallel tradition to test and to illustrate Vico's speculations. What Tacitus' *Germania* represented to Vico was a striking representation of an archetype of "first barbarism"—a way of retracing, or rethinking, one's way historically from culture to nature. For Tacitus was an observer both of a decadent civilization, imperial Rome, with its proliferating and inequitable laws, and of an innocent and unmixed society in the process of formation, the age of gods and giants and kings—and in this connection Vico recalled not only Tacitus' phrase describing the Germans, *magna corpora*, but also the opening words of the *Annals:* "Urbem Romam a principio reges habuere." In general Vico took the Tacitean stereotypes as illustrations of the *termini a quo* and *ad quem* of the courses of cultural history. The trajectory thus traced is embodied in the fifth of the seven primary aspects of the "new science," namely, "an ideal universal history traversed in time by the histories of all nations"—an epic history that would carry the story of humanity if not

[57] Vico (1953: par. 375, 594, 559, 584, 608, 992).

from Genesis to Revelation, then at least from the barbaric age begun by the offspring of Noah to the heights and depths of civilization and the emergence of a "second barbarism," whose features might be glimpsed in other works of Tacitus.[58] Thus Tacitus seemed to provide materials for a whole philosophy of history.

In modern times the work of Tacitus has had a very complex and colorful afterlife, with detractors as well as admirers. His questionable associations with Machiavelli in the Renaissance did considerable damage to his historiographical reputation, and so, in some circles did his uncanny literary virtuosity: in Joyce's *Finnegan's Wake,* for example, he appears as "Taciturn . . . our wrongstory shortener." The *Germania,* too, has had its critics, at least since Henry Cornelius Agrippa dismissed its portrait of the Germans as "poppycock."[59] Ever since its dramatic discovery in the fifteenth century Tacitus' essay has been interpreted as a sort of ethnic or *grossdeutsch* manifesto and has been placed in the service of various distasteful nationalist or racialist ideologies; and these modern by-products of Renaissance Tacitism have not done credit to "the greatest of Roman historians."

On the other hand—and what is of more interest here—the *Germania* revealed to the modern world fascinating glimpses of a bygone age and traces of a vanished culture, which nevertheless have seemed to have links with (or at least to offer lessons to) modern society. In its sublimated form "Tacitism" has given the study of cultural "antiquities" parity with narrative political history and Germanic tradition with the classical canon; it has encouraged the genetic and comparative approach so characteristic of philological and antiquarian study; it has helped to deepen and enrich modern historical scholarship by drawing attention to the study of "barbarian" language, myth, primitive religion, and social customs; and at least indirectly it has given sustinence and support to anthropological approaches to cultural history, theory, and prehistory. This is apparent not only in the work of a number of ingenious humanist commentators and antiquarians and their successors among nineteenth-century Germanist historians but also of more speculative contributors to the human sciences such as (to mention just a few) Bodin, Vico, Montesquieu, Marx, Henry Sumner Maine, Emile de Laveleye, and J. J. Bachofen, and finally—if only there were more time to pursue this posthumous story—of the more scientific historical, sociological, and anthropological projects of recent times.[60] For this reason, too, it seems proper not only for classical scholars but also for mere modern historians like myself to speak of, and even, in a collegial way, to honor *Tacitus noster.*

[58] Vico (1953: par. 349).
[59] Agrippa (1530: chap. 5).
[60] Kelley (1990).

BIBLIOGRAPHY

Aeneas Sylvius Piccolomini. (1571). *Opera*. Basel.

Agrippa, H. C. (1530). *De incertitudine et vanitate scientiarum declamatio invectiva*. Antwerp.

Aikin, J., trans. (1777). *Cornelius Tacitus: A treatise on the situation, manners and inhabitants of Germany, and the Life of Agricola*. Warrington.

Alexander, W. H. (1952). "The Tacitean 'non liquet' on Seneca," *Univ. Calif. Publ. Class. Philol.* 14.269–386.

Althamer, A. (1529). *In libellum Cornelii Taciti . . . Scholia*, in Schardius (1574).

———. (1536). *Commentarii Germaniae in P. Cornelii Taciti Equitis Rom. libellum de situ, moribus, et populis Germanorum*. Nuremberg.

André, J.-M. (1975). "Les 'ludi scaenici' et la politique des spectacles au début de l'ère antonine," in *Association G. Budé: Actes du IXe Congrès*, vol. 1, 468–79. Paris.

Aubrion, E. (1985). *Rhétorique et histoire chez Tacite*. Metz.

Auguet, R. (1972). *Cruelty and Civilization: The Roman Games*. Eng. trans. London.

Aventinus (1880–1886). *Johann Turmairs genannt Aventinus Sämmtliche Werke*. 6 vols. Munich.

Bacon, N. (1647). *An Historical Discourse of the Uniformity of the Government of England. The First Part: From the first Times till the Reigne of Edward the Third*. London.

Bain, D. (1987). *Actors and Audience: A Study of Asides and Related Conventions in Greek Drama*. 2d ed. Oxford.

———. (1988). "Some Reflections on the Illusion in Greek Tragedy," *BICS* 34.1–14.

Baldwin, B. (1979). "Nero and His Mother's Corpse," *Mnemosyne* 32.380–81.

Bardon, H. (1953). "Tacite et le Dialogue des Orateurs," *Latomus* 12.166–87.

———. (1956). "Tacite *Hist.* 3.21–24 et Thucydide 7.43–44," in *Hommages à M. Niedermann. Collection Latomus* 23.348–56.

Barnes, T. D. (1986). "The Significance of Tacitus' *Dialogus de oratoribus*," *HSCP* 90.225–44.

Baron, H. (1955). *The Crisis of the Early Italian Renaissance: Civic Humanism and Republican Liberty in an Age of Classicism and Tyranny*. (Rev. ed. 1966). Princeton.

Barrett, W. S. (1964). *Euripides: Hippolytus*. Oxford.

Bartsch, S. (1989). *Decoding the Ancient Novel: The Reader and the Role of Description in Heliodorus and Achilles Tatius*. Princeton.

Barwick, K. (1929). "Zur Erklärung und Komposition des Rednersdialogs des Tacitus," in *Festschrift W. Judeich*, 81–108. Weimar.

———. (1954). *Der Dialogus de oratoribus des Tacitus. Berichte der sächsischen Akademie des Wissenschaft* 101, 4. Berlin.

Beatus Rhenanus. (1519). *P. Cornelii Taciti De moribus et populis Germaniae libellus*. Leipzig.

———. (1551). *Rerum Germanicarum libri tres*. Basel.

———. (1542). *In P. Cornelium Tacitum Annotationes*. Lyon.

———. (1886). *Briefwechsel des Beatus Rhenanus*, ed. A. Horowitz and K. Hartfelder. Leipzig.

Beaujeu, J. (1960). "Le *mare rubrum* de Tacite et le problème de la chronologie des Arabes," *REL* 38.200–235.

Bebel, H. (1501). *Oratio ad regem Maximilianum Caesarem de eius atque Germaniae laudibus*. Pforzheim.

Bellen, H. (1982). "Antike Staatsräson. Die Hinrichtung der 400 Sklaven des römischen Stadtpräfekten L. Pedanius Secundus im Jahre 61 n. Chr.," *Gymnasium* 89.449–67.

Benario, H. W. (1977). "Gordon's Tacitus," *CJ* 72.107–14.

Betensky, A. (1978). "Neronian Style, Tacitean Content: The Use of Ambiguous Confrontations in the *Annals*," *Latomus* 37.419–35.

Blackwell, T. (1753–63). *Memoirs of the Court of Augustus*. 3 vols. Edinburgh.

Blount, T. P. (1697). *Essays on Several Subjects. . . . The third Impression*. London.

Boccalini, T. (1669). *I Ragguagli di Parnaso*. 2 vols. Amsterdam.

Boesche, R. (1987). "The Politics of Pretence: Tacitus and the Political Theory of Despotism," *History of Political Thought* 8.189–210.

Bolingbroke, H. St. John, Viscount (1752). *Letters on the Study . . . of History*. 2 vols. London.

Borchardt, F. L. (1971). *German Antiquity in Renaissance Myth*. Baltimore.

Borszák, S. (1969). "Das Germanicusbild des Tacitus," *Latomus* 28.588–600.

———. (1970). "Zum Verständnis der Darstellungskunst des Tacitus," *Acta Antiqua* 18.279–92.

———. (1973). "*Spectaculum*: Ein Motiv der 'tragischen Geschichtsschreibung' bei Livius und Tacitus," *ACD* 9.57–67.

———. (1982). "Alexander der Grosse als Muster taciteischer Heldendarstellung," *Gymnasium* 89.37–56.

Bowersock, G. W. (1975). "The Greek-Nabataean Bilingual Inscription at Ruwwâfa, Saudi Arabia," in *Le monde grec: Hommages à Claire Préaux*, ed. J. Bingen, G. Cambier, and G. Nachtergael, 513–22. Brussels.

———. (1987). "The Mechanics of Subversion in the Roman Provinces," in *Opposition et résistances à l'empire d'Auguste à Trajan*. Entretiens Hardt 33, 291–317. Geneva.

Braund, S. H. (1988) *Beyond Anger: A Study of Juvenal's Third Book of Satires*. Cambridge.

Brettschneider, H. (1880). *Melanchthon als Historiker*. Insterburg.

Briessmann, A. (1955). *Tacitus und das flavische Geschichtsbild*. Wiesbaden.

Bringmann, K. (1970). "Aufbau und Absicht des taciteischen Dialogus de oratoribus," *MH* 27.164–78.

Brink, C. O. (1989). "Quintilian's *De causis corruptae eloquentiae* and Tacitus' *Dialogus de oratoribus*," *CQ* 39.472–503.

II

Briscoe, J. (1981). *A Commentary on Livy Books XXXIV–XXXVII*. Oxford.

Brunt, P. A. (1960). "Tacitus on the Batavian Revolt," *Latomus* 19.494–517.

Burke, P. (1966). "A Survey of the Popular Ancient Historians 1450–1700," *History and Theory* 5.135–52.

———. (1969). "Tacitism," in *Tacitus*, ed. T. A. Dorey, 149–71. London.

Burnett, J., Lord Monboddo (1773–92). *Of the Origin of Language*. 6 vols. Edinburgh.

Buschmann, R. (1930). *Das Bewusstsein der deutschen Geschichte bei den deutschen Humanisten*. Göttingen.

Cameron, A. (1967). "Tacitus and the Date of Curiatus Maternus' Death," *CR* 17.258–61.

———. (1976). *Circus Factions. Blues and Greens at Rome and Byzantium*. Oxford.

Campano, G. A. (1505). *Opera omnia*. Venice.

Caplan, H. (1944). "The Decay of Eloquence at Rome in the First Century," in *Studies in Speech and Drama*, 295–325. Ithaca.

Champlin, E. (1989). "The Life and Times of Calpurnius Piso," *MH* 46.101–24.

Chilver, G.E.F. (1979, 1985). *A Historical Commentary on Tacitus' Histories I and II* and *Histories IV and V*, completed and revised by G. B. Townend. Oxford.

Christ, K. (1956). *Drusus und Germanicus*. Paderborn.

Christian, L. G. (1987). *Theatrum Mundi: The History of an Idea*. Ph.D. diss., Harvard University, 1969. New York.

Church, A. J., and Brodribb, W. J., trans. (1942). *Complete Works of Tacitus*, ed. M. Hadas. New York.

Cibber, C. (1725). *Caesar in Egypt. A Tragedy*. London.

Cizek, E. (1982). *Néron*. Paris.

Classen, C. J. (1988). "Tacitus—Historian between Republic and Principate," *Mnemosyne* 41.93–116.

Cochrane, E. (1972). Translation and edition of G. Spini, "Historiography: The Art of History in the Italian Counter Reformation," in *The Late Italian Renaissance 1525–1630*. London.

Coleman, K. M. (1990). "Fatal Charades: Roman Executions Staged as Mythological Enactments," *JRS* 80.44–73.

Concanen, M. (1730). *The Speculatist. A Collection of Letters and Essays, Moral and Political, Serious and Humorous: Upon Various Subjects*. London.

Cooper, H.H.A. (1984). *On Assassination*. Boulder.

Corsi Zoli, D. (1972). "Aspetti inavvertiti della congiura pisoniana," *Studi Romani* 20.329–39.

Costa, G. (1977). *Le antichità germaniche nella cultura italiana da Machiavelli a Vico*. Naples.

Courbaud, E. (1918). *Les procédés d'art de Tacite dans les Histoires*. Paris.

Courtney, E. (1980). *A Commentary on the Satires of Juvenal*. London.

Crook, J. A. (1970). "*Strictum et aequum*: Law in the time of Nero," *Irish Jurist* n.s. 5.357–68.

Curtius, E. R. (1951). *European Literature and the Latin Middle Ages*. Eng. trans. London.

The Daily Gazetteer. (1739). 7 April and 16 June. London.

Daitz, S. G. (1960). "Tacitus' Technique of Character Portrayal," *AJP* 81.30–52.

D'Amico, J. (1988). *Theory and Practice in Renaissance Textual Criticism: Beatus Rhenanus between Conjecture and History*. Berkeley.

D'Arms, J. H. (1975). "Tacitus, *Annals* 13.48 and a New Inscription from Puteoli," in *The Ancient Historian and his Materials*, ed. B. Levick, 155–65. Farnborough.

Dawson, A. (1968). "Whatever Happened to Lady Agrippina?" *CJ* 64.252–67.

Defoe, D. (1706). *The Review*, 3 January. London.

———. (1713). *The Review*, 3 February. London.

———. (1727). *History of the Principal Discoveries and Improvements in the Several Arts and Sciences*. London.

———. (1728). *Atlas Maritimus & Commercialis*. London.

De Lacy, P. (1952). "Biography and Tragedy in Plutarch," *AJP* 73.159–71.

d'Elia, S. (1979). "L'evoluzione della storiografia tacitiana," *RAAN* 54.27–63.

Deuse, W. (1975). "Zur *advocatus-diaboli*-Funktion Apers im *Dialogus* und zur Methode ihrer Deutung," *Grazer Beiträge* 3.51–68.

Dickison, S. K. (1977). "Claudius: Saturnalicius Princeps," *Latomus* 36.634–47.

Döpp, S. (1989). "*Nec omnia apud priores meliora*: Autoren des frühen Principats über die eigene Zeit," *RhM* 132.73–101.

Döring, K. (1979). *Exemplum Socratis. Hermes* Einzelschriften 42. Wiesbaden.

Drexler, H. (1939). *Tacitus: Grundzüge einer politischen Pathologie*. Frankfurt am Main.

Dryden, J. (1697). "Preface to the Aeneid," in *John Dryden: Of Dramatic Poesy and Other Critical Essays*, ed. G. Watson, 1962. 2 vols. London.

Duck, S. (1755). *Caesar's Camp: Or, St. George's Hill. A Poem*. London.

Dupont, F. (1985). *L'acteur-roi ou le théâtre dans la Rome antique*. Paris.

Du Tillet, J . (1607). *Receuil des roys de France*. 2 vols. Paris.

Dyer, J. (1740). *The Ruins of Rome*. London.

Edelmaier, W. (1964). "Tacitus und die Gegner Roms." Diss., Heidelberg.

Essay on Liberty and Independency: Being an Attempt to Prove, that the People under a Popular Form of Government, may be as much Slaves, as those subject to the Arbitrary Will of one Man, An. (1747). London.

Etter, E.-L. (1966). *Tacitus in der Geistesgeschichte des 16. und 17. Jahrhunderts*. Basler Beiträge zur Geschichtswissenschaft 103. Basel–Stuttgart.

Everts, P. S. (1926). *De Tacitea historiae conscribendae ratione*. Kerkrade.

Fabia, P. (1893). *Les sources de Tacite*. Paris.

Fabri, F. (1605). *Historia Suevorum*, in *Suevicar. rer. Scriptores*, ed. M. Goldast. Frankfurt.

Fantham, E. (1978). "Imitation and Decline: Rhetorical Theory and Practice in the First Century after Christ," *CP* 73.102–16.

Feiling, K. (1924). *History of the Tory Party*. Oxford.

Franck, S. (1538). *Germaniae Chronicon*. Augsburg.

Frazer, J. G. (1929). *P. Ovidii Nasonis Fastorum libri sex*. Vol. 3. London.

Frazer, R. M. (1966). "Nero the Artist-criminal," *CJ* 62.17–20.

Fredericks, S. C. (1969). "Mos Maiorum in Juvenal and Tacitus." Ph.D. diss., University of Pennsylvania.

Freed, J. (1750). *Stigand: Or, The Antigallican. A Poem in Miltonic verse.* London.
Furneaux, H. (1896, 1907). *Annals of Tacitus.* 2 vols. 2d ed. Oxford.
Garton, C. (1972). *Personal Aspects of the Roman Theatre.* Toronto.
Gebwiler, H. (1519). *Libertas Germaniae.* Strasbourg.
The Gentleman's Magazine. (1737). 7.411. London.
Gerber, A., A. Greef, and C. John. (1903). *Lexicon Taciteum.* Leipzig.
Gerlo, A., H.D.L. Vervliet, and I. Vertessen. (1967). *Correspondance de Juste Lipse conservée au Musée Plantin-Moretus.* Antwerp.
Gibbon, E. (1763). "Extraits de mon Journal," in *Miscellaneous Works*, ed. John, Lord Sheffield, 1796. 2 vols. London.
———. (1776–88). *The History of the Decline and Fall of the Roman Empire*, ed. J. B. Bury, 1900. 7 vols. London.
Ginsburg, J. (1981). *Tradition and Theme in the Annals of Tacitus.* New York.
———. (1986). "Speech and Allusion in Tacitus, *Annals* 3.49–51 and 14.48–49," *AJP* 107.525–41.
Glover, R. (1753). *Boadicea. A Tragedy.* London.
Goffman, E. (1974). *Frame Analysis: An Essay on the Organization of Experience.* New York.
Goodyear, F.R.D. (1970a). "Cyclic Development in History: A Note on Tac. *Ann.* 3.55.5," *BICS* 17.101–6.
———. (1970b). *Tacitus. G&R* New Surveys in the Classics no. 4. Oxford.
———. (1972, 1981). *The Annals of Tacitus.* Vols. 1–2. Cambridge.
———. (1976). "De inconstantia Cornelii Taciti," in *Acta conventus Latinis litteris linguaeque fovendis*, 198–204. Malta.
Goold, G. P. (1961). "A Greek Professorial Circle at Rome," *TAPA* 92.168–92.
Gordon, P., trans. (1974). *Two Renaissance Book Hunters: The Letters of Poggio Bracciolini to Nicolaus de Nicolis.* Eng. trans. New York.
Gordon, T. (1728–31). *The Works of Tacitus To Which are Prefixed Political Discourses on that Author.* 2 vols. London.
Gordon, T., and Trenchard, J. (1748). *Cato's Letters: Or Essays on Liberty, Civil and Religious, and other Important Subjects.* 3 vols. 5th ed. London.
Gowing, A. (1990). "Tacitus and the Client Kings," *TAPA* 120.315–31.
Graf, F. (1931). *Untersuchungen über die Komposition der Annalen des Tacitus.* Thun.
Grainger, J. (1756). Review of *Essay on Pope* by Joseph Warton, *Monthly Review* 14.58.
Grant, M., trans. (1956). *Tacitus: The Annals of Imperial Rome.* Harmondsworth.
Greene, E. B. (1779). *The Satires of Persius Paraphrastically Imitated, and Adapted to the Times.* London.
Gries, K. (1949). "Livy's Use of Dramatic Speech," *AJP* 70.118–41.
Griffin, M. T. (1976). *Seneca: A Philosopher in Politics.* Oxford.
———. (1984). *Nero. The End of a Dynasty.* London.
Griffiths, R. (1759). Review of a translation of Tibullus by James Grainger, *Monthly Review* 20.62–63.
Gudeman, A. (1914). *Cornelii Taciti Dialogus de Oratoribus.* 2d ed. Leipzig.
Guicciardini, F. (1951). *Ricordi*, ed. R. Spongano. Florence.

———. (1970). *Maxims and Reflections of a Renaissance Statesman (Ricordi)*, trans. M. Domandi. Gloucester, Mass.
———. (1977). *Ricordi*, ed. E. Barelli. Milan.
Güngerich, R. (1980). *Kommentar zum Dialogus des Tacitus*, ed. H. Heubner. Göttingen.
Gunn, J.A.W. (1983). *Beyond Liberty and Property. The Process of Self-Recognition in Eighteenth-Century Political Thought*. Kingston, Ontario.
Habicht, C. (1974). "Zwei römische Senatoren aus Kleinasien," *ZPE* 13.1–6.
Halfmann, H. (1979). *Die Senatoren aus dem östlichen Teil des Imperium Romanum bis zum Ende des 2. Jh. n. Chr. Hypomnemata* 58. Göttingen.
Hardinghaus, B. (1932). "Tacitus und das Griechentum." Diss., Münster.
Harrington, J. (1656). "The Commonwealth of Oceana," in *The Political Works of James Harrington*, ed. J.G.A. Pocock, 1977. Cambridge.
Harrison, J. E. (1927). *Themis*. 2d ed. Cambridge.
Hass-von Reitzenstein, U. (1970). "Beiträge zur gattungsgeschichtlichen Interpretation des Dialogus 'de oratoribus.'" Diss., Cologne.
Häussler, R. (1965). *Tacitus und das historische Bewusstsein*. Heidelberg.
———. (1969). "Zum Umfang und Aufbau des *Dialogus de oratoribus*," *Philologus* 113.24–67.
Heilmann, W. (1989). "'Goldene Zeit' und geschichtliche Zeit im Dialogus de oratoribus," *Gymnasium* 96.385–405.
Heinsius, D. (1607). *Epicedia*.
———. (1612). *Orationes*, Leiden.
Heldmann, K. (1982). *Antike Theorien über Entwicklung und Verfall der Redekunst*. Munich.
Helmbold, W. C. (1957). *Plutarch's Moralia*. Loeb ed. Vol. 6. Cambridge, Mass.
Hemelrijk, E. A. (1987). "Women's Demonstrations in Republican Rome," in *Sexual Asymmetry: Studies in Ancient Society*, ed. J. Blok and P. Mason, 217–40. Amsterdam.
Henrichs, A. (1982). "Changing Dionysiac Identities," *Self-definition in the Greco-Roman World*, ed. B. F. Meyer and E. P. Sanders, 137–60. London.
Herrmann, L. (1955). "Quintilien et le Dialogue des Orateurs," *Latomus* 14.349–69.
Herrmann, P. (1989). "Rom und die Asylie griechischer Heiligtümer: Eine Urkunde des Diktators Caesar aus Sardeis," *Chiron* 19.127–58.
Heubner, H., ed. (1972). *P. Cornelius Tacitus. Die Historien. Band III*. Heidelberg.
———. (1983). *P. Cornelius Tacitus Annales*. Stuttgart.
Hill, A. (1749). *Gideon: Or, The Patriot. An epic poem in twelve books. Upon a Hebrew plan*. London.
Hind, J.G.F. (1972). "The Death of Agrippina and the Finale of the 'Oedipus' of Seneca," *AUMLA* 38.204–11.
Hirschman, A. (1977). *The Passions and the Interests: Political Arguments for Capitalism before Its Triumph*. Princeton.
———. (1982). "Rival Interpretations of Market Society: Civilizing, Destructive, or Feeble?" *Journal of Economic Literature* 20.1463–84.
Hobbes, T. (1651). *Leviathan*. London.
———. (1682). *Behemoth, or The Long Parliament*. London.

Holborn, H. (1937). *Ulrich von Hutten and the German Reformation*. Eng. trans. New Haven.

Hopkins, C. (1697) *Boadicea Queen of Britain. A Tragedy*. London.

Hopkins, K. (1983). *Death and Renewal*. Cambridge.

Hotman, F. (1972). *Francogallia*, ed. R. E. Giesey. Eng. trans. Cambridge.

Houston, G. W. (1972). "M. Plancius Varus and the Events of A.D. 69–70," *TAPA* 103.167–80.

Howard, A. A., and C. N. Jackson. (1922). *Index verborum C. Suetoni Tranquilli*. Cambridge, Mass.

Hughes, J. (1702). *The House of Nassau. A Pindarick Ode*. London.

Hutten, U. von. (1859–62). *Ulrichi Hutteni Equitis Germani Opera quae reperiri potuerunt Omnia*, ed. E. Bocking. 7 vols. Leipzig.

The Illustrious Modern, with a commission to the Knight of the Solecism (1718). London.

Irenicus, F. (1518). *Germaniae exegeseos volumina duodecim*. Hagenau.

Jackson, J., trans. (1931). *Tacitus. Annals*. Loeb Classical Library. Cambridge, Mass.

Jacobsen, H. G. (1954). "Untersuchungen zur Darstellungsweise des Tacitus in den Historien (Buch IV)." Diss., Kiel.

Jacobson, D. L. (1965). "Thomas Gordon's Works of Tacitus in Pre-Revolutionary America," *Bulletin of the New York Public Library* 69.58–64.

Jal, P. (1968). "Tacite et la guerre civile, d'après les livres II et III des Histoires," *L'Information littéraire* 20.225–32.

Janson, T. (1964). *Latin Prose Prefaces*. Stockholm.

Jens, W. (1956). "*Libertas* bei Tacitus," *Hermes* 84.331–45.

Joachimsen, P. (1910). *Geschichtsauffassung und Geschichtsschreibung in Deutschland unter dem Einfluss des Humanismus*. Leipzig.

———. (1911). "Tacitus im deutschen Humanismus," *Neue Jahrbücher für das klassische Altertum, Geschichte und deutsche Literatur* 23.697–717.

Johnson, S. (1759). *Idler* 81, 3 November. London.

———. (1985). *Journey to the Western Islands of Scotland*, ed. J. D. Fleeman. Oxford.

Jones, C. P. (1968). "A New Commentary on the Letters of Pliny," *Phoenix* 22.111–42.

———. (1971). *Plutarch and Rome*. Oxford.

Judson, C. R., and C. Van de Velde. (1978). *Book-illustrations and Title-pages*. Corpus Rubenianum Ludwig Burchard 21. 2 vols. London–Philadelphia.

Kajanto, I. (1969). "Tacitus on the Slaves. An Interpretation of the *Annales*, XIV, 42–45," *Arctos* 6.43–60.

Kappelmacher, A. (1932). "Zur Abfassungszeit von Tacitus' *Dialogus de oratoribus*," *WS* 50.121–29.

Keitel, E. (1978). "The Role of Parthia and Armenia in Tacitus' *Annals* 11 and 12," *AJP* 99.462–73.

———. (1987). "Otho's Exhortations in Tacitus' *Histories*," *G&R* 34.73–82.

———. (1991). "The Structure and Function of Speeches in Tacitus' *Histories* I-III," *ANRW* II.33.4.2272–94.

Kelley, D. R. (1964). "De Origine Feudorum: The Beginnings of an Historical Problem," *Speculum* 39.207–28.

———. (1970). *Foundations of Modern Historical Scholarship*. New York.

———. (1976). "Vico's Road," in *Giambattista Vico's Science of Humanity*, ed. G. Tagliacozzo and D. Verene, 15–29. Baltimore.

———. (1990). *The Human Measure: Social Thought in the Western Legal Tradition*. Cambridge, Mass.

Kennedy, G. (1972). *The Art of Rhetoric in the Roman World*. Princeton.

Kenney, E. J. (1974). *The Classical Text*. Berkeley.

Keyssner, K. (1936). "Betrachtungen zum Dialogus als Kunstwerk und Bekenntnis," *Würzburger Studien* 9.94–115.

Kliger, S. (1952). *The Goths in England: A Study in Seventeenth and Eighteenth-Century Thought*. Cambridge, Mass.

Klingner, F. (1932). "Tacitus," *Die Antike* 8.151–69. Also (1961) *Römische Geisteswelt*, 4th ed., 490–513. Munich.

Koestermann, E. (1930). "Der taciteische *Dialogus* und Ciceros Schrift *De re publica*," *Hermes* 65.396–421.

———. (1956). "Die Feldzüge des Germanicus 14–16 n. Chr.," *Historia* 6.429–79.

———. (1957). "Die Mission des Germanicus im Orient," *Historia* 7.331–75.

———. (1963–68). *Cornelius Tacitus: Annalen*. Vols. 1–4. Heidelberg.

Köhnken, A. (1973). "Das Problem der Ironie bei Tacitus," *WS* 30.32–50.

Königer, H. (1966). "Gestalt und Welt der Frau bei Tacitus." Diss., Erlangen.

Krantz, A. (1520). *Saxonia*. Cologne.

Krapf, L. (1979). *Germanenmythos und Reichsideologie*. Tübingen.

Krohn, F. (1934). "Personendarstellung bei Tacitus." Diss., Leipzig.

[Lamplugh], T., Lord Bishop of Exeter. (1678). *A Sermon Preached before the House of Lords on the Fifth of November. In the Abby Church at Westminster*. London.

Leeman, A. D. (1985). *Form und Sinn: Studien zur römischen Literatur (1954–1984)*. Frankfurt.

Lehmann, G. A. (1971). "Tacitus und die *Imitatio Alexandri* des Germanicus," *AU* Beih. 1.23–36.

Leo, F. (1898). "Anzeige von: Taciti Dialogus de oratoribus, ed. A. Gudeman (Boston 1894)," *GGA* 160.169–88. Also (1960) *Ausgewählte kleine Schriften*, ed. E. Fraenkel, 2.277–98. Rome.

Levick, B. (1983). "The *Senatus Consultum* from Larinum," *JRS* 73.75–115.

L'Hoir, F. (1991). "Tacitus and Livy's Debate on the Lex Oppia," paper presented at the Classical Association of the Middle West and South, Hamilton, Ontario.

Lipsius, J. (1574). *C. Cornelii Taciti Annalium et Historiarum Libri Qui Exstant Iusti Lipsi studio emendati et illustrati*. 2d ed. 1581, 3d ed. 1585, 4th ed. 1588, 5th ed. 1589, 6th ed. 1595, 7th ed. 1600, 8th ed. 1607. Antwerp.

———. (1581). *Iusti Lipsi Ad Annales Corn. Taciti Liber Commentarius Sive Notae*. Antwerp.

———. (1584). *Iusti Lipsi De Constantia Libri Duo, Qui Alloquium Praecipue Continent in Publicis Malis*. Antwerp.

II

———. (1586–1607). *Iusti Lipsi Epistolarum Selectarum Centuriae Miscellaneae: Prima*. Antwerp and Leiden, 1586, *Secunda*. Leiden, 1590, *Tertia*. Antwerp, 1601, *Quarta (postuma)*. Antwerp, 1607, *Quinta (postuma) et De Calumnia Oratio*. Antwerp, 1607.

———. (1588). *Iusti Lipsi ad C. Cornelium Tacitum Curae Secundae*. Leiden.

———. (1589). *Iusti Lipsi Politicorum sive Civilis Doctrinae Libri Sex. Qui ad Principatum Maxime Spectant. Additae Notae Auctiores*. Leiden. 2d ed., Antwerp, 1596. 3d ed., Antwerp, 1604.

———. (1595). *Iusti Lipsi De Militia Romana Libri Quinque*. Antwerp.

———. (1596). *Iusti Lipsi Poliorceticon sive de Machinis, Tormentis, Telis, Libri Quinque*. Antwerp.

———. (1600). *Iusti Lipsi Dissertatiuncula Apud Principes: Item C. Plini Panegyricus Liber Traiano Dictus, Cum Eiusdem Lipsi perpetuo Commentario*. Antwerp.

———. (1602). *Iusti Lipsi Epistolarum Centuriae*. Antwerp.

———. (1604a). *Iusti Lipsi Manuductionis ad Stoicam Philosophiam Libri Tres: L. Annaeo Senecae Aliisq. Scriptoribus Illustrandis*. Antwerp.

———. (1604b). *Iusti Lipsi Physiologiae Stoicorum Libri Tres: L. Annaeo Senecae Aliisq. Scriptoribus Illustrandis*. Antwerp.

———. (1605). *Iusti Lipsi Monita et Exempla Politica. Libri Duo, Qui Virtutes et Vitia Principum Spectant*. Antwerp.

———. (1637). *Iusti Lipsi V.C. Opera Omnia*. 4 vols. Antwerp.

———. (1675). *Iusti Lipsi V.C. Opera Omnia*. 4 vols. Wesel.

Luce, T. J. (1986). "Tacitus' Conception of Historical Change: The Problem of Discovering the Historian's Opinions," in *Past Perspectives: Studies in Greek and Roman Historical Writing*, ed. I. S. Moxon, J. D. Smart, and A. J. Woodman, 143–57. Cambridge.

Luther, M. (1967). *Table Talk*, in *Luther's Works*, vol. 54. Eng. trans. Philadelphia.

MacDougall, H. A. (1982). *Racial Myth in English History: Trojans, Teutons, and Anglo-Saxons*. Montreal.

MacMullen, R. (1966). *Enemies of the Roman Order*. Cambridge, Mass.

Manuwald, B. (1979). *Cassius Dio und Augustus. Palingenesia* 14. Wiesbaden.

Marshall, A. J. (1975a). "Roman Women and the Provinces," *Ancient Society* 6.109–27.

———. (1975b). "Tacitus and the Governor's Lady: A Note on *Annals* III.33–34," *G&R* 22.11–18.

Martignac, J.B.S. Gay, Vicomte de. (1696). *Horace de la traduction de Mr de Martignac avec des remarques*. 2 vols. 3d ed. Paris.

Martin, J. R. (1972). *The Decorations for the Pompa Introitus Ferdinandi*. Corpus Rubenianum Ludwig Burchard 16. London.

Martin, R. H. (1967). "The Speech of Curtius Montanus," *JRS* 57.109–14.

———. (1981). *Tacitus*. Berkeley.

———. (1990). "Structure and Interpretation in the 'Annals' of Tacitus," *ANRW* II.33.2.1500–1581.

Martin, R. H., and A. J. Woodman. (1989). *Tacitus: Annals Book IV*. Cambridge.

McCulloch, H. Y., Jr. (1984). *Narrative Cause in the Annals of Tacitus.* Koenigstein.
Meinecke, F. (1962). *Machiavellism*, trans. of *Die Idee der Staatsräson* by D. Scott. New Haven.
———. (1963). *Die Idee der Staatsräson in der neueren Geschichte*, vol. 1 in *Werke*, 3d ed., ed. W. Hofer. München.
Meisterlin, S. (1522). *Ein schöne Chronik vn Hystoria.* Augsburg.
Melanchthon, P. (1834–60). *Opera quae supersunt omnia*, ed. C. Brettschneider and H. Bindseil. 28 vols. Halle.
Mendell, C. W. (1935). "Dramatic Construction of Tacitus' Annals," *YCS* 5.3–53.
———. (1957). *Tacitus: The Man and His Work.* New Haven.
Merklin, H. (1991). "'Dialogus'-Probleme in der neueren Forschung. Überlieferungsgeschichte, Echtheitsbeweis und Umfang der Lücke," *ANRW* II.33.3.2255–83.
Michel, A. (1962). *Le Dialogue des orateurs de Tacite et la philosophie de Cicéron.* Paris.
———. (1966). *Tacite et le destin de l'Empire.* Paris.
Miles, G. (1988). "*Maiores, Conditores*, and Livy's Perspective on the Past," *TAPA* 118.185–208.
Miller, N. P. (1964). "Dramatic Speech in Tacitus," *AJP* 85.279–96.
———. (1973). *Tacitus: Annals 15.* London.
Milton, J. (1648–71). *History of Britain*, in *Complete Prose Works of John Milton*, vol. 5, part 1, ed. F. Fogle, 1971. New Haven.
———. (1848). *Defense of the People of England*, ed. J. St. John. London.
Moles, J. L. (1988). *Plutarch: The Life of Cicero.* Warminster.
Molloy, C. (1676). *De Jure Maritimo et Navali: Or, a Treatise of Affairs Maritime and of Commerce. In three books.* 4th ed. 1690. London.
Momigliano, A. (1947). "The First Political Commentary on Tacitus," *JRS* 37.91–101.
———. (1977). "Eighteenth-Century Prelude to Mr. Gibbon," in *Gibbon et Rome à la lumière de l'historiographie moderne: 10 exposées suivis de discussions*, ed. P. Ducrey, F. Burkhalter, and R. Overmeer, Université de Lausanne Publications de la Faculté des Lettres 22.57–72. Geneva.
Montesquieu, C.-L. de Secondat, Baron de. (1748). *The Spirit of the Laws. A Compendium of the First Edition.* Eng. trans., ed. D. W. Carrithers, 1977. Berkeley.
———. (1989). *The Spirit of the Laws.* Eng. trans. Cambridge.
Morford, M. (1991). *Stoics and Neostoics: Rubens and the Circle of Lipsius.* Princeton.
Morris, J. M. (1969). "Compositional Techniques in Annals XIII–XVI." Ph.D. diss., Yale University.
Mossman, J. M. (1988). "Tragedy and Epic in Plutarch's *Alexander*," *JHS* 108.83–93.
Muret, M.-A. (1887). *M. Antonii Mureti Scripta Selecta.* 2 vols. Leipzig.
Murgia, C. E. (1978). "Loci Conclamati in the Minor Works of Tacitus," *CSCA* 11.159–78.

———. (1979). "The Length of the Lacuna in Tacitus' *Dialogus*," *CSCA* 12.221–40.

———. (1980). "The Date of Tacitus' *Dialogus*," *HSCP* 84.99–125.

———. (1985). "Pliny's Letters and the *Dialogus*," *HSCP* 89.171–206.

Murphy, A., trans. (1793). *The Works of Cornelius Tacitus*. 4 vols. London.

Nangle, B. C. (1934). *The Monthly Review First Series 1749–1789. Indexes of Contributors and Articles*. Oxford.

Newcomb, T. (1739). "Q. Horatii Flacci ad Curionem Epistola. Or, an Epistle from Horace in Elizium to Curio in England, faithfully translated into English from the Elizian copy. By J. M. of the Inner-Temple, Barrister," *Daily Gazetteer*, 16 June 1739. London.

———. (1740). *A Miscellaneous Collection of Original Poems*. London.

Nipperdey, K. (1908). *P. Cornelius Tacitus. II Ab Excessu Divi Augusti XI–XVI*. 6th ed. rev. G. Andresen. Berlin.

Nisbet, R.G.M., and M. Hubbard. (1970). *A Commentary on Horace: Odes Book I*. Oxford.

Norden, E. (1898). *Die antike Kunstprosa*. 2 vols. Leipzig. Repr. 1958, Stuttgart.

Nörr, D. (1983). "C. Cassius Longinus: Der Jurist als Rhetor (Bemerkungen zu Tacitus, *Ann.* 14.42–45)," in *Althistorische Studien. Festschrift H. Bengtson. Historia* Einzelschriften 40, ed. H. Heinen, K. Stroheker, and G. Walser, 187–222. Wiesbaden.

———. (1984). "Zur Biographie des Juristen C. Cassius Longinus," in *Scritti in onore di Antonio Guarini. Sodalitas* 6, 2957–78. Naples.

Oestreich, G. (1969). *Geist und Gestalt des frühmodernen Staates*. Berlin.

———. (1982). *Neostoicism and the Early Modern State*. Eng. trans. Cambridge.

———. (1989). *Antiker Geist und modernes Staat bei Justus Lipsius (1547–1606)*. Göttingen.

Ogilvie, R. M. (1965). *A Commentary on Livy Books 1–5*. Oxford.

Oldmixon, J. (1724). *A Critical History of England Ecclesiastical and Civil*. London.

A Parallel between the Roman and British Constitution. . . . Addressed to the Young Members of the Present Parliament, An. (1747). London.

Paratore, E. (1962). *Tacito*. 2d ed. Rome.

Parker, H. (1928). *The Roman Legions*. Oxford.

Pasquale, C. (1581). *C. Cornelii Taciti equitis Romani ab excessu divi Augusti Annalium Libri quattuor priores et in hos observationes Caroli Paschali Cuneatis*. Paris.

Paterson, W. (1740). *Arminius. A Tragedy*.

Pelling, C.B.R. (1983). Review of *Cassius Dio und Augustus* by B. Manuwald, *Gnomon* 55.221–26.

———. (1988). *Plutarch: Life of Antony*. Cambridge.

———. (1989). "Aspects of Plutarch's Characterisation," *ICS* 13.257–74.

———. (1990). "Childhood and Personality in Greek Biography," in *Characterization and Individuality in Greek Literature*, ed. C.B.R. Pelling, 213–44. Oxford.

Penn, W. (1675). *England's Present Interest Considered With Honour to the Prince. And Safety to the People*. 4th ed., 1698. London.

Percy, T. (1763). *Five Pieces of Runic Poetry*, trans. and introd. London.
Perret, J. (1949). *Tacitus, La Germanie*. Paris.
Philips, A. (1722). *The Briton. A Tragedy*. London.
Pichena, C. (1607). *C. Cornelii Taciti Opera Quae Extant iuxta veterrimos manuscriptos emendata notisque auctioribus illustrata per Curtium Pichenam*. Frankfurt.
Pinkerton, J. (1787). *Dissertation on the origin and progress of the Scythians or Goths*. London.
Plain Truth, or Downright Dunstable . . . With Some Critical Thoughts concerning Horace and Virgil. (1740). London.
Plass, P. (1988). *Wit and the Writing of History*. Madison.
Pocock, J.G.A. (1971). *Politics, Language and Time: Essays on Political Thought and History*. New York.
———. (1975). *The Machiavellian Moment: Florentine Political Thought and the Atlantic Republican Tradition*. Princeton.
———. (1985). *Virtue, Commerce, and Property*. Cambridge.
Poem on the Anniversary of the Birth-Day of His Majesty King George, An. (1719). London.
Pope, A. (ca. 1738). "Epitaph," in *Alexander Pope: Minor Poems*, ed. N. Ault and J. Butt, The Twickenham Edition of the Poems of Alexander Pope, 1954. London.
———. (1738). *One Thousand Seven Hundred and Thirty Eight . . . Something Like Horace*. London.
Potter, D. S. (1991). "The Inscriptions on the Bronze Herakles from Mesene: Vologeses IV's War with Rome and the Date of Tacitus' *Annales*," *ZPE* 88.277–90.
Powell, J.G.F. (1988). *Cicero: Cato Maior de Senectute*. Cambridge.
Power and Patriotism. (1748). London.
Prinz, W. (1973). "The *Four Philosophers* by Rubens and the Pseudo-Seneca in Seventeenth Century Painting," *Art Bulletin* 55.410–28.
Proverbia germanica collecta atque in Latinum traducta. (1508). N.p.
Puteolanus, F. (c. 1475). *Cornelii Taciti Historiae Augustae li.xi*. Milan.
Quinn, A. (1984). "Meditating Tacitus: Gibbon's Adaption to an Eighteenth-Century Audience," *Quarterly Journal of Speech* 70.53–68.
Raepsaet-Charlier, M.-T. (1982). "Epouses et familles de magistrats dans les provinces romaines aux deux premières siècles de l'empire," *Historia* 31.56–69.
Rech, H. (1936). "Mos maiorum. Wesen und Wirkung der Tradition in Rom." Diss., Marburg.
Reflections on Ancient and Modern History. (1746). London.
Reitzenstein, R. (1915). "Bemerkungen zu den kleinen Schriften des Tacitus," *GGA* 14.226–76. Also *Aufsätze zu Tacitus*, 70–120. Darmstadt, 1967.
Ridé, J. (1977). *L'image du Germain dans la pensée et la littérature Allemandes de la récouverte de Tacite à la fin du XVIe siècle*. 3 vols. Lille.
Robinson, R. P. (1935). *The Germania of Tacitus, a Critical Edition*. Middletown, Conn.
Ross, D. O., Jr. (1973). "The Tacitean Germanicus," *YCS* 23.209–27.
Rudd, N. (1976). *Lines of Enquiry*. Cambridge.
Russell, D. A. (1964). *"Longinus": On the Sublime*. Oxford.

Rutherford, R. (1982). "Tragic Form and Feeling in the *Iliad*," *JHS* 102.145–60.
———. (1989). *The "Meditations" of Marcus Aurelius: A Study*. Oxford.
Rutland, L. W. (1987). "The Tacitean Germanicus: Suggestions for a Re-evaluation," *RhM* 130.153–64.
Ruysschaert, J. (1949). *Juste Lipse et les Annales de Tacite. Humanistica Lovaniensia* 8. Turnhout.
———. (1979). "Juste Lipse, éditeur de Tacite," in *Atti del Colloquio La Fortuna di Tacito dal Sec. XV ad Oggi. Studi Urbinati* 53, ed. F. Gori and C. Questa, 47–61. Urbino.
Sage, M. M. (1990). "Tacitus' Historical Works: A Survey and Appraisal," *ANRW* II.33.2.851–1030.
Saint-Denis, C. de. (1692–94). *Miscellaneous Essays: By Monsieur St. Evremont*. 2 vols. Eng. trans. London.
Sandy, G. N. (1974). "Scaenica Petroniana," *TAPA* 104.329–46.
Scafuro, A. (1989). "Livy's Comic Narrative of the Bacchanalia," *Helios* 16.119–42.
Scaliger, J. J. (1666). *Scaligeriana*. The Hague.
———. (1695). *Scaligerana (Prima et Secunda)*. Cologne.
Scanlon, T. F. (1986). "Historia quasi fabula: The Catiline Theme in Sallust and Jonson," in *Themes in Drama 8: Historical Drama*, ed. J. Redmond, 17–29. Cambridge.
Schaeffer, P. (1976). "The Emergence of the Concept *Medieval* in Central European Humanism," *Sixteenth Century Journal* 7.21–30.
Schardius, S. (1574). *Historicorum opus. I: Germaniae antiquae illustrationem continet*. Basel.
Schellhase, K. C. (1976). *Tacitus in Renaissance Political Thought*. Chicago.
Schmidt, A. (1962). *Aeneas Sylvius "Germania" und Jakob Wimpheling "Responsa."* Cologne.
Schumann, G. (1930). *Hellenistische und griechische Elemente in der Regierung Neros*. Leipzig.
Seager, R. (1972). *Tiberius*. London.
———. (1977). "Amicitia in Tacitus and Juvenal," *AJAH* 2.40–50.
Shackleton Bailey, D. R. (1977). *Cicero Epistulae ad Familiares*. Vol. 1. Cambridge.
Sherwin-White, A. N. (1966). *The Letters of Pliny*. Oxford.
Shotter, D.C.A. (1968). "Tacitus, Tiberius and Germanicus," *Historia* 17.194–214.
———. (1974). "Cn. Calpurnius Piso, Legate of Syria," *Historia* 23.229–45.
Sidney, A. (1698). *Discourses concerning Government*. London.
Simar, T. (1907). "Notice sur les livres de Juste Lipse," *Revue des Bibliothèques* 17.261–83.
Slater, N. W. (1985). *Plautus in Performance: The Theatre of the Mind*. Princeton.
———. (1990). *Reading Petronius*. Baltimore.
Spence, J. (1966). *Joseph Spence: Observations, Anecdotes, and Characters of Books and Men; Collected from Conversation*, ed. J. M. Osborn. 2 vols. Oxford.
Spini, G. (1948). "I trattatisti dell' arte storica nella Controriforma italiana," in *Contributi alla storia del Concilio di Trento e della Controriforma*, 109–36. Florence.

Spitz, L. (1957). *Conrad Celtis, the German Arch-humanist.* Cambridge, Mass.
Squire, S. (1745). *An Enquiry into the Foundation of the English Constitution; Or, an Historical Essay upon the Anglo-Saxon Government both in Germany and England.* London.
Stackelberg, J. von. (1960). *Tacitus in der Romania: Studien zur literarischen Rezeption des Tacitus in Italien und Frankreich.* Tübingen.
Steinmetz, P. (1988). "Secundus im Dialogus de oratoribus des Tacitus," *RhM* 131.342–57.
Stintzing, R. (1875). *Das Sprichwort "Gut Juristen böse Christen."* Bonn.
Stolleis, M. (1980). *Arcana Imperii und Ratio Status.* Göttingen.
———. (1983). *Herman Conring (1606–1681): Beiträge zu Leben und Werk.* Berlin.
Straub, J. (1980). "Liberator haud dubie Germaniae," *WJA* n.s. 6a.223–31.
Strauss, G. (1959). *Sixteenth-Century Germany: Its Topography and Topographers.* Madison.
———. (1963). *Historian in an Age of Crisis: Johann Aventinus 1477–1534.* Cambridge, Mass.
———. (1971). *Manifestations of Discontent on the Eve of the Reformation.* Bloomington.
Stuart, G. (1768). *An Historical Dissertation concerning the Antiquity of the English Constitution.* Edinburgh.
Swift, J. (1704). *A Tale of a Tub to Which is added The Battle of the Books*, ed. A. C. Guthkelch and D. N. Smith, 2d ed. 1958. Oxford.
Syme, R. (1939). *The Roman Revolution.* Reprint 1968. Oxford.
———. (1958). *Tacitus.* 2 vols. Oxford.
———. (1970). *Ten Studies in Tacitus.* Oxford.
———. (1982). "Tacitus: Some Sources of His Information," *JRS* 72.68–82.
———. (1984–88). *Roman Papers.* Vols. 3–5. Oxford.
Talbert, R.J.A. (1984). *The Senate of Imperial Rome.* Princeton.
Taplin, O. (1978). *Greek Tragedy in Action.* London.
———. (1986). "Fifth-century Tragedy and Comedy: A *Synkrisis*," *JHS* 106.163–74.
Temple, W. (1758). *A Vindication of Commerce and the Arts: Proving that they are the Source of Greatness, Poverty, Riches, and Populousness of a State.* London.
Tenney, M. F. (1935). "Tacitus through the Centuries to the Age of Printing," *University of Colorado Studies* 22.341–63.
———. (1941). "Tacitus in the Politics of Early Stuart England," *CJ* 37.151–63.
Ternes, Ch.-M. (1976). "Recherches concernant la Gaule et les Germanies," *REL* 56.226–71.
Thomasson, B. E. (1984). *Laterculi praesidum.* Vol. 1. Göteborg.
Tiedemann, H. (1913). *Tacitus und das Nationalbewusstsein der deutschen Humanisten, Ende des 15. und Anfang des 16. Jahrhunderts.* Berlin.
Timpe, D. (1968). *Der Triumph des Germanicus: Untersuchungen zu den Feldzügen der Jahre 14–16 n. Chr. in Germanien. Antiquitas* 1.16. Bonn.
———. (1970). *Arminius-Studien.* Heidelberg.
Toffanin, G. (1921). *Machiavelli e il 'Tacitismo' (La 'politica storica' al tempo della Controriforma italiana).* Padua.

Treggiari, S. (1985). Review of *Death and Renewal* by K. Hopkins, *AJP* 106.256–62.

Tresch, J. (1965). *Die Nerobücher in den Annalen des Tacitus*. Heidelberg.

Ulery, R. W. (1986). "Cornelius Tacitus," in *Catalogus Translationum et Commentariorum* 6, ed. F. E. Cranz, V. Brown, and P. O. Kristeller, 87–174. Washington, D.C.

Ullmann, R. (1927). *La technique des discours dans Salluste, Tite-Live et Tacite*. Oslo.

Valla, L. (1962). *Opera omnia*, ed. E. Garin. Turin.

Van de Velde, C. (1977). "Rubens' illustraties bij klassieke auteurs," *Hermeneus* 49.207–16.

Van Gulik, E. (1975). "Drukkers en Geleerden—De Leidse Officina Plantiniana (1583–1619)," in *Leiden University in the Seventeenth Century*, ed. T. H. Lunsingh-Scheurleer and G.H.M. Posthumus Meyjes, 366–93. Leiden.

Verstegen, R. (1605). *Restitution of Decayed Intelligence*. London.

Vico, G. (1953). *La Scienza nuova seconda*, ed. F. Nicolini. Bari.

———. (1974). *Il Diritto universale*, ed. P. Cristofolini. Florence.

Vlieghe, H. (1987). *Rubens' Portraits of Identified Sitters Painted in Antwerp*. Corpus Rubenianum Ludwig Burchard 19.2. London.

Voet, L. (1977). *The Plantin-Moretus Museum*. Antwerp.

Volpilhac-Auger, C. (1985). *Tacite et Montesquieu*. Studies on Voltaire and the Eighteenth Century 232. Oxford.

Walker, B. (1952). *The "Annals" of Tacitus: A Study in the Writing of History*. Manchester.

Wallace-Hadrill, A. F. (1982). "Civilis princeps: Between Citizen and King," *JRS* 72.32–48.

Wallace-Hadrill, J. M. (1971). *Early German Kingship in England and on the Continent*. Oxford.

Walser, G. (1951). *Rom, das Reich und die fremden Völker in der Geschichtsschreibung der frühen Kaiserzeit*. Basel.

Walsh, P. G. (1961). *Livy, His Historical Aims and Methods*. Cambridge.

Watson, A. (1987). *Roman Slave Law*. Baltimore.

Watson, G. R. (1969). *The Roman Soldier*. Bristol.

Weinbrot, H. D. (1978). *Augustus Caesar in "Augustan" England: The Decline of a Classical Norm*. Princeton.

———. (1982). *Alexander Pope and the Traditions of Formal Verse Satire*. Princeton.

———. (1988). *Eighteenth-Century Satire: Essays on Text and Context from Dryden to Peter Pindar*. Cambridge.

Weinstock, S. (1971). *Divius Julius*. Oxford.

Wellesley, K., trans. *Tacitus. The Histories*. Harmondsworth.

Wesley, S. (1705). *Marlborough; Or, The Fate of Europe: A Poem. Dedicated to the Right Honourable Master Godolphin*. London.

Whitman, L. Y. (1978). *The Octavia: Introduction, Text and Commentary*. Noctes Romanae 16. Bern.

Williams, G. (1978). *Change and Decline*. Berkeley.

Wimpheling, J. (1501). *Germania ad rem publicam Argentinensum*. Strasbourg.

———. (1505). *Epithoma rerum Germanicarum usque ad nostra tempora*. Strasbourg.

Winterbottom, M. (1964). "Quintilian and the *Vir Bonus*," *JRS* 54.90–97.

Wirszubski, C. (1950). *Libertas as a Political Idea at Rome*. Cambridge.

Wolf, J. G. (1988). *Das Senatusconsultum Silanianum und die Senatsrede des C. Cassius Longinus aus dem Jahre 61 n. Chr.*. Heidelberg.

Woodman, A. J. (1975). "Questions of Date, Genre, and Style in Velleius: Some Literary Answers," *CQ* 25.272–306.

———. (1977). *Velleius Paterculus: The Tiberian Narrative*. Cambridge.

———. (1979). "Self-imitation and the Substance of History: Tacitus, *Annals* 1.61–5 and *Histories* 2.70, 5.14–15," in *Creative Imitation and Latin Literature*, ed. D. West and Tony [A. J.] Woodman, 143–55. Cambridge.

———. (1988). *Rhetoric in Classical Historiography: Four Studies*. London.

———. (1992). "Nero's Alien Capital: Tacitus as Paradoxographer (*Annals* 15.36–7)," in *Author and Audience in Latin Literature*, ed. Tony [A. J.] Woodman and Jonathan Powell, 173–88. Cambridge.

Zwicker, S. N., and D. Bywaters. (1989). "Politics and Translation: The English Tacitus of 1698," *Huntington Library Quarterly* 52.319–46.

Johann Sleidan and the Origins of History as a Profession*

I

Johann Sleidan was not only "the father of Reformation history," he was one of the greatest of all modern historians.[1] A man of action, he was also trained in the best traditions of classical scholarship and was a pioneer in the use of European archives. A passionate Lutheran, he was at the same time an extraordinarily accurate, fair- and international-minded observer of the upheavals of his time, the Thucydides as well as the Eusebius of early Protestantism. The period spanned by his life (1506–56) and book (1517–56) was one of the most revolutionary in European history. He was born into a world in the course of being illuminated by the humanist discovery of the classical and Christian past, his childhood coincided with the emergence of the national state and modern power politics, and his adult career with the Protestant Reformation, the first social and ideological revolution of modern times. Corresponding to these three transformations were three new perspectives on the European past: The first created by the humanist "sense of history" associated with scholars like Leonardo Bruni, Flavio Biondo, and Lorenzo Valla; the second shaped by the new politics observed and interpreted by such actor-critics as Niccolò Machiavelli, Francesco Guicciardini, Philippe de Commines, and Claude de Seyssel (whose work Sleidan translated into Latin); and the third a kind of fundamentalist church history derived from Martin Luther and Phillip Melanchthon's radical reevaluation of the Christian tradition.[2] Such was Sleidan's mixed heritage, and such the ingredients of his own contributions to modern historiography.

* A version of this paper was presented in March 1979 at the Shelby Cullom Davis Center for Historical Studies, Princeton University; for comments on that occasion the author is grateful to Eric Cochrane, Anthony Grafton, Lawrence Stone, Orest Ranum, and other participants in the seminar on the history of the professions.

[1] The best modern study is Walter Friedensburg, *Johannus Sleidanus, Der Geschichtsschreiber und die Schicksalmächte der Reformationzeit* (Leipzig, 1935). A comprehensive bibliography of Sleidaniana may be found in Karl Schottenloher, *Bibliographie zur deutschen Geschichte im Zeitalter der Glaubensspaltung 1517–1585* (Stuttgart, 1956–66), vols. 1 & 7. See below n. 50.

[2] The best survey is still, unfortunately, Eduard Fueter, *Geschichte der neueren Historiographie* (Berlin, 1936), and more particularly that of Paul Joachimsen, *Ges-*

[*Journal of Modern History* 52 (December 1980): 573–598]

Such, too, it seems to me, were three of the principal factors in the emergence of history as a professional field of study. The identification of humanism with the first phase of modern historical thought is a commonplace which has been qualified but which still commands widespread agreement; the association of modern historical study with politics is also conventional and certainly in keeping with the nineteenth-century view of the "science" if not with more recent revision of history; and finally the Protestant perspective, however secularized and sublimated, continues to inform our view of the career of Western Christendom, which is to say of European civilization. Not, of course, that such intellectual premises suffice to support the notion of "professional history" before the establishment of the historical profession in the nineteenth century, but they do suggest the framework within which this process was begun and in terms of which it was first justified—and subsidized. My suggestion is that history became at least a protoprofession in the sixteenth century, and my chief witness—or at least illustration—will be Johann Sleidan, who was at once a leading practitioner of the Renaissance "science of history," a pioneering developer of "political history," and one of the first to hear the Reformation "call" to historical studies as the central path to human wisdom. If the sixteenth century did not witness the establishment of professional history, it did possess, in the person of Sleidan, an early archetype of the professional historian. Before examining his historiographical career, let us survey briefly some of the main features of his intellectual heritage.

II

In one of his epistles Guarino da Verona registers an image which seems perennially appropriate to the profession of history—the muse Clio with a book in one hand and a trumpet in the other.[3] This symbolism suggests not only the trite choice between science and art but also the fundamental polarity, or perhaps balance, between private investigation and public notification, between history as an account of "what really happened" (as Lucian had long before written) and as a persuasive vehicle of ideology or celebrator of a cause. The

---

chichtsauffassung und Geschichtsschreibung in Deutschland unter dem Einfluss des Humanismus (Leipzig, 1910). On the three types mentioned see D. R. Kelley, *Foundations of Modern Historical Scholarship* (New York, 1970); Felix Gilbert, *Machiavelli and Guicciardini* (Princeton, N.J., 1965); and E. Menke-Glückert, *Geschichtschreibung der Reformation und Gegenreformation* (Leipzig, 1912); there is of course a massive specialized literature.

[3] Cited by Patricia Labalme, *Bernardo Giustiniani* (Rome, 1969), p. 251.

book of history demanded not only to be read and intrepreted but also broadcast in a form that would move, and possibly shake, the world. Such was the aim of civic historians like Bruni, and such even more urgently would be that of evangelical historicans like Sleidan. In the course of these efforts history received recognition as a "public thing" and its practitioners as "public persons"—*chose publique* and *personne publique* are term employed by the Huguenot historian La Popelinière.[4] The devotees of Clio began to form a public image, to achieve a social role and in effect to reach for professional status.

In the later Renaissance the herald's horn signified more than the conventional humanist pursuit of fame or the attention-getting mechanisms of rhetoric; it suggested also the commercialism of the emergent printing industry. A large public and still larger posterity seemed to beckon authors, and literary ambitions and strategies changed accordingly. Consider the attitude of a typical monastic chronicler. "In this book," runs one prescription, "there should at all times be a blank sheet on which you can note with a pencil such matters as the decease of a well known man or anything memorable about the affairs of state if you should chance to hear of it. And at the end of the year you should write out briefly in the body of the book itself, what you consider to be reliable and worth preserving for the knowledge of posterity."[5] Such advice is worlds away from self-conscious authorship and from the blurbs written for printed texts designed for popular consumption, as for instance the list of twenty precepts drawn up by Budé's publisher Badius for his edition of Sallust.[6] Included are not only Cicero's famous "first law of history," to avoid falsehood and bias, but also elaborate rules for narrative structure and literary tactics intended to enhance explanatory power and emotional effect. Such publicity announcements illustrate the transformation of historical writing not only from chronicle to reasoned narrative but also from private record to social commodity, a necessary condition for professional history. Of this phenomenon, too, Sleidan was a beneficiary; and his published writings, appearing in several languages, had international circulation and repercussions. The fact that, as a

[4] See D. R. Kelley, "History as a Calling: The Case of La Popelinière," in *Renaissance Studies in Honor of Hans Baron*, ed. A. Molho and J. Tedeschi (Florence, 1971), p. 781.

[5] E. Goldschmidt, *Medieval Texts and Their First Appearance in Print* (London, 1943), p. 174.

[6] P. Renouard, *Bibliographie des impressions et des oeuvres de Josse Badius Ascensius* (Paris, 1908), p. 174. The significance of printing for history has been recently discussed by Elizabeth L. Eisenstein, *The Printing Press as an Agent of Change* (Cambridge, 1978).

devout Lutheran, he was obliged also to bear public witness to his faith gave added impetus to Sleidan's historiographical ambitions.

In quantitative terms the growth of printing during Sleidan's lifetime was astonishing, and its importance for the study of history can be seen in a variety of ways: In the editions and especially translations of classical authors, in the upsurge of interest in medieval (national as well as universal) histories, in the publication of source collections and bibliographical aids (like Gesner's *Universal Library* of 1545),[7] and in the growth of private as well as public libraries. One example is the municipal library of Strasbourg, whose collection Sleidan must have used. Up to 1500 it possessed seventeen books of a historical character (about 5 percent of the total), while over the next century it acquired about 350 more (11 percent).[8] In this general increase one expert has detected "a real infatuation with history in the sixteenth century."[9] As for authors, La Croix du Maine's careless but vastly informed *French Libraries* (1584) lists almost 400 vernacular writers on some aspect of history (far outnumbering, he thought, their Italian rivals).[10] One selective analysis of 200 authors for the century shows one-eighth of their output to be historiographical, and at the peak during the 1560s the proportion had risen to more than one-fifth.[11] Of course this included medieval-style chronicles, textbooks, propaganda, and popular entertainments as well as classical and humanist histories. In any case, the expansion of historiographical activity and presumably of a literary market furnished another precondition for the profession of history in general. And if Sleidan was a pioneering professional historian, in another sense he was riding the crest of a great historiographical wave.

Conceptually, too, the study of history was given increasingly serious consideration in this period; and to begin with this centered on the old issue of whether history referred to bygone reality (*res gestae*) or human attempts to describe that past (*narratio rerum gestarum*). Answers to this question tended to extremes. On the one hand was the view of Saint Augustine that "history is not to be counted among human institutions, for events which have occurred and cannot be undone are to be considered as part of world order, whose founder

[7] K. Gesner, "De Historiis," in *Bibliotheca universalis* (Zurich, 1545), 2:xii.

[8] F. Ritter, *Catalogue des incunabules et livres du XVIe siècle de la bibliothèque municipale de Strasbourg* (Strasbourg, 1948).

[9] H. J. Martin, "What Parisians Read in the Sixteenth Century," in *French Humanism*, ed. W. Gundersheimer (London, 1969), p. 137.

[10] La Croix du Maine et Du Verdier, *Les Bibliothèques françaises* (Paris, 1772).

[11] D. Pottinger, *The French Book Trade in the Ancien Régime* (Cambridge, Mass., 1958).

and ruler is God."[12] At the other extreme was the humanist conception of history as a literary genre, or intellectual discipline—the "art of history" (*ars historica,* analogous to the *artes rhetorica* and *poetica*), which was a highly regulated task of exploration and expression.[13] This polarity again suggests the metaphor of the book and the trumpet, but in this case the book represents the past experience of humanity, the trumpeter the proclaimer, celebrator, or lamenter thereof. Of course the humanist view was modified in various ways that marked departure from a purely literary view. "For men are curious by nature," wrote Biondo, adapting the famous formula of Aristotle, to distinguish history from rhetoric, "and desire the wholly unadorned knowledge of things."[14] And the Machiavellian view of history as a natural process further estranged history from its passive place in the humanities. Still, the contrast remained—history as divine Creation and its aftermath, history as human recreation and its worldly potential. The richness of Sleidan's vision is that he drew upon both of these conceptions: paradoxically or not, he viewed history as at once divine order, political process, and literary expression.

The pivotal question of the intellectual status of historical studies in the sixteenth century can best be approached through that polymorphous academic construct known as the classification of sciences. In the simplest "trivial" organization, history acquired meaning in terms mainly of grammar and rhetoric, but in the wake of the Renaissance expansion of the classical "encyclopedia" history emerged, along with poetry, as an art in its own right. What is more, it had some claim to be regarded as prime vehicle of intellectual maturity and civilization. Renaissance encyclopedists like Georgio Valla and Barthélemy de Chasseneux defended its dignity by citing the Ciceronian formula that "without history men would be forever children."[15] Professional chauvinism led Lorenzo Valla to go further and claim that history, because of its emphasis on concreteness and utility, ranked above philosophy.[16] As a recent book by Arno Seifert has

[12] W. Green, "Augustine on the Teaching of History," *University of California Publications in Classical Philology* 12 (1944): 326.

[13] See G. Cotroneo, *I trattisti del"Ars Historica"* (Naples, 1971); R. Landfester, *Historia Magistra Vitae* (Geneva, 1972); and E. Kessler, *Theoretiker humanistischer Geschichtsschreibung* (Munich, 1971).

[14] Biondo, *De Roma triumphante* (Basel, 1531), p. 97: "Historia quoquemodo scripta delectat. Sunt enim homines natura curiosi, et quamlibet nuda rerum cognitione capiuntur."

[15] Georgio Valla, *De expetendis et fugiendis rebus opus* (Venice, 1501), sig. KKi^{v}; and Barthélemy de Chasseneux, *Catalogus gloriae mundi* (Cologne, 1617), p. 354.

[16] Discussion in Kelley, *Foundations,* chap. 1.

shown, the conceptual respectability of history was promoted further, and along similar lines, by the new empirical philosophy, which likewise prized concrete experience, under the banner of *historia*, or *cognitio historica*.[17] Sleidan's insatiable appetite for inside information and documentary sources is one reflection of just this attitude.

The final step in history's ascension, or self-promotion, up the ladder of Renaissance learning was its transformation, at least terminologically, from an art into a science. If the Italianate *artes historicae* represented the first position, the notion of history as a genuine *scientia* was the product of the French and German "methods" of history of the later sixteenth century. Most notable were the critical discussions of "universal history" by Christophe Milieu (who gave special attention to what he called the *professio historicorum*), François Baudouin (whose work constitutes the first handbook of historical method), and especially Jean Bodin (who incidentally included an extensive critique of Sleidan in his *Method of History* of 1566).[18] In various prefaces Sleidan also contributed marginally to this genre. These works all attempted to place the study of history on a more solid basis, especially by intensifying self-awareness, attending to the history of historiography, and providing some definition of the social role of the historian (*office du historiographe*, in the words of one of Bodin's—and Sleidan's—most professional-minded followers, La Popelinière). They also displayed a kind of intellectual imperialism hardly matched before the historical schools of the nineteenth century. For Bodin history was more than a science, it was "above all sciences" (*super scientias omnes*); for another disciple, it was the living source of all disciplines.[19] On such grounds La Popelinière, who was also the first serious historian of historiography, elevated the "profession of history" (*la profession de l'histoire*) to a quasi-religious vocation. So, with no less deliberateness and determination, Sleidan had done a generation before.

A more concrete measure of the professional status of history than its place in the classification of sciences or its independence as a literary genre is its support in the academic curriculum. Pedagogi-

[17] Arno Seifert, *Cognitio Historica* (Berlin, 1976).

[18] Christophe Milieu, *De scribenda universitate rerum historia libri quinque* (Basel, 1551), pp. 192 ff.; Baudouin, *De institutione historiae universae* (Strasbourg, 1608); and Jean Bodin, *Method for the Easy Comprehension of History*, trans. B. Reynolds (New York, 1945); and in general see A. Klempt, *Die Säkularisierung des universalhistorischen Auffassung* (Göttingen, 1960), and C. A. Patrides, *The Grand Design of God* (London, 1972).

[19] P. Droit de Gaillard, *Méthode qu'on doit tenir en la lecture de l'histoire* (Paris, 1579); La Popelinière, *Histoire des histoires, avec l'idée de l'histoire accomplie* (Paris, 1599); and see above n. 4.

cally, too, history was in the process of being promoted from an art to a science, which in another sense is to say being professionalized. In 1494 Theodorich Gresemund represented history (along with grammar, rhetoric, dialectic, and poetry) as a daughter of logic and granddaughter of philosophy; but in the later sixteenth century another German humanist (and, not incidentally, reader of Bodin) granted it a much higher status.[20] For David Chytraeus grammar, rhetoric, and dialectic were elementary subjects (*necessaria adminicula*), while the higher disciplines were of four kinds: theology; ethics and politics (including jurisprudence); physics (including medicine, mathematics, and astronomy); and history itself (broken down into Latin, Greek, and Hebrew).[21] And indeed this subversive reclassification of knowledge corresponded to a real development in academic terms, at least in German universities, a development which again illustrates a methodical building on Italian foundations. Much of the later construction would be carried out by Lutheran scholars of Sleidan's generation and attitude of mind.

University chairs of history represent one of the starting points for the modern profession of history; but the record does not permit a very clear description of their appearance. In some rudimentary sense the teaching of history did find a refuge in the trivium. In 1262 a certain Rolandinus of Padua, "doctor of grammar and rhetoric," read from his own historical work before an audience of students, faculty, and city magistrates; but this piece of academic lore, unearthed by Lynn Thorndike, was exceptional and perhaps without issue before the fifteenth century.[22] In that period promoters of the *studia humanitatis* began to teach history in the restricted sense of reading and explicating classical authors like Livy, Caesar, Tacitus, and Valerius Maximus. The practice is evident in Germany as well as Italy, and indeed as early as 1456 Peter Luder lectured on Valerius Maximus at the University of Heidelberg, where the humanities curriculum was divided specifically into history, eloquence, and poetry.[23] The fashion spread to other schools, especially under the influence of Conrad Celtes, and was intensified by a renewed interest in German history inspired above all by the discovery of Tacitus's *Germania*.[24]

[20] E. C. Sherer, *Geschichte und Kirchengeschichte an den deutschen Universitäten* (Freiburg in Breslau, 1927), p. 27; an indispensable survey.

[21] D. Klatt, *David Chytraeus als Geschichtslehrer und Geschichtsschreiber* (Rostok, 1908), p. 35.

[22] Thorndike, "Public Readings of New Works in Medieval Universities," *Speculum* 1 (1926): 101–3.

[23] Scherer, *Geschichte*, p. 14.

[24] K. Schellhase, *Tacitus in Renaissance Political Thought* (Chicago, 1976).

Nominally, the first *lectio historica* was given by Ivo Wittich in 1504 at the University of Mainz, and three years later another chair was occupied by Hermann Busch at the University of Leipzig; but many other German humanists were contributing to the same enterprise through teaching and publication. Their investigations were all the more intense—and arguably more broadly based—because of the ideological rivalry with Italian scholars and the need to justify their own "barbaric" traditions in the face of more complacent classicism.[25] So they turned, as Sleidan turned, to the old theme of universal empire, "translated" from Rome to the German nation.

This antiquarian enthusiasm was only one facet of a more general upsurge of national sentiment of which, in Germany, the Lutheran Reformation became the center and in many ways the directing force. Lutheranism not only conscripted historical scholarship but in many ways promoted it institutionally as well as emotionally. Luther himself posed the problem of reform in essentially historical terms: first portraying the corrupt "human traditions" from which men had to be liberated, and second proposing to reconstitute the true (which was to say the ancient and "primitive") tradition of the church.[26] Luther contributed to the criticism of tradition—which is to say the reevaluation of history—not only through his polemical writings but also through the encouragement of historiography (for instance, sponsoring Robert Barnes's hostile history of the popes) and the most extravagant praise of history.[27] In contrast with Calvin, who rejected the Ciceronian commonplace that history was the "mistress of life" by protesting that "scripture alone had that charge," Luther argued that "almost all laws, art, good counsel, warning, threatening, comforting, strengthening, introduction, prudence, wisdom, discretion, and all virtues well up out of the narratives as from a living fountain," and that "the historians, therefore, are the most useful people and the best teachers."[28] The great Lutheran enterprise of recasting history culminated a generation later, first in Flacius Illyricus's paradigmatic *Catalogue of the Witnesses of Truth,* which not only recalled conventional hagiography but also anticipated that "Whig view" derided by

[25] F. Borchardt, *German Antiquity in Renaissance Myth* (Baltimore, 1971).

[26] See John Headley, *Luther's View of Church History* (New Haven, Conn., 1963); P. Fraenkel, *Testimonia Patrum* (Geneva, 1961); and H. Berger, *Calvin's Geschichtsauffassung* (Zurich, 1955).

[27] Martin Luther, "Pio lectori in Christo," prefacing Barnes's *Vitae Romanorum pontificum* (Basel, 1535).

[28] "Preface to Galeatus Capelli's History, 1531," in *Works,* ed. L. Spitz, (Philadelphia, 1960), 34:275; cf. Calvin, *Commentariorum in Epistolam Pauli ad Romanos,* in *Joannis Calvini, opera quae supersunt omnia,* ed. G. Baum, E. Lunitz, and E. Reuss (Berlin, 1863–1900; 58 vols.), 49: col. 86.

Herbert Butterfield, and second in the massive *Magdeburg Centuries*, which provoked the equally massive counterhistory of Cardinal Baronius.[29] Even more than theology, as Pontien Polman and Sergio Bertelli have so exhaustively showed, history became the principal mode of explanation, justification, criticism, and especially partisan controversy in the age of reformation and counterreformation.[30] Here is the most immediate context of Sleidan's work, the ideological stage on which he occupied so central a position.

One of the other major protagonists in this great Kulturkampf, so destructive in religious and political terms but so seminal for the profession of history, was Philip Melanchthon, that "preceptor of Germany" who represented a primary link between humanist innocence and evangelical commitment.[31] Even more than Luther, Melanchthon was convinced of the need for historical perspective and, on behalf of the "new learning" as well as the Lutheran cause, repeated the aforementioned adage that "without history men will forever remain children."[32] Melanchthon's efforts to achieve a new vision of history might also be symbolized by the emblem of the book and the trumpet. Intellectually, he tried to explain Lutheran tradition as a doctrinal rather than insitutional succession, as the true vehicle of that German-imperial-universal history which, in his revised edition of Cario's chronicle, established the general framework of Lutheran history. Ideologically, he tried to reform Lutheran universities as part of a lifelong enterprise of indoctrination. In this indoctrination, history was to play a leading role; and like Sleidan, Melanchthon combined the transcendent Augustinian conception with the more down-to-earth humanist view already introduced into the curriculum by his elder German colleagues.

It was in this context of militant Protestant reform that the first chairs of history, in the modern sense of the term, were established. In the second quarter of the sixteenth century, professorships appeared in several German universities in the wake of curricular reform. In 1529 a *historicus* was established at the University of Marburg by Philip of Hesse; the next year one was established at Tübingen; in 1544 there was a *lectio historica* at Strasbourg; and others such followed: Greifswald, Königsberg, Heidelberg, Rostok, and Jena

[29] Flacius Illyricus, *Catalogus testium veritatis* (Basel, 1556).

[30] Besides the magisterial work of Pontier Polman, *L'Elément historique dans la controverse religieuse au XVIe siècle* (Gembloux, 1932), see S. Bertelli, *Ribelli, libertini e ortodossi nella storiografia barocca* (Florence, 1973).

[31] H. Brettschneider, *Melanchthon als Historiker* (Insterburg, 1880); and Fraenkel, *Testimonia Patrum*.

[32] Philip Melanchthon, Preface to *Chronicon Carionis* (Wittemberg, 1580).

among others.[33] These courses differed little from those taught by earlier, Italian "professors of poetry and history." At the University of Wittenberg, for example, Melanchthon lectured in a conventional way on Livy (book 21) in 1535 and later on Thucydides and Tacitus's *Germania*; he used historical illustrations in his lectures on Aristotelian ethics and Cicero's *De officiis*; and in various inaugural orations he sang the praises of history, especially universal history (*integrum corpus historiae mundi*, as he called it.)[34]

Under such circumstances and the pressure of contemporary issues Melanchthon contributed to the shift of attention to the examination of European and ecclesiastical tradition. Among the topics he took up in academic addresses were the lives of various emperors (Otto I, Henry III, Frederick Barbarossa, Louis of Bavaria, Sigismund), the revival of Roman law in the thirteenth century, and "Luther and the Ages of the Church."[35] A work symbolic of and central to this effort to reevaluate universal history in evangelical terms was the famous chronicle published in 1532 by Melanchthon's friend Johann Cario. Melanchthon not only reedited this book, prefacing it with his own contribution to the *artes historicae,* but from 1555 lectured on it. "The profession of history is above all in the church," he declared (if we may so render *opus historiae*).[36] There was in these years a rising wave of such textbooks of universal history, including, among others, the *Ephemeris Historica* of Michael Beuther, the *Chronique* of Bishop Jean du Tillet, and especially Johann Sleidan's book on the "four world monarchies." Translated as *The Key to History,* this interpretation of universal history served as a textbook in various universities well into the eighteenth century.[37]

The emergence of historical studies in a formal academic setting is most striking, and best documented, at the Academy of Strasbourg founded by Melanchthon's and Sleidan's friend Johann Sturm, who likewise followed the new learning which favored the *studia humanitatis* over scholastic philosophy. As early as 1541, according to the statutes, Doctor Nicolas Gerbel came to "read histories" (*liset historias*), and the subject as usual was taught indirectly within the liberal arts—but not (as so often claimed) by Sleiden, although he was residing in Strasbourg and working furiously on several historical

[33] Scherer, *Geschichte*; J. F. Hautz, *Geschichte der Universität* Heidelberg (Mannheim, 1862), 2:428; and Schindler, *Humanistische Hochschule und freie Reichstadt, Gymnasium und Akademie in Strassburg, 1538–1621* (Weisbaden, 1977).

[34] "De Studiis linguae Graeci," in *Opera* (*Corpus Reformatorum*), vol. 11, col. 862; cf. other "Orationes," in vol. 10, col. 746; vol. 11, cols. 8, 58, 383; vol. 12, col. 497.

[35] Calvin, *Opera,* vol. 11, cols. 509, 163, 306, 318, 350, 783; vol. 12, col. 286.

[36] See Melanchthon above n. 32.

[37] See below note 74.

projects.[38] It was in 1565, just before Strasbourg was transformed by Maximilian II from a gymnasium into an academy, that the first *historicus ordinarius* was appointed. Michael Beuther, another of Melanchthon's disciples, became *professor historiarum* and began, after the plan of Melanchthon, to lecture on universal history, beginning with the Old Testament and going on to Rome from the founding of the city through the caesars.[39] It is plausible but not proven that he followed the texts of either Cario or Sleidan. He also lectured on Tacitus's *Germania,* made critical observations (*animadversiones*) on Germanic and biblical antiques, and presided over thesis defenses on historical subjects. After Beuther's death in 1587, the chair of history was taken over by the theologian Johann Pappus, who in fact did make use of Sleidan's *Four World Monarchies.* By the late sixteenth century, the Academy of Strasbourg had established a firm tradition of academic history, joining others (especially in Germany) to form one of the two principal institutional bases of the modern profession of history.

Of course universities were not uniformly cordial to the new discipline. To a theologically oriented educational establishment, history could be as threatening as innovative natural philosophy, while, on the other hand, advocates of the new science like Galileo had little respect for a field managed by "memory experts."[40] But even without academic support, history would survive. "If history have no professorship, if all universities be closed," wrote the classical scholar Daniel Heinsius in the early seventeenth century, "she will always have an honorable reception in the innermost chambers of kings and princes."[41]

This brings us to the second institutional base of historical studies, a subject which has a longer, more complicated, and still more poorly documented record. Official historiography—"court history"—certainly antedates the Renaissance, and perhaps its origins are too diverse even to permit a synthetic interpretation. Monastic and city chronicles, national and civic historiographers, ecclesiastical and lay apologists all have some claim to be included in this tradition; but the official character of their charges, at least before the sixteenth cen-

[38] M. Fournier, ed., *Les Statuts et privilèges des universités françaises,* 4 vols. (Paris, 1894), 4:31. S. D'Irsay, *Histoire des universités françaises et étrangères* [Paris, 1935], 2:27, mistakenly says Sleidan was called in 1542 to the first chair of history.

[39] Fournier, pp. 118, 180, 187.

[40] Galileo, *Dialogue concerning the Two Chief World Systems,* trans. S. Drake (Berkeley, 1953), p. 113.

[41] Daniel Heinsius, *The Value of History,* trans. G. Robinson (Cambridge, Mass., 1943), p. 14.

tury, is often in doubt; and even afterward, when recorded commissions or stipends are lacking, the designation of "royal historiographer," or its equivalent, is often a matter of public repute, assumed title, or later convention. In Italy civic posts, whatever their institutional validation, were common from the time of Bruni; and later this Italian-style office, as well as the attendant literary and scholarly conventions, were transplanted to the courts of northern Europe, the most notable of these officeholders being Paolo Emilio in France and Polydore Vergil in England.[42] Unfortunately, the coherence of this Italianate tradition is less apparent in any common institutional pattern than in the form and style of neo-Livian historiography exemplified in Latin works devoted to the national and civic traditions of a variety of minor as well as major states.

In France the record is more complete. Here was a distinctive and at least quasi-official tradition of *historiographes du roi* beginning with the famous chronicle of Saint Denis, which came to enjoy legal authority as well as popular acclaim and which constituted a major source and even model for later official histories. Apparently Charles appointed royal historiographers, including Juvenal des Ursins and Jean Chartier, and so did Charles VIII for his Italian expedition, for which Octavien de Saint-Gelais and André de la Vigne wrote historical propaganda.[43] The first definitely commissioned "historiographer of the king" (from 1489) was Paolo Emilio (Paule-Emile), but his office was not continuous. About other historiographical servants of the crown less can be determined.[44] Commines hardly deserves such a title, but the brothers Du Bellay may, and so also the genealogist Bouchet. A special case might be made for the brothers Du Tillet: The elder wrote a patriotic universal chronicle often appended to Paule-Emile's history, while the younger was commissioned to assemble a source collection which, in published form, constituted the first scholarly survey of French history. Etienne Dolet made a bid for such a post but was unsuccessful. From the reign of Francis II the office of royal historiographer became more common if not more continuous, and a series of such commissions have been recorded. Among the

[42] K. Davies, *Late XVth-Century French Historiography* (Ph.D. diss., University of Edinburgh, 1954); and D. Hay, *Polydore Vergil* (Oxford, 1952). On Renaissance Italian historiography in general see the forthcoming, exhaustive work of Eric Cochrane.

[43] B. Guenée, "Histoire, annales, chroniques: Essai sur les genres historiques au moyen âge," *Annales* 28 (1973): 997–1016; and see now Orest Ranum, *Artisans of Glory* (Chapel Hill, 1980).

[44] See Kelley, *Foundations,* p. 233, and works there cited; also R. C. Christie, *Etienne Dolet* (London, 1880), pp. 365 ff.; and article of R. Barroux, "Histoire," in *Dictionnaire des lettres françaises XVIe siècle,* ed. G. Grente et al. (Paris, 1951), pp. 377–80. But there is no general discussion of official historiographers.

earliest was the hapless Pierre de Paschal, attacked by Ronsard for incompetence; and another was Ronsard himself, though his contributions were strictly in the epic (and mythic) mode. More productive were François de Belleforest, that champion of Gallican orthodoxy, and Bernard du Haillan, who was given 1,000 gold crowns for his general history of France (though he received it in 1581, five years after the first edition was published). Both of these *historiographes du roi* built directly on the work of Paule-Emile, though they incorporated the best of modern scholarship—Italian and German as well as French—and especially that of Etienne Pasquier, whose pioneering researches were carried on without benefit of official endorsement. From the later sixteenth century royal historiography—*pro patria scribere*—was a major force in both scholarly and ideological terms. From the perspective of the nineteenth-century authors like Augustin Thierry and Gabriel Monod it seemed to represent the earliest antecedents of the French historical profession.[45]

Commissioned histories were of course not confined to the national level. There were also works devoted to particular provinces and families, such as the house of Anjou, which assigned both Baudouin and Du Haillan the task of writing apologetic dynastic histories.[46] Scholarly studies with a historical approach were also devoted to particular institutions, such as the *Parlement* of Paris, and offices, such as the Admiral of France; and whether or not such publications can be placed within the genre of history, indirectly they certainly contributed to the professionalism of history. Equally effective as a spur to historical writing were the demands of propaganda, especially during the wars of religion, when both parties, Huguenots and Catholics, found it necessary to give historical as well as political legitimacy to their respective causes. For the opposition, the most conspicuous effort was the *History of France* by La Popelinière.[47] The book was not officially commissioned, but through the efforts of Henry of Navarre it was officially censured by the Synod of La Rochelle in 1585. In the course of the proceedings the author developed an extraordinary historiographical credo, which became the basis for his works of 1599, *The Idea of History* and *The History of Histories,* the most comprehensive of all contributions to the *artes historicae* as well as a sort of "mirror for historians" analogous to the

[45] A. Thierry, "Notes sur quatorze historiens antérieurs à Mezeray," in his *Dix Ans d'études historiques* (Paris, 1868), pp. 335–93; and G. Monod, "De progrès des études historiques en France depuis le XVIe siècle," *Revue historique* 1 (1876): 5–38, reprinted in centenary volume.

[46] Kelley, *Foundations,* p. 145.

[47] See article cited n. 4 above.

mirrors of the prince. More specialized, but equally important as an expression of historiography as a calling and a profession, were martyrological works such as those of Jean Crespin, John Foxe, and Ludwig Rabe and the *History of the Reformed Churches* sponsored by Theodore Beza and the Genevan church.[48]

But the great model, and in many ways the source book for these interlocking genres, was Johann Sleidan's monumental history of the Reformation. These *Commentaries on Government and Religion in the Age of Charles V* were published in 1556 and soon translated from the Latin into German, French, English, and Italian.[49] The book was written according to the historiographical values of Renaissance humanism, the realism of the "new politics" and diplomacy of the age, and the Lutheran perspective on the past, and it was supported by the Schmalkaldic League: Sleidan was writing, in other words, as official historiographer for the Lutheran party. For all of these reasons, and others which will appear, Sleidan may be taken as an archetype of the modern professional historian; and a survey of his career—neatly fulfilling Guarino's symbolism of the book and the trumpet—illustrates in a most comprehensive and concrete way a seminal phase in the history of the modern profession of history.

III

The future historian was born Johann Philippson in a small town in Lorraine, Schleidan, from which he took his Latin name (Sleidanus). Like Erasmus, Luther, and his boyhood friend Johann Sturm, Sleidan attended a school founded by the Brothers of the Common Life, the Gymnasium of Saint Jerome in Liège, and then went on to complete his classical studies in Cologne. By 1533 he was living in Paris in the company of Sturm, and somehow he finished his formal training by studying philosophy at Louvain and civil law at the University of Orleans, where he took a degree in 1535. By 1536 he had entered into the service of Cardinal Jean Du Bellay, succeeding Sturm, who left to begin his distinguished career as first rector of the Academy of Strasbourg.[50] Cardinal Du Bellay and his brother Guillaume (an expert

[48] See D. R. Kelley, "Martyrs, Myths, and the Massacre: The Background of St. Bartholomew," *American Historical Review* 77 (1972): 1325.

[49] See below note 54.

[50] The basis of this discussion is Hermann Baumgarten, ed., *Sleidans Briefwechsel* [Strasbourg, 1881], containing 182 letters. Over 200 more, no longer extant, have been identified by Adolf Hasenclever, *Sleidan-Studien* (Bonn, 1905), app. 2. A few others have turned up since (on which see Schottenloher, work cited n. 1). And see V. L. Bourilly, *Guillaume de Bellay, Seigneur de Langey 1491–1543* (Paris, 1904); and Charles Schmidt, *La Vie et les travaux de Jean Sturm* (Strasbourg, 1855).

historian in his own right) were diplomatic links between France and the German Protestants and engaged first in an attempt to reconcile Catholics and Lutherans then more modestly to establish a diplomatic liaison. Sleidan served them as translator, secretary, and representative, gaining thereby much valuable information and a wide circle of acquaintances including Luther, Melanchthon, Bucer, and Calvin.

The missions suited both Sleidan's temperament and his background. As a man of the Rhineland, he divided his attention and to some extent his allegiance between Germany and France. As a professional interpreter, he came naturally and bilingually to the idea of mediating between the two and, as a professional diplomat serving as a link between the two, to the idea of establishing a politico-ecclesiastical alliance. So it is not surprising that as a historian he tried to bring together this Franco-Germanic tradition: a modern version of the old "middle kingdom," linked not only by a common political heritage but also (he hoped) by a common religious destiny. Sleidanus was more realistic than Erasmus in his conciliatory designs, but even so historical studies seemed more attractive than an ineffectual *vita activa*. Two years after attending the crucial Diet of Hagenau in 1540, Sleidanus left active service to accept an invitation from his old friend Sturm. He settled down in Strasbourg and, aside from a few missions, including one to England and another to the Council of Trent, devoted his remaining years to the study and writing of history.

Sleidan, in fact, was already involved in his second but most engrossing vocation. In 1537 he had published a Latin version of Froissart's history and dedicated it to Jean Du Bellay.[51] In the introduction he presented his first defense of the study of history, rehearsing humanist themes but placing particular emphasis on political utility. He agreed with Thucydides that there was no substitute for firsthand experience; but since this takes too long, perhaps a lifetime, he proposed "useful learning" as a shortcut. The commonest way was the "science of equity," but studying the events of the past seemed more direct (and in any case, remarked Sleidanus, "I have always thought [the study of law] to have close affinity with the science of history"). "In order to manage such matters as war, peace, treaties, alliances, marriages, the means of increasing one's territory, the loyalty of a people, parties and other business of a kingdom," he wrote, "it seems to me that there is no more useful knowledge than the study

[51] Froissart, *Historiarum opus omne jampridum et breviter collectum et latine sermone a J. Sleidano* (n.p., 1548); English translation: "Preface to the History of Froissart, Dedicated to the Most Reverend Father and Lord, Jean du Bellay, Bishop of Paris and Cardinal of the Holy Roman Church" (July 12, 1537).

of history." He acknowledged that this commonly meant Greek and Roman history but added his own mite to the quarrel of the ancients and moderns by asking: "Who will deny that great deeds have been accomplished also among us?" Surely the examples are closer, the lessons more relevant, and "the events of our times are as remarkable as those of antiquity." Sleidanus chose Froissart because "he lived in a time that was indeed much troubled" and because, following the court for a considerable time, "he could speak of events with authority and set them down truthfully in his book."

In 1548 Sleidanus published his translation from Commines's *Memoires* and in the introduction presented a more urgent manifesto for objective history.[52] "The most important thing about history," he wrote, paraphrasing Cicero, "is not simply that it contains nothing false but also that the policies and motives of the statemen should be clearly described." Again he praised the firsthand testimony but warned against the dangers of self-serving judgments. "The same risk is run by historiographers who have been in the imperial court or army, for upon their successes they bestow all the riches of their eloquence, praising what they favor and showing themselves to be orators rather than historians." Inexperience created different problems, he continued. "On the other hand those who have no experience in affairs and who follow the accounts of others, while they may not be charged with bias, nevertheless . . . may be suspect because of their sources." "Those who desire fame through their writings should not be ambitious but rather try by every means to make the reader better and wiser." For these reasons Sleidanus chose to translate selections from Commines, an able and honest observer despite his ignorance of Latin. He, too, wrote in times of terrible trouble; and while he offered useful conclusions, "in no way did he praise those of his own country or race, even kings who had raised him to high honor, unless it was true . . . [and] everywhere he presented the facts in themselves."

This publication was dedicated to the young King Edward VI of England, one of the last hopes of moderate Protestantism, and so was the last of his translations, the *Monarchy of France* by Claude de Seyssel, who himself had made translations of classical historians into French.[53] In the introduction to his Commines, Sleidanus had in-

[52] *P. Comminaei de Carolo octavo . . . commentarii . . . J. Sleidano interprete* (n.p., 1548); English translation: "The epistle of John Sleidan to the high and mighty Prince Edward Duke of Somerset . . ." (Strasbourg, May 1548); also "A Short Declaration of Some Things Which Seem Difficult in the History of Commines . . . John Sleidan to the Reader with Health," both prefacing *The History of Philip Commines, Knight, Lord of Argenton* (London, 1665).

[53] Claude de Seyssel, *De Republica Galliae et regum officiis libri duo*, I. Sleidano

cluded a sketch of French geography and institutions; the *Monarchy of France* represents a more direct move from political history to problems of government, law, and what Sleidan refers to as "political and social science." Although ignorant of true religion ("for Seyssel wrote about thirty-three years ago when things were in darkness") and motivated by national pride, Seyssel accumulated the best of ancient and modern insights and, what is more, "accommodated them to recent conditions and explained their utility." He discussed "the bonds which hold a people together" and those three famous "bridles"—religion, justice, and police—which insure unity and guard against tyranny. Sleidan found "something to be desired" in the treatment of the first bridle by the orthodox Bishop of Turin, but on the whole he thought the advice appropriate for the young English king. "I only ask that you become familiar with these two books of Commines and Seyssel," he concluded, "one historical and the other political, both from another time. . . . You will not be displeased by the work, and I know of no other books written in French that will do more to improve judgment."

From at least 1539 Sleidan was also busy collecting materials for his own masterwork, which he first called a "history of the restored religion" (*historia restauratae religionis; histori der ernewter religion*) but which later included the political theme as well (*de statu religionis et reipublicae*).[54] The first fruits were a pair of addresses to Charles V, delivered in 1540 and published a year later, including a historical survey of the Empire from earliest times.[55] At about this time Sleidanus's commission came. With the recommendation of Bucer and the backing of Philip of Hesse, he was appointed historiographer of the Schmalkaldic league with a stipend of 250 gold florins.[56] The salary, to be paid by the Council of Strasbourg, Sleidanus evidently found difficult to collect, for he had to ask the Landgrave of Hesse to send a reminder to the magistrates of Strasbourg. But his commitment was not weakened or his efforts slowed. He continued work on his

---

interprete (n.p., 1562); English transiation: "To the Most Serene Prince, Edward VI, King of England, France, and Ireland, Greeting from Johann Sleidan" (June 1548). A modern English version of Seyssel's *Monarchy of France*, prepared by J. H. Hexter and myself, is forthcoming.

[54] Sleidan, *De Statu religionis et reipublicae* (Strasbourg, 1555), second English translation as *The General History of the Reformation of the Church*, continued to 1562 by Edward Bohun (London, 1689), preface to the Elector of Saxony March 23, 1555. The early translation was that of J. Daus [Daie], *A Famous Chronicle of Oure Time, Called Sleidanes Commentaries* (London, 1560). Sleidan's other designations appear in letters to William Cecil and John Cheke, March 15, 1553, and to Philip of Hesse, May 15, 1546 (Baumgarten, nos. 126 and 74).

[55] Sleidan, *Zwei Reden an Kaiser und Reich*, ed. E. Böhme (Tübingen, 1879).

[56] Jakob Sturm to Martin Bucer, May 2, 1545, and Philip of Hesse to the Thirteen of Strasbourg, September 1, 1547 (Baumgarten, nos. 23 and 79).

book almost to the day of his death—which occurred, as a result of the plague, on October 31, 1556, the thirty-ninth anniversary of the day that marked the birth of his cause and the starting point of his book.

Sleidanus was obviously a professional historian by contractual agreement and private interest as well as by public and confessional commitment. Yet if his status as hired apologist restricted his freedom of expression, it also gave him access to documentation not otherwise available (a justification offered by so many later court historians). "On the 10th of this month," he wrote to the *Stettmeister* of Strasbourg (Jakob—no relation to Johann—Sturm) in May 1545, "I sent letters to [the Elector of] Saxony and to [the Landgrave of] Hesse and enclosed a chapter, in German, of my future history, of which you saw the Latin version last year, in order that they might see my order of procedure and tell me what they want of me. I need more precise details, and perhaps they will furnish these when I give them the completed chapter. It should not be difficult for their secretaries to collect all this information, especially since I have everywhere indicated the dates and order of the subjects."[57] Both of these princes complied as best they could, though Philip of Hesse could find nothing in his father's records about the Diet of Worms and suggested applying directly to Luther. This Sleidan had already done. There is no evidence that Luther responded directly, but Sleidan did make full use of the first volume of Luther's works for this crucial period. For later times he drew not only on his own recollections and those of friends but also, whenever possible, on archival sources, especially those of Hesse (Marburg), Weimar, and Strasbourg. In this respect he was something of a pioneer, although it was probably true, as Sleidan's father-in-law complained, that he did not make use of a sufficiently wide range of archival sources even from Protestant states.[58]

He applied to many other friends and acquaintances for aid and information. "In December I asked you by letter," he reminded Sir William Cecil in March 1553, "to give me information about all that went on between Clement VII and Henry VIII of beloved memory, when he declared his own and his kingdom's independence."[59] A few

[57] To Sturm, May 15, 1545 (Baumgarten, no. 29). On Sleidan's archival inquiries, see Johann Friedrich of Saxony to Philip of Hesse, June 10, 1546 (Baumgarten, no. 76); cf. Sleidan to and from Hesse, May 29, 1545, and May 15 and May 20, 1546 (Baumgarten, nos. 31, 74, 75).

[58] Kaspar von Nidbruck to Sleidan, July 3, 1555 (Baumgarten, no. 147).

[59] To Cecil, March 1533 (Baumgarten, no. 126).

months later he wrote also to Calvin. "I think that you know of the task I undertook some years ago to write the whole history of the restored religion. I have now completed it from 1517 to 1546 and the war of the Emperor against us. But I want to know all about the Waldensian persecution. . . . I should be most grateful if you would send this to me."[60] He was referring to the royal campaign against the Protestants in Merindole which had shocked him a few years before. Sleidan owed many such debts—to Calvin's friend Jean Crespin, whose martyrology was to appear a few months later, to Pier Paolo Vergerio, Bucer, Martyr, Melanchthon, and others not recorded.

Well publicized before publication, Sleidan's book raised the highest expectations. Though not the first, it would be the most comprehensive and authoritative treatment of the greatest theme of the century. "Many little books have appeared which treat parts of the subject," he told the Elector of Saxony in June 1553, "but with such superficiality and partisanship that a more accurate book is made all the more urgent."[61] In the spring of 1555 it finally appeared under the imprint of Wendel Rihel of Strasbourg and dedicated to that same Elector, August I. It treated "the state of religion and government" from All Saint's eve 1517 to February 1555 in twenty-five books. For the remaining year and a half of his life Sleidan continued his work, and after his death a twenty-sixth book was assembled out of his notes, taking the story down to September 1556. The last entry that could be in Sleidanus's hand states that on the fifteenth of that month Emperor Charles V, the great nemesis of German Protestantism who (even more than Luther) dominated the narrative, retired into Spain, leaving his crowns to his son Philip and his brother Ferdinand. The final sentence was set down by another.[62] In the English translation (which appeared in 1560, three years after the French and German versions) it reads: "The last day of October, John Sleidan authour of this worke, a man of singular giftes of the minde, and excellent learnynge all prayse worthy, departeth out of this life at Strasbourg, and is there honorably buried."

Sleidan's *Commentaries on Government and Religion in the Age of Charles V* was much more than partisan propaganda. Epic in theme, European in scope, and annalistic in method, it was, however inadvertently, the first attempt to treat synthetically "the rise of modern Europe." Sleidan's first premise was to give equal weight to what Luther himself had referred to as *politeia* and *religio*. "In the history

[60] To Calvin, September 13, 1553, and April 2, 1554 (Baumgarten, nos. 128, & 132).
[61] Baumgarten, no. 127.
[62] Sleidan, *A Famous Chronicle*, fol. 470.

of religion," he explained in his preface, "I would not omit what concerned the civil government because . . . they are interwoven with the other, especially in our times, so that it is not possible to separate them."[63] He began *in medias res* with the epoch-making exhibiting of the Ninety-five Theses (and gives no support to the modern suggestion that this act was mythical). His narrative proceeds year by year, stopping occasionally to fill in background on particular topics, taking up persons and events as they appear without much regard for relevance except for great matters of state and war. One result is that as the Reformation spreads and ramifies, Sleidan's story, too, becomes more diffuse and broken up, except when a major scene furnishes coherence or dramatic possibilities. In general Sleidan displays intermittent control over classical dramatic style but—increasingly an occupational hazard—often falls victim to his accumulated documentation, which chronically overwhelms the story line. The reader, however, is impressed with a certain immediacy and abstinence from editorial intrusion. Not, of course, that this undiscriminating openness to facts prevented Sleidanus (any more than it prevented Ranke) from assuming that the events being chronicled were part of God's plan.

But if Sleidan's appetite for information distorted classical form, it did enrich the texture and deepen the explanatory power of his narrative. To some extent his criterion for inclusion was journalistic—newsworthiness—but his dual, politico-religious focus expanded his view of the historical process beyond the contemporary standards reflected, say, in Machiavelli or Guicciardini. In his political analyses, Sleidan was obliged to consider not only questions of interest but also ideological factors and sometimes the force of fanaticism. Because of his attention to the progress of the reformation in Europe, moreover, Sleidan also had to explore various levels of social history.[64] He had to treat not only great personnages and public confrontations but also conversions, the penetration of the gospel and religious dissent into less visible classes of society, and especially the official "pursuits" and persecutions of heresy and the tradition of martyrs. He had to attend also to the upheavals in the cities, especially his own Strasbourg, and most especially to the growing manifestations of social discontent and political resistance. This multiplicity of concerns also helps to account for the diffuseness of the book.

The first three books, based on Luther's own published works and debates, set the scene with a description of the posting of the

[63] Sleidan "Preface" in *The General History of the Reformation.*

[64] There is, however, no analysis or even appreciation of these qualities of Sleidan's masterpiece.

Ninety-five Theses and from there carry the story down to 1522. Imperial affairs, preceded by a sketch of the constitution of the Empire, are given parallel treatment with marginal attention to Erasmus, Zwingli, Henry VIII, and the "Bohemian sects." The central scene is the drama at the Diet of Worms in April 1521 when Luther took his archetypal stand (though Sleidan does not report the legendary "Hier steh' ich" inscribed on the monument in Worms). The next three books continue the dual story, especially the Italian wars and the dissemination of the gospel, down to the formation of the Protestant party in 1529, and then the focus widens again. With book 8 the Schmalkaldic League (in effect Sleidan's employer) becomes dominant, and for the first time he can draw on his own experiences. Among the topics in the next four books (the 1530s) are the defeat and death of Zwingli, the events of the English reformation, the sensational anabaptist uprising at Münster, the persecution of French Protestants, the reforming efforts of Pope Paul IV, the emergence of Calvin, the founding of the Academy of Strasbourg, and, as always, the European wars centering on Charles V. Books 13 through 21 cover the 1540s, which Sleidanus spent mainly in Strasbourg, and continue the narrative of the wars down to the Interim of Augsburg in 1548. In Book 22 we find summarized that *locus classicus* of revolutionary ideas, the Confession of Magdeburg. The last five books carry the story down to Sleidanus's death, with continuing focus on the civil wars, especially the relations between the French monarchy and the German Protestants, though events from England to eastern Europe are commented on. The last major topic is the Diet of Augsburg, which ended the first phase of the Reformation.

Reactions to the book were not long in coming. Among friends and coreligionists, Calvinists as well as Lutherans, responses were favorable and sometimes adulatory. "Letters have come to me from many places," Sleidan told one admirer, "expressing the great gratitude of learned men for my recently published book, though all praise belongs to God."[65] A French friend, sending along a copy of the remonstrances made by the *Parlement* of Paris, remarked, "Never have I seen a work so much sought after as yours." If there were 10,000 copies, he added, they would be bought up within an hour.[66] The general Protestant reaction is perhaps best expressed by the rhapsodic lines addressed several years before to Sleidan by one of his colleagues at the Academy of Strasbourg Nicolas Gerbel, who happened also to be

[65] To Caspar Lanus, September 9, 1555 (Baumgarten, no. 156).

[66] Anonymous, Paris, December 26, 1555 and January 30, 1556 (Baumgarten, nos. 164, 167).

the school's (and also one of Europe's) first "professors of history."[67]

> Press on, Sleidan, the omens are good, nothing can stop you.
> Press on, all the weight of history is on your side,
> And so, in the hands of such a master, is the task itself.
> Press on, then, it is worthy of your labor.
> What if it does not please our miserable age?
> The future will bring a better judgment.

There were many readers in Sleidan's "miserable age," of course, who were far from being pleased, especially French and German Catholics. Although this was only to be expected, Sleidan had no intention of taking criticism quietly. In May 1555 he wrote to the Council of Augsburg, where the imperial Diet has been in session for the previous three months to bring an end to the civil wars.[68] "It has been reported to me that my recently published history has provoked many discussions among you . . . and that some claim to have found untruthful passages in it," he began.

> Illustrious sirs, this report is so upsetting to me, so undeserved and baseless . . . , that I beg you not to be irritated and to listen to my own account. . . . What most disturbs me is the suggestion that truth is lacking in the work. That is the cruelest blow, yet the easiest to answer, for I am the enemy of all falsehood and do not boast when I affirm that I would rather die than say, still less write, anything without proof. . . . Should anyone object that my history is not true, he cannot be taken as a historian. For I have taken nothing on my own judgment, as charged, but everything out of authentic acts, which I have carefully collected over the past sixteen years.

But the attacks continued and indeed became more intense. In June Sleidan wrote to Nidbruck, then attending the Diet of Augsburg, about the calumnies against himself and his work. "Of those who seek my ruin," he complained, "your vice-chancellor is the first, then the chancellor of our bishop [Christoph Welsinger]. They are fit company for each other. I expected nothing better."[69] In the Protestant camp, too, Sleidan had critics, notably Markgraf Albrecht Alcibiades of Kulmbach-Bayreuth, also of the house of Hohenzollern. The story

[67] Sleidan to Vergerio, summer 1555 (?) (Baumgarten, no. 144):

> Perge bonis avibus, Sleidane diserte. Quid obstat?
> Perge, tibi historiae numina cuncta favent.
> Et res ipsa favet, talem sortita magistrum.
> Perge modo: res est digna labore tuo.
> Quod si te praesens malesana felfellerit aetas,
> Iudicium melius saecla futura ferent.

[68] Baumgarten, no. 139.

[69] To Nidbruck, June 18, July 20 and 30, 1555 (Baumgarten, nos. 143, 148, 152).

that this ultra-Lutheran prince inspired a book enumerating the "1,000 lies of Sleidan" is probably a fiction of later invention, but there is no doubt that he did lead an attack upon Sleidan's treatment of the Empire.[70]

It was to defend himself against the Catholic attacks, he told Nidbruck, that he had decided to compose a brief "apology" for his history. He had in no sense violated the law of history (Cicero's *prima lex historiae*), he continued, nor had he in any way discredited his fatherland.[71] "In all ages, he declared, "historians have been condemned for such reasons"; but his book was, he repeated a *vera historia*. "If it is not a true history, then there is no such thing as a credible political history (I except sacred histories)." Still more absurd, he went on, were charges of indiscretion. "I recall ten years ago, when my edition of Commines appeared, [such critics] were still attacking him, forty years dead, for discussing in his history the secret counsels of great princes." What really offended his enemies, he concluded, was the survival of the Reformation (*restauratae religionis series*). Sleidanus sent a German version of the apology to the Council of Strasbourg, and while they approved, they did not think it should be printed at this time. This was the advice, too, of Nidbruck, who argued that it would either seem to be a concession or provoke still sharper attacks. Sleidan finally agreed. "About suppressing the apology and letting moderation prevail," he told Nidbruck in July, "I have followed your advice."[72] His angry little essay appeared only after his death, as an appendix to his history.

In this apology Sleidan reaffirmed the arguments of his introduction.[73] In our times there has been, he wrote, "such a change in religion as is not to be parallelled since the apostles . . . [followed by] a great commotion in the civil state, as is usual." Though "not the fittest person to undertake this work," he continued, "yet at the request of many good men, I entered upon it, for the glory of God"; and "though I willingly profess the doctrine of the gospel . . . , yet I have carefully abstained from all exasperating language and simply delivered everything as it came to pass." Few historians have ever been satisfied with unadorned truth, and among those who insert their own judgments Sleidanus mentioned Platina, Pietro Bembo, Paolo Giovio, and even Commines. Others are filled with uncontrollable

[70] See K. Schottenloher, "Johannes Sleidanus und Markgraf Albrecht Alcibiades," *Archiv für Reformationsgeschichte* 35 (1938): 193–202.

[71] "John Sleidan's *Apology for his History*," in *The General History of the Reformation*.

[72] Baumgarten, no. 149.

[73] Sleidan, *Apology*.

bias, such as the writing of Cardinal Pole and especially Luther's libelous biographer Johann Cochlaeus, whose commentaries were "stuffed with horrible, unheard of, and invented slanders." By contrast Sleidan, giving up the incompatible "profession of civil law," gave himself wholly over to history and, thereby, to the glory of God.

The broader context in which Sleidan's view of contemporary history was set appears in his last published work, *The Four World Monarchies,* which follows the prophecy of Daniel and the historiographical model established by Orosius, preserved by Otto of Freising, and given new life by Cario and Melanchthon.[74] The date of composition is unknown, nor does Sleidan ever refer to it in his extant correspondence, but it is obviously related to his "Two Addresses" to the Emperor in 1540, and it can be assumed that the book was conceived, if not written, not long after this. The theme of the work is the old notion of the "translation of empire" (*translatio imperii*) from the Medes, Persians, and Greeks through the Romans and more recent German beneficiaries.[75] This universalist conception of history, though it was imperial rather than papal, was not popular in all circles, especially with the French, who rejected the Emperor's as well as the Pope's hegemony. On such grounds Sleidan's old-fashioned view was assailed a decade after his death by Bodin, who preferred a national and pluralistic perspective.[76] But despite the betrayal of Charles V (which he so carefully chronicled) Sleidanus never accepted the notion of "Europe divided" in either political or religious terms, and within the canon of academic history his universalizing ideal was preserved in one form or another down to the time of Hegel and Ranke.

IV

In general terms, it seems to me, Johann Sleidan represents a type which we have come to know as the professional historian. Not only did he fulfill many of the same requirements, including professional commitment, regular subsidization, academic associations, and conception of his discipline as an independent science, but he also belongs in a sense to the same intellectual continuum or tradition. This is suggested above all by several striking parallels and ties between his researches, attitudes, and writings, and those of the most famous

[74] Sleidan, *De quatuor summis imperiis* (Geneva, 1559), trans. as *The Key of History or Generall Chronicle from the Floode . . .* (London, 1631).

[75] See W. Goez, *Translatio Imperii* (Tübingen, 1958).

[76] Bodin, *Method* (cited above n. 18), chap. 7. "Refutation of Those Who Postulate Four Monarchies and the Golden Age."

of all models of the professional historian: Leopold Ranke, nineteenth-century champion of the science of history. Both the "father of Reformation history" and this "founder of scientific history" were born in time of rampant enthusiasm for the study of the past, of a belief in the public as well as the private value of history.[77] They were in conspicuous agreement about the need for a concern for religion as well as politics. In fact, Ranke's defense of this bifocal perspective is virtually a paraphrase of the formulation by Sleidan cited above: "For purposes of discussion or instruction, it may be possible to sever ecclesiastical from political history," reads the first sentence of Ranke's own history of the German Reformation; "in actual life they are indissolubly connected, or rather fused into one indivisible whole."[78] Although Ranke was critical of Sleidan's scholarly standards, he shared with him an obsession for firsthand information and especially archival research and made the same sort of extravagant claims about his objectivity. At the same time both Ranke and Sleidan had a (quasi-) religious commitment to their subject—in the sense not only of dedication to their calling (*Beruf* in the Lutheran sense) but also of an ideological attachment to Lutheran tradition. Both thought it possible and necessary to relate "how it really was" in the context of a larger, indeed providential, plan (Sleidan's *Four World Monarchies* being the pedagogical equivalent of the *Weltgeschichte* of Ranke's old age). Convinced of their functions as teachers and champions of a politico-religious cause, they fulfilled in their own way the old humanist ideal depicted in the symbolism of the book and the trumpet.

It is at least arguable that Sleidan fulfilled the role of professional historian. Can it also be maintained that his age saw anything like a profession of history? A sociologist has recently identified five major attributes of a modern profession: (1) systematic theory; (2) a sort of "authority" not shared by excluded amateurs; (3) community sanction, involving some sort of accreditation, perhaps privileged information and confidentiality; (4) a regulative code of ethics; and (5) a "professional culture" exhibited in some sort of collective behavior.[79] Artificial as these criteria are, they do furnish an approach to the

[77] See the recent interpretation of Leonard Krieger, *Ranke, the Meaning of History* (Chicago, 1977).

[78] Leopold Ranke, *History of the Reformation in Germany,* trans. Sarah Austin (London, 1905), p. 1. For Ranke's comments on Sleidan, see *The History of the Popes,* trans. Foster (London, 1907), 3:48–49.

[79] R. Pavalko, *Sociological Perspectives on Occupations* (Itasca, Ill., 1972). Cf. H. Duranton, "Le Métier d'historien au XVIIIe siecle," *Revue d'histoire moderne et contemporaine* 23 (1976): 481–500.

general (and, perhaps, likewise artificial) question of the origins of history as a profession. In the first place a "systematic theory" was surely realized in the proliferation of historical arts and methods which, in the wake of the Reformation and Counter-Reformation, provided the conceptual basis for enterprises like that of Cario and Sleidan. Second, quasi-professional authority was enjoyed, or at least proclaimed and widely acknowledged, by authors like Sleidan, Bodin, and La Popelinière. "Community sanction," third, was indirectly reflected in the professorships of history and official historiographical posts which provided institutional bases for what La Popelinière called "the office of the historiographer," as in a different way did the new medium of print. Fourth, a "regulative code of ethics" was certainly implied in the prescriptions expressed in the *artes historicae* and manifestos like Sleidan's apology—not to speak of the condemnations, unofficial as well as official, of particular historical publications, such as (again) those of Sleidan and La Popelinière. Finally, a professional culture might be seen emerging in various kinds of collective behavior, including cooperative research (such as that of the martyrologists and the Magdeburg Centuriators), critical reviewing by peers, the systematic publication of documentary and reference works, and journalistic and political exploitation.

Do these factors add up to a professional activity? Now obviously, the sixteenth century did not have anything quite so formal as historical journals, research centers, historical conferences, or history book clubs; nor did it possess anything like a guild structure. What this period did have, however, was the formulation of some standards of historical scholarship, the establishment of certain sources of revenue, and the fixing of various professional patterns. Perhaps the best answer to the question posed by this paper is that, while the sixteenth century did not see the establishment of history as a profession in a sociological sense, it did witness the appearance of a new intellectual type, comparable to the perfect orator, courtier, or ambassador, or perhaps better to Bacon's "men of science."[80] This was the learned and experienced, self-consciously dedicated, but reimbursed and publicized student of the past, who would likewise brook no superior in the study of the human condition. Men of this type are at least the protoprofessional forebears of modern practitioners of history.

[80] Cf. G. W. Sypher, "Similarities between the Scientific and the Historical Revolutions at the End of the Renaissance," *Journal of the History of Ideas* 26 (1965): 353–68.

IV

HISTORY AS A CALLING: THE CASE OF LA POPELINIÈRE

Nowhere in this temple
Are the works of God concealed.
It is to man in the center
That they are best revealed [1].

So one 16th-century French humanist expressed the view that man's unique « dignity » brought him not only immortality but also an ideal perspective from which to survey the world. In particular, as François Baudouin argued, « The study of history is the one way we can ascend to that knowledge of divine and human things, thus to see our haughty spirits as in a mirror and to gain some perspective on [*circumspiciamus*] what has been done in the world ...» . These were not new ideas, of course, but they were being given a new epistemological twist at this time. It was beginning to dawn upon some scholars that man's dignity involved a crucial ambiguity, that he was obliged to attend not one but two temples — that, in short, there was a fundamental distinction between God's creation and the world of man's own making. In precisely the same way that Vico would later distinguish between the *verum* and the *factum*, Baudouin marked off nature (*res naturales*) from the sphere of human action (*res humanae*) [2]. In the latter « ampitheater », he conti-

---

[1] Guy du Four, Sieur de Pibrac, *Les Quatrains* (Paris, 1574), no. 8:

« Il ny a coin si petit dans ce temple,
Ou la grandeur n'apparoisse de Dieu.
L'homme est planté justement au milieu,
Afin que mieux par tout il le contemple ».

It may be noticed that man's superiority to the animal world, expressed in this medieval commonplace, rests not only upon reason but also upon history; see, for example, the preface to Henry of Huntingdon's *Historia Anglorum*: « Historia ... maxime distinguat a brutis rationabiles ... ».

[2] *De Institutione historiae universae et ejus cum jurisprudentia conjunctione* (Strasbourg, 1561), opening and closing paragraphs. Almost identical language is used by J. J. Grynaeus, « De Historia in universum » (Zurich, Zentralbibliothek, MS B. 130).

nued, man was a performer (*actor*) as well as observer and critic (*spectator* and *judex* or *interpres*). Nature might be understood through reason and contemplation, but humanity had to be viewed in terms of memory and temporal sequence (*ordinibus temporum*). The significance of this argument, it seems to me, is that for the first time the historian's field of inquiry has been defined in explicitly philosophical terms. In this way history attained a certain intellectual parity with other established professions.

In more concrete ways, too, the study of history was coming of age in the 16th century. Through its reception into the university curriculum and through the various « methods » devised by Baudouin, Bodin, and others, history was transformed from a badly defined literary genre into a recognizable — if still badly defined — academic discipline. It was promoted literally from an « art » to a « science ». For some humanists, in fact, it outranked philosophy itself. « As the soul is nobler than the body », declared Pomponio Leto, « so history surpasses other bequests and offers the most authoritative part of wisdom, for in it may be found an imitation of life ».[3] Not only had history begun to invade and to inform the more established disciplines, including law, theology, and philosophy, not to mention literature and historiography itself, but it had begun to appear, at least in the eyes of some scholars, as the actual *source* of these disciplines [4]. Here are some of the assumptions underlying the various attempts to restore, or to recreate, the plenitude of history, most conspicuously in the « designs » of history proposed by Louis le Roy and Bernard du Haillan, in the « researches » of Etienne Pasquier, and in such humanist *summae* as Le Roy's *Vicissitude of Things in the Universe* (1575), Christophe Milieu's *Writing of Universal History* (1547), and perhaps Polydore Vergil's *Inventors of Things* (1499 and later editions) [5]. To judge

---

[3] Pomponius Laetus, *Opera ... varia* (Mainz, 1521), f. II r (letter to Francesco Borgia).

[4] P. Droit de Gaillard, *Methode qu'on doit tenir en la lecture de l'histoire* (Paris, 1579), p. 552: « Et pour dire en un mot, toutes disciplines ne prennent pas leur source ... que de l' histoire, comme d'une fontaine tresabondante ».

[5] C. Milieu, *De scribenda universitatis rerum historia* (Basel, 1551), proposed a threefold division, corresponding to natural history, social and

from such works the intellectual imperialism of history was unmatched since the triumph of Aristotelian philosophy in the 13th century.

But there is another factor in the establishment of history as an independent field of study that has not been sufficiently appreciated. This is the impulse provided by the ecclesiastical controversies of the 16th century. As Hans Baron has argued, the historical perspective of 15th-century Italy was shaped as much by political conflict as by « archeological enthusiasm », in Burckhardt's phrase. A similar view must be taken of 16th-century historical thought, which likewise became involved in the *vita activa* — and in a still more fundamental « crisis », namely, the Protestant Reformation. From the beginning this conflict, which of course had a social and national as well as an ideological dimension, was expressed in fundamentally historical terms; that is, as a clash not merely of religious values but of distinct historical « traditions ». Consequently, history was not merely a weapon of controversy but the characteristic mode of thought in which Protestants and Catholics expressed their differences. It was the Protestants, of course, who took the lead in the attempt to make a reevaluation — or perhaps transvaluation — of Christian antiquity and its later tradition [6]. It is no accident that the first chairs of history were set up in Protestant universities and devoted specifically to ecclesiastical studies, nor that the first comprehensive handbook of historical method, that of Baudouin, was inspired by the Protestant conception of « universal history ». The eventual result of the demands of religious polemic — together with the interest it aroused and the subsidization it provided — was to transform the investigation of history into a major scholarly industry.

By the end of the 16th century, in short, history was recognized not only as a distinct mode of thought but as a most demanding profession. From at least some enthusiastic students it elicited not only scholarly allegiance but a kind of religious

---

economic history (*historia prudentiae*), and the history of arts and sciences (*historiae sapientiae*). Le Roy's « Proiect ou dessein du royaume de France » appeared in his *Exhortation aux françois pour vivre en concorde* (Paris, 1570); cf. B. Du Haillan's *Promesse et desseing de l'histoire de France* (Paris, 1571).

[6] A prime example is Flacius Illyricus, *Catalogus testium veritatis* (Basel, 1556).

devotion; and it may be suggested that, because of its ideological function, it had become not only a science but a calling.

Of those who were « called » at this time, no one better illustrates the heritage and the ideals (I will not add, the accomplishments) of modern historical scholarship than Lancelot Voisin, Sieur de la Popelinière. In 1599 La Popelinière published a remarkable work which was at once the last of the 16th-century handbooks of historical method and the first comprehensive history of historiography and which illustrates all of the themes I have introduced [7]. Yet this *History of Histories*, together with the *Idea of Perfect History* and an ambitious « Design for the New History of the French », was still-born, not to say misbegotten. It is perhaps not surprising that La Popelinière should have been neglected in the 17th century, when historical knowledge was going out of fashion; but even in the history-haunted 19th century, when Bodin was resurrected as a father of historical methodology, his disciple La Popelinière was practically unknown. Gabriel Monod, one of the few to appreciate his significance as part of a *nouvelle vague* of French historical writing, tried to persuade Augustin Renaudet to take up the subject for his thesis, but that young man (fortunately for students of humanism and pre-reform) had other things on his mind, and in fact it is only recently that La Popelinière has attracted attention [8]. Yet, as one of his few 19th-century readers justly remarked, « La Popelinière has his place among those, who *helped* to bring historical literature from a rude and indiscriminate superstition, to the more philosophic position which it occupies in modern

---

[7] *L'Histoire des histoires* (Paris, 1599), published with the separately paginated *L'Idee de l'histoire accomplie*, followed by « Le Dessein de l'histoire nouvelle des François ». I take this « histoire accomplie » to be equivalent to Bodin's « historia consummata » and to Baudouin's « historia perfecta » or « integra ».

[8] Beginning with Herbert Butterfield, *Man on his Past* (Cambridge, 1955), appendix I. Most important are the articles by G. Wylie Sypher in the *Journal of the History of Ideas*, XXIV (1963), 41-54, and XXVI (1965), 353-68, and by Myriam Yardeni in *Revue d'histoire moderne et contemporaine*, XI (1964), 109-26, whose bibliographical references I shall not repeat. Cf. Lucien Febvre, « Un historien de l'humanisme: Augustin Renaudet », *Bibliothèque d'humanisme et Renaissance*, XIV (1952), x, and G. Monod, « De progrès des études historiques en France depuis le XVIe siècle », *Revue historique*, I (1876), 5-38.

times »[9]. Whatever its novelty and whatever its influence, La Popelinière's provoking and badly written treatise, brimming with opinions and half-baked ideas, was an incomparable illustration of the exalted status which history was beginning to claim for itself in the 16th century.

Soldier, diplomat, man of letters, La Popelinière was one of the most interesting and unconventional authors of the later 16th century[10]. Opinionated, bursting with ideas and projects, he was also one of the least successful. In 1577 La Popelinière's characteristic indiscretion got him involved in a duel, and he received a wound in the face as a result. After this he retired from military service to what he hoped would be a quiet life of literature. He was fascinated with maritime affairs and wrote two books on different aspects of this subject: *The Three Worlds* (1582), dealing with the discoveries of the past century and the revised physiognomy of the earth, which now consisted of the Old World, America, and « Australia », as he called Antarctica; and *The Admiral of France* (1584), a pioneering essay in comparative institutional history. It was his *History of France*, however, that produced most of his fame, that absorbed his energies, and that eventually changed the course of his life. The indiscretions committed by La Popelinière in this book had a still more disastrous effect upon his career, causing him to lose favor first with his party, the Huguenots, and then, more irreparably, with Henry of Navarre. Nor did any of his later writings, the *History of Histories* or even the laudatory *History of the Conquest of Bresse and Savoy* (1601), restore him to the king's good graces. La Popelinière kept his vision of historical truth but, it would appear, little else. In 1608 he died, as Pierre de l'Estoile cynically remarked, « of a disease common to men of learning and virtue, that is, of misery and of want ».[11]

---

[9] Note in the copy of the Houghton Library at Harvard, signed « C. Francis 1857 ».

[10] The only satisfactory biography is Sypher's dissertation (Cornell, 1961), in which many of the documents concerning La Popelinière's career and the « crisis » discussed below have been transcribed. A few of these have also been published in the appendix of Agrippa d'Aubigné, *Histoire universelle*, ed. A. de Ruble, I (Paris, 1886), 371 ff.

[11] *Journal de l'Estoile pour le régne de Henri IV*, ed. L.-R. Lefèvre and A. Martin, II (Paris, 1958), 412.

La Popelinière's « idea of history » was not a theory recollected in tranquillity; it was an ideal forged and tested in the course of a deep personal crisis that furnishes an almost archetypal illustration of the dilemma of the contemporary historian. It was widely assumed, as one of La Popelinière's better known countrymen remarked, that « the only good histories are those written by men who themselves managed or participated in the events ... » [12]. But in the midst of a bloody and fratricidal conflict how could a man rise above passion and partisanship? How could one who was at once spectator, actor, and critic achieve a truly historical perspective? La Popelinière's solution to the problem was simple and radical. Machiavellian, some might say, although La Popelinière himself, as the author of a conventional Calvinist « Anti-Machiavel », would have been shocked at the notion [13]. Professional, is perhaps a better way of putting it; for what he did was to establish a purely historical standard, dispensing altogether with value judgments. Evangelical, one might add; for he seemed to regard history, and to preach its saving graces, with an almost religious fervor. From the earliest version of his book, *The True and Whole History of these Recent Troubles of France and Flanders* (1571), La Popelinière addressed himself to a strictly unadorned account of the civil wars without any attempt at suppression or rationalization. It was a noble dream. But if this was proper for the writing of history, it was no way to run a war; and this is where La Popelinière's own troubles began.

L'Affaire La Popelinière was set off in 1581 with the publication of his *History of France*, which he had the temerity to dedicate to Henry III and to Catherine de Médicis. The attack was begun by a minister in La Rochelle, and in the summer the case was taken up by the national synod of Huguenot churches held in that city, where La Popelinière's book had appeared [14]. Among various minor indiscretions were certain uncalled-for

---

[12] Montaigne, *Essais*, ed. F. Strowski and F. Gébelin, II (Bordeaux, 1919), 116.

[13] « Contre Machiavel », in Bibliothèque Nationale, Paris, Manuscrits, Fonds français, vol. 20787, f. 19 v.

[14] B. N., MSS, Collection Dupuy, vol. 744, ff. 230-68 (« Lettres et memoires touchant l' Histoire de Lancelot du Voisin, Sr de la Popeliniere ») contains the documents concerning this episode, which Sypher discusses fully.

remarks about the cruelty of his former commander François de la Noue, who indeed had become an intransigent since St Bartholomew (and who was now a prisoner in the chateau of Limbourg). La Popelinière had also in several passages spoken not unfavorably about the Catholic « faith » (before Luther's time), and he had suggested that the Calvinists were not wholly blameless in preparing the way for the religious wars. It was the implied criticism of the Huguenot party, of course, that brought down upon his head the wrath of its leaders. The issue seemed so serious that Henry of Navarre himself took notice of it. « Messieurs », he wrote to the magistrates of La Rochelle in June, « I have learned that ... a certain Popellynyere, who lives at present in your city, has produced a book against the reformed religion and also against those of our house » [15]. Five weeks later the synod condemned La Popelinière and his book and insisted upon a public retraction. This, with some qualifications, they received three years later (February 1585), when « L. Voesin » signed a prepared statement of submission [16].

Not without a struggle, however. In the intervening years La Popelinière had been making frantic efforts to justify himself, denying that he had sold his pen to the Guises, protesting his fidelity to the reformed religion and to the house of Navarre as well as to historical truth, or rather denying that there was any difference between them. He wrote first to Theodore Beza in Geneva. « We have the same goal of illustrating God's glory by the clear truths of His doctrine in true accounts of the deeds of His church », (a reference to the *Ecclesiastical History* attributed to Beza), although being « far from your calling », he added, « I do not work as fortunately as you do » [17]. But he affirmed his sincerity and accuracy. The reason he had dedicated his book to the King and the Queen Mother, he explained, was in order to influence Catholics as well as his fellow reformers and so to give the work a bi-partisan character. In reply, Beza thanked him for his fraternal sentiments and remarked that he, Beza, had more to learn than to teach in such matters, though

---

[15] *Ibid.*, f. 248 r (3 June 1581).

[16] *Ibid.*, f. 255 r. The condemnation by the synod (9 July) appears on f. 254 r, and it has been printed in Haag, *La France Protestante*, IX (Paris, 1859), 530-31.

[17] *Ibid.*, f. 235 r-236 r (15 Jan. 1581).

he did not deny the attribution of the work mentioned. He made only two criticisms, that La Popelinière had not denounced vigorously enough the massacres of Vassy and St Bartholomew, and that he had falsely praised the wicked apostate François Baudouin, who twenty years before had learned how dangerous it could be to criticize Calvinism in the name of a historical ideal. All La Popelinière had said was that Baudouin was « learned and eloquent », but perhaps Beza detected a more reprehensible sympathy between the two authors [18].

With Henry of Navarre and the Prince of Condé, La Popelinière took a different tack. He admitted that he « might have written too briefly or unclearly and so have given material to men of bias or of weak understanding », but he protested his continued good faith. « Sire », he pleaded, « my only intention has been to represent to posterity the praiseworthy deeds of your predecessors ... And if those of your party do not write down what you and others have done, the Catholics will write to their own great advantage and to the detriment of the reformers » [19]. Elsewhere he elaborated on this argument that competition with the Romanists extended also to posterity, and he used one of the favorite examples of his generation. « Who does not see that the same causes and similar events have affected us in France as those whom our ancestors called Albigensians, Beggars of Lyon, Waldensians, Beguines, and others whom until now we have regarded as abominable heretics and rebels? This is due to the absence of a true history of the events and circumstances in which they took up arms against the Catholics for the defense of their religion, which was not different from our own. On the other hand, the Catholics wrote many books which were in no way contradicted ». It was La Popelinière's historical vocation even more than his Huguenot allegiance, in short, that had led him to and sustained him in his life's work.

---

[18] *Ibid.*, f. 237 r, referring to the *Histoire de France* (La Rochelle, 1581), f. 269 r, mispaginated and cited by Beza as « 299 ». Baudouin was attacked in two separate *responsiones* by Calvin in 1562, one by Beza in 1563, and again by Beza in the *Vie de Calvin* and in the *Histoire ecclésiastique*, where he is styled « apostat renommé ». In general, see my article on Baudouin in *Journal of the History of Ideas*, XXV (1964), 35-57.

[19] *Ibid.*, f. 240 r (undated) and f. 238 r (12 Aug. 1581), the latter (to Condé) published in *Bulletin historique et philologique* (1892), pp. 250-51.

This passage appears in what was La Popelinière's most serious attempt to defend his position at this time, a relatively formal, though unpublished, « Response for History », which may indeed have been a draft of his statement to the magistrates of La Rochelle [20]. It is remarkable how this little manifesto, though written in the heat of a disastrous law suit, parallels or even prefigures the more mature evaluation of the nature and purpose of history that appeared in La Popelinière's *Idea of History* some fifteen years later, when he could afford to take a more serene view of the historian's role. A comparison of La Popelinière's apologetic writings with his more theoretical work provides an interesting illustration of the ideological basis not only of his own thought but, to some extent, of historical scholarship in general.

Running contrapuntally through La Popelinière's work are two fundamental themes: fidelity to truth and, in a general sense, civic humanism. On the one hand the historian was set apart from other men of letters because of his concern for literal and factual truth; on the other hand he was superior to the philosopher because of the public services that he, like the rhetorician, could perform. Unfortunately, these two themes were not quite in harmony. Since history was, in La Popelinière's phrase, « une chose publique », it was inherently controversial and open to partisanship. Royal or municipal historiographers were hired as official propagandists, not as irresponsible gossips, and even a free-lance writer like La Popelinière recognized his public obligation (*devoir*). Like Baudouin he wanted not only to serve his country, he hoped also to remain, as he put it to Beza, « in conformity with the traditions of the Christian church ». At the same time history had to be written « for the profit of human society » [21]. This was difficult enough; for some people he would always be *trop Huguenot*, La Popelinière admitted, for others *trop Catholique*. What made the task impossible was La Popelinière's fanatical allegiance to historical truth. His dilemma, in other words, was to reconcile his role as « actor » with that

[20] B. N., MSS Fr., vol. 20297, ff. 458 r-463 v, entitled « Responce pour l'histoire ».

[21] « Responce », f. 458 r; *Histoire des histoires*, p. 26, and *Idee de l'histoire*, p. 47.

of « spectator ». « They are three and four times blessed », Baudouin had declared, « who descend into that lower arena » [22]; but as he and La Popelinière found out, there might be a curse awaiting them as well. It was for this reason that La Popelinière, again like Baudouin, expanded his perspective — not only to encompass earlier traditions but to focus upon « posterity », as the most appropriate audience for his work. So La Popelinière's view of history became at once more comprehensive and more detached.

This detachment was reinforced by, if it did not actually stem from, La Popelinière's growing alienation from his comrades. The ministers of La Rochelle, as he told a friend during his time of troubles, had condemned his book after a bare two hours' perusal and « in the style of the Spanish Inquisition ». They had set up a « papacy » more tyrannical than that of Rome, and they were hypocrites as well. « What would they say », he asked, « if they saw the secret memoirs I have that would make them blush? » — not, he added, that he would publish such scandals out of vindictiveness [23]. He did not deny that there were some lapses in his history, but after all this was only human weakness; Beza himself had allegedly made something like seventy-nine errors in his own book. Anyway, the important thing was that La Popelinière was fair-minded. A generation earlier Martin Bucer had warned Calvin himself about the dangers of bias: « We judge as we love », he wrote, « but we love as we please ». Baudouin, who as Calvin's former secretary had had access to his correspondence, noted this remark and later used it against Calvin, as if it were a personal rebuke. Now La Popelinière, attacked in much the same way as Baudouin had been, recalled this statement in his « Response » in order to justify the frankness of his history [24]. Like Baudouin, he sought a standard of judgment that transcended « passion » and « party », and so he took his stand upon « conscience ».

---

[22] *De Institutione historiae universae*, p. 2.

[23] B. N., MSS Dupuy, vol. 744, f. 263 r-v, to « Mon frere ».

[24] « Responce », f. 462 v. Cf. Baudouin, *Responsio altera ad Joannem Calvinum* (Cologne, 1562), p. 40. The incident is discussed — and the attack upon Baudouin renewed — by Emile Doumergue, *Une Poignée de faux* (Lausanne, 1900), pp. 104-15.

Of course every historical writer knew the Ciceronian « first law of history », to tell the whole truth and nothing but the truth. But La Popelinière thought that he had discovered something new. « I have practiced a new means of representing the design and actions of both factions », he explained to Beza, « being neutral and indifferent to the two parties, as befitting the historiographer ». In his *Idea of History* La Popelinière later stated this rule in a more generalized form. « One of the most certain premises of a good historian », he wrote, « is to leave the praise and blame of men to the merit of their actions, which he must represent faithfully » [25]. Above all one should never try to act as both prosecutor and judge, as his enemies had done. It was necessary to investigate the behavior of men, but always in terms of the intention and consequences (*la volunté, puis le bien et le mal qui en venoit*). Again La Popelinière later generalized this requirement by demanding that the historian seek out *la cause*, *le progres*, *bonne ou mauvaise issue* [26]. What is more, such judgment should always be made in the context of the particular time and conditions and not in an abstract or dogmatic way. This is why it was the business of the historian, not the philosopher or the theologian, to establish the sequence of cause and effect in human affairs.

It was in this way, led by the logic of his own argument and pushed by the objections of his opponents, that La Popelinière came to his view of history as an independent and indeed sovereign discipline. He emerged from his crisis with a particularly deep conviction that history was superior to theology, at least to that « scholastic theology » that divided Protestants and Catholics. Despite its pretensions, such « positive theology » was only a « human science » — and at that less certain than history. La Popelinière acknowledged that history dealt with « accidents », but he denied that this gave any grounds for « pirrhonisme ». On the contrary, the concern of history for incontrovertible facts made it more secure than other « human traditions », which rested upon mere « opinion ». The very fact that history had to be understood in terms of times and circumstances (*selon*

[25] « Responce », f. 462 v; *Idee de l'histoire*, p. 324, and *Histoire des histoires*, p. 413.

[26] « Responce », f. 458 v; Histoire des histoires, p. 52.

le tems, les personnes et les affair[*es*] *des hommes*) made it more reliable and more useful than either philosophy or political science (*la police*) [27]. Such indeed was the way in which history as a mode of thought was distinguished, that it represented the actions of men « according to the times, the places, their causes, progress and results ». Echoing Bodin, La Popelinière concluded that history was « above all arts and sciences » [28].

La Popelinière did not win his case, but for the rest of his life he continued to gather evidence, to devise arguments, and to seek support for his conception of history. After 1585, as part of his scholarly crusade, he embarked upon a vast program of reading in historical writers of all ages and societies. This included not only historiographers but political writers such as Seyssel and Machiavelli, philologists such as Guillaume Budé and Joseph Justus Scaliger, and the authors of the so-called *artes historicae*, such as Baudouin, Milieu, and above all Bodin. In general La Popelinière sided with the « moderns ». He was a militant, and indeed defensive, advocate of the vernacular, and he was contemptuous of those « fonder of antiquity than of reason ». This included both the philological tradition, whose celebrated « encyclopedia » he regarded as an inflated and disorganized « mélange of sciences », and most historians, who tended to have an « excessive respect for their predecessors » [29]. He complained in particular about the French tradition of royal historiographers (Robert Gaguin, Paolo Emilio, Guillaume du Bellay, Denis Sauvage, Du Haillan, and Jean de Serres), partly, it may be suspected, because he hoped for some such position himself in order to subsidize his projects. In any case it was to remedy this unfortunate situation — the fact that the French had no histories except rehashes of old chronicles — that La Popelinière offered to the public his own « idea of history ».

---

[27] « Responce », f. 460 r; *Idee de l'histoire*, p. 36, *Histoire des histoires*, « Avant-discours », and *Histoire de la conqueste des pais de Bresse et de Savoye* (Lyon, 1601), p. 9. For a contrasting view of the « sciences humaines » and their inferiority to theology, see the remarks of La Popelinière's enemy and one time captain, François de la Noue, *Discours politiques et militaires*, ed. F. E. Sutcliffe (Geneva, 1967), p. 603.

[28] *Histoire des histoires*, p. 461; cf. Bodin's *Methodus* in *Oeuvres*, ed. P. Mesnard (Paris, 1951), p. 113.

[29] *Idee de l'histoire*, pp. 1, 197; cf. his defense of the vernacular in *L'Amiral de France* (Paris, 1584), « Avant-discours ».

The foundation for this, the oldest of a long line of « new histories », was a hastily assembled yet carefully planned history of historiography. In this work La Popelinière offers not only critical comments upon practically all published historians down to his own day, but an interesting and ingenious periodization of the development of historical literature. He recognized a pattern of four « seasons », that is, four levels of historical consciousness and expression [30]. First came a period of « natural history », that is, oral tradition and superstition (such as Germany described by Tacitus, Gaul by Caesar, or Mexico by Sebastian Fox). Next, a period of « poetic » history (in Moses, for example, or Homer), which lasted until the establishment of a rational chronology (the Olympiads or the founding of Rome). « It is evident », wrote La Popelinière in an interesting anticipation of romantic theories of the origins of history, « that the poets were the first historians » [31]. This is followed by « continuous history », which means simple chronicles and annals, unilluminating but at least faithful to the facts. Finally comes a kind of civilized history characterized by the addition of eloquence to the narration of facts and consequently by consideration of cause and effect. This stage of history arises with the growth of human arts and sciences (beginning in Greece with Herodotus, in Rome in the 4th century) and lasts until the decay of civilization, coinciding roughly with the end of political dominion. Every nation moved through such a cultural cycle, La Popelinière believed, and so did its historiography.

For the first time, La Popelinière thought, a fifth stage was about to be reached, namely his own « perfect history ». No historian, ancient or modern, not even his predecessor Jean Bodin, had ever achieved the synthesis of knowledge, eloquence, and philosophy necessary for this. After laying down the rules for his « new history », La Popelinière went on to redefine its form and content. He proposed a simple five-stage periodization (ancient, Roman, Germanic, and Frankish Gaul, and modern France), and pointed out the crucial importance of the problem of racial origins [32]. In the second part of his

---

[30] *Ibid.*, p. 137.
[31] *Idee de l'histoire*, pp. 362-64.
[32] *Histoire des histoires*, pp. 25, 33, 49, 155, and esp. 66.

« Design », in fact, he presented a thorough, though by no means original, critique of the theory of Trojan origins. As for the content, La Popelinière, like some of the « new historians » of our own century, took the position that nothing human was alien to it. With Gaillard he believed that « all the arts, sciences, and other human inventions derive from history ». In addition, there must be consideration of the geography of France, the forms of government, the crown, various institutions, offices, legal organization, social classes, and religion [33]. For this purpose the historian should ransack all available primary sources, and above all the archives, though all too often, he added, these had been closed to public view.

How « new » was La Popelinière's new history? It is obvious that his views derive in general from the rhetorical conception of history revived by the humanists. This includes both the claim that history was, by virtue of its concreteness and social utility, superior to philosophy, and the hope that it would encompass all human activity. Despite his dismissal of the « long-winded » discourses of Baudouin and Milieu, La Popelinière remained well within the genre of the *ars historica* — and none more long-windedly so.

In one respect, perhaps, he helped to change this relatively sheltered tradition. He was even more aware than his model Bodin of the geographical basis of history and, especially, of the significance of the « new horizons of the Renaissance ». Near the end of his life he conceived a mad scheme for a kind of anthropological expedition to Africa and America designed, again, to extend the scope of history (*rendre l'histoire de particuliere generale*) and to perfect it (*afin de nous approcher de la perfection de l'histoire*) [34]. But, although he wrote to the great Scaliger in order to get

---

[33] *Idee de l'histoire*, pp. 269 ff., 358 ff. The latter passage has been translated and discussed by George Huppert, « The Renaissance Background of Historicism », *History and Theory*, V (1966), 48-60.

[34] La Popelinière's two letters to Scaliger appear in Jacques de Rèves (ed.), *Epistres françoises de personnages illustres et doctes, a Monsr. Joseph Juste de la Scala* (Harderwyck, 1624), pp. 151-53 (9 Jan. 1601) and 303-7 (4 Jan. 1604). The second letter has been reprinted in the valuable article by Corrado Vivanti, « Le Scoperte geografiche e gli scritti di Henri de la Popelinière », *Rivista storica italiana*, LXXIV (1962), 225-49. More generally, see the remarks of Geoffroy Atkinson, *Les nouveaux Horizons de la renaissance française* (Paris, 1935).

financial support from the Estates General of Holland, nothing more came of this enterprise than of his design as a whole. And his impact was even slighter than his accomplishment. None of the later propagandists for a « new history », neither James Harvey Robinson nor, curiously, Voltaire, bothered to read his work. If La Popelinière was « called », he was obviously not, from this point of view at least, one of those chosen.

Yet La Popelinière deserves better of that posterity to which he had devoted so much of his life. Like Bacon he had tried to open up a new road to knowledge; and if, like Bacon, he was more interested in pointing the way than in making the trip himself, he nonetheless illustrates a significant phenomenon in the history of thought, namely, history's declaration of independence from other disciplines, especially from philosophy, theology, law, and political science. For this reason his ideas must be distinguished from the more influential work of Bodin. As La Popelinière himself wrote of his distinguished predecessor, « Since the method of understanding and organizing something consists in comprehending and arranging its parts, and since history consists rather in truth and its order, it seems to me that he should have taken time to order or to illuminate particular history rather than to digress so on universal history » [35]. This is why Bodin's book was, in La Popelinière's opinion, a « method of law » rather than of history. To La Popelinière, on the other hand, history had no superior in temporal things. It was as much a « profession » as law itself and as such had its own distinctive mode of thinking [36]. The « method » of history, in fact, followed the pattern of human experience; that is, it proceeded according to the succession of times and the variety of circumstances, and it sought to reproduce the plenitude of the human past.

It may be true, as one of La Popelinière's intellectual descendants (and few readers) remarked, that his work was « less a method for studying history than judgments on historians » [37]. Certainly, in keeping with his autobiographical preoccupations, he was more interested in the character of the historian than in the teaching of history. Yet it is precisely here, it seems to me, that

---

[35] *Idee de l'histoire*, p. 29.

[36] « Responce », f. 458 r, « la profession de l'histoire ».

[37] Lenglet du Fresnoy, *Methode pour etudier l'histoire* (Paris, 1729), I, IX.

his major significance lies. What he offered in fact was a kind of « mirror for historians », an idealized description that deserved to be set beside those conventional pictures of the prince, the courtier, the ambassador, the citizen, the artist, and perhaps most revealingly Bacon's « man of science » [38]. Ideally, the historian had himself been literally « in the midst of things », an actor as well as an observer, and so epitomized the humanist view of man as poised between the world of experience and the world of ideas. At the same time, while the historian derived substantial benefit from his two-fold role, he had also to cut himself loose from particular sects and authorities, whether political or doctrinal. Only then could he become, in La Popelinière's phrase, a truly « contemplative historian ».

Finally, La Popelinière laid great emphasis upon the moral duty of the historian (*le devoir d'un vray historiografe*). Not that he maintained a Calvinist interpretation of history, but he does seem to have transferred the emotional energy of his faith to his profession, so that it became a deadly serious cause, almost a crusade. The reason he had struggled so intensely against censorship of his work was that he found it shocking to silence « a public person like the historiographer », as he called himself, « pushed by God for the common good, of which he is the faithful recorder » [39]. Indeed, what La Popelinière had done was to transmute his « first calling », as he called his religious belief, into a historical form; as Beza, the theologian, labored to extend the faith, so La Popelinière, the historian, labored to preserve the memory of the deeds of the faithful. Later, of course, this program was broadened and even detached from its original ideological context, but La Popelinière continued to believe that « the principal goal and true purpose of history is to bring not pleasure but profit to everyone » [40] — that Clio

---

[38] See M. E. Prior, « Bacon's Man of Science », *Journal of the History of Ideas* », XV (1954), 348-70. The parallel between Bacon and La Popelinière has been drawn out — very far out — by Sypher in the second of his articles (see note 8).

[39] B. N., MSS Dupuy, vol. 744, f. 263 v.

[40] *Idee de l'histoire*, p. 306, echoing Cicero's « esse utilitatem in historia, non modo voluptatem » (*Brutus*, 228). The phrase « duty of the historiographer » appears often, e. g., B. N. MSS Dupuy, vol. 744, ff. 242 r, 244 v, 264 r, 266 r.

was not so much a muse as a missionary. The Protestant view of a « calling », according to the famous formulation of Max Weber, required one to labor in a single-minded and above all methodical fashion for the benefit of the whole community. La Popelinière's conception of history owed more than a little to the Protestant ethic, it seems, if not to the spirit of capitalism.

In such *chiaroscuro* tones, then, La Popelinière painted his portrait of the complete historian. He was at once the involved participant and the disinterested observer, the omnivorous autodidact and the duty-bound professional, the *uomo universale* and the man with a calling.

V

Martyrs, Myths, and the Massacre: The Background of St. Bartholomew

HOW, FROM A DISTANCE of four hundred years, can we obtain a clear view of the Massacre of St. Bartholomew? The refractory powers of time always present difficulties, but in this case our vision is further distorted by a screen of false and conflicting evidence and by an endless stream of partisan debate. Perhaps the answer is that we should discard altogether the idea of describing some objective set of circumstances independent of ideological presuppositions and the passions aroused in witnesses and interpreters. Perhaps we should try rather to restore the event to its various contexts, conceptual as well as historical, and from a point of view that accommodates political and religious consciousness as well as social reality, that recognizes the mythical as well as the historical dimension. For it is upon some such symbolic level that the historical significance of events is to be found.

Over the past four centuries the Massacre of St. Bartholomew has presented many faces. It has been seen as a sensational explosion of violence fired by a half-century of mounting religious hatred; as a tragedy so shocking, according to one contemporary witness, that posterity would never believe it; as a turning point in a great world conflict; as a storm center of religious polemic and a seedbed of political theories; as a legend of gigantic proportions promoted by publicists and sanctioned by men of letters; as a puzzle and topic of debate for generations of historians; as an occasion for Catholic masses, Protestant lamentations, and historical conferences.[1] It was all these and more. It was also an archetypal occurrence that transcended its

This paper is an offshoot of two projects, a biography, *François Hotman, A Revolutionary's Ordeal,* forthcoming from Princeton University Press, and a study in progress of sixteenth-century propaganda. A shorter version of this paper was read at a meeting of the Newberry Library Renaissance Conference in May 1972 devoted to "The Massacre of St. Bartholomew in Historical Perspective."

[1] The most important source material is the anonymous pamphlet literature, which is fairly exhaustively listed in the following publications: Robert Lindsay and John Neu, *French Political Pamphlets, 1547–1648* (Madison, 1969); the *Catalogue de l'histoire de France,* 1 (Paris, 1845), which is a listing by shelf mark of the Bibliothèque Nationale (BN), principally the range Lb.33 to Lb.35; the catalog of the Bibliothèque de l'Arsenal, unfortunately unpublished, in nine MS volumes, 8°H. 12868; and F.-A. Isambert, ed., *Recueil général des anciennes lois françaises,* 12 (Paris, 1822–33), numbered consecutively.

historical context—transcended it not only in the direction of the future (by endless debates over premeditation, guilt, and consequences) but also in the direction of the past (by seeming to symbolize, summarize, and confirm long-standing fears and anticipations and indeed to repeat earlier misfortunes on a grander scale). It was, in other words, an almost generic human experience that came as no surprise in the event, that followed a familiar pattern in its course, and that would be relived in various ways afterwards.

In order to suggest the basis and dimensions of this historical epiphenomenon, we must look beyond the conventional narrative and diplomatic sources that help to show (in Ranke's view) "what really happened." One of the most convenient as well as fashionable procedures is to choose some analyzable model. This seems to be all the more appropriate since the model in this instance does not have to be imported from any of the more structured social disciplines. On the contrary, it is suggested, indeed imposed upon us, by the historical context of the sixteenth-century wars of religion. Here is a clear case of history repeating itself, or at least of men seeing it as a repetition. For the witnesses, participants, and interpreters of the events of late summer 1572 knew what the phenomenon was practically before it happened: it was not a "tumult" or a "disorder" or the suppression of a "conspiracy" as various observers supposed; it was a massacre, by no means unexpected and not even the first in that generation. And they knew what part they might ultimately have to play: it was that highly stylized and stereotyped role called "martyrdom," the most exalted and yet in some ways the simplest form of sainthood. The fundamental psychological model for this phenomenon, then (again with a nominal bow to intellectual fashion), was what can only be called the martyr complex.[2]

The remaining problem is where to find reflections of this model, or in other words, how to gain access to this aspect of the Protestant conscience. The most obvious and direct source would seem to be that most human and down-to-earth variety of Protestant historiography, the martyrology. The tradition of latter-day martyrs was inherent in Protestant self-consciousness from the beginning—Luther's stand at Worms in 1521, so reminiscent of Hus's a century before, was potentially that of a martyr—but not for another generation did this tradition take a consciously literary form. The first fruits came within a few years and showed a pronounced family resemblance. Most significant were Jean Crespin's *The History of the Martyrs* and the first Latin version of John Foxe's *Acts and Monuments,* both appearing in 1554, in Geneva and Strasbourg respectively. Ludwig Rabe's *Stories of God's*

[2] A convenient bibliography on the question of martyrdom may be found in W. H. C. Frend, *Martyrdom and Persecution in the Early Church* (New York, 1967). In all the massive literature I find no useful studies from a psychohistorical or sociohistorical point of view. General Catholic treatments—of which the best is perhaps Henri Leclercq's in Fernand Cabrol and Henri Leclercq, eds., *Dictionnaire d'Archéologie chrétienne et de liturgie* (Paris, 1924–53), vol. 10, pt. 2—tend to be so rigidly legalistic and orthodox that Protestant experiences do not even come into the discussion.

Chosen Witnesses and Martyrs, published in Strasbourg in 1552, antedated these two but was limited to martyrs in antiquity until later, derivative editions. Also related were Heinrich Pantaleone's *History of the Martyrs,* Johann Sleidan's great history of the Reformation, published in Strasbourg in 1555 and soon translated into German, French, and English, and Matthias Flaccius Illyricus's *Catalog of the Witnesses of Truth,* published in Basel in 1556.[3]

Though independently conceived, these works were all products of the international Protestant community and had a collective, to some extent cooperative, character. The links between Geneva and Strasbourg, the two leading Calvinist centers, were particularly strong and were strengthened by the presence of the exiles from Marian England. Crespin was in close touch with Calvin's friend Sleidan, drew upon Sleidan's book, and in 1556 published a French translation of it in Geneva. For later versions of his own *History* Crespin drew also upon Foxe's concomitantly growing *Book of Martyrs.* Foxe himself had gone to Strasbourg in 1555 and then settled in Basel to continue his work, but he continued to receive materials from his friend Edmund Grindal, and no doubt indirectly from Sleidan. Foxe also made use of Flaccius Illyricus's *Catalog,* which was printed in 1556 by Foxe's own publisher, Johann Oporinus. In addition Foxe's work was continued by Pantaleone, who was also Sleidan's German translator. The relation of Rabe, a leading theologian in Strasbourg's Lutheran congregation, is not known, but in any case it seems clear that the first generation of martyrologists constituted something approaching a literary circle, a kind of Protestant pleiade of the exile circuit, which drew upon a common fund of experience, a common ideological commitment, a common historical perspective, and a common reliance upon what Foxe called the "miracle" of printing.[4]

In many respects the groundbreaking work was Crespin's, and for France, certainly, it provided the model. Crespin was himself an exile from the Netherlands and, along with his friend François Baudouin, had barely escaped from his native Artois with his skin. That was in 1545. Afterwards Crespin settled in Geneva, set up his printing press, and launched into his life's work. The *History of Martyrs* was based on a wide range of printed and unprinted sources and on several other independent works, including those of Foxe, Antoine de la Roche Chandieu, and François Hotman, the first historian of the Massacre of St. Bartholomew. Crespin also

[3] Ludwig Rabe, *Der heiligen aus erwohlten Gottes Zeugen Bekennen und Martyren* (Strasbourg, 1552), with a treatment of the modern period in the expanded edition (Strasbourg, 1571); Jean Crespin, *Le Livre des martyrs* ([Geneva], 1554); John Foxe, *Commentarii rerum in ecclesia gestarum* (Strasbourg, 1554), dedicated to Christoph von Württemberg, Aug. 31, 1554; Heinrich Pantaleone, *Martyrum historia* (Basel, 1563); Johann Sleidan, *De Statu religionis et reipublicae, Carolo Quinto, Caesare, Commentarii* (Strasbourg, Sept. 1556); Matthias Flaccius Illyricus, *Catalogus testium veritatis* (Basel, 1556).

[4] For some of these complex interrelations, see G. Moreau, "Contribution à l'histoire du livre des martyrs," *Bulletin de la Société de l'histoire du protestantisme français,* 103 (1957): 173–99.

drew on the *Ecclesiastical History of the Reformed Churches of France,* long attributed to Theodore Beza. The *History of Martyrs* appeared in successively augmented and altered editions between 1554 and 1570 (the last published by Crespin) and thereafter was continued by Simon Goulart, the prolific polemicist who issued the most comprehensive edition in 1619, when he had succeeded Beza as head of the Genevan church. This book is the centerpiece, as far as France is concerned, of the modern martyrological canon.[5]

Perhaps the most fundamental theme of this whole genre was, in Crespin's words, "the conformity of the modern history of the martyrs with that of antiquity." This parallel was perhaps what Lefèvre d'Etaples had in mind when he began to compile his *Agonies of the Martyrs,* as did Rabe, who referred explicitly to the "proto-martyrs" of antiquity. "The memory of the first persecutions," as Chandieu put it, "is a school that teaches how to remain true to one's calling." Indeed the purpose of collecting these biographical accounts included all of the basic ingredients for the humanist prescription for history. They offered "consolation," as Crespin wrote in his first preface; they constituted a treasury of *exempla* for imitation and a kind of moral and anagogical "mirror" for Christians; and they were commemorative, preserving for posterity the "deeds and writings" of exemplary men of faith.[6]

Yet there is no doubt that these humanist commonplaces were transformed by their conscription into the service of militant Protestantism. The biographical form of martyrology resembled less the *de viris illustribus* of classical tradition than the *vitae sanctorum* of the medieval Church. In each biography Crespin wrote, it was his intention to describe the doctrine as well as the life of the martyr and above all his "happy ending"; and to

[5] Besides the invaluable edition by Daniel Benoit of Crespin and Simon Goulart, *Histoire des martyrs* (Toulouse, 1885–89), see Arthur Piaget and Gabriel Berthoud, *Notes sur le livre des martyrs de Jean Crespin* (Neuchâtel, 1930); C.-L. Frossard, *Le Livre des martyrs de Jean Crespin* (Paris, 1880); and more generally, Ferdinand Vander Haeghen *et al., Bibliographie des martyrologies protestants néerlandais,* 2 (La Haye, 1890); also the article on Crespin in Eugène Haag and Emile Haag, eds., *La France Protestante* (2d ed.; Paris, 1877–88); the notes to Calvin's correspondence in Calvin, *Opera quae supersunt omnia,* ed. J. W. Baum, Eduard Cunitz, *et al.* (Strasbourg, 1863–1900), vols. 38–39; and J.-F. Gilmont, "Une édition inconnue du martyrologie de Jean Crespin," *Bibliothèque d'Humanisme et Renaissance,* 30 (1969): 363–71. The latter article and that by Moreau, "Contribution à l'histoire du livre des martyrs" (p. 174), refer to the work of E. E. Halkin and his students, which is important though devoted mostly to the martyrs of Belgium and the Netherlands. On Rabe's book, see Robert Foncke, *Duitse Vlugschriften van de Tijd over het Proces en de Terechtstellung van de Protestanten Frans en Nikolaas Thys te Mechelen* (Antwerp, 1937), 60–65; and William Haller, *Foxe's Book of Martyrs and the Elect Nation* (London, 1963), 55–73. The other related works are Antoine de la Roche Chandieu, *Histoire des persecutions et martyrs de l'eglise de Paris depuis l'an 1557* (Lyons, 1563), BN, Rés. Ln.25. 91; *Histoire ecclésiastique des églises reformées au Royaume de France,* ed. J. W. Baum and Eduard Cunitz (Paris, 1883); [François Hotman], *De Furoribus Gallicis* ("Edinburgh" [probably Basel], 1573); and [Hotman], *Gasparis Colinii Castelonii, magni quondam Franciae amiralii vita* (hereafter *Vita Colinii*) (n.p., 1575).

[6] Crespin, *Histoire des martyrs,* vol. 1, prefaces of 1570 and 1554, *passim;* [Lefèvre d'Etaples], *Agones martyrium mensi ianuarii. Libro primo* (Paris, 1529) (no more published); Rabe, *Heiligen aus erwohlten Gottes Zeugen Bekennen und Martyren* (1571), vol. 2; Chandieu, *Histoire des persecutions,* xiii.

suit this purpose Crespin did not hesitate to stretch the already flexible standards of sixteenth-century editorship, improving in various ways upon the texts of even original documents. Chandieu took pride in declaring his "fidelity" to truth and especially to his sources, but his partisanship was still more flagrant. The purpose of his book was both to afford "profit" to his brothers and to demonstrate the justice of his "Cause" to the "poor ignorant ones" outside of it. The book was quite literally a call to arms. "We are not in this world to rest," he declared, "but rather to fight."[7]

The most direct source of inspiration for these martyrologies was clearly the Protestant view of ecclesiastical history, as variously expressed by Luther, Melanchthon, and Calvin. "From all authors and histories," declared Flaccius Illyricus, "it is evident that our church . . . is truly ancient and takes its origin from the time of Christ and the apostles."[8] In the subsequent life of this true church the persecutions of the faithful constituted a major source of continuity, which according to Crespin paralleled the progress of Grace on earth and indeed represented its carnal counterpart. "The blood of martyrs is the seed of the church" was the invariably quoted motto of Tertullian, and its life-giving force was continuous over the centuries. Moreover, like Christian tradition in general and in sharp contrast to the national orientation of pagan historiography, the history of martyrs was truly universal in scope and included, as Crespin remarked, "all conditions, ages, sexes, and nations."[9] It differed from medieval historiography, too, especially from the saints' lives with which it had undeniable resemblances, in that it was concerned not with the idolatrous relics but with the spiritual legacy of the faithful—with their "words and deeds." Like the view of ecclesiastical tradition held by Melanchthon and Flacius Illyricus, the view of the Crespin-Goulart martyrology was not merely "human" but doctrinal or confessional.

Between the first, archetypal age of Christian martyrs and the moderns came a time that seemed darker to Crespin than it did to many of the most critical of humanists (which may serve as a reminder, though surely not a revelation, that the myth of the "Dark Ages" was as much a creation of the Reformation as it was of the Renaissance). After the primitive church came the papal monarchy—"la monarchie papistique" is Crespin's phrase—and then, at a still lower level, a third age ridden with Scholasticism, canon law, relic worship, and other forms of idolatry.[10] Throughout this period there was a tradition of "pure religion," but it was tenuous and took the form only of scattered "witnesses to the truth"—"precursors" is the word modern

[7] Chandieu, *Histoire des persecutions*, xxviii.

[8] Flaccius Illyricus, *Catalogus testium veritatis*, preface.

[9] Crespin, *Histoire des martyrs*, 1:1; Chandieu, *Histoire des persecutions*, lxii. See also Hans Campenhausen, *Die Idee der Martyrium in der alten Kirche* (Göttingen, 1964), and the references there to Augustine, Luther, and Calvin.

[10] Crespin, *Histoire des martyrs*, 1: 41; see also Heinrich Bullinger, *Origines errorum* (Zurich, 1549).

historians prefer for this still no less mythical phenomenon. Finally came the revival of true doctrine begun by Luther, which brought with it, according to Crespin, a renaissance of martyrdom as well.

SO MUCH FOR MARTYROLOGY as a model. The original, martyrdom itself, is more difficult to define. A legal concept, a value judgment, a psychological condition, a social role, a weapon of propaganda—again it was all these, and more. The idea, if not the terminology, long antedated Christianity. As early as the fifth century, for example, Athenians killed in war were assured of deification; and this notion of dying in battle for a just cause has always been associated with that of martyrdom.[11] But it was Christianity that adopted the Greek term *martys* to this general behavior pattern. Although the original signification was lost in the Latin West, Protestant martyrologists quite consciously, in the spirit of Biblical humanism, restored it and identified the martyrly condition with one "testifying" to the faith.[12] It was not the fact of death, in other words, but the inner attitude that admitted one to the pantheon of martyrs and so, though theologically this could not be explicit, to the certainty of salvation as well as earthly immortality. The vital importance of the act of testifying in early Protestantism is further highlighted by the counterconcept—"Nicodemitism" was the term coined by Calvin in 1543—referring to the concealment of one's faith, one of the most heinous of all sins.

Martyrdom was a highly conventional as well as highly painful process: it was a form of mimesis—*imitatio Christi* with a vengeance. And to follow Christ, "captain of the martyrs," as Crespin put it, entailed a heavy weight of ritual, rhetoric, etiquette, and symbolism, as reflected in interrogations, confessions of faith, execution scenes, crowd reactions, and contemporary graphic representations. The stereotyped character of the role is clearly evident in the martyrologies—not only in the "ten marks of the martyr," which Crespin established for purposes of identification and as the Protestant equivalent of canonization, but also in the unarticulated categories, including the status of the accused and the types of punishment, which modern scholars have extracted and applied in an almost quantitative fashion.[13] These categories were confirmed, and in some cases created, by the more or less predictable reactions of established authority, which in France

[11] Ernst H. Kantorowicz, "*Pro Patria, Mori* in Medieval Political Thought," *AHR*, 56 (1950–51): 472; included also in his *Selected Studies* (New York, 1965), 308.

[12] See H. A. M. Hoppenbrouwers, *Recherches sur la terminologie du martyre de Tertullien à Lactance* (Nijmegen, 1961); and Carlo Ginzburg, *Il Nicodemitismo* (Turin, 1970).

[13] Crespin, *Histoire des martyrs*, preface of 1570. A modern example is Piaget and Berthoud, *Notes sur le livre des martyrs*, drawing upon Vander Haeghen, *Bibliographie des martyrologies*. Such attempts deserve to be followed up by more statistically grounded studies, not only along the lines suggested by Geoffrey Nuttall, "The English Martyrs, 1535–1680," *Journal of Ecclesiastical History*, 22 (1971): 191–97, but also, and indeed at the same time, along those of Lacey Baldwin Smith, "English Treason Trials and Confessions in the Sixteenth Century," *Journal of the History of Ideas*, 15 (1954): 471–98.

was determined to uproot all heresy. The result was to intensify the impression of Protestants that they were recapitulating the experiences of early Christians—confronting the same style of interrogation, the same inseparable charges of blasphemy and sedition, and the same sorts of repression and punishments. It may be added that they also anticipated the same kind of vengeance, that is, the decline and fall of the persecuting state; for such was the judgment often expressed by Protestants about the fate of France in the later sixteenth century.[14]

It is not going too far to suggest that the coherence of the modern tradition of martyrs was created as much by external pressures as by the sharing of a common ideology and a common "Cause."[15] Catholic attempts to discredit individual martyrs only provided further publicity. Stories about last-minute recantations were always being circulated, remarked Erasmus, rejecting one such rumor about Louis Berquin, the first notable French martyr (who indeed, against Erasmus' advice, had chosen to stand upon his conscience).[16] Catholics were always as ready to attribute a "Virgin, intercede for me" to a man about to be killed as Protestants were to find a martyrly defiance; what counted most, however, was the fact of execution. The Catholic solution was to create a kind of countermythology about heretics and, ultimately, an "antimartyrological" tradition to undo the work of Crespin and his fellow authors.[17] In ideological wars, it seems, demonology has often been the response to hagiography.

This dialogue was also pursued on the official level. From the mid-1520s Protestants were plagued by a wide range of repressive legislation that constituted a kind of mirror image of their own propaganda and was an almost continuous effort to regulate their behavior on every level. The legislation was not always consistent (alternating between prescribing banishment and forbidding emigration, for example, and between controlling the printing press and abolishing it altogether), but its tone was unmistakable. Except for intermittent periods of crisis or compromise, it reflected an almost totalitarian, off-with-their-heads attitude toward heresy and disobedience that was hardly less intense than the fanaticism of the Huguenots themselves. The royal ordinances are filled with repetitive orders banning weapons, expelling vagabonds and such dangerous elements, forbidding Protestants the right to inheritance, officeholding, and burial, and prescribing death for the printing, selling, or even possession of heretical or seditious literature and for the convening of "illicit assemblies." Again and again government policy was declared to be "the extirpation and extermination" of

14 See, for example, Chandieu, *Histoire des persecutions,* lxv.

15 "La CAUSE," i.e. of the Huguenots, became a central theme of debate between Protestants and Catholics immediately following St. Bartholomew; see especially Pierre Charpentier, *Epistola ad Franciscum Portum* (n.p., 1572); Franciscus Portus, *Responsio* (n.p., 1573); and Jean de Montluc, *Oratio* . . . (Paris, 1573).

16 Erasmus, *Opus epistolarum Des. Erasmi Roterdami,* ed. P. S. Allen and H. M. Allen, 8 (Oxford, 1934), no. 2188.

17 Jacques Severt, *L'Anti-Martyrologie* . . . (Lyons, 1622).

heresy.[18] The most spectacular expression of official disfavor, of course, was the unending series of executions staged as public exhibits at strategic spots, especially market places like the Place de Grève and the Place Maubert in the university section of Paris.[19] It was this campaign, more than anything else, that gave French Protestantism its persecution complex and Protestant propaganda its paranoid style.

From the time that the winds of Lutheran doctrine first reached France, bracing to some, to others bringing an odor of heresy and sedition, the production of martyrs became a familiar feature of religious opposition. In many cases, of course, the pattern of early Christianity was consciously and pridefully followed. From the execution of the self-styled hermit Jean Vallière on August 8, 1523, the honor roll of this special echelon of the elect grew and was carefully preserved by religious chroniclers and martyrologists. From 1534—the notorious "year of the placards," when heretical posters were distributed in the streets of Paris and even affixed to the king's chamber door in the castle of Amboise—the official reaction became more intense, and within a few months the list of martyrs increased considerably. It was at this time, Crespin reported, that the practice of cutting off the tongues of heretics before execution was initiated, although this symbolic act was notably unsuccessful in silencing French Protestantism in general.[20]

It was the "miracle" of printing that gave Protestantism its voice, but this same miracle also produced one most unattractive offshoot—the institution of preventive censorship. Book burning was by no means a Catholic monopoly, as Luther's sensational act of throwing the corpus of canon law into the fire demonstrates, but it was specifically Protestant literature that furnished most of the fuel at the beginning. Bearing witness in the embarrassingly public form of print often entailed equally drastic retaliation by established authority; and condemning and destroying books may well be regarded as one of the preliminaries of martyrdom itself, since more than one printer and propagandist followed his books into the flames. So it was with Berquin, so it would be with Étienne Dolet (that unwilling "martyr of the Renaissance" who did in fact recant),[21] and so it would have been with Calvin and Beza if they had returned to France.

One crucial factor in the ideological polarization of society was the alienation of the younger generation. A year before the affair of the placards there was an indication of this alienation in an edict that sought to bring greater discipline into the university of Paris. Specifically the order banned "the impudent books of the heretics" and called for interrogation of younger students if such books were found in their possession. The edict

[18] Isambert, *Recueil,* vol. 12: no. 128 (June 10, 1525), no. 211 (Jan. 29, 1534), no. 367 (July 23, 1543), no. 382 (July 24, 1557).

[19] See John Viénot, *Promenades à travers le Paris des martyrs, 1523–59* (Paris, 1913).

[20] Crespin, *Histoire des martyrs,* 1: 297.

[21] R. C. Christie, *Etienne Dolet, The Martyr of the Renaissance: 1508–1546* (London, 1899).

also frowned upon long whiskers (*prolixa barba*) worn by masters, and it was later derided by Beza, a student in these years, as the "edict of the beards."[22] In the course of the reaction to the placards (in which university persons were deeply implicated), Francis I issued a special warning to the university community about the danger of heresy. "I pray that you . . . be especially solicitous of the youth," he told the faculty in the spring of 1535, "and see that they are well instructed and indoctrinated [*indoctriner*] so that they do not fall into the evil and forbidden opinions."[23]

This incipient conflict of generations affected the family as well as education. One striking but not unusual example is that of François Hotman, who was converted to the "new opinions" at precisely the time that his father was taking his place on that special tribunal of the Parlement of Paris, the *Chambre ardente,* which took over the official campaign of suppression in 1547. The conflict was so intense that the next spring the younger Hotman made his decision—after a crisis very much like that of his friend Beza a few months later—to break ties with his home and go into exile; and he made quite clear the significance of the martyr complex in his choice. "My father ended his career by oppressing more than a thousand martyrs," he later told Melanchthon. "As long as I was with him he tried to keep me forcibly from impiety, but God kept me for His church, and here I intend to spend the rest of my life." He denounced the way of the Nicodemite and chose Calvin, quite literally, as his new "father." "He [Hotman] abandoned the hope of a fine inheritance," Calvin later told Heinrich Bullinger, "in order to fight for Christ."[24] A contemporary scholar has suggested that the martyr is a kind of religious adventurer,[25] and it was in some such spirit that Hotman, like many another young man in these years, committed this act of rebellion.

In the spring of 1549 Hotman left Geneva (in the company of Beza, who had just decided not to go into the printing business with Crespin) to take a position in the Calvinist academy of Lausanne. Even here Hotman was not out of reach of the royal campaign of persecution. Less than four years later five students from Lausanne, on their way to join congregations in southern France, were imprisoned by the Catholic authorities of Lyons and became a *cause* more *célèbre* than that of the placards. Despite Calvin's efforts and despite pleas from various Swiss cities these young men were condemned in 1553 and, one by one, were burned at the same stake. Crespin

[22] Beza to Maclou Popon, May 7, 1542, in Beza, *Correspondance,* ed. Fernand Aubert and Henri Meylan (Paris, 1960–), 1: 43.

[23] Francis I, quoted in C. E. Bulaeus, *Historia Universitatis Parisiensis* (Paris, 1673), 6: 252–53.

[24] François Hotman to Melanchthon, May 24, 1556, BN, MS, Collection Dupuy, vol. 797, fol. 212v. The record of the elder Hotman's activities has been published by Nathaniel Weiss, *La Chambre ardente* (Paris, 1889); the son's conversion and flight may be followed through his correspondence with Calvin, published in the *Opera.* See Calvin to Bullinger, Nov. 25, 1549, *Opera,* vol. 44, no. 1324.

[25] Michael Walzer, *The Revolution of the Saints* (London, 1965), 9. This study contains many interesting suggestions concerning the psychology of martyrdom.

publicized the fate of these latter-day "martyrs of Lyons" by printing their prison correspondence with Calvin in the first edition of his *History,* which appeared the following year (and which provided Sleidan with his account).[26] Whether these letters were authentic or assembled in some way by Crespin himself, they provided most effective Protestant propaganda and took their place in the martyrological tradition.

THE CREATION OF MARTYRS seriatim was alarming enough, especially when it was the result of institutional persecution, but far worse was the creation of martyrs en masse. According to a famous distinction of the Huguenot historian Agrippa d'Aubigne, massacre victims, though their names often went unrecorded, constituted a second type of martyr, and these were still more disturbing to the Protestant conscience.[27] The first sensational episode was the notorious persecution of the Waldensians in Mérindole, which Crespin called "as memorable as anything within the memory of man" and in fact thought worthy of a separate volume.[28] In 1545 a veritable campaign of extermination was waged in which twenty-two villages were destroyed and hundreds of persons killed; others were put to flight, and many went to Geneva, as was becoming increasingly common. This episode, together with the work of the *Chambre ardente,* haunted Protestants with the prospect of martyrdom or exile, which represented a kind of political martyrdom. Further incidents and the repressive legislation of the 1550s served to magnify such fears among the Huguenots, as they were beginning to be called, as well as to bring civil war closer.

Such fears played a part, too, in that complex set of uprisings referred to as the Conspiracy of Amboise, which such Protestants as Hotman, Beza, and Crespin looked upon as in effect the opening phase of the wars of religion. The conspiracy, brewing already in the fall of 1559 after the death of King Henry II, aimed at breaking the power of the Guise family by gaining possession of the young King Francis II. It was further stirred up by the famous trial of Anne du Bourg, who was executed at the end of that year.[29] In his responses to interrogators and in his last words, widely publicized by Crespin and others, du Bourg provided a *locus classicus* not only for Huguenot political propaganda but also for the tradition of martyrs.

The conspiracy itself was a fiasco. Hotman, one of the conspirators as well as the historian of this attempt to overthrow the Guise "tyranny," described the terrible fate of the captured "rebels." Some of them were hanged from the parapets of the castle of Amboise and others decapitated, and Hotman quoted in particular the words of his old friend the Sieur de Villemongis:

[26] Crespin, *Histoire des martyrs,* 2: 595.

[27] Agrippa d'Aubigné, *Histoire universelle* (Paris, 1616–20), ed. Alphonse de Ruble (Paris, 1886–1909), 1: 227.

[28] Crespin, *Histoire des martyrs,* 2: 381; and Crespin, *Histoire memorable de la persecution et saccagement du peuple de Merindole et Cabrieres* . . . ([Geneva], 1556); see also Isambert, *Recueil,* vol. 12, no. 316 (Nov. 8, 1540).

[29] Crespin, *Histoire des martyrs,* 2: 675.

Fig. 1. Execution of conspirators at Amboise, 1560. Contemporary engraving. Photograph from Jean Héritier, *Catherine de Medici,* tr. Charlotte Haldane (New York, 1963), facing p. 208.

"Having dipped his hands in the blood of his headless companions, he lifted them as high as possible to the heavens and cried, 'Here is the blood of your children, O Lord; for this you shall be avenged.' "[30] This scene, depicted in an often-reproduced contemporary engraving (see fig. 1), was another to treasure in that martyrological canon that Hotman and Crespin were in the process of compiling.

The villain of this piece, of course, was the cardinal of Lorraine. He was denounced a few weeks later by Hotman as the "Tiger of France" in a pamphlet that was in effect the *J'accuse* of the religious wars. The cardinal, supported by his brother, the duke of Guise, was the true conspirator, Hotman charged, the one responsible for spilling the blood of so many innocents. "If Caesar was killed trying to gain the sceptre justly," he asked, "can we permit you to live, who pretend to it unjustly?" It must be added that Hotman himself was responsible for the creation of at least one more martyr, for during the summer the printer of his *Tiger* was seized by the police, who were apparently chasing a murderer at the time. The printer, a certain Martin Lhommet, was executed a month later in the Place Maubert near the university. Only three copies of Hotman's book seem to have survived: one in Strasbourg, one in Switzerland, and the other in Paris, which was to be discovered in the nineteenth century, reprinted, and made the center of an extensive controversy over the "freedom of the press."[31]

The next two years were a time of indecision, wavering duplicity, and futile attempts at compromise. Persecutions continued, especially against the Waldensians, and a recent historian has spoken with justice of "the impossible toleration of the Colloquy of Poissy" in the fall of 1561.[32] Few hoped to prevent war; it was only a question of time, and the time came the following spring. The spark was provided by the tragic confrontation at Vassy between a force led by the duke of Guise and a Huguenot congregation—the "Sarajevo of the religious wars," as it has been called.[33] As Guise and his men approached, perhaps looking for trouble, they heard singing from the Protestant church—"I am afflicted and ready to die" is one of the verses from the psalm—and were outraged at this violation. Whichever side cast the first stone, the result was seventy-four Huguenots dead or dying and a political situation out of control. "If you will forgive a snap judgment," wrote one observer, "this is the beginning of a tragedy that we shall all be playing."[34] No Protestant hesitated to regard the affair as a full-fledged massacre. So within a few weeks Hotman and other observers represented it, and so later it would be interpreted by Huguenot historians, again including Hotman as well as Crespin.

The blood of these martyrs rapidly nourished the seeds of civil war. Barely a month later Huguenot forces gathered at Orleans and prepared for a major conflict. Hotman was among them and made the connection most explicitly. "In this event," he remarked of the affair of Vassy, "our leaders see the signal for a general massacre being prepared by our enemies in all parts of the kingdom."[35] Underlying this view one may see not only a kind of conspiracy theory of history, which was to become increasingly common, but also a doctrine of political expediency, which was to become a central feature of Huguenot propaganda and self-justification.[36] In either case the Massacre of Vassy was transformed into a myth—not a "nonevent" but a kind of "hyper-event," which served at once as an excuse for resist-

[31] [Hotman], *Epistre envoiee au tigre de la France* (Strasbourg, 1560), ed. Charles Reade, *Le Tigre de 1560* (Paris, 1875), and the offprints among Reade's papers located in Paris, Bibliothèque de la Société de l'Histoire du Protestantisme Français, MS 816, vol. 4; see also *Calendar of State Papers, Venetian,* 8: 234.

[32] Alain Dufour, "L'impossible tolérance au Colloque de Poissy," *Musées de Geneve,* n.s. 4 (1963): 8–11.

[33] H. O. Evennett, *The Cardinal of Lorraine and the Council of Trent* (Cambridge, 1930), 21.

[34] Etienne Pasquier, *Les Lettres* (Paris, 1617), bk. 4, no. 15; other accounts of the massacre are in Crespin and Goulart, *Histoire des martyrs,* 2: 209; and *Memoires de Condé* (London, 1743–45), 3: 111.

[35] Hotman to Bonifacius Amerbach, Apr. 12, 1562, Universitätsbibliothek, Basel, MS G. II. 19, fol. 148r.

[36] See, e.g., *Advertissement sur la falseté de plusieurs mensonges semez par les rebelles* (Paris, 1562), in Lindsay and Neu, *French Political Pamphlets,* no. 258, which is a Catholic response to the *Histoire comprenant en brief ce qui est advenu depuis le partement des sieurs de Guise . . .*

ance, as a means of shifting all guilt to the Guise party, and as a most satisfactory explanation for the coming of the wars of religion.

There were other "massacres" over the next decade, of course, but Vassy remained the archetype; and for the rest of the century Huguenots operated upon the assumptions generated—or rather confirmed—by this tragedy. The Massacre at Vassy fitted in perfectly with the belief, based upon countless statements of official policy, that the government was literally intent upon the "extermination" of those of the religion. The theme recurred again and again over the next decade. The most famous illustration is the meeting in 1565 between Catherine de' Medici and the duke of Alba. Although their conversations were generally inconclusive, they immediately provoked suspicions among Huguenots about a universal Catholic conspiracy, turning upon a Paris-Madrid axis linked in turn with the Council of Trent, whose canons and decrees had been published only the year before. This meeting between Catherine and the duke of Alba has always been associated with St. Bartholomew seven years later, but it should be understood that the legend surrounding it came earlier and was in fact part of the general fear of that Florentine woman, Catherine de' Medici. Hotman later published a letter by her, supposedly written in 1569 and intercepted; and although it is undoubtedly spurious, it sounded quite convincing to her Protestant critics. "To restore the crown of France," she is supposed to have written, "there is no better way than to kill all the Huguenots."[37]

It was at this same time, that is, during the third war, that Admiral Gaspard de Coligny emerged as the leader of the Huguenots and as a figure of international influence. Protestants began looking to him as their savior, and indeed a number of cities and congregations placed themselves under his protection. In September he was officially condemned by the Parlement and deprived of his offices. According to this *arrêt,* which was printed in eight languages and widely distributed, Coligny was "giltie of traison, distourber and breaker of peace, ennemy of repos, and tranquillitie of the commonwealth: the Captain, author, and ringleder of the rebellion, conspiracie, and faction that hath bin made against the King and his State." It is very interesting to note that when Coligny perished in the Massacre of St. Bartholomew three years later, this same charge was resurrected and in fact the *arrêt* itself republished.[38]

(Orleans, 1562), BN, Lb.[33] 48; see also *Bref discours et veritable des principales coniurations de ceux de la maison de Guyse . . .* (Paris, 1565), in Lindsay and Neu, *French Political Pamphlets,* no. 407, one of the many pamphlets carrying on the attack inaugurated by Hotman's *Tigre.*

[37] Quoted in [Hotman], *Vita Colinii,* 57. On "le desseing de Bayonne" see, e.g., the Huguenot pamphlets collected as *Les Requests, Protestations, remonstrances et advertissements, faits par Monseigneur le Prince de Condé . . .* (Orleans, 1567), BN, Lb.[33] 206; and *Discours au vray des conseils et moyens qu'on a tenus pour exterminer la pure doctrine . . .* (Heidelberg, 1568), BN, Lb.[33] .195.

[38] *Arrest de la Court de Parlement contre Gaspart de Colligny, qui fut admiral de France, mis en huict langues, a sçavoir, François, Latin, Italien, Espagnol, Allemant, Flament, Anglois et Escoçois* (Paris, 1569), republished (Paris, 1574), in Lindsay and Neu, *French Political Pamphlets,* nos. 652, 653, 754.

In these same years there was a growing tendency among Protestants to attach these fears and threats to malicious foreign, especially Italian, influence. Among other suspected imports during the early stages of the religious wars came "Papemania" and the practice of assassination—murder "Italian style," as Hotman's friend Henri Estienne called it—which was another source of martyrs.[39] Nor was the overall apprehension in any way allayed by specific pacification agreements, which on the contrary were suspected of being duplicitous arrangements made to trick Huguenots into letting down their guard. This was especially the case with the "limping and uneasy peace" of Saint-Germain of 1570, which Huguenots would later condemn as an evil trick and, according to one of Hotman's imaginative friends, as the diseased offspring of Catherine and her alleged consort, that devil of a cardinal (of Lorraine), who was accumulating his own share of "legends."[40]

All of these proliferating and intertwining anti-Catholic legends tended, as legends will do, to group themselves together around a more visible and concrete symbol that could serve as the center of a grander construct. The symbol that finally emerged to take this sovereign position was the figure, or at least the public image, of Catherine's countryman Machiavelli, who came to represent a kind of devilish counterpart to the Protestant martyr ideal. Machiavelli could not assume this posthumous role, however, until there was a crime worthy of his evil genius; and such a "crime" was indeed provided on August 24, 1572. Taken together, this massacre, the Protestant conspiracy theory, and the patterns of martyrdom created a mythology of monumental proportions.

It is in such a conceptual and emotional context, it seems to me, that the events surrounding and succeeding St. Bartholomew's Day 1572 must be understood; and so must the leading actors in the drama. The Huguenot chief Coligny was the very prototype of the Protestant saint, as represented in the official, and indeed hagiographical, account written by Hotman.[41] Coligny's days, even his meals, were filled with prayers, sermons, and psalm singing, and he was most solicitous about spreading the word through education and missionary work as well as by personal example. Yet he never ceased being a fighter, and in the name of these very ideals he had been playing a most dangerous political game, purportedly at the expense of that

[39] Henri Estienne, *Apologie pour Hérodote*, ed. Paul Ristelhuber (Paris, 1879), 1: 353; and *La Papemanie de France* (n.p., 1567), Arsenal, 8°H. 12774, vol. 1; see also Rabelais, *Pantagruel*, bk. 4, ch. 48.

[40] Anonymous poem, "La Paix Valois," in *Le Reveille-matin des François* ("Edinburgh" [Basel?], 1574); see also *Legende de Charles Cardinal de Lorraine*, vol. 6 of *Memoires de Condé*. In general, see my "Murd'rous Machiavel in France," *Political Science Quarterly*, 85 (1970): 545–59; and Salvo Mastellone, *Venalità e Machiavellismo in Francia (1572–1610)* (Florence, 1972).

[41] [Hotman], *Vita Colinii*, 130; see also Crespin and Goulart, *Histoire des martyrs*, 3: 663.

Tridentine "conspiracy," which by now had taken on the appearance of a Madrid-Rome axis. Indeed he was doing a bit of conspiring himself, though apparently not without royal permission, and had committed himself to supporting William of Orange's projected invasion of the Netherlands. But in July Coligny's credit had fallen off sharply when a force of Huguenot troops, sent to Mons to relieve William's lieutenant Louis of Nassau, was ambushed and slaughtered by the Spanish.

Meanwhile in Paris tensions were mounting. The scheduled wedding of Henry of Navarre and Catherine's daughter Marguerite, a kind of nuptial prefiguring of the conciliatory policy later adopted by the Politiques, was a hopeful sign; but it had to be postponed because of the death of Henry's mother, Jeanne d'Albret, in June. Stories immediately began to circulate, and to be believed by Huguenots such as Hotman, that she had been poisoned by the enemy. In such a heated atmosphere the wedding was set for August 18. Alarming rumors continued to fly, and in July Charles IX issued another in a long line of ordinances banning weapons and expelling vagabonds and *mauvais garçons* within twenty-four hours. Just before the wedding, it seems, Jean de Montluc, a moderate Catholic friend of the Huguenots and a diplomatic agent for Catherine, warned one of Coligny's men to get out of the city. This Coligny himself could not do, and he took up residence in a house belonging, ominously enough, to the family of Anne du Bourg. "I would rather be with you than at court," he wrote to his young and pregnant wife a few hours after the ceremony, "but I must set public advantage above private pleasure."[42]

The first act of the tragedy came on Friday of the same week. On that morning of August 22, as he was returning from court, Coligny was shot and seriously wounded by a certain Maurevert, called the "king's killer" because of a more successful attempt made against one of Coligny's lieutenants a few years before. The next two days Coligny spent in his quarters, attended by friends and his physician, Ambrose Paré, and visited by embarrassed members of the royal family. Coligny spoke at length and in saintly tones, providing political advice for the king, a confession of faith for his followers, and forgiveness for his would-be assassin, if not for the duke of Guise, whom he held responsible. Already, according to Hotman's secondhand account, Coligny was beginning to sound like a martyr. A royal guard was given to him but was placed under the command of an old enemy. The ban on arms was still in effect, but it did not apply to the king's men, who were rattling their weapons ostentatiously in the streets. So, as

[42] Quoted in [Hotman], *Vita Colinii,* 105, but differing significantly from the extant original (which has been published in the *Bulletin de la Société de l'histoire du protestantisme Français,* 1 [1852]: 369) by adding a statement to the effect that the admiral would take care not to offend his enemies (presumably to offset the charges of hostility and militancy); see also *Ordonnance du Roy portant injonction a tous ses subjects de vivre en amitie les uns avec les autres* (Paris, 1572), Arsenal, 8°H. 12778, vol. 3.

Huguenots looked back on the situation, the trap had been set; indeed the events of that weekend all seemed to fall into one terrible pattern.

The second and successful attempt on the admiral early in the morning of August 24 set off the mythopoeic process. "I am ready for death," the admiral had said before the assassin struck, and soon the "Matins of Paris" began. "Away with him, cut of his head and handes,/ And send them as a present to the Pope," the duke of Guise has been represented as saying. The words are Christopher Marlowe's,[43] but the deed itself has been documented and has taken its place alongside of many other atrocity stories; babies dropped from windows, bodies stripped and thrown into the Seine, some to be seen for days afterwards, a few as far as Rouen, according to a Huguenot song. As usual Paris set the fashion for the provinces, and the attacks signaled by Coligny's murder, carried out by laborers as well as by gentlemen, spread to a dozen or so towns throughout France. Many Protestants fled into the countryside. "I am sure that the wild beasts are kinder than those in human form," Hotman remarked to a friend. Later he reported that "Huguenot-hunting"—*la chasse des huguenots*—was becoming a popular sport.[44]

In the international Protestant community the reactions included shock and outrage but little real surprise. The inhabitants of La Rochelle had been warning Coligny of some such plot for two months, Hotman had heard, and throughout France men had been saying that Coligny was deceived at court.[45] "What an atrocity!" was Beza's reaction to the admiral's death. "How many times have I predicted this! How many times did I warn him about it!"[46] Streams of refugees carried the news in greater detail, but there seems to be little doubt about the underlying cause of the massacres. The plot was "undoubtedly general and the work of the Council of Trent," declared the Council of Geneva, which indeed feared that it would extend into their own territory.[47] During the fall one French agent confessed under torture that the invasion would be launched from Savoy, and though the attack did not materialize, the fear continued for the rest of the century. Hotman, then exiled in Geneva, shared and broadcast this apprehension about what he called "the Tridentine web and popish alliance called the Holy League."[48]

43 Christopher Marlowe, *The Massacre at Paris,* based on Hotman's well-known *De Furoribus Gallicis;* see also Paul Kocher, "François Hotman and Marlowe's *The Massacre at Paris,*" *PMLA,* 56 (1941): 349–68.

44 Hotman to Rodolphe Gualter, Nov. 5, 1573, Zentralbibliothek, Zurich, MS F. 39, fol. 214v; the same phrase is used by Nicolas Pithou, *Histoire ecclesiastique de l'eglise pretendue reformee de la ville de Troyes,* published by Charles Recordon as *Le Protestantisme en Champagne* (Paris, 1863), 144.

45 Hotman to William of Hesse, Oct. 6, 1572, published in Ludwig Ehinger, *Franz Hotmann,* Beiträge zur vaterländischen Geschichte, vol. 14 (Basel, 1896), no. 24.

46 Beza to Thomas Tilius, Sept. 10, 1572, published in *Bulletin de la Société de l'histoire du protestantisme français,* 6 (1858): 16.

47 Registres du Conseil, Sept. 4, 1572, Archives d'état, Geneva, vol. 67, fol. 201r.

48 Hotman to Bullinger, Oct. 25, 1572, Zentralbibliothek, Zurich, MS S. 127, fol. 95r.

One conspicuous sign of the meta-historical impact of the massacre was the extremism of the reactions to it from all quarters. The Huguenots, of course, screamed bloody murder. The leaders were all "assassins," Hotman proclaimed, "the likes of whom no age has tolerated."[49] And this specifically included the king, by whose "express command" the deed was admittedly done. On the other side Catholics, arguing that the attacks were designed to crush a Huguenot "conspiracy" arising from the "Theodor-Bezian infection," concluded that it was simply retribution. "There is no gallows, cross, or torture severe enough to punish the crime of a traitor or rebel," one royalist wrote.[50] Others celebrated the event as providential. So François de Belleforest, later one of Hotman's chief critics, declared it to be no less than a miracle; and he found this judgment to be confirmed by the appearance of the great nova (the first in modern history) of November 1572. "I know the heretics will laugh and tax me with superstition," he added.[51] In fact the "heretics" were not laughing and had an explanation of the phenomenon hardly less "superstitious": to them it was the Star of Bethlehem returned, and it signified the salvation to come.

Quantitative estimates were likewise inflated. The massacre was so enormous, said one commentator, "that I doubt if posterity will ever believe it."[52] And in fact posterity has not believed the figures given by contemporary critics. At first Beza himself cried that over 300,000 of his brothers had been killed.[53] Later estimates were commonly placed at 100,000 deaths and revised downwards to 50,000. A decade later a certain "N. Froumenteau" published what purported to be a statistical survey of the costs, social as well as economic, of the religious wars, and his figures offer evidence of the depth of contemporary feeling if not of exact totals. By that date, 1583, Froumenteau estimated that about 765,000 persons had perished in the wars; 76,010 were civilian casualties, and of these 36,000 could be classified as "massacred"; 4,500 bodies had passed Paris on the Seine, while 6,000 had been carried by the Loire. In addition he estimated that 12,000 women and girls had been raped, and he went on to remark that, since this sort of thing so often went unreported, the total was probably twice as great. If the war continued, he remarked, the total would indeed be 100,000 instead of only 36,000.[54]

49 Hotman to Abraham Sulzer, Oct. 3, 1572, *ibid.*, fol. 47r. See also *Declaration du roy de la cause et occasion de la mort de l'admiral* (Paris, 1572), in Lindsay and Neu, *French Political Pamphlets*, no. 729.

50 Artus Desire, *La Singerie des Huguenots . . .* (Paris, 1574), 22; and *Discours de la mort et execution de Gabriel comte de Montgomery* (Paris, 1574), fol. 2v, in Lindsay and Neu, *French Political Pamphlets*, no. 790.

51 François de Belleforest, *Discours sur l'heur des presages advenus de nostre temps significantz la felicité de regne de nostre Roy Charles* (Paris, Nov. 18, 1572), fol. 10r.

52 *Resolution claire et facile sur la question . . . de la prise d'armes par les inférieurs* (Reims, 1577), 97, in BN, Lb.34 .103.

53 Beza to Bullinger, Sept. 1, 1572, Zentralbibliothek, Zurich, A. 44, p. 679, cited by P. F. Geisendorf, *Théodore de Bèze* (Geneva, 1949), 306.

54 The book in question is the fascinating *Secret des finances de France* (n.p., 1581), dedicated to Henry III, by N. Froumenteau (no doubt a pseudonym), a friend of Hotman and author also

Whoever he was, Froumenteau was a Huguenot and had nothing but contempt for the "Machiavellistes" who had so ravaged France. Yet, though his statistics are inflated by partisanship, it should be added that he did make some effort to indicate his sources (*preuves*) and often omitted provincial figures for lack of evidence, so that his conclusions are relatively far closer to reality than those of most chroniclers.[55] While it would be an error to take his figures at face value (as certain nineteenth-century scholars have done), it would be equally mistaken to deny this pioneering work a significant place in the history of statistics, which like other social sciences emerged at least in part from (and has never quite disassociated itself from) ideological conflict. In any case a great effort went into the making of the book, and it testifies again to the enormous intellectual impact of the wars of religion and of St. Bartholomew in particular.

In the field of political thought, of course, the impact of St. Bartholomew was even more spectacular. The massacre immediately took its place as the pivotal event in the martyrological tradition and became a central force in the flood of propaganda that poured from Protestant presses at a greater than average rate in succeeding years. It was at this point that the enlarged community of martyrs began to take on a more special political significance because of its association with the opposition party led by Henry of Navarre, who succeeded Coligny as the leader of the Huguenots. The point was made best by Beza in his *Right of Magistrates,* a tract so radical that he was refused permission to publish it in Geneva. "And this I conclude," he wrote, "that we must honor as martyrs not only those who have conquered without resistance, and by patience only, against tyrants who have persecuted the truth, but those also who, authorized by law and by competent authorities, devoted their strength to the defense of the true religion."[56] Here is expressed the complete politicization not only of the Calvinist cause

---

of the anonymous *Miroir des François* . . . (Paris, 1581), *Le Cabinet du roy* . . . (Paris, 1581), and, if only in part, of the *Reveille-matin,* which is one work that estimates the massacred of St. Bartholomew as 100,000 (p. 78). The first book includes a dialogue between "Provence" and "Le Politique" (who figures also in the *Reveille-matin* and the *Miroir des François*) and a listing, province by province, of the taxes, charges, and expenditures, especially military, over the previous thirty-one years. The second book discusses the social costs, again province by province (pp. 378–79). The categories of the dead are ecclesiastics, nobles (Catholics and Huguenots distinguished), soldiers (again Catholics and Huguenots), those executed (many for lese majesty), Huguenots "massacred," foreigners, houses destroyed, villages burned and razed, and *filles violees.* Froumenteau's *Preuves* (pp. 401–09) include records of the Chambre des Comptes and *controlles de la gendarmerie* as well as "chronicles and memoirs," but he adds that no "proof" is needed to describe the horror of the massacres.

[55] Froumenteau, *Le Secret des finances,* 418. The work has not received its due in the history either of economic thought or of statistics; the judgment of Fernand Faure, "France," in John Koren, ed., *The History of Statistics* (New York, 1918), 236–37, contradicting such credulous nineteenth-century opinions as that of Henri Baudrillart, is probably excessively severe and certainly unhistorical.

[56] Beza, *Du Droit des magistrats* (Geneva, 1574), critical edition by R. M. Kingdon (Geneva, 1970), 67, and translated in Julian Franklin, ed., *Constitutionalism and Resistance in the Sixteenth Century* (New York, 1969), 135.

but also of the tradition of martyrs—an unmistakable shift from passive to active resistance.

Another conspicuous by-product of St. Bartholomew was the mythology, or demonology, associated with Machiavelli, whose ideas of political behavior were widely regarded as the cause both of the massacre itself and of the political and social degeneration of France in general over the previous ten years and more. Much of this material, especially the *Reveille-Matin* and Hotman's *French Fury,* consisted of highly colored accounts of the event itself or of extravagant elegies of the "hero-martyr" Coligny,[57] but there was also a growing quantity of polemic and theorizing about the problem of war guilt (which has always played so fundamental a role in historical thinking) and about ideas of political resistance, constitutional government, sovereignty, and the structure of society in general. Not only the work of the Monarchomachs but also Jean Bodin's *Republic,* which may be taken as a response to the work of the Monarchomachs, grappled quite directly with the problems that the Massacre of St. Bartholomew defined in a way that made them impossible any longer to ignore.[58]

In more concretely historical terms the effect of the massacre was traumatic. Anticipated for a decade, after its coming it haunted an entire generation of Protestants, who suspected that it might be revived at any time and who were prepared, ideologically if not emotionally, to take their place among the future martyrs. Hotman, for example, having been sent into permanent exile, lived out his remaining eighteen years in almost perpetual fear that the fate he had just barely missed in 1572, and that had claimed so many of his friends, including Petrus Ramus, would overtake him. The tone of his correspondence is consistently that of a victim and even martyr. At one point he was convinced that the pope had hired a man to assassinate him, and in his last years he became obsessed with the idea of dying in battle for his Cause—one of the established "marks of martyrdom." Only the thought

[57] See, for example, *Epicedia illustri heroi Caspari Colignio . . . Beato Christi martyri, variis linguis a doctis piisq. poetis decantata* (n.p., 1572), in Lindsay and Neu, *French Political Pamphlets,* no. 725, of which Beza's own presentation copy is in the possession of Yale University Library. Professor Samuel Kinser of Northern Illinois University points out a most interesting example of the hero-martyr dichotomy in d'Aubigné's account of Coligny's death. Following the account of Jacques-Auguste de Thou, *Historiarum sui temporis opera* (Frankfurt, 1614–21), 1: 993, and of [Hotman], *Vita Colinii* and, with some modifications [Hotman], *De Furoribus Gallicis,* d'Aubigné first represented the admiral, on the point of death, as adopting a hero's stance and lamenting the fact that he was about to be killed at the hands not of a "cavalier" but only of a common servant. But a few years later, in the second edition (1626), d'Aubigné changed the picture so that Coligny appeared as a passive victim, "on his knees beside his bed" and making only the martyrly comment, "My friends, save yourselves." See *Histoire universelle,* 3: 313.

[58] For discussions of this large subject, see Ralph Giesey, "The Monarchomach Triumvirs: Hotman, Beza and Mornay," *Bibliothèque d'Humanisme et Renaissance,* 32 (1970): 41–56; and J. H. M. Salmon, "Bodin and the Monarchomachs," in a forthcoming volume based upon the international conference on Jean Bodin held in Munich in 1970. It has recently been argued that the monarchomach author of the *Vindiciae contra tyrannos* (n.p., 1578) was not Philippe du Plessis Mornay but rather Johan Junius de Jonge: see Derek Visser, "Junius: The Author of the Vindiciae contra Tyrannos?" *Tijdschrift voor Geschiedenis,* 84 (1971): 510–25.

of his children, he said, restrained him.[59] In many ways his attitude was typical of the French exile community of his generation, whose politics, perspective, and very lives had been shaped by the massacre.

Situated as it was at the center of such swirling emotions, revolutionary implications, festering resentments, and indeterminate intellectual repercussions, the Massacre of St. Bartholomew became a legend almost before it happened, and it grew with the telling and with the passage of time. As it furnished a target and motive for endless polemic, so it furnished a target and motive for scholarly debate—a classic "problem" for historians, though ultimately insoluble, at least in the guild-oriented, legend-prone, history-transcending terms of sixteenth-century propaganda, from which we have hardly yet escaped.[60] "The blood of martyrs is the seed of the church": it has also been fuel for the labors of generations of historians, and by now more ink than blood has flowed as a result of the events of that weekend in Paris four hundred years ago. Catholic masses have ceased, Protestant lamentations have been muted, but the historical discussion continues: such is one of the forms, it seems, that myths take in our time.

[59] Hotman to Simon Grynaeus, Nov. 27, 1586, in B. F. Hummel, ed., *Celebrium virorum . . . epistolae ineditae* (Nuremberg, 1777), 81; and Hotman to Daniel Tossanus, Feb. 26, 1588, in *Hotomanorum epistolae* (Amsterdam, 1700), no. 162, citing *Aeneid,* bk. 2, line 353.

[60] Herbert Butterfield, "Lord Acton and the Massacre of St. Bartholomew," in his *Man on His Past* (Cambridge, 1955), 171–201, is a useful survey.

VI

HISTORY AND THE ENCYCLOPEDIA

The study of history was central to Renaissance learning both explicitly and implicitly—both as an ancient "art" raised to the level of a modern "science" and as a repository of cultural memory and instruction. My purpose here is to explore more specifically the way in which "history," without losing its more general meaning (narrative description), came also to signify a particular mode of thought, or at least a way of organizing human experience, behavior, and learning in order to assert, to accommodate, or to change, contemporary priorities and values. In various ways the medieval *Studium* was transformed from a hierarchy into a historical process—from a structure into an adventure.[1] The idea not of a ladder but rather of the advancement of learning illustrates what may be regarded as a historical recasting of the the classification of sciences, analogous to the "temporalizing" of the Great Chain of Being traced by Arthur O. Lovejoy more than half a century ago.[2] The road from Vincent of Beauvais's *Speculum Mundi* to Diderot's *Encyclopédie* is hardly straight, but from our perspective the growing prominence of historical perspective and the idea of cultural progress seem undeniable.

The encyclopedic ideal is no longer much with us, but it is evident in certain modern descendants of Renaissance scholarship; and here I come to the second aspect of this discussion, which is the modern study of intellectual and cultural history; for it is here, I would suggest, that we can see what remains of the alliance between history and the encyclopedia. The history of ideas in particular may be regarded as a modern offshoot of the Renaissance encyclopedia.[3] In any case what I am offering here, in this bifocal perspective, is a preliminary and very general effort to map the role of history in the shaping and reshaping of knowledge from Renaissance to Enlightenment.

On this encyclopedic road there are many significant landmarks, and I begin with one modest example, Polydore Vergil's popular encyclopedia,

D. R. Kelley and R. H. Popkin (eds), The Shapes of Knowledge from the Renaissance to the Enlightenment, 7–22.

De Rerum inventoribus, which appeared in many editions beginning in 1496.[4] In this work Vergil organized the arts and sciences according to their ancient founders, legendary or historical, and their modern continuators. After an account of Creation, the origins of letters, the liberal arts, philosophy, and the various sciences are treated in the first two books, followed by systematic discussions of social and political organization, the mechanical arts, and other aspects of human and particularly religious culture. The humanist and critical face of Vergil is not especially evident in this pedestrian compilation, but the historical orientation of his early book is in accord with the assumption that the disciplines have been fundamentally human creations to be investigated historically even though their origins are often lost in myth and fable. In a human and historical perspective the arts of speech were expressed first in poetry, which was a product of natural language, and only later by more refined and rational modes of expression, while philosophy emerged from magic and religion, and history itself advanced from poetic forms of expression.

Another encyclopedic effort informed by historical awareness was the work of Juan Luis Vives on the transmission of learning (*De Tradendis disciplinis*), where history appears as an aspect of prudence essential for Christian doctrine. In this pursuit of "true wisdom" (*vera sapientia*) Vives invokes the methods of Roman law, which was likewise drawn from historical experience (*jus totum ex historia manet* is Vives's striking aphorism, associated with the famous work of Pomponius on the origin of law enshrined in Justinian's Digest).[5] A similarly encyclopedic view is evident in Vives's subsequent discussion of the related theme of the corruption of disciplines (*De causis corruptarum artium*), in which history again appears as a vehicle of learning, though unfortunately subject to the instability and self delusions that, despite the historical ideal of truth, marked the human condition.[6]

In the course of the sixteenth century the idea of "encyclopedia" went far beyond such popular or pedagogical summaries of knowledge and came to embrace the new, or renewed, agenda of classical philology, for instance in the work of the French hellenist Guillaume Budé.[7] In theoretical as well as practical terms Budé celebrated the ancient encyclopedia (*orbs doctrinae*) and identified it in particular with the modern science of "philology"—"philology," he wrote, "once an ornament but now the restorer and interpreter" (*philologia . . . olim ornatrix, hodie instauratrix atque interpolatrix*).[8] For Budé the myth of Prometheus was an allegory of the achievement not only of the mechanical arts but also of philosophy, "discoverer of the disciplines" (*inventrix disciplinarum*), while the figure of Minerva stood for the legacy of the arts and sciences assembled by various nations—*Minerva Attica*, *Minerva Romana*, and more recently the *Minerva* or "genius" of France. However, Budé also came to insist that the legacy of antiquity, and especially "Hellenism" (*Hellenismus*), received its perfection only in the higher wisdom of Christian doctrine.

In the view of humanists like Budé and Vives history became prominent not only as one of the *studia humanitatis* but also as a way of defining other fields of study, including philosophy, law, political science, literature (vernacular as well as classical), and history itself. In the effort of popularizing the humanist encyclopedia, Louis Le Roy, who was Budé's biographer and regius professor of Greek in Paris, published studies of what he represented as "the origin, progress, and perfection of philosophy, with a comparison of Plato and Aristotle," and similarly of "the origin, antiquity, progress, excellence and utility of the political art," again concentrating on Plato and Aristotle, while his more famous *Vicissitude of Variety of Things in the Universe* of 1575 encompassed a comparative history of civilization from mythical and fabulous beginnings (Vergil's "inventors of things") in the near east down to the age of modern cultural revival and the triumph of the moderns over the ancients.[9]

Abel Lefranc thought that Le Roy's book was the first history of civilization in a general sense, but there is at least one other candidate for this honor. A quarter of a century earlier Christophe Milieu (or Mylaeus) published a book entitled *De Scribenda universitatis rerum historia* (1551), which reorganized the arts, sciences, and technical aspect of human culture under five rubrics, or historical categories; namely, the history of nature (*natura*), of prudence, (*prudentia*), of government (*principatus*), of wisdom (*sapientia*), and of literature (*litteratura*).[10] Milieu's work was arranged as a series of "narratives" and focussed on "writing" (thus anticipating Derrida by four centuries in proclaiming the primacy of *écriture*); yet it is deeply concerned with the substance of human culture and displays an encyclopedic vision of history—or a historical vision of the encyclopedia. Like Vergil and Le Roy, Milieu was impressed by the vicissitude of cultural things. He was inspired in particular, he tells us, by the fall of Constantinople and the translation of learning resulting from the emigration of Byzantine scholars.[11] These importers of Greek Paideia began those comparisons between Plato and Aristotle which have figured so centrally in western philosophy and in the history of philosophy. But Milieu's survey covered much more than the tradition of academic philosophy; like Le Roy's work, it reached out for the totality (and in this sense the *universitas*) of things—the realms both of nature and of "second nature" (*altera natura*), which was founded not in abstract philosophy and theory but rather in prudence, practical knowledge, and what the Greeks (he remarked) called *phronesis*.

For Milieu human action defined the realm of prudence which encompassed what he called "administration of the things of the earth"—agriculture, technology, civil and military, typography, commerce, and laws. These expressions of man's "second nature" led to the next category, political organization, which Milieu traced from antiquity down to the empire of Charles V.[12] The third rubric, or stage, was "wisdom," by which Milieu meant not only philosophy but the whole range of disciplines, including the profession of history itself (*historicorum professio* is his phrase) and the modern arts of public discourse.[13] *Historia sapientiae* was in effect the Renaissance equivalent of intellectual history. "Through history and poetry," Milieu remarked in this connection, "all sorts of doctrines have been disseminated" (*ex historia et poesia omnia doctrinarum genera dimanasse*), including the liberal arts and the sciences corresponding to the three university faculties of law, medicine, and theology. Finally, Milieu took up "literature", in which he included all the efforts of human writing—poetry, history, civil law, and all the philosophical sects that succeeded the Platonic system (referring to what he called the *doctrinae Platonica integritas*) down to his own point of departure, which was the revival of Greek learning (*literarum renovatio* is his phrase), culminating in the encyclopedic work of Budé.[14]

In the following century the history of the advancement of learning continued to be pursued but in ways at once reflective and more restricted than the humanist celebrations of erudition and indiscriminate "literature" as defined, or left undefined, in Milieu's survey. In particular the impulse toward historical understanding intersected with questions of scientific "method," which was a major theme of all of the disciplines and especially of philosophy in the sixteenth century; and concerns tended to shift from the human to the natural sciences.[16] This was especially the case with the Cartesian skeptical attack on both history and encyclopedic learning and the more positive Baconian classification of knowledge, which became the dominant model for the history of the practical as well as the theoretical sciences for two centuries and more. More general interest in the history of *sapientia*, in *principatus*, in *prudentia*, and in *literatura* continued in a number of forms, and above all in what was still the central theme of the Renaissance encyclopedia, which was the study of "philosophy." Frequently, however, this was the "new philosophy" that called all—and especially all traditional learning—in doubt, so that history as well as the encyclopedia became suspect as sources of truth.

Despite these restrictions the history of philosophy, between the fifteenth and the eighteenth century, was transformed from an incidental aspect of the humanist encyclopedia into a major genre devoted both to the advancement of learning in a general sense and to the emergence of philosophy as a true and independent "science."[17] In the Renaissance the definition of philosophy continued formally to be the "love of wisdom" (*amor sapientiae*), but under the weight of scholastic controversy and humanist erudition this love, though it could be Platonic, could not be pure. Philosophers had to confront the mythical past and pagan heritage of philosophy. While identifying perhaps with the ancients, they had perforce to be moderns, that is, historians and critics; and from this circumstance came not only the modern study of the history of philosophy—and, it seems to me, the history of ideas—but also that curious sub-field which since the Enlightenment has been called the "philosophy of the history of philosophy" and which continued to be involved in the encyclopedic tradition. In this connection the problem was not only telling the story of the "career of philosophy" but also determining the conceptual role of history, if any, in the project of philosophy. Although the vast literature accumulated on the *Philosophie der Philosophiegeschichte* has been surveyed many times over the past three centuries, there is nothing at all comparable for the history of the encyclopedia, the classification of knowledge, or the history of ideas more generally. Yet there are significant overlaps with this genre that need to be considered.

There are several ways in which philosophers could deal with their past, and I would point to four in particular, at least three of them based on firm classical precedent.[18] The first of these is skepticism, pure and simple, or complex and philosophical—rejecting not only the writings of philosophers but the whole project to which they had been devoted. In the sixteenth century the most conspicuous example of this is the negative encyclopedia of Henry Cornelius Agrippa of Nettesheim, *The Vanity of Arts and Sciences*, which dismissed all the disciplines as products of human pride and presumption.[19] Prometheus would be punished, and his gift was spurious in any case. True learning resided "not in human arts but in faith," Agrippa declaimed (*non in humanis artibus sed in fidei disciplina*), and he invoked among other things the "learned ignorance" taught by Nicholas of Cusa.

A second way of viewing the philosophical past was to accept it in its own terms—in the terms, that is, of the story of particular "sects." Like forms of religion or heresy, these sects could be viewed critically or embraced dogmatically, but the historian's task was basically to write their literary history. The founder of this doxographical method was Diogenes Laertius, and indeed historians of philosophy from Thomas Stanley to Bertrand Russell have followed and exploited this mode of interpretation.[20] At its worst doxography limited itself to biography and anecdotes; at its best it sorted out traditions and philosophical schools—those eponymous"-isms" founded by *magistri* and continued by *discipuli*—according to the generational patterns preserved in universities and intellectual life more generally.

A third approach, or perhaps set of approaches, was the effort to reconcile earlier philosophical works with current systems of thought and belief, characteristically Christian religion. This conciliatory view could take the form of a sympathetic "comparison" between Platonism, Aristotelianism, and Christian doctrine, for example, as in the work of fifteenth-century Byzantine scholars like Pletho and Trapezuntius; or it could be more broadly syncretistic and produce a *philosophia perennis* (to invoke a famous sixteenth-century formula) that aspired to dissolve all human speculation in a non-sectarian, non-partisan, superhuman, metahistorical, and perhaps mystical vision.[21] Among the more controversial associates of this view were pantheism, natural religion and, in a later age, psychologism and anthropologism.

The fourth way of looking at the history of thought also has ancient precedents, but its modern form represents a significant departure from earlier ones and was contrasted by its devotees with syncretism as well as skepticism and dogmatism. I refer to what by the later seventeenth century was being called the "eclectic method" (*methodus eclectica*) and what was especially in accord both with the search for a proper method of historical understanding and writing, and with the growing fondness for ideas of an accumulation of knowledge and an advancement of learning.[22] The history of philosophy, like the history of religion, was divided between the history of error (*historia stultitia*) and the history of wisdom (*historia sapientiae*), and it was the historian's mission to extricate the latter from the former—often in the light of contemporary doctrinal commitments, to be sure, such as Cartesian philosophy or Christian revelation. One early survey of the history of philosophy compiled from the standpoint of a sort of Christian eclecticism, Thomassen's *Method of Studying and Teaching Philosophy with Respect to the Christian Religion and Scriptures in a Solid and Christian Manner* (1685), treated poets and rhetoricians as well as the philosophical canon. [23] In general, from the seventeenth century this "eclectic" or "elective" approach—in contrast to skeptical, sectarian, or syncretistic methods—aimed at an "adult philosophy" purified of the errors and misconceptions of the past.

Among the champions of this method, which has survived down to the present day, were Christian Thomasius, J.F. Buddeus, and J.G. Heineccius; but the pivotal work, and the modern classic, was J.J. Brucker's *Historia critica philosophiae* (1742–44), which not only summed up generations of Renaissance learning but also established the standard plot for the modern story of philosophy down to the (still flourishing) handbook of Ueberweg, not to mention the popular surveys of Will Durant and Bertrand Russell.[24] In a general way Brucker, like Lovejoy, took Platonism and its *fortuna* as the basis of his plot, and "ideas" in a classic Platonic sense (*ideae purae, intellectus purus*) as his main characters. For Brucker, in other words, the history of philosophy treated the permutations and combinations of "ideas" as expressed by various "sects," "schools," and "systems" emerging in the wake of Plato, his disciples, epigones, and critics; but it was aimed at a modern, purified synthesis of these partial visions arising from the advancement of learning and the progress of enlightenment.

For Brucker modern Eclecticism had nothing in common with the ancient variety. "The true Eclectic philosophy," he wrote, "renouncing every prejudice in favor of celebrated names of ancient sects, makes reason his sole guide, and deliberately investigates the nature and properties of the objects which come under his observation, that he may from these deduce clear principles, and arrive at certain knowledge."[25] Antiquity possessed many truths but also many falsehoods, as Heineccius put it; and the authority of "prjudice" derived from a "sectarian" method could not lead to wisdom. Heineccius concluded his own survey by drawing several inferences: No one should be satisfied with his own knowledge and reason, or build on his own knowledge, nor despise that of others, but should suspect his own ideas. Finally, no one "should seek truth by himself, nor should indiscriminately accept or reject all that Ancients and Moderns have written; and therefore there should be no other reasonable method of philosophizing except the Eclectic Method" (*Folglich kein anderer Methodus philosophandi raisonnable sey, als: METHODUS ECLECTICA*).[26]

One of the characteristics of the modern history of philosophy has been its increasingly narrow and abstract nature, especially in the dominant

German tradition which culminates in Kant's famous "a priori history of philosophy."[27] Moreover, the "criticism" of critical philosophy was bound up not with erudition and history but rather with pure ideas and pure reason—with logic, ontology, epistemology, and psychology (and, in that connection, ethics). The professional tradition of philosophy has become alienated in many ways from the encyclopedia, if not entirely from practical philosophy in an abstract, individualistic, and characteristically Kantian sense.

Yet within the debate of the "philosophy of the history of philosophy" there arose a fundamental divergence between Kantian and Hegelian views of philosophy as an independent "science" and what Richard Rorty has called the "richer and more diffuse genre" of the history of ideas and intellectual history."[28] In this divergence, it seems to me, the grounds for the modern "history of ideas" appear clearly for the first time. The term "history of ideas" was itself a coinage from an earlier work of Brucker—his *Historia philosophica doctrinae de ideis* (1723)—and it was soon after adapted by Giambattista Vico as one goal of his own "new science" (a concept which he initially identified with Renaissance "philology" in Budé's sense).[29] In one of its manifestations, wrote Vico, the *scienza nuova* was a "history of human ideas" (*storia delle idee umane*), and for Vico of course this meant not only metaphysics but the whole range of human knowledge going back to its linguistic and poetic origins—a radical historicization of the encyclopedic tradition.

Vico's historical and philological approach to the said history of ideas is expressed in his famous maxim, "the sciences must begin where their subject matter begins", applied in this context to the new science, which Vico continues, "took its start when the first men began to think humanly, and not when the philosophers began to reflect on human ideas (as in an erudite and scholarly little book"—referring to Brucker's aformentioned work, published two years before the first version of Vico's *Scienza nuova*). According to a late eighteenth-century admirer, Vico was "the first who tried to trace the progressive march and stages of the moral world, as Newton before him had calculated that of the natural world."[30]

What Vico proposed to do in his new science was to restore the connections between philosophy and philology—that is literature and historical criticism—and indeed to recall the whole encyclopedic tradition into the service of philosophy. In this effort he was of course not alone, and within the German tradition itself, as Frederick Beiser has recently written, "Herder is intentionally pushing philosophy in the direction of literature" and not (as Kant had charged) confusing the two.[31] Quite independently of Vico, Herder's "metacritique" of Kantian philosophy (following the earlier "metacriticism" of Hamann) reinforced his arguments by asserting the primacy of language over pure ideas.[32] Both Herder and Vico urged the expansion of the horizons of philosophy to include all the facets of human culture and thus to promote, once again, the old humanist alliance between history and the encyclopedia.

In his *Critical History of Philosophy* of 1737 A.F. Bourreau-Deslandes, for example, descended from the peaks of metaphysical speculation to the lower rungs of the ladder of learning in order to to describe what he called the "origins, progresses [note the plural], and revolutions" of philosophy lead by the party of the "Moderns" in the Republic of Letters. "Looked at in a certain way," he wrote, "the history [of philosophy] amounts to a history of the human spirit [*histoire de l'esprit humaine*], or at least a history in which the human spirit appears from the highest point of view."[33] Another example of the return of an encyclopedic scope in the history of philosophy may be seen in Appiano Buonafede's popular survey (published in 1786 and soon translated into French and German), which celebrated modern restorations and revolutions of philosophy—"le grandi rivoluzioni" and "la restaurazione di ogni filosofia."[34] Buonafede cited the work of Bourreau-Deslandes and other "philosophes" as well as Brucker, and he admitted into the philosophical canon many humanist authors, including the likes of Petrarch, Erasmus, Rudolph Agricola, Ramus, and the younger Scaliger, not to mention the skeptic and occultist Henry Cornelius Agrippa.

There was much talk in the eighteenth century about the history of the "human spirit" in broad cultural terms (*historia intellectus humani; histoire de l'Esprit humaine; Geschichte des menschlichen Geistes*), even by Brucker, contemptuous as he was of Bourreau-Deslandes's "superficial" work—and usually it was in sharp contrast to the concerns of the canon of professional philosophy. In 1791 Karl Leonhard Reinhold, for example, working in the shadow of Kant but standing on the shoulders of Brucker, distinguished the history of philosophy proper from the "history of the human spirit," which included considerations not only of technological and commercial achievement but also of cultural context, anthropological (i.e., psychological) factors, and even external circumstances and environment.[35] In his *Ideen zur Geschichte der Philosophie* of 1809 F. A. Carus distinguished a philosophy following doctrinal development from one concerned with questions of originality, causality, individuality of thought, the force of nationality, and the role of language; and he resurrected the old notion that the history of error as well as truth should be considered (*Die Geschichte der Philosophie darf also nicht bloss* historia sapientiae *sondern auch* historia stultitiae *seyn*).[36]

In a less critical way many self-styled "philosophes" undertook to humanize, to vulgarize, and thus to politicize philosophy by extending the notion of "progress" beyond the lecture halls to larger issues, treated extensively by Renaissance scholars, of material well-being and civilization, that is, "the arts of commerce and technology." These extensions of the old mechanical arts, together with the theme of progress, were celebrated most famously in D'Alembert's "Preliminary Discourse to the Encyclopedia," which expanded and up-dated the Baconian scheme of learning—and its "advancement"—by transforming the old encyclopedia into a modern and enlightened "reasoned dictionary of the sciences, arts, and professions." Indeed the historical dimension here is obscured by the desire to reduce the arts and sciences to a rational order and what D'Alembert termed a "mappemonde" of learning. For D'Alembert the arts and sciences were bound together as by a chain; and in order to arrange them in a system it was necessary to determine "the genealogy and the filiation of the parts of our knowledge, the causes that brought the various branches of our knowledge into being, and the characteristics that distinguish them." "In short," he concluded, "we must go back to the origin and generation of our ideas."[37]

The French conception was further extended by Dugald Stewart (writing the article on "encyclopedia" for the *Encyclopedia Britannica*), who praised Bacon's "magnificent design" but who criticized D'Alembert's rigid classification, especially his undervaluation of the faculty of imagination and his failure to recognize the benefits of modern interdisciplinary encounters—between geometry and physics, for example, and between etymology and ancient history—in the "Progress of philosophy," which Stewart traced, in his words, "since the renaissance of letters in Europe."[38] It was through the French translation of his work, to which Stewart's "friend" Victor Cousin added "reflections" and a supplement, that a knowledge of Vico's work first reached a significant French audience.

There were efforts in the eighteenth century to draw together ideas and historical context, as in the question (posed by the Academy of Dijon) confronted by Rousseau in 1750 concerning the effects of the restoration of the arts and sciences on morals. In 1781 the Academy of Sciences of Berlin posed a more general question: "What has been and is still the influence of the constitution of states on the sciences and that of the sciences on the constitution?" In this case the victorious prize essay was Christoph Meiners's study of "the history of the human spirit" and "the history of philosophy" in its seminal Greek period.[39] Later, with reference to Rousseau's prize essay, Meiners broadened his vision to include the "morals, constitutions, laws, trade, commerce, religion, sciences, and education of the middle ages," tracing them through the "first renaissance" (*Ueber die ersten Wiederherstellen nützlicher Kentnisse im viertzehnten und funfzehnten Jahrhunderts*) and comparing these in great detail with those of the Enlightenment. In this connection he reviewed Kant's famous question—"Was ist wahre Aufklärung?" in Meiners's phrasing—and the more historical problem of the possibility of progress (*Der Frage, ob wir einem Fortgang im Guten zu hoffen, oder ein Rückfall in's Böse zu fürchten haben?"*).[40] For Meiners "true enlightenment" began not with the founders of natural philosophy but with Petrarch and his humanist followers, who began the resurrection of the "human spirit" (*menschlicher Geist*), and its history entailed a comprehensive survey of human culture in the broadest sense.

This enterprise was carried on in the nineteenth century by the modern school of Eclecticism (which had roots in Thomasius's and Brucker's conceptions of the history of philosophy). The leading figure of this much maligned doctrine (or metadoctrine) was Victor Cousin, but an earlier illustration is provided by the work of Cousin's elder colleague, Baron Degérando's comparative history of philosophical systems, which was published in 1804 and which surveyed the career of philosophy from antiquity down to contemporary Idealism, Skepticism, the Scottish and Kantian (*Criticisme*) schools, and, especially, Eclecticism.[41] Like D'Alembert, Degérando aimed at a kind of "historical map" (*une tableau historique des systèmes* and *une carte géographique des doctrines et des opinions*) which "will be to philosophy what philosophy itself has been to the other arts and sciences." Degérando's justification for his history of ideas was founded on a rejection of the notion of metaphysics as "first philosophy," because (as he explained) "the universal principles of all the sciences can be resolved only within the nature of science itself, since before deciding about the three great objects of all learning, God, the Universe, and Man, one must ask on what basis man decide questions."

Degérando's answer to this problem turned on a rejection of naive idealism and an affirmation of the perspective achieved after the Baconian "revolution of ideas," which is to say the "philosophy of experience" or "experimental philosophy," which represented at once a remedy for the "prejudices" of rationalism, especially the notion that "the operations of the spirit are the model for the laws of nature," and a justification for historical understanding.[42] Yet history remained in a sense subordinate to philosophy; for as Dégerando wrote, his purpose was, "by studying the history of different sects, their birth, development, successions, conflicts, and mutual relations, to seize upon their true point of divergence, the cause of their oppositions, and the origins of their disputes," and finally to judge their value for modern thought, thus making the history of philosophy itself the basis of (in the words of Leibniz cited by Degérando) a "perennial philosophy" (*perennis quaedam philosophia*).

This was in brief the position of Cousin, who drew also on the work of Brucker as well as German idealists, French philosophes, Scottish moralists, and even Herder and Vico. Cousin's work marked an intersection between the old and the new encyclopedic traditions and the history of "ideas" in a more general sense: *Histoire des idées, de principes, de doctrines particuliéres* is the phrase he used to characterize the genre of the history of philosophy from Brucker down to that of the Kantian Tennemann, whose manuel (used by Degérando) Cousin translated.[43] That Cousin produced no conceptual synthesis out of this doctrinal pandemonium is not surprising, and his philosophical reputation is past redemption. As a historian of ideas, however, he was more successful; and his so-called "new philosophy" of the Romantic period reinforced the "new history" of the new period, which likewise tried to broaden cultural and social—and more surreptitiously political—horizons. Cousin defended what, after the German historians, he called "external history," which meant looking not only at the lives of the philosophers, the trajectory of ideas, and the fate of their systems but also at cultural environment and material causes, including climate and historical factors, and indeed at historiography.[44]

There were other practitioners of this sort of history of ideas in the Restoration period, but suffice it to mention the name of professor Eugène Lerminier—almost as famous as Cousin during the July Monarchy and even more neglected in later times. Before his appointment at the College de France Lerminier had been a Saint-Simonian and had been concerned with the social basis of human thought, especially in its potential for the "younger generation," and in "the relations between ideas and manners." In his *Influence of Eighteenth-Century Philosophy on the Legislation and Sociability of the Nineteenth* (1833) Lerminier celebrated "the power of ideas" for the creation of "social harmony," focussing in particular on "the history of one of the essential ideas of humanity," which was the theory of law in social and historical context."[45] Lerminier traced the generation of "new ideas" from Locke to Montesquieu, who represented "the philosophical restoration of social history" in the Englightenment and whose teachings were still relevant. "From one century to another ideas prolong their existence," Lerminier wrote; "and the more powerful and effective they are in a particular period, the slower they are to perish and to give way to the new ones which they generate."[46] Lerminier preserved an affection for the eighteenth-century, but he rejected the mixed heritage of "eclecticism" for the doctrine of modern Liberalism, which was the source both of his own "influence" and of his discrediting in the period of the "Bourgeois Monarchy."

This eclectic offshoot of the "philosophy of the history of philosophy," in short, seems to me to mark a renewal, or a continuation and culmination, of the old alliance between the modern—Renaissance and Enlightenment—conception of the encyclopedia and history (both as a method of interpretation and as a principle for the organization of knowledge). It marks also a link with the modern canon of intellectual history, or history of ideas, associated with that modern eclectic scholar (philosopher-humanist-historian), Arthur O. Lovejoy. As the idea of evolution was produced by a temporalizing of the "great chain of being," so intellectual history represents a historicizing of the old "encyclopedia." The story does not end here, of course; and in particular the various literary, historical, and philosophical—textual, contextual, and metatextual—approaches to knowledge and the understanding of culture continue to be debated. All I can hope is that the perspective suggested here helps to throw some light on the sophisticated but often derivative and epigonic controversies of our own times, and the significance of these for the current shapes of knowledge.

Notes

1. See especially Ulrich Dierse, *Enzyklopädie: Zur Geschichte einer philosophischen und wissenschaftstheoretischen Begriffs* (Bonn, 1977); Wilhelm Schmidt-Biggeman, *Topica Universalis: Eine Modelgeschichte humanistischer und barocker Wissenschaft* (Hamburg, 1983); Giorgio Tonelli, *A Short-title Catalogue of Subject Dictionaries of the Sixteenth, Seventeenth and Eighteenth Centuries as Aids to the History of Ideas* (London, 1971); Jean Bollack, "Vom System der Geschichte zur Geschichte der Systeme," *Geschichte—Ereignis und Erzählung*, ed. Reinhart Koselleck and Wolf-Dieter Stempel (Munich, 1973), 11–28; A. Diemer (ed.), *Der Wissenschaftsbegriff: Historische und systematische Untersuchungen* (Meisenheim, 1970); Robert Collinson, *Encyclopedias: Their History Through the Ages* (New York, 1964); Otto Ritschl, *System und systematische Methode in der Geschichte der wissenschaftlichen Sprachgebrauchs und der philosophischen Methodogie* (Bonn, 1906); and Robert Flint, *Philosophy as Scientia*

Scientiarum and a History of the Classification of the Sciences (New York, 1904); also the classic essay by P. O. Kristeller, "The Modern System of the Arts: A Study in the History of Aesthetics," *Journal of the History of Ideas,* 12 (1951), 496–527 (reprinted in *Renaissance Thought II*, [New York, 1965]), and Wilhelm Dilthey, *Introduction to the Human Sciences*, ed. Rudolph Makreel and Frijhof Rodi (Princeton, 1989), 72–76 (bk. I, ch. 6, tr. Michael Neville). According to Henri Ahrens, *Encyclopédie juridique*, tr. A. Chaufford (Paris, 1880 [1855]), 5, "An encyclopedia may be regarded in general as a synthetic plan embracing a science in all its parts."

2. Lovejoy, *Great Chain of Being* (Cambridge, Mass., 1936), and "Reflections on the History of Ideas," *Journal of the History of Ideas*, 1 (1940), 3–23; also the recent comments by Daniel J. Wilson, Edward P. Mahoney, and Francis Oakley in *ibid.*, 48 (1987), 187–263; all now in D. R. Kelley (ed.), *The History of Ideas* (Rochester, 1990), 5–21, 158–212.
3. See D. R. Kelley, "Horizons of Intellectual History: Retrospect, Circumspect, Prospect," *Journal of the History of Ideas,* 48 (1987), 143–169 and "What Has Become of the History of Ideas?" *ibid.*, 51 (1990), 3–25.
4. *De Rerum inventoribus* (Basel, 1536 [1496]), and see D. R. Kelley, "The Theory of History," *Cambridge History of Renaissance Philosophy*, ed. Quentin Skinner and Charles Schmitt (Cambridge, Eng., 1988), 746–161.
5. Vives, *De Tradendis disciplinis sive de doctrina*, in *Opera omnia* (Valencia, 1782–90), VI, 386ff; and cf. *De Initiis, sectis, et laudibus philosophiae*, in *Opera*, III, 3ff.
6. *De Causis corruptarum artium*, in *Opera*, V.
7. Budé, *De Asse et partibus eius* (Paris, 1532), fol. 179; and see D. R. Kelley, *Foundations of Modern Historical Scholarship* (New York, 1970), 63–66.
8. *De Philologia* (Basel, 1533), 217; and cf. *De Transitu Hellenismi ad Christianismum* (1535), also ed. M. Lebel (Sherbrook, 1973), and ed. and tr. D. F. Penham (Columbia U. diss., 1954).
9. Le Roy, *La Vicissitude ou varieté des chose en l'univers* (Paris, 1575); and cf. *G. Budaei vir clarrisimi vita* (Paris, 1540); also Werner Gundersheimer, *The Life and Works of Louis Le Roy* (Geneva, 1967), Kelley, *Foundations*, 80–85, and Abel Lefranc, "De la traité De la vicissitude ou variété des choses de Louis Le Roy et sa véritable date," *Mélanges Lanson* (Paris, 1922).
10. *De Scribenda Universitatis rerum historia libri quinque Christophoro Mylaeo autore* (Basel, 1551), 20: "Et in Natura quidem inchoata communiter in omnibus caussae rerum conditarum: in Prudentiae alteram quandam Naturam efficiente, usus et commoditates rerum terrenarum: in Sapientiae rationes, consensu eruditorum firmatae, et multis elaborantibus completae: in reliquis autem duabus, armorum et literarum clarissima exempla continentur."
11. *Ibid.*
12. *Ibid.*, 81.
13. *Ibid.*, 133.
14. *Ibid.*, 192.
15. *Ibid.*, 244.
16. Still fundamental is Neal Ward Gilbert, *Concepts of Method in the Renaissance and their Ancient and Medieval Antecedents* (New York, 1956).
17. In a vast literature see now the exhaustive work of Giovanni Santinello *et al.* (ed.), *Storia della storia della filosofia* (Brescia, 1981), three vols. so far down to Kant, with extensive bibliographies.
18. See Richard Rorty, "The Historiography of Philosophy: Four Genres," in *Philosophy in History*, ed. Richard Rorty, J. B. Schneewind, and Quentin Skinner (Cambridge, Eng., 1984), 49–75—although my four approaches differ from Rorty's, which are philosophical rather than historical.

19. *De Incertitudine et vanitate scientiarum atque declamati* (Antwerp, 1530), cap. 5, "De historia;" and see Charles Nauert, *Agrippa and the Crisis of Renaissance Thought* (Urbana, 1965).
20. Santinello (see above, n. 17) not only surveys but also sums up this tradition; see also H. S. Harris's review of vol. III in *Journal of the History of Ideas*, 51 (1990), 115–120.
21. See Agostino Steuco, *De prenni philosophia* (Lyon, 1540), on which see Charles Schmitt, *Studies in Renaissance Philosophy and Science* (London, 1981).
22. Santinello, II, index and passim. On ancient skepticism there is a huge literature, beginning with Brucker and including Diderot's entry in the *Encyclopédie*, but no satisfactory study of modern Eclecticism from its seventeenth-century beginnings.
23. *Le Methode d'etudier et d'enseigner Chretiennement et Solidement la Philosophie par rapport a la religion Chrestienne et aux Ecritures* (Paris, 1685).
24. J. J. Brucker, *Historia critica philosophiae* (6 vols., Leipzig, 1766).
25. The translation of Brucker's book published as William Enfield, *The History of Philosophy* (London, 1819), II, 468–469.
26. Heineccius, *Elementa historiae philosophiae* (8th ed., Berlin, 1756 [1728]), 292, which is the concluding passage of this text book, treating the history of "philosophia antiqui, medii aevi, et nova" down to his own time.
27. Kant, *Preisschrift uber die Fortschritte der Metaphysik*, in *Gesammelte Schriften* (Berlin, 1942), XX, 264.
28. Rorty, "The Historiography of Philosophy," 68.
29. Vico, *La Scienza nuova seconda*, ed. F. Nicolini (Bari, 1953), 128 (par. 127), citing Brucker, *Historia philosophia doctrinae de ideis* (Augsburg, 1723).
30. Salfi's *eloge* of Filangieri, ed. Dusart, in Dugald Stewart, *Historire abrégée des sciences metaphysiques, morales et politiques depuis la Renaissance des lettres*, tr. J. Buchon (Paris, 1820), III, 369.
31. Frederick Beiser, *The Fate of Reason: German Philosophy from Kant to Fichte* (Cambridge, Mass., 1987), 153; and cf. Goldfriedrich, *Die historischen Ideenlehre in Deutschland* (Berlin, 1902).
32. Herder, *Metakritik*, in *Sammtliche Werke*, XXXVII (Stuttgart, 1853), 17.
33. A. F. Bourreau-Deslandes, *Histoire critique de la philosophie ou l'on traite de son origine, de ses progrés, et des diverses Révolutions qui lui sont arivées jusqu' à notre tems* (Amsterdam, 1737).
34. [Buonafede], *Della storia di ogni filosofia nei secoli XVI, XVII e XVIII* (Venice, 1785).
35. K. L. Reinhold, "Uber den Begriff der Geschichte der Philosophie," *Beyträge zur Geschichte der Philosophie*, ed. G. G. Fulleborn (Zullichau, 1791), 21 ("Geschichte des menschlichen Geistes"); cf. (among many examples in all languages) Brucker, *Historia critica*, 21 ("historia intellectus humani"), A. Y. Goguet, *De l'Origine des lois, des arts et des sciences* (Paris, 1758), preface ("l'histoire de I'esprit humaine"); and in general see Lutz Geldsetzer, *Die Philosophie der Philosophiegeschichte im 19. Jahrhundert* (Meisenheim, 1968), Martial Guéroult, *Histoire de l'histoire de la philosophie*, 3 vols. (Paris, 1984–88), and, on the semantic history of the term *Spiritus* (*Lessico intelletuale europeo*, XXXII, ed. M. Fattori and M. Bianchi, Rome, 1984).
36. Carus, *Ideen zur Geschichte der Philosophie* (Leipzig, 1809), 110.
37. D'Alembert, *Preliminary Discourse to the Encyclopedia of Diderot*, tr. Richard N. Schwab (Indianapolis, 1963), 5. See Grazia Tonelli Olivieri, "Per una storia della classificazione delle scienze: Il 'Prospectus' dell 'Encyclopedie,'" *Studi e ricerche di storia della filosofia,* 103 (1977).
38. See above, n. 29.
39. See the French translation by J. Laveaux of Meiners's work, *Histoire de l'origine, des progrès et de la décadence des sciences dans la Grece* (Paris, an VII [1800]), I.
40. Meiners, *Historiesche Vergleichung der Sitten und Gewerbe, des Handels, und der*

Religionen, der Wissenschaften, und Lehranstalten des Mittelalters mit denen unsers Jahrhunderts in Rücksicht auf die Vortheile und Nachtheile der Aufklärung (Hanover, 1793), III, 465.

41. Degérando, *Histoire comparée des systémes de la philosophie* (Paris, 1847), I, xvi.
42. *Ibid.*, II, 463ff.
43. Cousin in his translation of Tennemann, *Manuel de l'histoire de la philosophie* (Paris, 1839), I, 36.
44. Cousin, *Cours de l'histoire de la philosophie moderne* (Paris, 1843), and *Histoire générale de la philosophie*, many editions.
45. Lerminier, *De l'Influence de la philosophie du XVIIIe siécle sur la législation et la sociabilité du XIXe* (Paris, 1833), xv; and see Bonnie Smith, "The Rise and Fall of Eugene Lerminier," *French Historical Studies*, 2 (1982), 145–153.
46. Lerminier, *ibid.*, 297.

VII

ANCIENT VERSES ON NEW IDEAS: LEGAL TRADITION AND THE FRENCH HISTORICAL SCHOOL

> Let us change into our honey their most ancient flowers;
> To paint our idea let us use their colors;
> Let us light our torches with their poetic fire;
> On new ideas let us make ancient verses.[1]

These lines by André Chenier famously locate the emotional thrust of romantic literature and art, but they suggest also the more general fascination with the past displayed by writers of many persuasions. They highlight one essential feature of that cast of mind which early nineteenth-century scholars were already beginning to call "historicism" and which was best realized, perhaps, in what, at least from the 1820s, Augustin Thierry and others were celebrating as the "new history."

During the Restoration and July Monarchy this "new history" was the subject of much discussion and many pretensions. About "l'histoire nouvelle" Jean Sarazin marvelled in 1835: "This restoration of classes and secondary races has not only rendered justice to humanity but has also been an important conquest for history."[2] Not only Thierry and Michelet but even the aged Chateaubriand applauded the achievements of *l'école moderne* and the foreign impulses which had inspired it, especially through the work of Vico, Herder, and the "historical school of law" headed by Savigny.[3] The novelty of this particular "new history" (which was neither the first nor, certainly, the last to be so-called) has been much celebrated and often exaggerated, but seldom fully appreciated. It derived not only from the literary artistry of romantic narrative but also from an emphasis (fashionable then as now) on social as distinguished from political and military concerns and from a fascination with the more remote and inaccessible stretches of the past. This shift, reflected particularly in the study of legal and institutional history, was illustrated most notably, perhaps, by Thierry's researches into the history of the Third Estate and by Michelet's *Origins of French Law*, both launched in

1. André Chenier, "L'Invention," *Oeuvres complètes* (Paris, 1958), 127: "Changeons en notre miel leurs plus antiques fleurs; Pour peindre notre idée, empruntons leurs couleurs; Allumons nos flambeaux à leurs feux poétiques; Sur des pensers nouveaux faisons des vers antiques." On the MS appears the note (877) "Cotoyer toujours les anciens auteurs."

2. Jean Sarazin, *Du Progrès des études historiques en France au dixneuvième siècle* (Strasbourg, 1835).

3. François René de Chateaubriand, *Etudes historiques* (Paris, 1831), preface.

the 1830s.[4] Each of these projects in its own way illustrated Alfred de Vigny's famous conceit that "History is a novel and the people are its author." This sort of "social Romanticism" was a primary source of Michelet's equally famous conception of history as a form of disinterment or, as he called it is his rhapsodical book on *Le Peuple*, "resurrection."[5]

Yet was this new historical school so innovative after all (except, perhaps, in its rhetorical claims)? Its champions were obviously obsessed not only with national traditions but also (though not without some "anxiety of influence," in Harold Bloom's phrase[6]) with their own intellectual forebears; and their interest in the Old Regime extended not only to its historical sources but also to its methodologies and its ideologies. The "new history" praised by Thierry from the left and Chateaubriand from the right relied on many, sometimes covert, conduits of prerevolutionary learning and mentality; and Michelet's "resurrection" had elements of traditionalism as well as nostalgia and curiosity. Without being able to forget their postrevolutionary predicament, practitioners of the "new history" hoped to find understanding in a remote past made all the more inaccessible because of the shattering experience of revolution, which had tried to destroy that past. In their antiquarian enthusiasm they could not help but resume old themes, though of course they had to do so under new conditions.

In a recent book I examined the relations between the legal tradition and historical scholarship in the postrevolutionary period, especially in the wake of the Civil Code and controversies generated by it.[7] What I propose here is to follow some of the major themes linking the "new history" of that period with the legal ideas, scholarship, and practice of the old regime, and to suggest that in many ways, though the words might be different, the music was often the same. In a sense this was the peculiarly Romantic, sometimes nostalgic, sometimes hagiographic, sometimes almost necrophiliac, form of mimesis and myth-making which André Chenier referred to as "making ancient verses on new ideas."

I

There were many expressions of this attempt to maintain, or to restore, contact with the wisdom of the prerevolutionary fathers. Among the most prominent testimonies to intellectual continuity were a series of "great historical enterprises" which had been started in the Old Regime and which were resurrected after the

4. Jules Michelet, *Les Origines du droit français* (Paris, 1837), and Augustin Thierry, *Essai sur l'histoire de la formation et le progrès du Tiers Etat* (Paris, 1853), introduction to *Collection des documents inédits sur l'histoire de France*, 4 vols. (1850–1856), XIII, a work which Thierry began in 1834. Vigny is cited by Maxime Leroy, *Histoire des idées sociales en France* (Paris, 1950), II, 425.

5. Jules Michelet, *The People*, transl. G. Smith (London, 1846), 25.

6. Harold Bloom, *The Anxiety of Influence* (Oxford, 1973).

7. Donald R. Kelley, *Historians and the Law in Postrevolutionary France* (Princeton, 1984), and further literature cited there; and see also my "Mythistory in the Age of Ranke," forthcoming in a volume from the Ranke conference held at Syracuse University in 1986. For the earlier stages of this tradition see my *Foundations of Modern Historical Scholarship: Language, Law and History in the French Renaissance* (New York, 1970).

Revolution, such as the *Histoire littéraire de la France* (1733-), the *Gallia Christiana* (1715–1865), the *Rerum Gallicarum et Francicarum* (1738–1904), the collection of royal ordinances (1723–1849) begun by Eusèbe Laurière *et al.*, the works of many prerevolutionary jurists, editions of provincial customs, and of course the *Archives Nationales* (to which Michelet was appointed in 1833).[8] Equally important—since the aim of "doing justice" as well as making "conquests for history" persisted—was the scholarly aim of the legal profession, which had long been a major vehicle of historical inquiry and interpretation and which had produced many distinguished legal and institutional historians, beginning in the sixteenth century with Estienne Pasquier and the *historiographe du roi*, Bernard du Haillan, whom Thierry honored as the "father of French historiography."[9]

Perched on the very watershed between Revolution and Restoration was one of the most famous of all creations of the lawyers—the "Civil Code of the French People," as Napoleon's masterpiece was originally called. The Napoleonic Code, which in its own way also "made ancient verses on new ideas," embodied and symbolized the intersection between Old Regime learning (on which in large part it rested) and postrevolutionary ideas and experiences, which formed the context of the jurisprudence produced in the wake of the Code and the modern scholarship vital for its interpretation.[10] This jurisprudence was also a major vehicle of various old-fashioned (neo-feudal as well as neo-monarchist) notions and attitudes, which intruded on and in some ways helped to modify the revolutionary legacy and to shape the "new history" of the Restoration and its intellectual offspring.

In the assessment of the French past one of the major bodies of evidence was, and still is, the vast and richly ambiguous tradition of provincial customs, which had been collected and "redacted" from the thirteenth century, "reformed" in the sixteenth century, rationalized and to a degree systematized from the seventeenth century, and technically abolished at the end of the eighteenth century, only to be resurrected by historical scholarship (and, more surreptitiously, by jurisprudence) in the nineteenth century.[11] In 1789 these *coutumes* numbered well over two hundred, and the commentaries on them many more—a dozen or more each, for example, for Paris, Burgundy, and Normandy. More than a century before that, customary law had, like its civilian and canonist rivals, claimed to be part of moral philosophy and had developed its own distinctive methodology. According to Paul Challine's *General method for interpreting the customs of France*, published in 1666, provincial customs, which were reflections of local

8. Henri Bordier, *Les Archives de la France* (Paris, 1855), 2ff, 15ff.

9. Augustin Thierry, "Notes sur quatorze historiens antérieurs à Mézeray," in *Dix ans d'études historiques* (Paris, 1868), 355–393.

10. See especially Julien Bonnecase, *La Pensée juridique française* (Bordeaux, 1933); also Thierry, *Dix ans*, "Sur l'ancien esprit et sur l'esprit actuel des légistes français" (1820), 244ff.

11. André Gouron and Odile Terrin, *Bibliographie des coutumes de France* (Geneva, 1975); Jean Caswell and Ivan Sipkov, *The Coutumes of France in the Library of Congress* (Washington, D.C., 1977); and see André-Jean Arnaud, *Les Origines doctrinales du Code Civil français* (Paris, 1969), with a "dictionnaire biographique" of seventeenth- and eighteenth-century jurists (301–319).

culture and dispositions, or "humors," had to be explained in their own terms, not those of Roman law.[12] In invidious contrast to Roman rigidity, Challine celebrated the geographical variety and historical adaptability of French law, especially that of Paris, which expressed the "general spirit of French customs." The vast complex of this customary law was interpreted by a wide range of monographs and studies in comparative law and legal history, going all the way back to the fundamental researches, historical as well as juridical, of Charles Dumoulin, Etienne Pasquier, Antoine Loisel, and other Renaissance pioneers in the long search for the "spirit" of French law and culture.

Historical and legal scholars of the Restoration were themselves aware of belonging to a long intellectual tradition beginning with just these sixteenth-century jurists. Among jurists one of the most conspicuous examples was Henrion de Pansey, a disciple and biographer as well as an editor of Dumoulin's authoritative annotations on all of the provincial customs of France. Professionally, Henrion survived, though he did not serve during, the Revolution. Under Napoleon he reappeared as a champion of the old legal tradition, and between 1812 to 1829 he continuously weathered political storms to maintain his position, first as judge and finally as President of the Cour de Cassation. Henrion was also the author of a number of scholarly works, especially an historical study of "judicial authority," which was one of the major repositories of conservative attitudes.[13] The Revolution might abolish the institutions of the Old Regime, including the entire legal profession, but it could not destroy the underlying *mentalité*, at least in the memories, attitudes, and judgments of judicial Talleyrands like Henrion de Pansey.

Of the younger generation of the "new history," Henri Klimrath was the most promising medievalist and legal historian. Born and educated in Strasbourg, Klimrath was a disciple of Savigny and the German *Rechtsschule*; but intellectually he also identified himself with the French historical tradition which went back directly to Dumoulin (and would continue through Emile Chenon, Paul Viollet, François Olivier-Martin, and others). Among modern representatives of this tradition Klimrath admired two in particular – Henrion de Pansey, whom he admitted posthumously into the "historical school," and J. E. M. Portalis, one of the conservative redactors of the Code, who hoped to accommodate this revolutionary creation not merely to the imperial dreams of Napoleon but, more lastingly, to the inertial pressures of the past and the dynamic forces of the future.[14] Klimrath's own major "historical enterprise," though he died too early to finish

12. Paul Challine, *Méthode générale pour l'intelligence des coustumes de France* (Paris, 1666), 10, 134.

13. Henrion de Pansey, *Traité des fiefs de Dumoulin analysé et conféré avec les autres feudistes* (Paris, 1773), with the *éloge* of Dumoulin (1769), and *De l'Autorité judiciaires*, ed. L. Rozet (Paris, 1843), 467; also Renée Laude, *Henrion de Pansey, 1742–1829* (Lille, 1941). And cf. the contemporary opinion in the *Globe* 3 (1826), 35: "M. Henrion de Pansey est à nos yeux un jurisconsulte de l'école historique qui pense, comme MM. de Savigny et Hugo en Allemagne, qu'une jurisprudence mûrie lentement par le temps est supérieure à une législation créée d'une manière subtile et d'un seul jet."

14. Henri Klimrath, *Travaux sur l'histoire du droit français*, ed. L. A. Warnkoenig (Paris, 1843), I, 16, 146–157.

it, was the effort to carry on in an historical mode Dumoulin's great work of interpreting, in a national context and a comparative fashion, the entire range of provincial customs. Like Dumoulin, Klimrath had practical as well as antiquarian goals; for in keeping with the views of Portalis (as well as Savigny), he assumed that an historical understanding of the law would produce a more equitable interpretation (*equité historique* was his term). Like the traditionalism of Henrion and Portalis (not to speak of Dumoulin), the "historicism" of Klimrath rested on a vision of the future as well as an interpretation of the past.

II

Let me try to place this Romantic "historicism" in a larger perspective. Hans-Georg Gadamer has defined hermeneutics as an "experience of tradition"; and this certainly suits the jurists and historians I have been referring to.[15] From the time of Dumoulin and Du Haillan to that of Klimrath and Michelet, French feudists and historical scholars have shared such an experience. As a consequence they have constituted not so much an ideological movement as what Karl O. Apel calls a hermeneutical "community of interpretation," a community based on a common language, sources, assumptions, methods, and issues—though not necessarily goals.[16] The cast of mind shared by the new historians and the old jurists was alien and indeed antagonistic to the superficial rationalism which they attributed, somewhat vaguely, to the "philosophical school"—those "hastening enlighteners," as Coleridge called them, who wanted to bury the past. They tended to believe deeply, if instinctually, in what Gadamer (and Heidegger before him) have identified as the "forestructure of knowledge," and in effect they devoted themselves to the rehabilitation of that eighteenth-century *bête noire*, "prejudice"—*praejudicium* originally signified a legal precedent or preliminary judgment—by insisting on the historical grounding of knowledge and judgment.[17] Along with "prejudice" in this epistemological sense they also restored credit to ideas of tradition and authority even as they cloaked their social and often political conservatism in "scientific" rhetoric.

The coherence of this intellectual and professional continuum and the central place of historical scholarship is strikingly illustrated in various professional publications, including the annual anthologies of jurisprudence, such as that of Guyot and Merlin de Douai, first issued in the 1780s and still appearing in 1830, and in certain commentaries on French law, such as that of P. L. Gin, who hardly changed his views, or even the text of successive editions of his book, as he shifted from the old law of the Bourbons, through the so-called "intermediary law" of

15. Hans-Georg Gadamer, *Truth and Method*, transl. G. Barden and J. Cumming (New York, 1975), 345 ff. and 289 on the "exemplary significance of legal hermeneutics" for the method of the human sciences.

16. Karl O. Apel, *Transformation der Philosophie* (Frankfurt, 1976), II, 178–219 ("Szientismus oder transzendentale Hermeneutik?").

17. Gadamer, 238, and Heidegger, *Being and Time*, transl. J. Macquarrie and E. Robinson (New York, 1962), 191.

the 1790s, to the new law of Napoleon.[18] But the best illustration of this intellectual bridge is the authoritative handbook for lawyers originally published by A. G. Camus in 1772 and, in much augmented and modernized form, by Andre Dupin just fifty years later.[19] Like their book and their profession, these authors, collaborating across two generations and a revolution, were conservatives and survivors. In 1789 Camus became the first director of the National Archives and died in 1804. In that same year Dupin became the first graduate of Napoleon's new law faculty, a member, librarian, and finally *bâtonnier* of the Order of Advocates (abolished in 1791 and restored by Napoleon in 1810), member of the Institut, and famous in the Restoration as defender of several of Napoleon's marshals. In 1823 an English observer called him "possibly at the present moment the most influential man in France."

The Camus-Dupin handbook, entitled in its last incarnation *Profession d'Avocat*, was mainly an anthology of professional panegyrics going back to the *Dialogue des Advocats*, published by Antoine Loisel in 1602 and named in honor of his friend and colleague Estienne Pasquier. The bibliography of Dupin's book began as a shelf-list of the library of the Order of Advocates (dispersed after the dissolution of the Order); it ended as the most concrete illustration of legal continuity and the best guide to the sources needed for the historical "resurrection" envisaged by Michelet, Camus's successor in the archives. In terms of the hermeneutical "community of interpretation," the difference between Old Regime jurists and restoration historians was largely nominal; for what the former had as "proofs" (*preuves*), the latter preserved as "monuments": both approached and interpreted their sources with a mixture of antiquarian and utilitarian motives. They sang the same words but made different music.

In such works historicism and legalism were inextricably entangled and mutually reinforcing, and the alliance became firmer in the age of the "new history" and the "historical schools." As jurists learned from Michelet to invoke Vico and to celebrate the popular source of law, so Michelet was introduced by them to the legal mysteries of liberty and property. Agreeing on the value of history, lawyers and historians also tended to reinforce each other's myths. As the "feudalism" resurrected by Romantic historians was a sort of reincarnation of the "feudal law" (*ius feudale* or *ius feudisticum*) constructed and interpreted by old regime jurists, so modern "liberalism" and the "bourgeoisie" were given a pedigree and a certain legitimacy by association with the "liberties" of the medieval communes and *coutumiers*. Notwithstanding the ideological divide created by the Revolution, then, jurists and historians alike were locked to some extent into old sources,

18. [P. Guyot], *Repertoire universelle et raisonné de jurisprudence* (Paris, 1775-86), and many later collections of this title edited by Merlin; and P. L. C. Gin, *Analyse raisonnée du droit françois par la comparaison des dispositions des loix romains et de celles de la Coutume de Paris* (Paris 1782), later edition with the same title extended, . . . *et du nouveau Code des Français* [sic] (Paris, 1803).

19. A. G. Camus, *Lettres sur la profession d'avocat et bibliothèque choisie des livres du droit* (Paris, 1772); editions also in 1777, and in Dupin's name, 1805, 1818, 1830; and finally *Profession d'Avocat* (Paris, 1832); on Dupin see my *Historians and the Law*, esp. 56–60. Cf. "Speeches of M. Dupin Ainé at the bar" *Law Magazine* 9 (*Choix des oeuvres oratoires* [Paris, 1823]).

scholarly traditions, and interpretations. In a sense there was a professional *mentalité* of extraordinary persistence which shaped — and in this sense "prejudiced" — their questions and arguments, if not always their answers and values.

The fundamental question linking Romantic history with Old Regime scholarship, of historicism with traditionalism, was that of "origins" — institutional, legal, social, intellectual, and cultural origins. Over many generations and the revolutionary caesura, jurists and historians were carrying on what Hans Blumenberg calls "work on myth."[20] They were doing this in the sense not only of giving national meaning to local customs and legal authority to certain privileged scholars but also of finding historical and prehistorical grounds for particular ideological structures, distributed finally across a spectrum ranging from Revolution to Counter-Revolution — the most potent myths of them all, unless we reserve that honor for "historicism" itself.

The Romantic desire to "think back" in time (*remonter* is the characteristic term) has often been pointed out for poets like Vigny and Lamartine, but it is no less remarkable in historical and legal studies. To understand French law, wrote Louis La Ferrière, citing Portalis, one must go back to Roman law (*remonter au droit romain*), which was in effect a part of the French "community of interpretation."[21] Indeed, Dupin's first book was a précis of Roman legal history, celebrating especially the sixteenth-century "historical school" (*Jurisprudentia Cujaciana* was his term). In a similar spirit an historian of property law, J. M. Carou, invited his readers to return with him in thought (*remonter par la pensée*) to the very beginnings of history in order to see how this institution originated.[22] Such was the aim, too, of Michelet, who took Vico's "new science" as the key to understanding prehistory, especially in his highly speculative quest for the "origins of French law."

What these Restoration historians were doing in a sense was historicizing the Enlightenment myth of the "state of nature." Although they could not entirely escape from the realm of speculation, their aim was not to hypothesize about a "natural" stage of existence before civilization but rather to reconstruct "original" institutions such as the Roman *ager publicus*, which consisted of conquered land distributed to citizens presumably representing an ancestor of modern private property. With the help of Vico's "new science," itself based in part on legal scholarship, Michelet tried to imagine what amounted to the absolute origin of property — "first occupation" — through hints in Germanic customs establishing boundaries of possession by the throwing of a stick or stone and the marking of such boundaries by a similar object.[23] In general Michelet, adapting the kind

20. Hans Blumenberg, *Work on Myth*, transl. R. Wallace (Cambridge, Mass., 1985).

21 Louis La Ferrière, *Histoire du droit civil de Rome et du droit français* (Paris, 1846), I, xvi.

22. J. M. Caron, *Traité théorétique et practique des actions possessoires* (Paris, 1841), 3; and see E. Laveleye, *De la Propriété et de ses formes primitives* (Paris 1901).

23. Jules Michelet, *Les Origines du droit français*, in *Oeuvres complètes*, ed. P. Viallaneix (Paris, 1973), III, 608, 657. See Armelo d'Amato, *Il Mito di Vico e la filosofia della storia nella prima metà dell'ottocento* (Naples, 1977), and M. Donzelli, "La Conception de l'histoire de Vico et son interprétation par J. Michelet," *Annales historiques de la révolution française* 53 (1981), 633–658; and cf. also Klimrath, *Travaux*, I, 146–157, and Heine, *Lutèce* (Paris, 1855), 272.

of speculative philology practiced by Vico to read the minds of primitive peoples, tried to retrace the trajectory of thought from words back to things, from reason back to the "material symbols" of a pre-logical and poetic age – back indeed to what he called the "enchanted forest" of Germanic law. In such efforts of imaginative reconstruction Michelet may have fallen too far into the "deep well of the past." Careful scholars like Klimrath were dismayed to see him resorting to the "poetic" and "symbolic" (and therefore unprofessional) methods of philologists like Jakob Grimm and Friedrich Creuzer (not to speak of Vico). "The 'symbolic' of law is not the law itself," protested Klimrath in a review; and Heinrich Heine dismissed Michelet's hermeneutical experiment as an "historian's dream."

III

Yet Michelet was not alone in this sort of dreaming. Long before his effort of resurrection, and indeed before Vico's "new science," some French jurists and historians had tried to rethink their way back to the medieval, Germanic, Roman, and even prehistorical beginnings of French law and, inferentially, of society. In general this meant exploring the wilderness of French customary law, which opened up not only legal quandaries but also fascinating questions of oral culture and prehistory. As Jacques Godefroy wrote in the early seventeenth century, "If one wishes to go back [*rétrograder*] to the origin of law, one will have to admit that customs have preceded and even form the first part of positive law, although they were set down last."[24] In this way French jurists hoped to find an original "spirit" of French law, hence of society and culture, not unlike the "immemorial custom" posited more or less contemporaneously by Coke and the common-law "community of interpretation." The assumption that national tradition was to be found in native custom rather than in imported Roman law or imposed royal ordinances or certainly in some putative "natural law" opened up the adventurous and speculative trail later chosen by Michelet, which led back, with the help of historical imagination, toward ultimate "origins."

This fascination with "origins" and with an historical approach, it should be noted, was in a sense inherent in the tradition of civil law as it was restored in the twelfth century. "The most important part of anything is its beginning," declared the classical jurist Gaius, justifying his work on "the origin of law," which was placed in the first title of Justinian's *Digest*.[25] One may hear an echo of this in the famous warning of Vico (whose "new science," in its first form,

24. Jacques Godefroy, *Commentaires sur la coustume reformee du pays et duché de Normandie* (Rouen, 1626), 1. Cf. Claude Ferrière, *Commentaire sur la coutume de la prévôté et vicomté de Paris* (Paris, 1714).

25. *Digest*, I, 2, 1: "et certe cuiusque rei potissima pars principium est. deinque si in foro causas dicentibus nefas ut ita dixerim videtur esse nulla praefatione facta iudici rem exponere: quanto magis interpretationem promittentibus inconveniens erit omissis initiis atque origine non repetita atque illotis ut ita dixerim manibus protinus materiam interpretationis tractare." Cf. the virtual paraphrase by Vico, *Scienza nuova*, 314, "Le dottrine debbono conciare da quando cominciano le materie che trattano"; also my "The Rise of Legal History in the Renaissance," *History and Theory* 9 (1980), 174–194, repr. in *History, Law and the Human Sciences* (London, 1984).

was based on civil law), that "doctrines should begin where the material which they treat begins." That this was a common view of jurists is evident from the contemporary observation of Claude Ferrière (made earlier than and independent of Vico's principle), that "It is an established maxim that no Man can arrive at a perfect Knowledge of any SCIENCE, without having examined its *Rise* and *Progress*."[26]

Like their nineteenth-century successors, of course, Old Regime scholars had practical and political as well as methodological and "scientific" motives for their researches into beginnings, pedigrees, and priorities. This was especially the case in the field of legal and institutional history, since interpretations of the past were inevitably tied to contemporary issues, including the relationship between legislative and judicial authority, the legitimacy of popular government, the nature of property, the desirability of constructing—and how to interpret—a code, and, in connection with all of these, the provenance and value of Roman and French law and culture.

The question of origins was also directed to that most crucial and sensitive legal topic, the "status of persons," which concerned the revolutionary issue of liberty but which historically meant the rival claims of *noblesse* and *bourgeoisie*. Long before the revolution, and anticipating in historical fashion the famous question of Sieyès ("What is the Third Estate?"), this class struggle was going on in the realm of historical and legal interpretation. On the one hand the Abbé Gourcy, basing his views on racialist theory as well as the authority of "les feudists," traced the nobility back to prehistory.[27] On the other hand C. J. Perriciot argued that it had been the product of later feudal usurpation and royal *annoblissement*, which had had the result of eroding the ancient liberties flourishing originally in the "forests of Germany" (*les forêts de la Germaine* being the historical equivalent of the state of nature); and Perriciot, writing in 1786, expressed the hope that Louis XVI would support the third estate against the nobility.[28] Perriciot's work (along with its volume of *preuves*) suited the assumptions of the "new history" enough to merit republication in 1845.

It is evident that long before Thierry had begun tracing the historical pedigree of liberalism through the "monuments" of "la Roture," Old Regime scholars had been studying some of the same sources, and tracing the "liberties" of the medieval communes and of the *coutumiers* back to Carolingian, Merovingian, and even Salian precedents. The principle that "by nature all men are free" (*natura omnes homines liberi sunt*) was defended not only by philosophers on the basis of natural law but also by feudists by appeal to French positive law, such as the

26. Claude Ferrière, *The History of the Roman or Civil Law*, transl. John Beaver (London, 1724), introduction.

27. Abbé Gouray, *Quel fut l'état des personnes en France, Sous la première et la seconde Race* (Paris, 1769), 160. And cf. François Bertrand, *Les Prerogatives de la robe* (Paris, 1701), and Gilles André de La Roque, *Traité de la noblesse* (Paris, 1678).

28. C. J. Perriciot, *De l'Etat civil des personnes et de la condition des terres dans les Gaules, des les temps celtiques jusqu'à la redaction des coutumes* [1786] (Paris, 1845), 20 ff., including observations on the work of Gourcy and, regarding the origins of fiefs (224), of Montesquieu.

coutumes of Bourges and Burgundy.[29] And long before Romantic medievalism and celebrations of the Hercynian forests, historians had been "romanticizing" about the laws of the original "free French"—*liberi Franci* being a centuries-old pun, since "francus" signified both "free" and "French."

Most controversial of all was the debate over the origins of feudalism, which had raged among historians since the sixteenth—and among lawyers since the thirteenth—century. The classic work on the "origins of fiefs" was that by Dumoulin, published in 1539, and thereafter the topic was debated by historians and feudists alike. A comprehensive review of the contributions of both, together with the usual collection of "proofs," was offered by Louis Chantereau, in his *Traité des fiefs et de leur origine* of 1662, but the subject was far from academic.[30] Indeed the debate became explosive as "la féodalité" became the first and most crucial issue on the revolutionary agenda, since it involved not only fashionable speculations about the social contract and "first occupancy" but also the most basic social question of the Old Regime. The theoretical and practical questions converged on the night of 4 August 1789, when the National Assembly formed, under Merlin de Douai's leadership, the committee to abolish "la féodalité" and to establish rights of "absolute" private property.[31] It is worth remarking that feudal tenure was transformed into modern property with the help of a very old legal distinction between feudal title and simple use (*dominium directum* and *dominium utile*), of which the second became private property, properly speaking. In other words this most fundamental break with history, the destruction of feudalism, was accomplished by application not of natural rights theory but of a time-honored principle developed with the old law, which was itself being abolished in the name of those rights.

In general, from the fourteenth to the nineteenth century and after, the poles of historical interpretation were set by the "Romanist" and "Germanist" theories of legal, hence, cultural origins of France. Within the juridico-historical "community of interpretation," the division could be traced back to the ground-breaking work of the two heroes of the French legal tradition, namely, the arch-feudist Dumoulin and the quintessential Romanist, Jacques Cujas, whose rival legacies and legends were still potent in the nineteenth century. (Their busts appeared in the gallery of the Cour de Cassation, and each of them was honored with an *éloge* by Dupin in the 1830s.)[32] The intellectual rivalry was given institutional

29. Nicolas Bohier, *Consuetudo Biturigenses* (Paris, 1543), fol. 1; and cf. Argou, *Institutes du droit françois* (Paris, 1771); the phrase is to be found in royal ordinances as early as Louis X.

30. See D. R. Kelley, "De Origine Feudorum: The Beginnings of an Historical Problem," *Speculum* 39 (1964), 207–228, repr. in *History, Law, and the Human Sciences*, and J. Q. C. Mackreel, *The Attack on "Feudalism" in Eighteenth-Century France* (London, 1973), 48–76.

31. See D. R. Kelley and Bonnie Smith, "What Was Property? Legal Dimensions of the Social Question in France (1789–1848)," *Proceedings of the American Philosophical Society* 128 (1984), 200–230; cf. E. Meynial, "Notes sur la formation du domain divisé (domain direct et domain utile) du XIIe au XIVe siècle dans les romanistes," *Mélanges Fitting* (Montpellier, 1908), II, 409–461.

32. Dupin, *Eloge des douze magistrats et jurisconsultes composant la galerie de la Cour de Cassation au palais de justice* (Paris, 1836), including addresses also on L'Hopital, Henrys, and D'Agues-

reinforcement in 1679, when Louis XIV established professorships of French law to counterbalance the traditional chairs of civil law dating back to the thirteenth century—a rivalry that was revived in Napoleon's University and that has continued ever since.[33] Romantic historians like Michelet extended this oppposition through their sentimental belief that Germanic institutions were more liberal, or closer to nature and to "the people," and had been devitalized by the Roman tendency toward generalization and centralization—toward an historical logic producing a syllogism of which, as Michelet wrote, "monarchy was the minor premise."

The *Kulturkampf* between Romanists and Germanists reached an historiographical high point in the later nineteenth century, especially in the controversial interpretations of Fustel de Coulanges, Paul Viollet, and others. Once again most of the arguments and much of the evidence had been aired long before the revolution, most notably in the rival works of the Abbé Dubos and of Boulainvillers. Most interesting for the postrevolutionary period was the extraordinary work of Boulainviller's disciple Mlle. de Lezardière, who formulated a "theory" of French legal and institutional tradition.[34] Lezardière's book, replete with extensive *preuves*, provides a fascinating, if unfamiliar, link between Old Regime and July monarchy, since the work, though completed in the early years of the Revolution and even set up in print, had to wait another forty years for publication, partly through the good offices of Guizot, who had himself made liberal use of the lady's researches.

IV

Historians continued to claim to be authorities and critics of national tradition. In many ways, however, the lawyers were closer to historical issues, to their implications, and indeed to their sources. If, as Keith Baker has suggested, the "control of history" had to be carried on at the level of sources as well as "symbolic representation," jurists had more direct claims to this control, since they were the "authorities" of legal tradition and its meaning.[35] What is more, they, and of course their clients, often had a larger stake in defining and interpreting an historical tradition. For the question of Germanic or Romanist provenance involved not only questions of knowledge but also of power, up to and including that of the state and its relation to judicial and popular sources of power and to private "interests."

---

seau. Cf. his *Des magistrats d'autrefois, des magistrats de la Révolution, des magistrats à venu* (Paris, 1814). On the French legal tradition see also Charles Giraud, *Essai sur l'histoire du droit français au moyen age* (Paris, 1846), I, "avertissement."

33. Christian Chêne, *L'Enseignement du droit français en pays de droit écrit (1679–1793)* (Geneva, 1982).

34. Mlle. de Lezardière, *Théorie des loix politiques de la monarchie française* (Paris, 1844), and *Ecrits inédits*, ed. E. Carcassonne; and in general see Carcassonne, *Montesquieu et le problème de la constitution française au XVIIIe siècle* (Paris, 1927).

35. Keith Baker, "Memory and Practice: Politics and the Representation of the Past in Eighteenth-Century France," *Representations* 11 (1985), 134–164.

The Romanist position, still the most firmly entrenched, was defended most authoritatively by academic jurists like Claude Henrys, François Boutaric, and Jean Bouhier, who argued that Roman law was the "common law" of France and stood in relation to provincial customs more or less as the law of nature did to Roman law. In his "praise of Roman law" and its "holy spirit," Henrys displayed textual "proofs" from a wide range of sources, culminating the grand tradition of civil law going back to Cujas.[36] Boutaric warned about undermining the authority of law by inquiring too curiously and speculatively into its "origin," and he rehearsed the old formula that Roman law had been received in France "not by reason of imperial authority but by the imperial authority of reason."[37] One aspect of this imperial "reason," he added, was the absolutist principle declaring the will of the ruler to be law (*quod principi placuit, legis habit vigorem*).

More systematic was the work of Jean Bouhier, president of the Parlement of Dijon, and last of a distinguished line of commentators on the Burgundian custom beginning with Barthélemy de Chasseneux in the sixteenth century. Bouhier, too, regarded Roman law as *ius commune* and (citing Henrys) as "written reason," or even "raison par excellence."[38] Custom, Boutaric added, had been made by ignorant men—not lawyers is what he meant—and he was contemptuous of any who believed in a national, prehistorical, and mystical "spirit" and even of feudists like Dumoulin who attributed special authority to the custom of Paris. Nor did he approve of that intuitive judgment which jurists, invoking unwritten law, called "equity" but which he regarded as "a species of prevarication." By contrast Roman law was the work of learned jurists who had given it, over the ages, rational form; and again Bouhier referred to the great line of Romanists going back to Cujas and his colleagues. From the first (*de toute ancienneté*) Roman law had been common law, and in modern times there was a true "reception" (*receptio*) of Roman law in France just as there had been in Germany. Bouhier defended this position against all the "French" chauvinists, including not only Dumoulin and vernacular jurists like Pasquier, Loisel, and Louis Le Caron but also Jean Bodin, who (as Bouhier put it) "reasoned rather as a *politique* than as a *jurisconsulte*."

On the other side of the debate were the "partisans of customary law," as Boutaric referred to the anti-Romanists, champions of the vernacular tradition and in many cases holders of the professorships of French law established by Louis XIV. One of these was François de Launay, who argued that the common law of France resided not in the Roman law taught in the universities but exclusively in provincial customs, which could be traced back at least to the capitularies of Charlemagne and which constituted, he argued, a "general rule of the whole

36. Claude Henrys, *Oeuvres* (Paris, 1738), esp. vi-xxxvii, "Eloge du droit romain."

37. François Boutaric, *Les Institutes de l'Empereur Justinien, conferées avec le droit françois* (Toulouse, 1740), viii.

38. Jean Bouhier, "Observations sur la coutume de Bourgogne," in *Ouevres de jurisprudence* (Dijon, 1787), I, 356, 364, 382, 430ff. And see his *Histoire des commentateurs de la Coutume du duché de Bourgogne* (Dijon, 1742); also Marcel Bouchard, *De L'Humanisme à L'Encyclopédie. L'Esprit public en Bourgogne sous l'ancien régime* (Paris, 1930).

kingdom, a Law universally observed in all of France."[39] In support of this allegation Launay cited the medieval Gloss, according to which custom might supersede written law (*consuetudo superveniens vincit legem*). He cited, too, the famous "fundamental laws" of the monarchy and the royal ordinances forbidding the citation of the "emperor's law." Instead of deploring the irregularity and inconsistency of French custom, Launay celebrated, in a kind of proto-Romantic way, their richness, diversity, and "free and frank" character. Not the law of Rome, he concluded, but the provincial *coutumes* were the basis of what he envisioned as the "Temple of French Justice," a temple which was later reinforced and adorned by an accumulation of native jurisprudence and interpretation, finally overlaid by his own commentary.

One of the most distinguished defenders of customary law was Pierre Grosley, another admirer and indeed product of Renaissance scholarship, who had singled out President Bouhier as a target for his Romanist opinions. Through his study of the vast literature on the *coutumes*, Grosley claimed to have grasped the true spirit of French law (*l'esprit particulier de notre Droit coutumier actuel*) and to have located it in the period before the emergence of feudalism.[40] In many ways Grosley's thesis resembles the mythopoeic—and similarly anti-Romanist—view taken by Sir Edward Coke toward English common law as "immemorial custom"; for French customs, too, had a continuity and a "unanimity" going back to a distant Germanic past—which is to say, for Grosley, "to the manners and usages of the ancient inhabitants of septentrional [that is, Frankish] Gaul." This "spirit of French law," Grosley added, was something altogether different—and arrived at independently—from the celebrated but more speculative work by his friend Montesquieu on the "spirit of laws" in general. Montesquieu, too, was a Germanist, but his legal methods were too abstract to suit Grosley's historical tastes.

Such were the premises of the "feudist" tradition in France; such, too, were the hermeneutical "prejudices" of national legal historiography from Du Haillan and Pasquier—if not their own medieval antecedents—down to Klimrath and Michelet. It is no wonder that, long before the emergence of the German historical school, French scholars were deploring the empty prescriptions of the advocates of natural law. French jurists were fond of recalling, and boasting, that French customs had originally been established by consent (*per turbam; par tourbe*), that is, by deliberation and consent of the three estates; and so historically they had always been regarded as a reflection of society and conditioned by environment, "climate," and "humors," as well as linguistic and cultural tradition—the French counterpart, in a sense, of the German *Volksgeist* celebrated by Herder and Savigny.[41] This, it seems to me, is one of the main sources of the perennial French fascination with "geohistory," from Bodin (who perhaps coined the term) down to Braudel (who also used it), and with other factors of *longue*

39. Francois de Launay, *Institution du droit romain et du droit françois* (Paris, 1786).
40. Pierre Grosley, *Recherches pour servir à l'histoire du droit françois* (Paris, 1752), 122ff.
41. See Hippolyte Pissard, *Essai sur la connaissance et la preuve des coutumes* (Paris, 1910).

durée so essential to social history. As P. G. Michaux wrote in 1783, "We emerged into a social and political order . . . not as imagined by Pufendorf and other [theorists of a social contract] but rather as revealed in our customs." In his enthusiasm, Michaux referred to French customs as "fundamental" and "social" laws and as "the creation of the nation as a whole" (*le propre ouvrage de ce nation en corps*).[42]

V

In these debates there was of course more at stake than the "philosophy of history," in Voltaire's catchy phrase. More basic were the issues of legal and social order, especially as expressed in the so-called "codification movement"; and this too links the old law with the "new history."[43] In the old regime this problem had arisen in connection with various efforts to unify French law, whether through a Romanist "code" or, as Dumoulin had proposed, through correlation and correction of provincial customs, with the *coutume* of Paris serving as the standard. It was again President Bouhier who, assembling all the Romanist testimonies, rejected the feudist position as a fiction invented by Dumoulin and kept alive by his many successors.[44] The notion that the Parisian *coutume* had any precedence over others, especially that of the Burgundian Parlement court which he served, Bouhier found offensive and historically unacceptable.

The Romanist view no doubt represented the *communis opinio* of the legal profession, as Bouhier suggested; but the "party" of Dumoulin still had its supporters before (and indeed during and after) the revolution. Several of his disciples spoke of a generalized, uniform, and presumably national "feudal system" (*le système féodale, la Doctrine féodale* are terms used by Hervé in 1785, for example),[45] and in the seventeenth century some jurists tried to give feudal custom rational form and "natural" order. In 1747 François Bourjon spoke of the "common law of France" as "l'exact explication de la Coutume" and as an expression of the French "genius" (*le génie François*, a term used two centuries earlier by Pasquier).[46] As Claude Ferrière wrote of the legal function and historical significance of the Parisian custom, "It unites our law, interprets it, and sometimes corrects it."[47] Even civil lawyers had to agree in principle, since one of their basic maxims was that "custom is the best interpreter of law." To some extent,

42. P. G. Michaux, *Les Coutumes considerées comme loix de la nation dans son origine et dans son état actuel* (Paris, 1783), 108ff.

43. G. Tarello, *Le Ideologie della codificazione nel secolo XVIII* (Genoa, 1971).

44. Bouhier, *Oeuvres*, 382.

45. Hervé, *Theorie des matières féodales et censuelles* (Paris, 1785), 1, and Henrion de Pansey, intro. to Dumoulin, *Traité des fiefs* (Paris, 1773), 24–25. Cf. Le Conte, *Coutume de Normandie, dans un ordre naturel* (Paris, 1779), and Poullain du Parc, *La coutume et jurisprudence coutumière de Bretagne, dans leur ordre naturel* (Rennes, 1759).

46. François Bourjon, *Le Droit commun de France et la Coutume de Paris reduits en principes* (Paris, 1770), "Epitre."

47. Ferrière, *Commentaire sur la coutume . . . de Paris*, 1, adding (preface): "En rassemblant icy les maximes du Droit Coutumier, je n'ay pas cru devoir negliger l'origine." Cf. *Digest*, I, 4, 37.

then, French custom, and especially that of Paris, could be regarded as a primary vehicle of French social and cultural history.

"Historians look backwards," Nietzsche wrote; "eventually they also believe backwards";[48] and this insight seems even more applicable to the juridico-historical community of interpretation in France after as well as before the Revolution. Some scholars looked back into French tradition, especially prefeudal tradition, in hopes of finding a time of greater freedom, sociability, and humanity; and indeed the historical school of the nineteenth century drew upon this sort of utopian or proto-socialism which posited some form of primitive communism (*biens de la terre . . . originairement communs*, in the disapproving words of Portalis).[49] Yet it is undeniable that interest in French customs and the feudal past inclined some scholars toward the sort of political conservatism later associated with Edmund Burke.

One example of this is Gabriel Dubuat-Nançay, who was also interested in historical beginnings, though his major historical work, treating "the origins of monarchical government," was not destined to become a best-seller after its publication in 1789; and his pessimistic attitudes gained him the contempt of liberal historians like Thierry, who wanted to make their "ancient music" on "new ideas." In his *Maximes du gouvernement monarchique*, published anonymously in London in 1778, Dubuat rejected the fashionable natural-law theories of "enlightened" politics, left or right. In this dialogue he updated the old "quarrel" of ancients and moderns.[50] One speaker, the "philosophe," celebrated the marvels of that age, including not only the discovery of electricity and the tracking of comets but also the questioning of authoritarian rule. But this was not progress, objected the other speaker, the "author"; it merely suggested another Augustan age, when mechanical arts served only to amuse a fickle people and when fanatics were undermining ancient wisdom with appeals to pleasure and the false "equality" of natural law. All laws are the product of human history, Dubuat argued, the deposit of "many rules produced by the relations between men and goods"; and therefore, "the law of nature does not exist."

The ideals and ambitions of Jacobinism and Bonapartism overshadowed these conservative views (whether or not joined to royalism) – or rather sent them into exile. Count Portalis, that champion of an historical approach to legislation and critic of what he called "abuses of the philosophical spirit during the eighteenth century," had himself been an émigré.[51] Yet like the émigrés, conservative ideas and historical "prejudices" returned; and the "new history" and the "historical school of law" were major repositories of this mentality, whatever the political and social values attached to it.

48. Nietzsche, *Götzen-Dämmerung*, 24, in *Werke in drei Banden* (Munich, 1955), II, 946.

49. *Discours, rapports et travaux inédits*, ed. F. Portalis (Paris, 1844), 209–210.

50. Gabriel Dubuat-Nançay, *Les Maximes du gouvernement monarchique* (London, 1778), 50. The work criticized by Thierry is *Elements de la politique, ou Recherches des vrais principes de l'économie sociale* (London, 1773).

51. Portalis, *De l'usage et de l'abus de l'esprit philosophique durant le dix-huitième siècle* (Paris, 1827).

The "ancient music" of the *coutumes* was especially evident in connection with the old question of codification. The "unification of customs" had been a goal of the monarchy for centuries, and again opinions diverged along Romanist and Germanist lines. In the end it took a revolution to realize this aim, and in general it was the Romanists who won out over the Germanists in forming the Civil Code after the customs were abolished. Or so it first appeared, and so Bonapartists hoped. In fact, however, history did not stop for Napoleon; and the complex task of interpreting his Code, of adapting it to the inertial as well as innovating forces of modern French society, led naturally to a renewed appreciation for history. Portalis was the champion of this legal kind of "historicism," but other jurists and historians were more active in giving concrete meaning to the rather abstract texts of the Civil Code by reviewing, and often surreptitiously resurrecting, the substance of the old customs and crypto-feudal practices. As Henrion de Pansey– himself a Germanist and an Anglophile – concluded, "The ancient constitution is the best commentary on the new."[52]

In his discourse delivered in 1829 at the library of advocates, Dupin preferred to cite the famous advice of Montesquieu, "to illuminate laws by history, and history by laws" – and then to recite the honor roll of French jurists: Bodin, Coquille, Dumoulin, Pithou, Loisel, Pasquier, and other conveyors of what he called *l'esprit parlementaire*. He ended by quoting the words addressed by Pasquier to Loisel's son, words which he rendered in capitals in his new edition of Loisel's *Pasquier, ou Dialogue des avocats*, published in the same volume: "You should attempt to preserve for our Order the rank and honor which our forebears gained by their merit and by their labors and then pass it on to your successors."[53]

The historical school of law added some new ideas to this old music. After 1815 Savigny became a critic not only of the Code Napoleon but of the very idea of a Code, at least in the context of postrevolutionary jurisprudence (or "jurisignorance," as another critic put it). Savigny's own monumental work on the history of Roman law in the Middle Ages was in part an effort to counteract the myopia and amnesia of modern legal and social thought. So was the work by his former student Jacob Grimm on German legal antiquities, which so profoundly influenced Michelet's *Origins of French Law.*[54] Like history itself, according to the view of these legal historicists, law was a creation of the "people," an expression of their culture, a reflection of their "spirit," and so had to be established not by pure reason but by historical investigation and interpretation. In this context, too, the achievements of the "new history" were entangled in the old habits, assumptions, and prejudices of the legal tradition.

The dominant theme of the Code, sounded by the Revolution and sanctified by Bonapartist and Restoration commentators alike, was private property; and after 1815 the question of the "origins" of this institution came to overshadow virtually all public issues, whether legal or historical. By both jurists and historians,

52. Cited by Laude, *Henrion de Pansey*, 188.
53. *Profession d'avocat*, I, 18.
54. Kelley, *Historians and the Law*, 72, 101, etc.

by Portalis no less than by Guizot, property was virtually identified with civilization, and its origins with the beginning of history. In the nineteenth century the debate between Romanists and Germanists resolved itself into a choice of myths: whether social origins (and implicitly cultural values) ought to be sought in Roman paterfamilial property (*dominium*) or simpler Germanic arrangements of possession and *saisine*. In the most extreme form the opposition was between the thesis of primitive communism suggested by Germanizers like Michelet and publicized by socialists of all stripes, and on the other hand the belief in the primordial and "natural" character of the patriarchal family and its attendant *dominium*, held by Romanists like Fustel de Coulanges and most liberal ideologists.[55] For most recent scholars both parties were essentially wrong; and yet the controversy was a valuable incitement to further research as well as argument.

The convergence between the old law and the "new history" had other implications that outlived the ideological heat and political uses of postrevolutionary society. One area of common and long-standing concern was the relationship of law and popular culture, which was expressed with great eloquence and erudition by Michelet in his *Origin of French Law*. Through the influence of the German historical school as well as Vico, Michelet joined to the *Volksgeist* that medico-astrological concept of *espirit* or *génie* of French culture which for generations had been an object of faith or investigation by the legal tradition. The most seminal work was probably the *Institutes coutumières* published in 1607 by Loisel, who ransacked poetry, proverbs, and oral culture as well as conventional legal monuments in his quest for the "spirit" of French law.[56] In the later seventeenth century François de Launay produced a commentary on Loisel's work which, after a ringing denunciation of Roman law, proceeded to defend the native tradition of customs, ordinances, and vernacular jurisprudence, along with the judicial power of "interpretation," which preserved, extended, and legitimized them. This was the tradition restored, a century and a half later, by Klimrath and other successors of Launay in the law faculty of the University of Paris, including André Dupin, who self-consciously edited the works both of Pasquier and of Loisel—and thereby built another intellectual bridge between the Old Regime and the Restoration.

It would be easy, though no doubt tedious, to multiply examples of intellectual *longue durée* in French juridico-historical discourse extending from Dumoulin to Klimrath, more tenuously from Beaumanoir to Fustel and perhaps even Marc Bloch. The more general (and these days rather unfashionable) point is the dependency of historians on a tradition of scholarship—and the "anxiety of influence," which operates (as Bloom suggests) even, or perhaps especially, when originality is sought. Enlightenment historiography, fearful of influence as well as "prejudice," hoped to put an "end to myth"; but, as Blumenberg argues and

55. Fustel de Coulanges, "Le Problème des origines de la propriété foncière," in *Questions historiques*, ed. C. Julian (Paris, 1893), 17–117.

56. *Commentaire sur les Institutes Coutumieres de M. Antoine Loisel* (Paris, 1688), xxxiii, lxx, etc.

as legal tradition and various "new histories" abundantly illustrate, this aspiration is itself a form of myth.[57]

In general, nineteenth-century historians fell easily into old patterns of questioning, controversy, and selection of "authorities," and in many ways constitute a further extension of the old juridico-historiographical community of interpretation. The champions of "new history" carried on the old regime's "work on myth"—in this case the mythology of the French legal tradition, especially with regard to the problem of national origins, the development of "liberty," and especially the "spirit" of national culture. It is of course true that in the wake of the Revolution the "nation" was increasingly identified with the Bourgeoisie, and so efforts were directed to the origins of this class and its institutions. Yet if the social orientation was transformed by the revolution, the intellectual and perhaps the emotional habits were in many ways preserved by defenders of national tradition.

One of the best illustrations is the case of the founder of the "new history." Thierry's major scholarly effort, to which he devoted the last two decades of his life until his death in 1856, was a kind of *collection pour servir à l'histoire* of the answer to Sieyès's famous question of 1789, "What is the Third Estate?"[58] In this work, the result of an assignment given him by Guizot in the 1830s, Thierry sought evidence for the "sovereignty" and "will" of the people in urban charters and customary law, in royal legislation, in the records of the Estates General and the Parlement, and in the work of the royal legists ("bourgeois du roi," he called them). On the basis of such sources (which were assigned historical but, since the Revolution, enjoyed no legal "authority") he proceeded to trace the "progress in liberty" of the *tiers état*, or *la Roture*, under the protection of royal government and culminating in the "bourgeois monarchy" (which he as well as Guizot served), when the "third estate" and the "nation" truly—or at least officially—became one.

More generally the scholars of the old and the restored monarchies shared certain attitudes and assumptions—"prejudices" in a hermeneutical sense—which were best expressed in the theories of the historical school but which had long been practiced by historians and jurists alike. In a sense Meinecke's old definition of "historicism," as a combination of the principles of individuality and development, locates the most fundamental of these assumptions:[59] that national character was the product of long-standing (but inexorably changing) particular customs, which originated in the popular will and which, though often thwarted by special interests or political forces, continuously resists the channels cut by political history and chronically emerges to alter the direction of "progress."

Another shared assumption was that this popular "will"—in the sense of social meaning as well as authorial intention of legal "acts"—could be extracted

57. Blumenberg, *Work on Myth*, 627.

58. See above note 4; also Lionel Gossman, *Augustin Thierry and Liberal Historiography, History and Theory, Beiheft* 15 (1976).

59. Friedrich Meinecke, *Die Enstehung des Historismus* (Berlin, 1936).

from the written records, official and unofficial, produced by antiquarian- and legal-minded scholars over many generations, especially in the early ages of print culture. The consequence was an extraordinary fetishism of texts and what Louis Halphen called *la chasse aux documents*, which led to a revival, or continuation, of massive documentary research and publication, and to that mythopoeic process which literary scholars call "canon-formation"—and which is no less fundamental, though it may be less doctrinaire, in historiography.[60] Although there was an institutional shift from a political to a scholarly base, the aim of enterprises like the *Monumenta Germaniae Historica* (founded in 1819), the *Ecole des Chartes* (1822), and the English Rolls Series (1822), continued to be the commemoration, the defense, and the furthering of national values through memorable written remains and the learned interpretation thereof: *sanctus amor patriae dat animum*, according to the motto of the *MGH*.

In this connection it might be noticed that recent emphases in the philosophy of history, which have fixed on the logic and especially the rhetoric of historical expression, have tended to neglect the equally fundamental question of the discovery, selection, and exploitation of source material (*Quellenforschung* and *Quellenkritik* being an essential part of the historical hermeneutics of Droysen and others, though figuring only marginally in recent discussions of historical thinking). In nineteenth-century historical conceptualization the question of *heuristic*, which has its own epistemological and narratological aspects, constituted a vital link with the old regime. To a large extent the problems, protagonists, and the plots of the Romantic "resurrection" of the past (to use Michelet's famous term) were inherent in the "record," both written and (in the case of the customs expressing popular will) unwritten.

All this suggests more, perhaps, than merely the legacy of Romantic historicism; it suggests the premises and the limits of the historiographical—and the hermeneutical—condition in general. To be relevant and "usable," a cultural past must be subjected to a certain myopic self-regard, social provincialism, and cultural "prejudice," as well as the limitations imposed by a retrospective posture. It will not do for us to take at face value, then, the self-advertising rhetoric of the so-called "new history" of any age, including ours—which can likewise be seen as part of an extended "community of interpretation." Historians are forever claiming to be unprecedentedly critical—but critical rejection is a rhetorical topos (*anasceua*) as well as a rational claim.[61] They are forever pretending to overcome myth, but at the same time adept at devising alternative myths. And they are forever finding and asserting novelty; but novelty and innovation, too, represent an ancient trope as well as a modernist pose—"make it new," Ezra Pound

60. Louis Halphen, *L'Histoire en France depuis cent ans* (Paris, 1914), chap. 4; on canon-formation the classic study is Ernst Robert Curtius, *European Literature and the Latin Middle Ages*, transl. W. R. Trask (New York, 1953), 256, pointing out that "the formation of a canon serves to safeguard a tradition," whether literary, juristic, or religious, and (265) showing how the process was taken up by historians.

61. See Frank Borchardt, *German Antiquity in Renaissance Myth* (Baltimore, 1971), 55.

demanded, while trying to light his own torch with the "poetic fire" of the *dolce stil nuovo* of the late thirteenth century. The words are often changing; but often, too, if we listen hard enough (and if we are not distracted by surface meaning and bright novelty, or overcome by the "anxiety of influence" or the myth of "post-modernism"), the music remains much the same.

VIII

MYTHISTORY IN THE AGE OF RANKE

"VERY DEEP is the well of the past. Should we not call it bottomless?" With these ominous words Thomas Mann begins his "Descent into Hell," the Dantesque prelude to his Joseph series, and poses what he calls "the alpha and omega of all our questions"—that is, the question of human origins, of cultural memory, and thus of myth. According to an older and still not wholly discredited view of history, it was the special destiny of western civilization to bring myth to an end, to move from *mythos* to *logos*,[1] up from the darkness of a brutish and hellish past into a bright, and brightening, future; and in many respects our scientized and technologized civilization has indeed tried to erase cultural memory, to throw off the burden of the past, and to make history irrelevant. The Cartesian *Cogito* has no memory, presumably has no need of it; and post-Cartesian champions of the Enlightenment have conspired to promote this conception, or rather this counter-myth, of rational progress.

Yet Cartesian rationality has exacted a psychic price. Fears about the inadequacy of pure reason have produced a state of mind which Richard Bernstein has identified as "Cartesian anxiety."[2] It seems to me, however, that the anxiety of the modern solitary, secularized, amnesiac ego is due not only to its isolation from religious absolutes but also to its detachment from cultural tradition, the separation of reason from memory, and the eclipse of historicism by naturalism in the course of a long struggle which, according to Ernst

Troeltsch, went back precisely to the rise of the new science in the seventeenth century.[3]

Historicism may still be in eclipse (or in "crisis" as Ernst Troeltsch would say), but in recent years the myth of pure reason and the claims of naturalism have come under fire from various quarters. Especially noteworthy have been the critiques of the Enlightenment presented by Theodor Adorno (as well as Wilhelm Dilthey and Ernst Cassirer), the attempts of Martin Heidegger and Hans-Georg Gadamer to rehabilitate "prejudice" (understood as the prerational grounds for rational understanding), and especially the efforts of Hans Blumenberg to appreciate the continuing force of myth and its inseparability from the establishment of meaning.[4] Each of these enterprises proposes in a way a "descent into hell," an expedition into the "fore-structure of knowledge," an exploration of what Hans Blumenberg calls "the chaos of the unnamed," and a critical reappraisal of history in its broadest sense. Moreover, each takes its point of departure and, ambivalently, its source of inspiration, from the Romantic attitude toward history and attraction to the deepest levels of the "well of the past," that is to say, to myth and mythology—which represent, it seems to me, the ultimate goal of Romantic historicism.

The roots of historicism (*avant la lettre*) may be traced back into the old regime and even down into the rich soil of humanist learning (or so some Renaissance historians like to think).[5] For the most part these roots did not flourish in the tradition of conventional historiography, however; rather, they grew out of the textual and aesthetic attitudes of philology and antiquarian scholarship. As Lord Acton wrote a century ago in his classic essay on the "German school" of history: "When Germans assert that their supremacy rests with their historians, they mean it in the sense of Bentley and Colebrooke, not of Machiavelli and St Simon"—in the sense of Barthold Niebuhr and Friedrich August Wolf, we may add, not of Leopold Ranke.[6] Elsewhere Acton underlined this point by comparing the Romantic revival of historical studies with the Renaissance revival of classical learning; and in general, I think, it suggests the true, though often concealed, character of nineteenth-century historicism, as it should be historically, if not philosophically, understood—*wie er eigentlich gewesen ist.*

This is not the place to enter into a detailed examination of

Romantic historicism, but exception must be taken to Meinecke's prescription, which reduces *Historismus* to a combination of the principles of individuality and development, is inadequate and, in its effort at philosophical abstraction, in violation of the intellectual movement it purports to define. For present purposes the significant point about Romantic historicism is that it did not so much establish a philosophical program as cultivate a variety of cultural insights—including the discovery, or rediscovery, that poetry does not merely lie, that mythology may be (as Herder said) the "oldest history," that imagination is a portal to a kind of historical truth not accessible to pure reason, and that history promises a sort of wisdom as well as knowledge not accessible to abstract thought.

In its nineteenth-century phase historicism may be defined as well by what it opposed as by what it favored, and what it opposed was above all the so-called "philosophical school," which was usually associated with Ranke's still more senior colleague Hegel, but which included also the old tradition of natural-law philosophy going back to G. W. Leibniz and Christian Wolff.[7] Not universal and unchanging law but particular and changing custom was the concern of the historical school; not abstract and classifying reason but concrete and localized memory; not mechanical or mathematical models but human language and culture; not the imperialism of liberal economics but the realities of national development—not, in short, the way the world should be (according to revolutionary, Bonapartist, Liberal, or Hegelian prescription) but the way it really was.

Yet historicism (if I may be permitted to keep this shorthand term) has always been subject to internal contradiction, suffering as it did from a deep and long-standing division going back to the very beginnings of *historia* as a term and a concept. The debate arose with Thucydides, who rejected Herodotus' tall tales and the notion that a true historian could reach beyond memory or direct testimony, and it persisted over many centuries—Tacitus versus Livy, for example, William of Newburgh versus Geoffrey of Monmouth, Guicciardini versus Flavio Biondo, or Voltaire versus Vico. On the one hand "pragmatic history," as Polybius called it; on the other hand "antiquities" or (in another nineteenth-century coinage) "prehistory."[8] On the one hand *histoire*, according to the *Encyclopédie*, on the other *érudition*. On the one hand, in other words, those who stuck to the sources and were content to describe directly accessible phenomena; on the other hand those who, with the poets, ventured to descend into Mann's "deep well of the past."

On this question Ranke's own opinion was unmistakable. "History cannot discuss the origin of society," he declared at the outset of his *Weltgeschichte*, "for the art of writing, which is the basis of historical knowledge, is a comparatively late invention. . . . The province of history is limited by the means at her command, and the historian would be overbold who should venture to unveil the mystery of the primeval world, the relation of mankind to God and nature. The solution to such problems must be entrusted to the joined efforts of Theology and Science."[9] In striking contrast to this were the aspirations of scholars like Herder, the Grimms, and even Niebuhr, who rejected the limitations of scribal culture and looked for other means of divining the mysteries of a remote antiquity.

Another way of representing this opposition is, following good classical usage, to contrast "history" and "mythistory" (*mythistoria* was a coinage of Thucydides). According to Nathan Bailey's *Dictionarium Brittanicum* (1730), mythistory is "an history mingled with false fables and tales."[10] Today we tend to take a less pejorative view of myth and its relation to history, as indeed did many contemporaries of Ranke, and we are more willing and prepared to look beyond the bounds of scribal culture. By "mythistory," I mean to invoke some of the broader and deeper, if more speculative and questionable, aspects of Romantic historicism, which have nevertheless had an essential and continuous role in the history of modern historical scholarship.

In this connection I must return to the point made earlier, that the pioneers of this radical branch of Romantic historicism, or "mythistoricism," were for the most part not the celebrated craftsmen and entertainers of narrative history. Rather they were the inglorious cultivators of those more specifically cultural and antiquarian fields, such as language, literature, law, religion, and even political economy, which all came to be dominated by "historical schools" even before the emergence of Ranke as a force in historical studies. The basic methods of these historical schools, moreover, derived not from historiography but rather from the old tradition of philology, which had enjoyed an equally extensive career, going back, by way of Renaissance humanism, to Homeric and Biblical criticism, and forward to the works of such modern scholars as Erich Auerbach, Ernst Robert Curtius, and Leo Spitzer—not to mention more recent and vulgar epigones, who call themselves the "new historicists."[11]

One of the defining features of historicism has always been attitudes toward language. We hear much about the "linguistic turn" of this century, but in fact the philological tradition has produced more than one such *Kehre* in the endless struggles between rhetoric and philosophy. One of the most conspicuous of these linguistic turns was expressed in the work of J. G. Herder, that "Copernicus of the historical world," as Cassirer called him. In his "Meta-critique of Kant's Critique of Pure Reason," Herder rejected the "transcendental" order which Kant had inferred from Newtonian naturalism. He argued that not "pure" but human reason was the proper object of criticism, that this reason may not be divorced from other human faculties, and finally that the human mind operates only through words (*die menschliche Seele denkt mit Worten*).[12]

A similar position had been taken earlier in the century by Giambattista Vico, who may be seen both as the last of the Renaissance humanists and as a prime specimen (according to Erich Auerbach as well as Friedrich Meinecke and Benedetto Croce) of modern historicism. Vico, too, took philology, not philosophy, as his starting point. "Philology is the study of speech," he wrote in his *Diritto universale*, "and it treats of words and their history, shows their origin and progress. . . . But since the ideas of things are represented by words, philology must first treat the history of things. Whence it appears that philologists must study human governments, customs, laws, institutions, intellectual disciplines, and the mechanical arts."[13] Philology was the first form taken by Vico's "new science"; and his expectation was that, through linguistic analysis and speculative, comparative etymology, it would be the key to reconstructing the history of humanity from its mythic and poetic origins. It is hardly surprising that his work, like Herder's, produced a shock of recognition among members of the historical schools, after the translation of the *Scienza nuova* into German in 1822 and into French (by Jules Michelet) in 1827.

Reacting to the excesses of naturalism, this late eighteenth-century "linguistic turn" was greatly reinforced by its intersection with two extraordinary scholarly movements of the Romantic period. One was what Edgar Quinet, Michelet's colleague and translator of Herder, called the "oriental renaissance," stemming especially from the discovery of Sanskrit, which underlay the resurgence of classical philology in German universities, and which placed classicism in a broad Indo-European perspective.[14] "I venture to predict," wrote Friedrich von Schlegel in 1797, "that the Indian study . . . will prove no less grand and universal in its operations and have no less influence" than the Italian Renaissance. And as Edward Moor wrote in 1810, "There can, I think, be but little doubt of the mythological legends of the Hindus being the same whence have been derived the fables and deities of *Greece* and *Italy*, and other heathen peoples of the West."[15]

The other movement was Romantic hermeneutics, the theory and practice of textual and inter- and para-textual interpretation, which likewise sought to reconstruct historical experience through the medium of language. The goal was—by moving from words to meaning, from *Wort* to *Geist* and perhaps to *Zeit-* and *Volksgeist*—to understand an author as he would have wished to be understood, according to Wolf—or, as Friedrich Schleiermacher hoped, even better.[16] Through hermeneutics a bridge was to be built not only between I and Thou, but also between present and past—a scientific way, as Schleiermacher saw it, of sharing a common meaning over a large expanse of time.

It was above all through the study of language, then, that scholars hoped to reach the apparently bottomless well of the past. In 1797 Friedrich Schlegel, like Vico before him, celebrated "the great importance of the comparative study of language, in elucidating the historical origins and progress of nations";[17] and after a generation of extraordinary achievement in historical linguistics, Karl Otfried Müller continued to press the argument: "Language, the earliest product of the human mind, and the origin of all other intellectual energies," he wrote, "is at the same time the clearest evidence of a nation and of its affinities with other races. Hence the comparison of languages enables us to judge the history of nations to which no other kind of memorial, no tradition or record, can ascend."[18] The discovery of Sanskrit suggested to Franz Bopp an original tongue (not unlike the pre-Babel language posited by Dante), from which all European languages had descended according to determinable linguistic laws; and from this *Ursprache*, some inferred, one might go on to reconstruct the elements of an Indo-

European *Urzeit* and so to decipher what J. A. Kanne called "the Sybelline pages of the book of human life."[19] Unlike Galileo's "great book of nature" (which Kanne's image recalls) this book calls not for mathematics but for comparative linguistics, a new form of speculative etymology beyond anything dreamed of by Vico, and great powers of what some Romantic scholars thought of as divination.

In this way philologists seem to have created their own kind of transcendental—and mythistorical—world, like Vico aspiring to ascend from philology to a new kind of philosophy. While invoking linguistic and historical "science" (*Sprachwissenschaft, Geschichtswissenschaft, Kulturwissenschaft*), they carried on the old search for the essential link between nature and culture—employing not, of course, a hypothetical social contract but a historical, or mythistorical, boundary between society and a "state of nature," marking the threshold of language, law, and (so philosophers would infer) consciousness. "In interpreting myth," wrote C. G. Heyne, "we must transport ourselves back into the manner of thought and expression which belonged to that remote period."[20] To that extent Romantic hermeneutics required a kind of retrospective mind-reading; and it is significant to note that to the dawning consciousness, which was the object of this inquiry, nineteenth-century scholars gave precisely the same name and some of the same connotations as old-fashioned critics had given to the original, intended, and true meaning of a text or a law—the Latin *mens* or *spiritus,* the French *esprit* and the German and especially Hegelian *Geist.*[21]

Philosophers and theologians might applaud this spiritualist or *geisteswissenschaftlich* goal; after all, as Ranke noted, this was their proper business, even if they did seek conceptual or confessional shortcuts. "But," to quote the words of a recent student of historicism, "it was the classicists and neohumanists—Friedrich Ast, Wilhelm von Humboldt, August Boeckh, and Friedrich Schleiermacher—who formulated what Hans-Georg Gadamer called the theory of 'romantic' hermeneutics that became the epistemological rationale of German historicism and linguistic studies. Reduced to their common denominator these views insisted that all historical understanding (including all philological understanding) that is mediated through a text or similar evidence is mediated only through an overriding metaphysical unity that unites author and interpreter: Ranke's God, Ast's Spirit, Humboldt's Ideas."[22]

To these we should perhaps add a further "metaphysical unity," and this is Creuzer's Symbol, a still more controversial and "overriding" device of nineteenth-century philology. In the quest for cultural origins classical philologists like C. G. Heyne and Kanne were led (as Vico in his "new science" had been led) back to the old tradition of mythology—and led to look at it with new eyes, neither blinded by overbright modern "reason" nor overawed by literary worship of the "genealogy of the gods" as pursued by Boccaccio for example. In short, mythology too would become a modern science as the nineteenth century (in Frank Manuel's phrase) "confronted the gods," and did so in more sympathetic ways—and certainly on firmer scholarly grounds—than their Enlightenment predecessors had done.[23] Language was in a sense, as F. W. J. Schelling put it, "a faded mythology"; and its investigation along historical and comparative lines promised to yield the secrets of those "Sybelline pages" of which Müller had spoken.[24]

Here we catch a glimpse of that view of the divinatory power of philology which underlay the so-called "new mythology" of the nineteenth century, whose guiding spirit was Friedrich Creuzer.[25] In the spirit of Vico, Herder, and Heyne, Creuzer rejected the Enlightenment's tendency to oppose *mythos* and *logos* and in effect sought a distinct "mytho-logic," equivalent to Vico's "poetic wisdom," for the prehistorical period. Creuzer's fascination with origins had also been evident in an early work which attempted to trace the Greek "art of history" back to its roots in the symbols of the priests and the writings of the poets and logographers preceding Herodotus, a work which thus forged another primordial link between history and mythistory. Creuzer's way of thinking was closer to that of Hegel and especially Schelling than to that of Ranke or even of Niebuhr, and it is no wonder that his masterwork, his *Symbolik und Mythologie der alten Völker, besonders der Griechen*, which began to appear in 1810, was endorsed by these two classically trained idealists.[26] In his "organic" and idealist interpretation of mythology, published in the 1840s, Schelling, who had commended Creuzer's "philosophical penetration," attempted his own synthesis of poetry and philosophy, but unfortunately he had missed the "linguistic turn" taken by Herder and others and had small patience with the empirical bent of contemporary historical science; and his views were consigned by most serious scholars to the limbo of speculation.

For Creuzer, unlike Ranke, history was not limited to written testimony; rather it was the expression of a "regular relationship between consciousness and nature" (*ein gesetzmässiger Verhältnis zwischen Geist und Natur*).[27] To establish this relationship, to make the leap from culture to nature, Creuzer proposed a method of interpretation through the symbol, understood in a prehistorical, prelinguistic and perhaps (anticipating Jung and Karl Kerenyi) preconscious sense. In this connection Creuzer relied extensively on the sources of art history, especially pictorial representations of gods and heroes interpreted symbolically and allegorically. Creuzer's assumption was that nature first spoke to man through symbols, aural as well as visual; and myths were the stories (pre-logical *logoi*) told in this preverbal language, expressing the forces of nature and experiences of birth, acquisition, production, reproduction, and death. In other words language was the product of apotheosis, or theogony—*logos* a cultivated form of *mythos*.

Creuzer's was a synthetic and one might say mythopoeic mind—a *philomythos* (as Aristotle would say, by analogy with *philosophos*). A student and devotee of neo-Platonism, he pursued his *Symbolen*, bespeaking the union of nature and culture (as well as suggesting the religious connection between humanity and divinity through a method he called "symphilosophy" or "symphilology."[28] His thesis was that myth originated not in the superstitious worship of nature but in the concept of God—in a primeval monotheism extending to all Indo-European cultures. There was an original *Ur-Religion*, in short, corresponding to the *Ur-Sprache* posited by orientalists like Schlegel and Franz Bopp, and likewise Indian in provenance. Like Vico's "new science, Schleiermacher's hermeneutics, and to some extent Ranke's universal history, Creuzer's interpretations were set in a basically theological framework. In terms of the Lutheran theology which Ranke would have understood (though rejected) Creuzer sought not the deadening letter but the life-giving spirit of texts—though this spirit now would be the revelation not of faith but of a human power of divination.

For most nineteenth-century philologists and historians Creuzer had descended too far into the well of the past and, in his transcendental enthusiasm, had in effect lost his linguistic bearings.

12

After its initial success the *Symbolik* became the target of a series of criticisms aimed at its "mysticism" and muddle-headed speculation, in effect its violation of conventional historicism; and within a generation advances in philology, or historical linguistics, art history, archeology, ethnology, and folklore had largely discredited it, though admittedly rival theories did not often fare better. Despite the alliance with *Sprachwissenschaft,* modern mythology has repeatedly been led down blind alleys, or up garden paths, because of methodological or ideological excesses—from Creuzer and Kanne to J. B. Bachofen, Friedrich Nietzsche, Erwin Rohde, and Karl Kerenyi, who have perhaps transgressed the bounds of scholarly propriety as defined by historians like Theodor Mommsen and Ranke.[29]

Yet the impulse and aspirations of mythistoricism were by no means exhausted in terms of historical scholarship. Creuzer's own influence persisted, especially in France, and was decisive in at least one line of inquiry. This brings us back to the historical school of law, dominated by Creuzer's lifelong friend Friedrich Karl von Savigny—that "Hermes nature," as Creuzer called him—who carried on the campaign against the philosophical school, and whose students, especially Jacob Grimm, brought his methods from Roman into European and especially Germanic law.[30] Like Ranke, Savigny himself preferred not to stray from the texts; and indeed his monumental history of Roman law in the middle ages was criticized by one of his Hegelian rivals at the University of Berlin for neglecting the "internal history" of his subject. Other scholars, however, did not hesitate to take up the quest for origins through the medium of language. Again it was Vico who had opened the way, not only in his *New Science* but also in his earlier book on the universal law of nations. For Vico, law was derived literally from myth, since according to Vichian etymology *jus* was descended from *Jous,* or Jove, Jupiter, the father god of all the nations and the first principle which the new science found in its descent into the "dark ages" (*tempus obscurum*) of human history.[31]

The intersection of law, language, and myth was examined much more "scientifically" by Grimm, especially in his essay of 1816, *Von der Poesie im Recht,* which was the foundation of his monumental *Rechtsalterthümer* of 1828. The immemorial, pre-historical character of law Grimm illustrated by citing the famous verse prefacing Eike von Repgow's thirteenth-century collection, the *Sachsen-*

spiegel: "Das Rechts hab ich nicht erdacht / es haben von Alter uf uns gedacht / unsere gute Vorfahren."[32] (The Law's not something that I thought / But something ancient to us brought / By our good forebears.) In his juridico-lexicographical researches Grimm sought out natural symbols as well as poetic expressions of ancient German custom, with all of its characteristic alliterations, rhymes, repetitions, and shameless puns. It takes a man not a mouse (as we might illustrate from Anglo-Saxon examples) to fight with might and main to keep his house and home safe and sound. Such was the currency of the law- and word-"finders"—*trovères, troubadours, Dichter, Richter*—and so were such material symbols as earth (for property), a stick (for authority) and an endless list of other objects, natural and man-made. Laws present the "deep history" of a country, as one of Grimm's disciples put it in 1845, for "to study laws is to study the origin and causes of historical facts."[33] And if "symbolic" was a blind alley for classical philology and Indo-European theogony, it was most illuminating for the history of law, custom, and institutions.

The classic work of a radical (root and branch) plumbing of mythistory in this sense and in the linguistic and legal terms I have been suggesting is Jules Michelet's *Origines du droit français,* published in 1837 and representing a confluence of virtually all of the intellectual forces I have tried to identify. Of these the most significant were Vico's *New Science,* which Michelet had translated a decade earlier; second, the "oriental renaissance," which had brought to European scholarship the fascinating collection of the *Laws of Manu;* third, Creuzer's controversial *Symbolik,* translated into French in 1822; and above all the work on Germanic legal antiquities by Grimm, who became Michelet's correspondent and mentor in *Germanistik.* To these should be added the shaping force of literary imagination, which informs all of Michelet's work and which seems to have monopolized recent critical studies of his work, especially in the wake of Hayden White's *Metahistory.* In my view, in any case, Michelet seems to be a prime specimen of nineteenth-century "mythistoricism."

Michelet conceived of his book as a treatise on the "poetic origins of European law" and a "symbolic of law," conscious invocations of Grimm and Creuzer; but it is the spirit of Vico that haunts the Sybelline pages of the book. If Creuzer provided the basic method and Grimm the source materials, it was Vico who inspired the philosophic form. Michelet's thesis was simple and uncannily anticipated Ernst Cassirer's philosophy of symbolic forms: God created man, and man (perhaps in emulation) created symbols. He was *homo symbolicus*, and the language of symbols still reflected in the "poetry of law" preceded and subsumed spoken and written language. On this basis Michelet ranged over the whole trajectory of human experience, from birth to death, from definition of self to confrontation, cooperation, and conflict with others, from the eternal "moi" of ancient Roman and modern bourgeois culture to the idealized "nous" of primitive Germanic society and revolutionary vision.

What is perhaps most remarkable about this "juridical biography of man," as Michelet characterized his book, was the way in which it opened up the social and cultural dimensions of history.[34] Questions of the status of children and women, property and inheritance, social structure and ceremony, the impact of war and crime, the significance of old age, death, and burial—all of these subjects were reflected in ancient Indo-European law in terms not only of language but also of gestures, colors, devices, arms, flags, and other kinds of silent symbolism. Because of its novelty, the book enjoyed a mostly sympathetic reception, aside from complaints by professional jurists like Henri Klimrath about Michelet's lack of legal expertise and his tendency to romanticize the law.[35] Yet the work had curiously slight long-range impact and practically no posterity, except for certain esoteric areas later defined as legal anthropology and legal archeology.

One notable exception was the remarkable but now largely forgotten book published by Joseph-Pierre Chassan in 1847 and called *Essai sur la Symbolique du Droit, précédé d'une introduction sur la poésie du droit primitif*. More comprehensive than Michelet's or Grimm's work, Chassan's treatise often resorted to them but displayed a more professional grasp of Roman and French law, including the civil code as well as a variety of older sources, and he presented the results of his studies of legal symbolism (*Rechtssymbolik*) in a more accessible form. Chassan accepted Vico's scheme of three ages (divine, heroic, human) and Creuzer's belief in a primitive religion; and he assumed that symbolic expression in art, especially in sculpture, preceded the poetic language which was still detectable in legal monuments. Nevertheless, philology remained the key to Chassan's investigations. "Philology alone can establish civil history," he wrote. "Languages are a sort of intellectual cosmogony where the archives of the human race are deposited. Philology possesses the secret of reading these mysterious archives and sometimes of discovering there, in the debris accumulated by the ages, certain expressions which, though meaningless to the layman, are for reflective scholars the revelations of an entire past."[36]

Like Michel Foucault (anti-historicist though this modern mythistorian always affected to be), Chassan regarded language as an "archive," a multi-layered deposit inviting a kind of archeological investigation. Like Foucault, too, Chassan was aware of the metahistorical—may we say implicitly synchronic?—nature of his subject. For Chassan it was impossible to establish a chronology of symbols. One might determine when they died, he remarked, but rarely when they were born—any more than one can say when a custom had first appeared. "Custom and symbols have no fathers," he concluded; "they are at once within time, as it were, and outside of time."

Nevertheless Chassan did not reject historicism, or mythistoricism. Like his Romantic forebears, he strained literally to hear the ancient voices, to see the primordial symbols reflected and resounding in the ancient texts, at least for readers learned and imaginative enough to make the historical and mythistorical leap. He wanted, in the famous lines of André Chénier, to "make ancient verses on new ideas." Also implied in Chassan's kind of mythistoricism was not only that the present was a continuation and an outgrowth of the past, but also that it contained, in legal and institutional as well as in linguistic and symbolic terms, substantial residues of that past and factors of *longue durée*—despite mighty revolutionary efforts to escape or efface it. "Modern France has no doubt broken entirely and irrevocably with feudalism as a political system," Chassan wrote; "but who can say that we do not continue to live at this very moment on the debris and in the bonds of the feudal regime, which organized Europe and created the landed property of the middle ages, an institution still evident today in our *propriété foncière?*"[37]

What, from philological analysis, do legal texts have to say about ancient civilization? Like Vico, Grimm, and Michelet, Chassan began by emphasizing the connections between law and poetry—illustrated by the fact that Solon was both poet and lawgiver, and that the Twelve Tables had a poetic form (a "serious poem," in Vico's words) and had originally been chanted. Chassan surveyed the remnants of poetic language in Germanic legal tradition. Following Grimm, he gave examples of alliteration, assonance, rhyme, and tautology—sometimes illustrated by up to five repetitions (though this may sound to us more like modern legal jargon): *voluimus, jussimus et mandavimus; wir setzen, ordnen und machen; disons, déclarons, voulons et ordonnons;* we wish, order, affirm, declare, etc.).[38]

Following a tradition going back to Antoine Loisel and Erasmus in the sixteenth century, Chassan cited proverbs and verses embodying ancient custom: "Ist das Bett beschritten / So is das Recht erstritten." (On the bed if they lie, / Then the law does apply.) And the famous lines from Loisel's *Institutes Coutumiers:* "Boire, manger, coucher ensemble, / C'est le mariage ce me semble." Expressions of political wisdom took a similar mnemonic form: "Sic rex, sic judex. / A Deo rex, a rege lex. / Si veut le roi, Si veut la loi." And so did expressions of common sense: "Noth, Hat kein Gebot." Necessity has no law, which may also be found among the runes of ancient Roman law. Like Erasmus' *Adages,* such jingles, proverbs, and commonplaces seemed to open window on antiquity.

In his critique of romantic hermeneutics Gadamer has argued that we cannot "get behind the back of language"; and yet this is precisely what Chassan, following Michelet and Grimm, was presuming to do. In modern law, for example, the term "conjoined" (*conjoints*), referring to the married couple, recalled the wooden yoke (*jugum*), symbolizing the Roman marriage (*conjugium*).[39] For somewhere behind these formulas, fictions, images, and symbols so carefully classified by Chassan there lay, surely, a whole world of belief and action—a world accessible to "symbology," perhaps, if not to philology. In pursuing this line of inquiry Chassan was continuing the exploration of fields then hardly defined, including not only mythology and art history but also folklore, ethnology, archeology, social history, the history of material culture, and perhaps psychohistorical research, though his ostensible target remained the science of law.

While Grimm's arrangement had been lexicographical and that of Michelet biographical (that is, according to the stages of human life), Chassan's classification was basically hierarchical, following in effect the great chain of being. On the lowest level juridical symbols were natural—a bit of earth or stone representing personal property and a branch political authority, as noted earlier, while colors had a wide range of meaning which often seemed universal. Also important were parts of the human body—the hand (for swearing, stealing, or striking), the mouth (for kissing or libeling), and symbolically that part of the body, that is, the tongue, was often excised for criminal transgressions.[40] Roman slaves had been castrated for adultery, for example, and the tongues of heretics or blasphemers ordered cut out by Christian rulers. Publicly, the kiss had a variety of meanings, depending on where bestowed—foot, hand, mouth, etc. When a Norman nobleman and an old clerical enemy were, after long negotiations, brought together for reconciliation and the kiss of peace, and when at the last moment the aristocratic *derrière* was offered to the bishop, the symbolism was not lost on the onlookers, or on the historian who recorded the incident.[41]

Animals were richly represented in legal lore, symbolism, and art. Birds could stand for power or freedom—and, unlike the liberty bestowed by city air (*Stadtluft macht frei*), to be "free as a bird" (*vogelfrei*) could mean on the loose and fair game as well as liberated. About the relationship between mankind and the animal world there was considerable ambivalence; and Chassan recalled what his contemporaries (though not necessarily his old-regime predecessors) would have regarded as another fiction, which was the attribution of criminal liability to certain animals, down at least to the level of rats, and their subjection to appropriate punishment.[42]

Another striking example of animal symbolism was the horse, especially the white horse. In the fourteenth century King Charles V of France gave a brown horse to the visiting Emperor Charles IV in order to demonstrate his own precedence by appearing on a white steed, a *cheval blanc*, which had long been a symbol of dominance for popes and ecclesiastical as well as secular rulers. Chassan goes on plausibly to link this with the white horses (*equi albi*) ridden by conquering Roman generals and, more remotely, Greek and Indian mythical figures.[43] One can imagine tracing this symbol over the centuries from Vishnu in his tenth incarnation down to the Lone Ranger, who has likewise enjoyed many ups and downs and revivals and intercultural transmissions.

Woman had a special, but also ambivalent, place in legal symbolism. On the one hand she was regarded in some laws as little more than an inhabitant of the animal world or a piece of property, a legitimate subject of trade and corporeal punishment. On the other hand she was the source of life and, as Chassan and Michelet quoted from the *Laws of Manu*, "A woman should not be beaten for a fault even if she commits it a hundred times, and not even with a flower" (which of course had its own non-violent symbolism).[44] And as Chassan further rhapsodized, "Woman is herself poetry" (*Car la femme, c'est la poésie même*—or is it "woman is poetry itself"?). But of course Germanic as well as Roman family and property law, founded on paternalism, often nullified this idealized view which attracted Romantic historians.

If language was a "faded mythology" (and mythology a most ancient history), so too was law, though perhaps in a better state of preservation for historians. In general, European jurisprudence retained the memory of a variety of myths, such as the werewolf (*homme-loup*), and more useful fictions such as the instantaneous passing of succession and inheritance (*le mort saisit le vif*) and, in public law, *le roi ne meurt jamais*).[45] It kept, too, a variety of symbols, allegories, and formulas preserving the aura of ancient word-magic and the symbolism and formalism of ancient law. The presumption of historicism, or mythistoricism, was that such formulas, generated by religious consciousness, progressed through various interpretations to a more secular and rational level until they reached, in some cases, the level of rational—indeed hyperrational—propositions and axioms, especially in the hands of seventeenth-century natural lawyers. The impulse of Vico, Michelet, and many members of the historical school was mainly to retrace this process of secularization and rationalization back to the primitive, poetic, preverbal, prerational origins. In this sense historicism was (as Emilio Betti remarked of modern hermeneutics) the reverse of the creative process.[46]

Here is the basis of the "poetry of history," as Emery Nef called it, the key to Romantic historicism, or mythistoricism.[47] What is at issue, however, is not merely the fascination, experienced by Michelet and even the young Ranke, for colorful narrative as fashioned by the likes of Walter Scott and Fenimore Cooper (an aspect of historical thought which has received more than its share of attention recently).[48] More than that, it was the attempt to recreate the life and thought of the remote past through a new combination of human faculties. For mythistory required the union not of memory and reason, as in Baconian method or the *histoire raisonnée* of the Enlightenment or perhaps the scientific history of Ranke, but rather of memory and imagination, which was the basis, too, of Romantic hermeneutics. Through the imaginative reconstruction of cultural remains—and especially of law, language, and symbols—the historian could plumb the depths of the "well of the past."

The legacy of what I have called mythistoricism over the past two centuries or so has been considerable—especially in various projects of modernist and post-modernist thought. Students of mythology from Bachofen to Georges Dumezil, for example, have continued the efforts of historical reconstruction of myth begun by Creuzer (and indeed have to some degree restored his reputation), and Jungian psychology has pursued the investigation of myth and symbol—archetypes—in even more speculative terms into prehistory as well as the subconscious.[49] Philosophers as disparate as Nietzsche, Cassirer, and Heidegger have tried in their own ways to see things "as they really are" by searching what Paul Ricoeur has called "our Greek memory" (the discovery of the Dionysian side of humanity in particular was in large part due to Creuzer),[50] and the philosophical hermeneutics of Gadamer and his students seems even more directly related to the sort of mythistoricism I have been discussing (though more exclusively literary in orientation). Born in a religious context, mythistoricism—much like modern hermeneutics—has survived in quasi-religious fields in which big questions are still asked, and big answers are still expected.

Another sign of the vitality of mythistorical pursuits appears in the contemporary German movement which has (like its Romantic antecedent) been called "the new mythology," which looks back to Creuzer and Schelling for questions, if not answers, which are still significant for a historical understanding of the human condition. In particular Hans Blumenberg has been in the process of exploding the illusions of "secularization" and "the end of myth," and showing that "myth" continues to be part of the very substance of history—a very un-Rankean view, of course.[51] The progress of this discussion bears watching, I think—especially since it has implications for modern as well as ancient history.

As for what (after Thomas Kuhn) we might call the "normal science" of history there is less to say. Historically, one might single out scholars like Jacob Burckhardt and Johan Huizinga (especially the Huizinga of *Homo Ludens*) as sympathetic to certain kinds of mythistory and to imaginative interpretation, but neither attracted a following in any way comparable to that of Ranke, who (despite his fascination with Walter Scott) was professionally (and theoretically) as suspicious of the faculty of imagination as he was of idealistic philosophy. This has also been the case with most of his epigones and indeed with devotees of any number of "new" social, economic, cultural, and even supposed "interdisciplinary histories," which seem generally to share a focus on the most "modern" phases of the historical process, a reliance on hard, often quantitative evidence and causal explanation, and an emphasis on reason rather than imagination in historical reconstruction.[52]

None of this is objectionable, but such preoccupations may lead us to forget that the past is truly a "foreign country," that people really "do things differently there"—and that historical significance requires qualitative as well as quantitative investigation. There really is a "deep well of the past" to explore even if we never reach bottom—and there really are big questions in history, even though we may be unable to supply suitably big answers. Recent critical developments in intellectual history arising from a new (perhaps neo-Romantic) linguistic "turning" and hermeneutical mode of understanding suggest at least a small posterity for a once powerful, heaven-storming, and soul-shaking, intellectual enterprise.[53] It is too soon to write an obituary for mythistory, but it surely deserves remembering here as a part (and conceptually perhaps the most significant part) of historicism "as it really was" in the age of Ranke.

NOTES

1. MYTHISTORY IN AGE OF RANKE

1. Cf. Wilhelm Nestle, *Vom Mythos zum Logos,* 2d ed. (Stuttgart: Krömer, 1942).

2. Richard Bernstein, *Beyond Objectivism and Relativism* (Philadelphia: University of Pennsylvania Press, 1983), 16.

3. Ernst Troeltsch, *Der Historismus und seine Probleme* (Tübingen: Mohr, 1922), 104. Meinecke and Troeltsch to the contrary notwithstanding, the term *Historismus* appeared first in the early, not the late nineteenth century, and conceptually is more properly associated with the historical thought of Romanticism and its descendants than the distorted interpretations of Karl Popper and others—who have in effect reduced "historicism" to a vulgar form of its "philosophical" opposite. On this corrected perspective, which is assumed in the present paper and which will be developed in a later study of which this is a part, see Erich Rothacker, "Das Wort 'Historismus,' " *Zeitschrift für deutsche Wortforschung* 16 (1960): 3–6; the entry in *Geschichtliche Wörterbuch der Philosophie,* and Gunter Scholz, *"Historismus" als spekulative Geschichtsphilosophie: Christlieb Julius Braniss (1972–1873)* Frankfurt: Klostermann, 1973): 130ff.

4. Theodor W. Adorno, *Dialectic of Enlightenment* (New York: Herder and Herder, 1972); Hans-Georg Gadamer, *Truth and Method,* trans. G. Barden and J. Cumming (New York: Seabury Press, 1975), 238ff; Hans Blumenberg, *Work on Myth,* trans. R. Wallace (Cambridge, Mass: MIT Press 1985), 34; and see Manfred Frank, *Der kommende Gott: Vorlesungen uber die neue Mythologie* (Frankfurt: Suhrkamp, 1982), and William Bouwsma, "Work on Blumenberg," *JHI,* 48 (1987), 347–54.

5. D. R. Kelley, *Foundations of Modern Historical Scholarship* (New York: Columbia University Press, 1970), 4.

6. John Emerich Dahlberg, Lord Acton, *Historical Essays and Studies* (London: Macmillan, 1919), 344–45; cf. *Lectures on Modern History* (London: Macmillan, 1906), 14.

7. Donald Kelley, *Historians and the Law in Postrevolutionary France* (Princeton: Princeton University Press, 1984). On this *Methodenstreit* in political economy see Joseph Schumpeter, *History of Economic Analysis (London: Oxford Uni-*

veristy Press, 1954), and Gottfried Eisermann, Die Grundlagen des Historismus in der deutschen Nationalökonomie (Stuttgart: Enke, 1956).

8. Glyn Daniel, *The Idea of Prehistory* (Baltimore: Penguin Books, 1964), 9; and see Lionel Gossman, *Orpheus Philologus: Bachofen versus Mommsen on the Study of Antiquity (Transactions of the American Philosophical Society,* LXXIII, pt. 5 (1983), and James Whitman, "Nietzsche in the Magisterial Tradition of German Classical Philology," *JHI*, 47 (1986): 453–68.

9. Leopold von Ranke, *Universal History*, trans. G. W. Prothero (London: Kegan Paul, Trench, 1884), preface.

10. *Dictionarium Brittanicum*, II.

11. Reviews of this phenomenon include Jonathan Goldberg in *English Literary History*, 49 (1982): 514–42, and *Studies in English Literature*, 24 (1984): 57–91; Louis Montrose and Jean E. Howard in *English Literary Renaissance*, 16 (1986): 5–12, 13–43; Kevin Sharpe in *History*, 71 (1986): 235–47; and David Sacks, "History in Literature: The Renaissance," *Journal of British Historical Studies* 26 (1987): 107–23. The term "new historicism" is commonly credited to Stephen Greenblatt, *Power of Forms in the English Renaissance* (Norman, Okla.: Pilgrim Books, 1982), 5, but this unfairly—and unhistorically!—slights Wesley Morris, *Toward a New Historicism* (Princeton: Princeton University Press, 1972).

12. J. G. Herder, "Metakritik," in *Sämmtliche Werke*, XXXVII (Stuttgart: J. G. Cotta, 1853), 17; and see Ernst Cassirer, *The Problem of Knowledge*, trans. W. Woglom and C. Hendel (New Haven: Yale University Press, 1950), 218; *Philosophy of Symbolic Forms*, trans. R. Manheim (New Haven: Yale University Press, 1953), II, *Language*, 152ff, and James H. Stam, "Perspectives on 'Linguistic Relativity,'" *Psychology of Language and Thought*, ed. R. W. Rieber (New York: Plerium Press, 1980), 239–62; also Hermann Josef Cloeren ed., *Philosophie als Sprachkritik im 19. Jahrhundert* (Stuttgart: Fromman-Holzboog Verlag, 1971); and Georges Gusdorf, *Fondements du savoir romantique, vol. IX of Les Sciences humaines et la pensée occidentale* (Paris: Payot, 1982).

13. Giovanni Battista Vico, *Diritto universale*, II 2, 1, in *Opere*, Vol. 2, ed. F. Nicolini (Bari: Laterza, 1936), 318; and see Donald Kelley, "Vico's Road," in his *History, Law, and the Human Sciences* (London: Variorum Reprints, 1984).

14. See Raymond Schwab, *The Oriental Renaissance*, trans. G. Patterson and A. Reinking (New York: Columbia University Press, 1984), and A. Leslie Willson, A *Mythical Image: The Ideal of India in German Romanticism* (Durham: Duke University Press, 1964); and, in general, Theodor Benfey, *Geschichte der Sprachwissenschaft und orientalischen Philologie in Deutschland* (Munich: Cotta, 1869); Rudolf Pfeiffer, *History of Classical Scholarship from 1300 to 1850* (Oxford: Clarendon Press, 1976); Ulrich von Wilamowitz-Moellendorff, *History of Classical Scholarship*, trans. H. Lloyd-Jones (London: Duckworth, 1982); Helmut Flashar, K. Grunder, and A. Horstmann eds., *Philologie und Hermeneutik im 19. Jahrhundert* (Göttingen: Vandenhoeck und Ruprecht, 1979); James Whitman, "From Philology to Anthropology in Mid-Nineteenth-Century Germany," *Functionalism Historicized*, ed. G. Stocking (*History of Anthropology*, II, Madison: University of Wisconsin Press, 1984), 214–29; Martin Bernal, *Black Athena: The Afroasiatic Roots of Classical Civilization*, I (London: Free Association Press, 1981), and J. E. Tashjean, "Indo-European Studies and the Sciences of Man," *History of Political Theory* 2 (1981): 447–68.

15. Friedrich von Schlegel "On the Indian Language, Literature, and

Philosophy," in *Works*, trans. E. J. Millington (London: G. Bell and Sons, 1849), 427, and Edward Moor, *The Hindu Pantheon* (London: J. Johnson, 1810), xi.

16. In general, Joachim Wach, *Das Verstehen* (Tübingen: Mohr, 1926), I, 62, 83ff, and Manfred Frank, *Das individuel Allgemein* (Frankfurt: Suhrkamp, 1977). Cf. Ernst Behler, "What it Means to Understand an Author Better than He Understood Himself," in Joseph P. Strelka ed., *Literary Theory and Criticism, Festschrift in Honor of René Wellek* (New York: Peter Lang, 1985), I, 69–92, and D. R. Kelley, "Hermes, Clio, Themis: Historical Interpretation and Legal Hermeneutics," *JMH*, (1983) 55: 644–68, also in his *History, Law and the Human Sciences*, with further literature.

17. Schlegel, *op. cit.*, 429.

18. Karl O. Müller, *A History of the Literature of Ancient Greece*, trans. J. W. Donaldson (London: Longmans, 1858), 4.

19. J. A. Kanne *Pantheum der aeltesten Naturphilosophie* (Tübingen: Cotta, 1811), 1; and see Erich Neumann, *Johann Arnold Kanne, ein vergessener Romantiker* (Berlin: Reuther, 1928).

20. Cited in K. O. Müller, *Introduction to a Scientific System of Mythology*, trans. J. Leitsch (London: Longman, 1844), 256.

21. Kelley, *History, Law and the Human Sciences*, especially chaps. IV & VII, and literature there cited.

22. R. Steven Turner, "Historicism, *Kritik*, and the Prussian Professoriate, 1790 to 1840," *Philologie und Hermeneutik im 19. Jahrhundert*, II, 470.

23. Frank Manuel, *The Eighteenth Century Confronts the Gods* (Cambridge, Mass.: Harvard University Press, 1959), especially ch. 6.

24. See Ernst Cassirer, *Language and Myth*, trans. S. Langer (New York: Dover Publications, 1946), 85, and his *Philosophy of Symbolic Forms*, II, *Mythical Thought*, 3–15; also Adolf Allwohn, *Der Mythos bei Schelling (Kant-Studien* 61 [1927]), Robert F. Brown, *Schelling's Treatise on "The Deities of Samothrace" (American Academy of Studies in Religion*, 12 [1974]), and Xavier Tilliette, *La Mythologie comprise: L'Interprétation schellingienne du paganisme* (Naples: Bibliopolis, 1984).

25. On the original "new mythology" see especially Marc-Matthieu Münch, *La "Symbolique" de Friedrich Creuzer* (Paris: Ophrys, 1976); also Ernst Howald ed., *Der Kampf um Creuzers Symbolik* (Tübingen: Mohr, 1926), Werner Paul Sohnle, *Georg Friedrich Creuzers "Symbolik und Mythologie" in Frankreich* (Göttingen: Kümmerle, 1972), and Benedetto Bravo, "Dieu et les dieux chez F. Creuzer et F. G. Welcker," *History and Anthropology* 3 (187): 263–301.

26. Friedrich Creuzer, *Religions de l'antiquité considérées principalement dans leurs formes symboliques et mythologiques*, trans. J. D. Guignaut (Paris: Treuttel et Würtz, 1825–); and Marc-Matthieu Münch, *Joseph-Daniel Guignaut et sa traduction de la Symbolik de Creuzer* (typed copy, Library of Congress, 1978), with reference to Guignaut's MS correspondence; for the illustrations see Joseph-Daniel Guignaut *Nouveau galérie mythologique* (Paris: Firmin Didot, 1850). Cf. G. W. F. Hegel, *The Letters*, trans. C. Butler and C. Seiler (Bloomington: Indiana University Press, 1984), 369.

27. Friedrich Creuzer *Die historische Kunst der Griechen*, ed. J. Keyser 2d ed. (Leipzig: G. J. Goschen, 1845), 11.

28. Friedrich Creuzer, *Briefe Friedrich Creuzers an Savigny (1799–1850)* (Berlin: Schmidt, 1972), 11–12.

29. See Jan De Vries, *Forschungsgeschichte der Mythologie* (Munich: Alber, 1961), Heinz Gockel, *Mythos und Poesie* (Frankfurt: Klostermann, 1981), Charles Rearich, *Historians and Folklore in Nineteenth Century France* (Bloomington: Indiana University Press, 1974), and the classic work of Otto Gruppe, *Geschichte der klassischen Mythologie und Religionsgeschichte* (Leipzig: Teubner, 1921).

30. See "Su Federico Carlo di Savigny," *Quaderni fiorentini per la storia del pensiero giuridico moderno*, 9 (1980), and the bibliography compiled by Klaus Luig in *ibid.*, 8 (1979), 501–59.

31. Giovanni Battista Vico, *Scienza nuova*, no. 391; and see Armelo d'Amato, *Il Mito di Vico e la filosofia della storia in Francia nella prima meta dell'Ottocento* (Naples, 1977), and Paolo Becchi, "Origini della 'Wirkungsgeschichte di Vico in Germania,'" *Materiali per una storia della cultura giuridica* 11 (1981): 275–323.

32. Jakob Grimm, "Von der Poesie im Recht," *Zeitschrift für geschichtliche Rechtrswissenschaft*, II (1816), and *Deutsche Rechtsalterthümer* 4th ed. (Leipzig: Dieterich, 1899), 27. See Wilhelm Ebel, *Jacob Grimm und die deutsche Rechtswissenschaft* (Göttingen: Vandenhoeck und Ruprect, 1963), Hans Fehr, *Die Dichtung in der Recht* (Bern: Francke, 1936), and Eduard Graf and Matthias Dietherr, *Deutsche Rechtsprichwörter* (Nordlingen: C. H. Beck, 1864); G. C. J. J. Van den Bergh, *Themis en de Muzen: de functie van de gebonden vormen in het recht* (Haarlem, 1964); also Gerald Strauss *Law, Resistance, and the State* (Princeton: Princeton University Press, 1986), 100.

33. G. A. Davoud-Ogyilou, *Histoire de la législation des anciens germains* (Berlin: Reimer, 1845), ix.

34. *Origines du droit français*, in *Oeuvres complètes*, ed. P. Viallaneix, III (Paris: Flammarion, 1973), 604ff.

35. *Travaux*, I, 146–57.

36. Joseph-Pierre Chassan *Essai* (Paris: Violecoq fils, 1847), xxiii. In general see Karl von Amira, *Rechtsarchäologie* (Berlin: Ahnenerbe-Stiftung, 1943), and Walter Pollack, *Perspektive und Symbol in Philosophie und Rechtswissenschaft* (Berlin: Rothschild, 1912).

37. Essai., cxxiii.

38. Essai., 349, 319, 360, 351, 366, etc.

39. Essai., 235.

40. Essai., 113ff.

41. Reported in Robert Fawtier, *The Capetian Kings of France*, trans. L. Butler and L. J. Adam (London: Macmillan, 1960), 102, quoting the chronicle of Saint-Pierre-le-Vif: as the Archbishop of Sens was about to give the kiss of peace to Count Renaud, "ille, vultum avertans, in posterioribus suis pacem ei offerabat."

42. *Essai*, lxxxviii.

43. *Essai*, lxxxviii, 105.

44. *Essai*, xci; and cf. Michelet, *Origines*, L. I, chap. 2.

45. *Essai*, xci, 361.

46. Emilio Betti, *Teoria generale della interpretazione* (Milan: Giuffrè, 1955), I, "prolegomeni."

47. Emery Neff, *The Poetry of History* (New York: Columbia University Press, 1947).

48. See, e.g., Robert H.Canary and Henry Kozicki eds., *The Writing of History: Literary Form and Historical Understanding* (Madison: University of Wisconsin Press, 1978), and other works appearing in the wake of Hayden White, *Metahistory* (Baltimore: Johns Hopkins University Press, 1973); also now Lionel Gossman, "History as Decipherment: Romantic Historiography and the Discovery of the Other," *New Literary History* 18 (1986): 23–57.

49. Carl Jung, *Symbols of Transformation*, trans. R. F. C. Hull (New York: Pantheon Books, 1956), refers once favorably, to Creuzer (238–354). The great Indo-Germanist Dumezil is unexpectedly becoming a cult figure among French intellectuals, overshadowing (at least in the media and in some scholarly circles) even Lévi-Strauss, Lacan, and Derrida, if not Foucault—suggesting a resurgence of "historisme" also in French intellectual circles. (This was noted barely a month before Dumezil's death in Oct. 1986.)

50. *Freud and Philosophy*, trans. D. Savage (New Haven: Yale University Press, 1970), 48; and see Walter F. Otto, *Dionysius, Myth and Cult*, trans. R. Palmer (Bloomington: Indiana University Press, 1965). As Martin P. Nilsson remarks in *A History of Greek Religion*, trans. F. J. Fielden (Oxford: Clarendon Press, 1949), 42, "No literature has so quickly gone out of date as the numerous writings on mythology."

51. *Work on Myth*, 34. Frank, *Der kommende Gott*, links the "new mythology" of the early nineteenth century and that of the later twentieth (including also the work of H. E. Richter and L. Kolakowski) and follows its political and literary offspring, with reference to the work of Bachofen, Nietzsche, and other errant philologists who lusted after strange, or merely old, gods, yet who have had their own impact on historical thinking.

52. There is obviously some exaggeration here, especially for ancient history, for which one might invoke the work of Fustel de Coulanges (the Fustel of the *Cité antique)*, Vernant, Gernet, Dodds, Nilsson, Benveniste, Detienne, Dumezil, among many others; but these scholars all seem to have operated on the margins (some might say the frontiers) of professional, or at least normal and consensual, scholarship. What is called for in this connection, it seems to me, is a full and critical history of classical scholarship, which recognizes the infidels and the heretics (and perhaps even, for historical purposes, the lunatic fringe) as well as the orthodox, the blessed, and the canonized of philological tradition.

53. Further suggestions on these points may be found in D. R. Kelley, "Horizons of Intellectual History," *JHI*, 48 (1987): 143–69.

IX

ROBERT FLINT, HISTORIAN OF IDEAS

Robert Flint was one of the most remarkable intellectuals, scholars, and «historians of ideas» (his phrase) of the nineteenth century. He drew variously and voraciously on the learning, philosophy, and theology of several national traditions — French, German, Italian, and Belgian as well as English and Scottish — and his interests ranged from classical antiquity to the most modern-*isms*. In some ways Flint seems most sympathetic to French thought. He was a *philosophe* after the Enlightenment had faded into memory, an *érudit* in a period of modernism and positivism, an Eclectic in the style of Victor Cousin after this doctrine had fallen into discredit, and «the last original thinker of the Scottish school»[1]. Yet he was also a patriotic Scotsman who revered the past and believed in the future of his country and in 'rendering to Caesar'. Flint was an enthusiast for a wide range of modern ideas from Vico and Condorcet to late-nineteenth-century Socialists; yet he was also a devout minister of the Scottish Reformed Church who always put theology above secular learning. He was a man of many parts, and if his intellectual make-up seems confusing and contradictory from a recent and more secular standpoint, there is little evidence that he entertained serious doubts about the relationship between his scholarly efforts and his religious calling[2].

I.

Flint was born in Dumfriesshire, Scotland (14 March 1834) — though it might have been in New England, he later recalled, except for the fact that his mother opposed his father's desire to emigrate. He was educated in Glasgow, following 'the old seven subjects' (liberal arts) and some natural history and in 1848, at age of fourteen, entered the University of Glasgow, where «the spirit of the polymath was upon him already». Here he spent a decade, five years each in arts and

1 George Elder Davie, *The Democratic Intellect: Scotland and her Universities in the Nineteenth Century* (Edinburgh, 1961), 272.

2 The only study is the commissioned and well-informed but laudatory and uncritical work of Donald Macmillan, *The Life of Robert Flint, D. D., Ll. D.* (London, 1914), which draws on Flint's papers, then in the hands of his sister, Janet Johnstone Flint. Besides this essential biographical source, I also make use of the extensive collection of Flint manuscripts in the Edinburgh University Library, MSS Gen. 631-689 (56 notebooks and 3 boxes), unused until now, as far as I know, since being deposited there.

divinity; and for the rest of his life his attention was divided between secular and sacred learning[3]. He was an avid and successful student, collecting at least sixteen prizes, mostly in theology. Among his teachers he was especially impressed by the up-to-date but unpublished Prof. Jackson, nephew and secretary to Dugald Stewart, who lectured on the history of theology. Flint had an activist side, too, and very likely may be counted among those who, as a contemporary recalled, «thought ourselves to be keen 'Radicals': believing in the 'people', 'progress', 'free education', 'wider suffrage', 'rights of man', 'rights of women', etc. etc.»[4]. To Flint such ideas represented the Christian as well as the enlightened way of thinking about the modern world. Writing many years later about the errors of the Socialists of that period, Flint recalled:

> In my early youth I myself held the views which they maintain, having been acquainted to some degree with a man whose name should not be forgotten in connection with the doctrine — a man of talent, almost a genius, an eloquent writer, as eloquent a talker — Patrick Edward Dove [...] [who] advocated the nationalisation of the land ardently and skilfully[5].

This was an age of revival in the Scottish Church, with the work of popular preachers like Norman MacLeod (whom he knew and very much admired) and Thomas Chalmers. The Church was just recovering from the traumatic 'Disruption' of 1843, followed by a decade of conflict, in which the Free Church, under the leadership of Chalmers, separated itself on the 'non-intrusion' principle that no minister should be imposed against the will of the congregation. At first Flint followed his father into the Free Church, but soon he turned back to the Established Church, presumably as more in keeping with an ecclesiastical and academic career and with his appetite for learning. According to a later scholar, «He was no Latitudinarian, but one who sought to gather all the relevant data whether gathered from Ethnic Religion, Natural Theology, Science or Christian Revelation and to build them into a systematic theology»[6]. Flint saw no contradiction in combining his Christian calling with the most eclectic and potentially subversive erudition. As he later explained, «The historian of ideas is no more bound to constitute himself the judge of their truth or falsity than the historian of events is bound to pronounce on their wisdom, or folly, rightness or wrongness»[7]. These kinds of value-judgments were to be formed only within the separate sphere of his religious faith and doctrinal commitment.

At first Flint was wholly devoted to his religious calling. In his last year at the university he contributed directly to the progress of Christian enlightenment as a

3 «Robertus Flint» (14 Mar. 1834-25 Nov. 1910), in *The Matriculation Album of the University of Glasgow from 1728 to 1858* (Glasgow, 1913).

4 Reminiscences of J. Nichol, quoted in Henry Jones and John Henry Muirhead, *The Life and Philosophy of Edward Caird* (Glasgow, 1921), 16.

5 *Socialism* (London, 1908, 2nd ed.), 142.

6 J. H. S. Burleigh, *A Church History of Scotland* (London, 1960), 383-84.

7 Preface to Bernhard Pünjer, *History of the Christian Philosophy of Religion from the Reformation to Kant*, tr. W. Hastie (Edinburgh, 1887), IX.

missionary in a district representing «the worst in Glasgow». In 1857, according to his biographer, he made 1736 visits, 213 to the sick and infirm, and held 33 meetings; and so he exposed himself to the 'social question', which he addressed more theoretically in later years[8]. In 1858, with his formal missionary appointment, Flint assumed his first position, as minister in the east Parish of Aberdeen, thus beginning a long and productive vocation as a preacher, which continued even after he shifted from an ecclesiastical to an academic career line. In 1862 he moved to a parish in Kilconquhar, where he delivered regular sermons, some of which appeared in his first published book, *Christ's Kingdom upon Earth* (1865). For Flint, even after he had plunged into historical scholarship, theology remained queen of sciences and Christianity the «Absolute Religion» — «from which all the religions of the world may be seen as they really are»[9]. His life goal was eventually to create a system of natural theology based on a synthesis of encyclopaedic learning and religious faith.

The world of Flint was one of small horizons. First came his family: mother, father, and sister, who, until their deaths, followed him in his pastoral and academic career from Glasgow to Aberdeen to Kilconquhar to Edinburgh; his father remained head of the family and led prayers even after his son's accumulation of degrees and eminence. Then his church, and later university, which Flint served with great conscientious and distinction; and though his administrative activities were limited and subordinate to his duties as preacher and teacher, his correspondence shows concern for theological issues, pedagogical policy, and the welfare of friends. Next Scotland, which Flint (to judge from his sermons) regarded with critical pride and solicitude for the mutual «duties» of people, church, and state. Then the larger European scene, which Flint (often in the company of his sister) visited as a tourist — especially France, Switzerland, and Germany — and across which he held an extensive correspondence. Mostly, Flint was a private man, a confirmed bachelor, dutiful son and brother, immersed in his preaching, teaching, (no doubt praying) and writing.

Flint has a mostly successful career. In 1864, before he was thirty, he entered the competition for the chair of moral philosophy at St. Andrews, left vacant in 1864 by the death of James Frederick Ferrier. With the help of friends Flint was successful in this effort, and on 16 November, two days after his election, he gave his inaugural lecture, praising Ferrier (though he had not known him) and celebrating the value of moral philosophy[10].

Two years later Flint was an unsuccessful candidate for a chair in his own University of Glasgow, and two years after that for the professorship in moral philosophy at the University of Edinburgh, a victim of the 'religious party', who (according to George Davie) found his faith «lukewarm»[11]. In 1876 William

8 Macmillan, *Life of Flint*, 75.

9 *Christianity in relation to other religions* (Edinburgh, 1882), 409.

10 Macmillan, *Life of Flint*, 149ff.

Crawford died, leaving open the chair of theology at Edinburgh (formerly held by Chalmers), and this time Flint was more fortunate. No doubt Flint would have preferred a chair of philosophy to accommodate his affection for secular learning, but he was assured that he was much needed by the Church of Scotland. Nor was the salary very satisfactory, though (over the objections of some) it was increased. On 7 February, while at the University of Glasgow delivering his Baird lectures on theism, Flint was elected professor of divinity; and on 14 November he gave his inaugural lecture, this time singing the praises of theology — which he regarded still as «queen of the sciences»[12]. He remained at Edinburgh for the rest of his life, continuing to lecture, to write, and to give occasional sermons, and actively engaging in the affairs of both University and Church.

II.

Flint came to intellectual maturity and commitment in a period crucial for Scottish philosophy as well as for European thought more generally[13]. In the early nineteenth century the old Scottish philosophy of common sense had experienced decline and then revival arising from a turn to evangelical religion, led by preacher-scholars such as Thomas Brown, who in 1810 succeeded Dugald Stewart in the chair of moral philosophy in Edinburgh, and Thomas Chalmers, professor of theology in the same university until his involvement in the Disruption of 1843. Chalmers's lectures on natural theology, reverting to the positions of Butler and Paley, was an attempt to reconcile evangelical religion with new philosophical ideas with reference to old notions of natural and historical «evidences» for Christianity, the existence of a providential deity, and even miracles[14]. Turning its back on the sensationalism of Reid and the skepticism of Hume, Scots philosophy opened a counterattack on incredulity and infidelity. In contrast to the agnostic inclinations of Leslie Stephen, W. E. H. Lecky, and T. H. Buckle in England, the Scottish antecedents of Flint made belief crucial to their conception of human progress. «This dissertation», wrote Flint's old hero Patrick Edward Dove, «attempts to trace the progress of human thought and human reasoning from the absolute negation of belief to the highest and most complex forms of credence»[15]. This agenda was the opposite of Stephen's, which set deism and its radical offshoots at the center of the history of thought.

This insistence on «the reality of spiritual things», in the words of the Scottish

[11] *The Democratic Intellect*, 319.

[12] *The Democratic Intellect*, 242ff.

[13] James McCosh, *The Scottish Philosophy, Biographical, Expository, Critical, from Hutcheson to Hamilton* (New York, 1875); Henry Laurie, *Scottish Philosophy in its National Development* (Glasgow, 1902); and the useful compendium edited by Daniel Sommer Robinson, *The Story of Scottish Philosophy* (New York, 1961).

[14] *Select Works*, V (Edinburgh, 1857), *Natural Theology: Lectures on Butler's Analogy*, and VI, *Evidences of the Christian Revelation and Lectures on Paley's Evidences* (Edinburgh, 1879).

[15] Patrick Edward Dove, *The Logic of the Christian Faith* (Edinburgh, 1856), preface.

Hegelian Edward Caird (brother of John, who defeated Flint in 1866 in the competition for the chair of moral philosophy in Glasgow), was not merely an expression of renewed religiosity but also a concern for metaphysics, mental science (as the philosophy of mind was then called), and the history of philosophy — a concern reinforced by the influence of German idealism (Kant and Hegel) and French spiritualism (Cousin's Eclecticism)[16]. Here the key figures were Chalmers, William Hamilton, who in 1836 became professor of logic and metaphysics at Edinburgh, J. D. Morell, who had studied philosophy with Fichte in Bonn and published a large and rather amateurish history of western philosophy in 1846, and James Frederick Ferrier, Flint's predecessor in the chair of divinity at Edinburgh. All these philosophers, while they were active in renewing contacts with continental thought, resisted the fashionable doctrines of Positivism and Utilitarianism, which threatened the new spiritualism which they championed[17].

These predecessors of Flint in «Scottish national philosophy», as Hamilton called it, were especially interested in mental science and the philosophy of the subject, or what Morell called «the philosophy of the me», derived from Fichte's *Ich* (and *Nicht-Ich*) and Cousin's *Moi*, which was the conceptual aspect of the individualism and selfishness celebrated by idealists and deplored by social and religious critics[18]. Hamilton created a sensation in the article he published in 1829 in the *Edinburgh Review*, in which he rejected Cousin's (likewise «spiritualist») position that the mind was able to grasp the absolute, arguing that all it could know was the unconditioned and the limited[19]. Hamilton's views about the relativity of knowledge and the old scholastic doctrine of «learned ignorance»[20] were extended by Ferrier, who created a whole new «science of ignorance» — «agnosiology» — in his efforts to understand the self and its intellectual limits[21].

Ferrier's skeptical and (for some) Germanizing tone produced a reaction from orthodox critics, including the town council of Edinburgh, whose efforts of censorship he resisted. In 1856 the Disruptionist Presbyterian minister John Cairns (who had himself studied in Berlin) complained that Ferrier was responsible for «a

16 Caird, *Essays on Literature and Philosophy* (Glasgow, 1892), 228 («The Problem of Philosophy at the Present Time»). On «mental science» see Richard B. Sher, *Church and University in the Scottish Enlightenment: The Moderate Literati of Edinburgh* (Princeton, 1985), 313ff.

17 See Morell, *On the Philosophical Tendencies of the Age: being four lectures delivered at Edinburgh and Glasgow, in January 1848* (London, 1848), on Positivism, Individualism, Traditionalism, and the philosophy of Progress.

18 See Thomas Brown, *Lectures on the Philosophy of the Human Mind* (Edinburgh, 1824).

19 «On the Philosophy of the Unconditioned; in reference to Cousin's Infinito-Absolute», *Discussions on Philosophy and Literature Education and University Reform* (Edinburgh, 1866, 3rd ed.), 35.

20 «On the Philosophy of the Unconditioned», II, 630, referring to Nicolas of Cusa, Lorenzo Valla, J. J. Scaliger, Grotius, Descartes, Pascal, and Locke.

21 *Institutes of Metaphysic: The Theory of Knowing and Being* (Edinburgh, 1875 [1854]), 405; and see Frederick Copleston, *A History of Philosophy*, VIII (London, 1967), 157-61; also Davie, *The Democratic Intellect*, 253ff, and *The Scottish Enlightenment* (Edinburgh, 1991), 89-98 («The Discovery of Ferrier»).

renunciation on the part of the most distinguished University of Scotland, of those views which have given it a place, and even a pre-eminence among the seats of Intellectual Philosophy»[22] — his grounds being that on such «agnosiological» grounds proof of God's existence was impossible. Ferrier defended himself and his Scottishness («to the core») in his *Scottish Philosophy, the Old and the New*, published that same year. In his inaugural lecture at Edinburgh eight years after this episode Flint gave cautious praise to Ferrier, but he may well have learned to tread carefully in matters of theological import, and later he took a severe stand against «agnosticism» in lectures he gave in 1880.

A last predecessor of Flint that deserves mention here is James McCosh, whose early career was almost a prototype of Flint's own — education at the University of Glasgow, several years spent in the ministry and missionary activities, efforts as educational reformer, and defense of Scottish philosophy in its latter, evangelical phase. The differences arose from the fact that McCosh, twenty three years older, was an active participant in the Disruption of 1843 and became more deeply involved in educational reform, first at Queens University in Belfast and then in the Presbyterian college of Princeton, of which he was president for the remainder of his life.

Like Flint, McCosh failed to obtain the philosophical appointments he coveted but unlike him refused to settle for positions in theology; while retaining his original evangelical impulse, McCosh's ambition was rather to continue the secular work of the Scottish tradition «from Hutcheson to Hamilton» — and beyond. As he wrote in an American Presbyterian periodical, «[O]f all the departments of natural knowledge, the science of the human mind comes nearest to religion; and of all the mental sciences Moral Philosophy stands in closest relation to Christian Theology»[23]. His own efforts were directed to bringing together the secular and the sacred through a sort of «Intuitive Realism» which, avoiding the extremes of idealism and materialism, would — in the words of his recent biographer — «correct the Scottish philosophy's rationalism and confidence by the Evangelical's sense of human sin and the fact of an omnipotent deity who judges sin»[24]. These words apply equally well to Flint, who was heir to the same tradition of Scottish moral philosophy as modified by nineteenth-century revivalism and continental philosophy — although his own contributions are derivative, and scattered in works devoted to theology and scholarship, and almost never mentioned in this connection.

Like Flint, finally, McCosh had an important scholarly contribution to make — «a contribution to what may be regarded as a new department of science, the history of thought, which is quite as important as the history of wars, of literature, or of civilization»[25]. McCosh made this claim just a year after the appearance of

22 *An Examination of Professor Ferrier's 'Theory of Knowing and Being'* (Edinburgh, 1856).
23 *James McCosh and the Scottish Intellectual Tradition* (Princeton, 1981), 166-67.
24 *James McCosh and the Scottish Intellectual Tradition*, 106.
25 *The Scottish Philosophy: Biographical, Expository, Critical*, III.

Flint's own major work in the history of thought, which (as far as this essay is concerned) constitutes Flint's main claim to fame.

III.

Flint was the most bookish of men — a phenomenally diligent and ambitious scholar, as is attested by the notebooks which he kept from at least 1864 to 1906. These notebooks are filled with reading notes and bibliography (in French, German, and Italian as well as English), exercises in Greek and Hebrew, plans for courses, lectures, and books, examination questions, prayers, and homilies as well as finished drafts of essays, lectures, and sermons. In this unsorted material one finds preparations for many of Flint's major publications and for works projected but never completed — from student papers on natural religion to his plans for his Gifford lectures, which were to be given in 1906-7 but which he was too ill to deliver. These reading notes covered a wide range of authors, including ancient Greek philosophers, seventeenth- and eighteenth-century English philosophers and theologians (not only Locke, Berkeley, and Hume but also Lord Herbert of Cherbury, Cumberland, Clarke, Norris, Butler, and Paley), Kant, Hegel, Hamilton, French Positivists and Socialists, and others. They also touched on many subjects philosophical (epistemology, skepticism, and cosmology), theological (theism, agnosticism, atheism, miracles, and immortality), moral (suicide, «sensitivity», and temperance), social (capital, exchange, wages, and value), and scholarly (Biblical criticism, historiography, and «historiology», or philosophy of history).

Corresponding to Flint's omnivorous and apparently indiscriminate reading was the wide range of courses which he taught (and sermons which he gave) in a professional career extending over half a century. He gave lectures on the history of philosophy, ancient (Chinese and Indian as well as Greek) and modern, on theology and the philosophy of religion, on the philosophy of history, on political economy and socialism, and on the modern encyclopaedia which encompassed all of these subjects — «the relations of the Sciences to one another, to Philosophy, Religion, and Morality». As a teacher he was most conscientious and exacting, depending heavily on examinations and written essays, and he evidently expected students to rehearse precisely the material they were fed from prescribed authors and from the lectures which he delivered from carefully prepared texts. Flint's method, like his own training, was scholastic and authoritarian, and it left small room for original or creative thinking. He permitted himself very little independent speculation; how could he grant such freedom to his impressionable young charges?

This rigorous method was surely reinforced by his commitment to theology and in particular to the doctrines of the Scottish Church, which he served and championed his whole life. It is true that Flint believed in scholarly objectivity, but at the same time — in his teaching and in his books — he never failed to join this with strict judgments arising from his theological convictions. His exposition of the arguments of Sextus Empiricus, for example, was fair and comprehensive, but his judgments were uncompromising; and so were his treatments of Hobbes, Spinoza, Hume, Voltaire, Comte, Marx, and other products of modern secular thought. Because of his theological commitment and pedagogical responsibilities Flint was constrained to defend a providential view of Creation, including the existence of miracles and other evidences of a spiritual world transcending the experience of history, and to devote some of his energies to missionary efforts, including not only indoctrination of students in theology but also «the glorious work of bringing back the lost sheep of the house of Israel into the fold of the Good Shepherd». «The Earth is the Lord's» (a sermon delivered in the east Church of Aberdeen on 18 September 1859) was Flint's first published work; and it expresses well the providentialist and Christocentric conception of the condition of humanity which he retained in all of his work — whether speaking from the lectern or from the pulpit, whether writing for scholarly or for devotional publications.

In his lectures on «anti-theistic theories» he made clear the doctrinal bias underlying all of his work.

> What chiefly threatens us is atheism in the form of agnosticism, positivism, secularism, materialism, etc.; and it does do directly and seriously. The most influential authorities in science and philosophy, and a host of more popular representatives of literature, are strenuously propagating it[26].

For Flint 'the cause of Christianity,' its missionary expansion as well as its intellectual defence, always came first.

IV.

The books published by Flint were virtually all the products of his preaching and his teaching. The was true of his works on theism (his Baird lecture for 1876), on «anti-theistic theories» (a follow-up for 1877), on agnosticism (his «Croall lectures» for 1880), on socialism (from lectures delivered in Edinburgh in 1890 «before an audience chiefly of working men»), on the classification of sciences, and especially on his unfinished masterwork on the philosophy of history in Europe. In 1866 he had been invited by the Philosophical Institute of Edinburgh to give lectures on the history of philosophy, and between 1867 and 1874 he delivered a dozen such prepared talks: four on the progress of the history of philosophy, two on the philosophy of history in its later development, two on Hobbes, two on Spinoza, and two on J. S. Mill.

Flint's career as a historian of ideas began with these early lectures, which were written down, laboriously read (Flint was 'a slave to his paper'), and very likely over the head of most of his lay audience. From them came his major scholarly work, the *History of the Philosophy of History* (1874), translated into

26 *Anti-Theistic Theories* (Edinburgh, 1885, 3rd ed.), 37.

French four years later by Ludovic Carrau, published in expanded form in 1893 as *Historical Philosophy in France and French Belgium and Switzerland*, or (according to another title-page) *The Philosophy of History in Europe, vol. I.* In this later version the book was reviewed widely, and for the most part favorably, in French, German, Dutch, Italian, and Spanish as well as English periodicals[27]. Flint projected a second volume which would have included also German thought, and indeed (as his manuscript notebooks show)[28] he had done reading and planning for this, but he never completed the task.

In this work his declared purpose was «to trace the course of human thought in its endeavors to explain human history; or, in other words, to give an account of the rise and progress of reflection and speculation on the development of humanity»[29]; but it was also to offer critiques of the authors treated in this connection. Flint's works on theism and anti-theism, though more dogmatic and polemical, followed much the same pattern, beginning with consideration of the relevant terminology, the *-isms*, in his words, and proceeding to chronological exposition and criticism. He took up the historical aspect of theism — that is, monotheism, as distinguished from deism — in the article he wrote for the *Encyclopaedia Britannica*, referring not only to the theological debates of the previous two centuries, especially in England and Scotland, but also to modern historical and ethnographic scholarship, including Ernest Renan and Max Müller[30]. Flint acknowledged that there was insufficient evidence to prove a primitive monotheism, but he did insist that there had been a sense of divine unity even in early polytheism; and John Stuart Mill to the contrary notwithstanding, he denied that modern progress had made the world outgrow theistic religion. On the contrary (rehearsing here the old arguments from rational design of Butler and Paley and historical evidence) both nature and history demonstrated the existence of a divine and creator, the worship of which Christianity, as described in Scriptures, was the supreme form. As Flint argued in another lecture, «Christianity is the Absolute Religion, in the sense of the perfect realization of the idea which underlies and gives significance to all religions»[31].

With this conviction in mind Flint pursued the various «anti-theisms», that is, criticisms of religion short of dogmatic atheism, according to which a man «must virtually declare himself a god»[32]. In a long historical perspective Flint saw the beginnings of antitheism in ancient materialism, especially as reflected in the Sophists and Epicurean philosophers, and which found modern descendants in the ideas of Holbach, La Mettrie, French Ideology, and in the Positivism of Auguste Comte. According to Flint, «Positivism is the phenomenalism of the Greek

27 See, e.g., the essay of Flint's translator Ludovic Carrau, «La Philosophie de l'histoire d'après de récens travaux», *Revue des Deux Mondes*, 45 (1875), 568-86.

28 Notebook n. 25 (Edinburgh U., MS 655).

29 *History of the Philosophy of History* (New York, 1894), 1.

30 «Theism», *Encyclopedia Brittanica* (8th ed.).

31 *Christianity in relation to other religions*, 409.

32 *Anti-Theistic Theories* (Edinburgh, 1885, 3rd ed.), 15.

sophists revived and adapted to the demands of the present age»[33]. Not only Comte but also Hume, Kant, and Saint Simon represented this subversive cast of mind. Other forms of antitheism include pantheism (which had been inaugurated by Bruno even before Spinoza), secularism, and pessimism; and Flint traced the history of each of these and described its failings.

Still more threatening was the concept, or anti-concept, which took its name of «agnosticism» (in the ungrammatical coinage of Huxley) from St. Paul's 'unknown god'. Philosophically, agnosticism was the opposite of gnosticism and was a kind of «know-nothingism» which denied the possibility of knowledge — whether of God, of religious belief, or of knowledge of God. Again Flint set this *–ism* in a very long historical perspective, including ancient Chinese, Indian, and Greek skepticism and the 'learned ignorance' of Nicolas of Cusa and others[34]. Among modern authors Kant was a prominent target because of his rational theology and the «imaginary» construct of «pure reason».

V.

It was against this apologetic background, though less explicit, and again in a long perspective of the development of civilization, eastern as well as western, that Flint told the story of historical thought. Throughout his teaching career he sang the praises of history, though by this he often meant just the Bible[35]. In his *Philosophy of History* he began with a survey of history, in practice and theory, as understood from Herodotus and Lucian down to the historical and scientific schools of his own century; and he offered a rich assortment of definitions[36]. History, Flint recited, was «the exhibition of what has happened» (Wilhelm von Humboldt), «the biography of society» (Thomas Arnold), «past politics» (Edward Freeman), «the record of human action» (Mandell Creighton, criticizing Freeman), «the knowledge of the development of men in their workings as human being» (Eduard Bernheim), «the knowledge of the development of reason» (Louis Bourdeau), etc., and «all that men have suffered, thought and executed» (Flint himself).

For Flint history was also a cornerstone of moral education, although for beginners he preferred sacred history over the dry facts of secular strivings. While science could show the wonders of «the starry skies above us», only history (he told an audience of working men) could reveal the greater marvels of «the moral law within us»[37]. Flint was convinced that in order to have meaning and validity, history had to be joined to the «religious spirit». Modern history taught the value of precise

33 *Anti-Theistic Theories*, 176.

34 *Agnosticism* (Edinburgh, 1903), 97; and see Notebooks nos. 11 and 17 and Box no. 1 (Edinburgh MSS 641, 647, 657).

35 «Scientific Education in relation to the Industrial Classes», unpublished lecture (Box no. 1, Edinburgh U., MS 57).

36 *Philosophy of History*, 6ff.

37 «Scientific Education», [8].

evidence and critical techniques, but Flint also recognized the contributions made by his countrymen Walter Scott and that «higher style» of history created by «the greatest of all Scotsman, Mr. Thomas Carlyle»[38]. But as yet, Flint added, no one had told the full story of the development of historiography.

On a higher level than narrative history was the philosophy of history — a phrase derived from Voltaire which enjoyed great currency in the nineteenth century. The philosophy of history, which sought the underlying causes of human development, was almost as old as history itself; but only since the Renaissance, when philosophy became independent of theology, could it appear in modern form. However, none of the first modern philosophers — Bacon, Descartes, Locke, and Spinoza — had any significant ideas about history; indeed it was not until the rise of «scientific history» that a valid philosophy of history could be established. The story of this new secular discipline, which was the main subject of Flint's book, had itself to be told philosophically, that is, with respect to the causes, conditions, and contexts of historical thought and writing. Flint, hoping to rise above an abstract history of ideas, argued that «The historical theories of individual thinkers will always be found largely explicable by the contemporary political conditions of the communities to which these thinkers belong»[39]. Not that this dash of relativism applied to Flint's own 'absolute' religion or his proselytizing concerns, but at least it figured in his assessments of secular and extra-Christian thinking about the human condition.

VI.

History, according to Flint, began with poetry, myth, and primitive efforts of religious expression; and — setting aside the unique experience of Israel — eastern civilizations such as those of China, Japan, and India seemed to him more richly endowed with historical sense and curiosity than the West. By contrast the Greeks had undermined historical awareness through their turn to speculative thought, which subordinated memory to reason and which, as in the case of Thucydides, neglected religious factors in their search for causes of historical change. Christianity enormously enriched and enlarged historical thought, beginning especially with the vision of Augustine and such followers as Orosius and, some seven centuries later, Otto of Freising. As Flint noted,

> What may be called in a lax and general way Augustine's philosophy of history was substantially the only one known in medieval Europe, and it has emerged in modern times with more or less important modification in the hands of Bossuet, Schlegel, and many others[40].

But the Middle Ages was largely innocent of any serious sense of history,

[38] «Scientific Education», [15].
[39] *Philosophy of History*, 35.
[40] *Philosophy of History*, 64.

which, according to Flint, was inseparable from the emergence of the modern European languages. If Adam of Bremen had written in his own tongue, Flint speculated, he might indeed have become «the Herodotus of the north». As it was, despite the efforts of some medieval chroniclers, it was Philip of Commines (as Hallam had judged) who merits recognition as the first modern historian, though he was soon to be surpassed by Machiavelli[41].

Yet even these pioneering historians had not achieved the philosophical sophistication which Flint found in his own age.

> We are no longer content with records of external transactions, but seek also to know the growth of reason and culture themselves, — the development of humanity in all its aspects and activities, industrial, aesthetic, political, moral, religious, and scientific. But all this is modern. The men of medieval times were so ignorant of scientific law and method as to have no conception of any forms of history in which a knowledge of them is implied[42].

One exception was Ibn Khaldun, who was «the first writer to treat history as the proper object of a special science» and who «as a theorist of history had no equal in any age until Vico appeared, more than three hundred years later». Only then did reason and learning finally begin to be joined.

> Vico and Montesquieu were the morning stars of a brighter and broader day, the light of which is now reflected from almost all the historians of recognized ability, not excluding even those who speak despairingly of everything of the nature of historical science in philosophy[43].

In this tradition, too, were contemporary scholars such as George Grote, Ernst Curtius, B. G. Niebuhr, and Theodore Mommsen, who have displayed, Flint continued, «a light not to be found in Herodotus, Thucydides, and Polybius».

What, according to Flint, were the principal attributes of the modern philosophy of history? Most essential was the new science of history as represented by scholars such as Niebuhr and Ranke. Beyond this Flint recognized three fundamental ideas on which historical understanding in the Victorian period depended: the laws of progress, the unity of mankind, and human freedom — ideas which had been formulated in the previous century but which were being realized only in Flint's day[44]. The idea of progress had been unknown to the peoples of the ancient world, including the Jews, though there were intimations of in Augustine, Vincent of Lerins, and Joachim of Flora; that of humanity had antecedents in Roman tradition and the medieval church; the idea of liberty is «as wide as history itself», though it achieved a higher spiritual dimension only under the impulse of the «Christian spirit» and still, according to Flint, lacked full political expression.

41 *Philosophy of History*, 77.

42 *Philosophy of History*, 78.

43 *Philosophy of History*, 77. Flint's tribute is cited by Charles Issawi, in his translations of selections from the *Prolegomena* of Ibn Khaldun, *An Arab Philosophy of History* (Princeton, 1987), 25.

44 *Philosophy of History*, 87-137.

These considerations are all prelude; Flint's main story begins with sixteenth-century France:

> Only when French nationality, civilisation, and literature had reached a certain stage of development could reflection on history make its appearance it France[45].

He reviewed the earlier chroniclers, jurists, memorialists, antiquarians, and political commentators but concluded that «The first writer who took a philosophical view of history was John Bodin». From this point Flint's survey becomes bibliographically exhaustive, with few authors of secondary or even tertiary importance escaping at least brief notice. As a theorist of history Bodin had been preceded by Christoph Milieu, Francesco Patrizi, and other authors included in Johann Wolf's anthology of the «arts of history» (1579). Flint found it «curious», however, that there was no sign of the idea of progress in Bodin's «method» of history[46], nor in that of his (then little-known) successor, the sometime Huguenot Lancelot Voisin de la Popelinière — an author of small talent but of «independent judgment», who wrote critically on the history and the «idea» of history at the end of the sixteenth century. Flint summed up the early modern period in this way:

> The sixteenth century was predominantly an age of pamphlets and occasional writings meant for defense or attack. The seventeenth century was predominantly an age of collections and compilations, and, in a lesser degree, of works designed to gain favour of literature[47].

In general, while historical research made significant progress, neither the art nor the method of history produced important work despite rhetorical treatises on the writing of history, such as those of St. Evremond and Rapin. La Mothe le Vayer «endeavored to find in history confirmation and illustrations of scepticism», but in general the Cartesian spirit had little value for historical understanding, and in fact disciples like Malebranche issued warnings against wasting time reading histories. At most Cartesianism helped, by emphasizing the superiority of the modern age to antiquity, to give currency to the idea of progress.

Where the idea of progress appeared most conspicuously in this early period was the notorious controversy between Ancients and Moderns, «which gave rise to much heat and noise» and many books and which, more importantly, suggested the further question «whether the movement of civilisation was toward improvement or deterioration»[48]. The original contribution of Fontenelle in particular (though Saint Simon and Émile Littré later claimed it as their own discovery) was the notion that

[45] *Philosophy of History*, 175.

[46] *Philosophy of History*, 200. This is contradicted by the famous but more cursory survey of J. B. Bury, *The Idea of Progress* (London, 1920), 39, which also takes Bodin as its main point of departure.

[47] *Philosophy of History*, 203. See D. R. Kelley, «History as a Calling: the Case of La Popelinière», *Renaissance Studies in Honor of Hans Baron* (Florence, 1971), 771-89.

[48] *Philosophy of History*, 213. Flint draws here on the classic work of Henri Rigault, *Histoire de la Querelle des anciens et des modernes* (Paris, 1859).

> the life of each nation has ages corresponding to the life an individual. In infancy individuals and nations are absorbed in the satisfaction of their physical wants; in youth they are chiefly occupied with poetry and art; and in manhood with science and philosophy[49].

Nor, Fontenelle added, was any degeneration from this mature state to be expected. These notions of progress and perfectibility were defended even more enthusiastically by the Abbé de Saint-Pierre and such successors as Turgot and Condorcet. Aside from the work of Bishop Bossuet, which looked back to the old Augustinian plan, this was the most important contribution made by the seventeenth century to the philosophy of history.

VII.

In the eighteenth century philosophy became a mighty force, but in a diluted form virtually to be identified, Flint thought, with public opinion, and in that form came to oppose the French state[50]. French «philosophism» displayed the liveliest interest in the study of history. It is true that «they carried their passions and prejudices» and «their polemical and proselytizing zeal» with them and «grievously erred» in their crude attacks on religion. Yet «in less that half a century far more historico-philosophical writing appeared than in all previous time»[51].

What was most significant in the history-writing of the Enlightenment came not in the large narratives but in studies of historical method and criticism. The work of Lenglet du Fresnoy was the first comprehensive survey of historical method — «the first systematic Historic» (Flint's rendering of the German term, *Historik*) — after two centuries of effort since Bodin's treatise, and its translations into English, Italian, and German were some measure of its success. Another study of «the method of studying history» was that of the popular historian, Charles Rollin, but even less than Lenglet du Fresnoy did he rise above rhetorical convention to a philosophical appreciation of history. In general Flint had little use for advocates of extravagant skepticism like the Jesuit Hardouin, important as was his work in numismatics.

Much more valuable were the contributions of the *érudits*, especially the Benedictines and the Academy of Inscriptions. In the former Montfaucon enlarged the horizons of history by showing the importance of art, while the latter helped raise the history of literature to a scientific level, Nicolas Fréret and La Curne de Saint-Palaye being the most prominent representatives[52]. Most impressive was the

49 *Philosophy of History*, 215.

50 *Philosophy of History*, 240.

51 *Philosophy of History*, 244. So Flint long anticipated the famous refutation of «the common opinion that the eighteenth century was an 'unhistorical' century» by Ernst Cassirer, *The Philosophy of the Enlightenment*, tr. Fritz C. A. Koelln and James P. Pettegrove (Princeton, 1951), 197.

52 *Philosophy of History*, 254ff. See the recent rehabilitations by Lionel Gossman, *Medievalism and the Ideologies of the Enlightenment: The World and Work of La Curne de Sainte-Palaye* (Baltimore, 1968), and Blandine Barret-Kriegel, *Les Historiens et la monarchie* (4 vols.; Paris, 1988).

work of Fréret, who, while avoiding historical pyrrhonism, nonetheless «threw off the fetters of traditionalism» and anticipated best historians living in Flint's own day. Fréret explored geography, religion, mythology, philosophy, historical linguistics, and especially chronology, in which he surpassed Scaliger and other earlies scholars.

In the achievements of historical erudition Flint pointed in particular to the seminal question of the origins and early history of Rome, which was the subject of study by French scholars associated with the Academy of Inscriptions beginning in 1720[53]. First came two inconclusive papers presented by Antoine Anselme and then, more importantly, the dissertation of Pouilly (though he did not know Vico's work) «on the uncertainty of the first four centuries of Roman history», three discourses of the Abbé Sallier, and especially Fréret's «reflections» on the question in 1724. Philosophy for Fréret was not the credulous «spirit of system» but criticism applied to facts in the service of historical proof. On this particular subject Fréret was suspicious of tradition, as contrasted with eyewitness testimony, but argued that Roman history did rest in part on «contemporary records, in the form of inscriptions, acts, treaties, and written registers, from very early times». This French debate, which «marked an epoch in the progress of Historic», was revived in 1738 by Louis de Beaufort, whom Niebuhr later discussed as a «precursor», without mentioning Pouilly or the earlier phase of the controversy and (according to Flint) mistakenly associating Beaufort with the skepticism of Bayle.

There was of course a larger background to this dispute, the topic having been taken up «in a critical spirit» first by Valla and Glareanus and, more profoundly, by Giambattista Vico, who «so remarkably anticipated the conclusions reached by Niebuhr, Mommsen, and others in the present century»[54]. In 1884 Flint published the pioneering study in English of Vico, in which he celebrated in particular Vico's «notion of finding a philosophy in the tools and phrases of Latin speech» and his principle of «the convertibility of truth with fact» — the famous *verum-factum* formula[55]. «For Vico, as for Hegel, the real is rational, and the rational real», Flint concluded[56]. As for the famous Vichian cycles, Flint confessed that

> I could have wished that he had spoken more clearly and more hopefully of the future, but I have been unable to find anything justifying the common

[53] Flint, *loc. cit.*; and see Barret Kriegel, *Les Historiens et la monarchie*, III, *Les Académies de l'histoire*, 221ff.

[54] *Philosophy of History*, 256.

[55] *Vico* (Edinburgh, 1884), 77, 86. Michael Mooney, *Vico in the Tradition of Rhetoric* (Princeton, 1985), 119n, speaks of the «enduringly valuable monograph» of Flint. It had little impact in the Victorian period, as indicated by Isaiah Berlin, *Vico and Herder* (London, 1976), 94; but it is a significant presence in contemporary Vichian scholarship, as suggested, e. g., by Max Harold Fisch and Thomas Goddard Bergin (tr.), *The Autobiography of Giambattista Vico* (Ithaca, 1944), 77, and Donald Verene, «Vico's Science of Imaginative Universals and the Philosophy of Symbolic Forms», in *Giambattista Vico's Science of Humanity*, ed. Giorgio Tagliacozzo and Donald Philip Verene (Baltimore, 1976), 295.

[56] *Vico*, 160.

> representation that he believed that it would be a mere plagiarism of the past, without any new disclosures of the glory of God and the capacities of man[57].

But Vico was an anomaly, and France remained the center of Flint's attention. In particular he turned to three authors who were «the chief initiators of the reflective or philosophical study of history which now prevails». On this basis Montesquieu, Turgot, and Voltaire were elected to the canon which Flint was constructing, if only as precursors. Montesquieu was a highly original writer despite the many sources on which he drew (not including Vico, despite the conjectures of some). Unlike Bossuet, who applied a theological doctrine to history, Montesquieu drew his theory from the facts of history and commendably introduced economics into historical explanation. Unfortunately, Montesquieu overemphasized the influence of physical factors (showing a tendency to the error of «fatalism» so feared by nineteenth-century spiritualists), vacillated between inductive and deductive methods, and failed to offer a clear idea of what he meant by «law».

Not that this was surprising, Flint added: «To those who have never tried to trace the history of ideas this may seem incredible; to those who have it will be in no wise strange», since this ideas had never been defined by either ancients or moderns. Nevertheless, for Flint, this deficiency left Montesquieu's analysis less than scientific and its author undeserving of the claim made by Alexander Alison to be founder either of the philosophy of history or of historical method (as Comte, Henry Maine, and Leslie Stephen had argued); for «He propounded no theory of the general movement of humanity, nor attempted any survey of the course of universal history»[58].

Closer to this ideas was the work of the tweenty-three-year-old Turgot, «one of the wisest and best men of the eighteenth century». The discourses delivered at the Sorbonne in 1750 on the benefits of Christianity and the advances of the human mind made him the friend not only of secular progress but also, unlike his follower «Condorcet and other atheists of the eighteenth century», of religion. Here Flint becomes enthusiastic:

> here, for the first time, the idea of progress was made, as M. Caro has said, 'the organic principle of history'. In contrast to the movement of the physical phenomena of nature [...], history is represented as the life of humanity, ever progressing toward perfection, from generation to generation, from stage to stage, from nation to nation, and by alterations of rest and agitation, success and failure, decay and revival. None before Turgot, and few after him, have described so well how age is bound to age, how generation transmits to generation what it has inherited from the past and won by its own exertions[59].

Turgot's ideas, for which (Flint believed) Condorcet had received undue credit, also anticipated Auguste Comte's famous law of the three stages of history; but

57 Box 1 (Edinburgh U. MS 687).

58 *Philosophy of History*, 273.

59 *Philosophy of History*, 281. Flint's canon has also been followed by Frank Manuel, *The Prophets of Paris: Turgot, Condorcet, Saint-Simon, Fourier, Comte* (Cambridge, Mass., 1962).

unfortunately his political activity did not permit him to realize the profound vision of universal history which he left in his notes dating from this period.

As for Voltaire, Flint could not deny his prominence — «With as much truth as Louis XIV had said 'L'État, c'est moi,' might Voltaire have said, 'Le siècle, c'est moi'» — nor his originality in coining the term 'philosophy of history'[60]. Characteristically, however, Flint very much disapproved of Voltaire's secular cast of mind. It was true that Voltaire became «the first to write a general history in which the *esprit* and *moeurs* of nations were throughout regarded as of more importance than their outward fortunes and actions». Yet he was neither profound nor very original but mainly a popularizer — an educator and a fighter, a reformer and a revolutionist, and not really «philosophical» or (the constant refrain) appreciative of religion and the idea of progress as Flint conceived it. Flint complained that «Voltaire failed to recognize clearly in history a comprehensive plan, a pervasive order, such as implies a Divine will operating through human wills, a first cause working through secondary causes»[61]. Even so, Voltaire had unrivalled «wit and worldly wisdom», and despite his «want of philosophy», he performed a valuable service in shifting the focus of history from politics to culture and in popularizing this view.

Voltaire's conception of civilization was very sincere but also very defective, Flint admitted, and it was no wonder that Rousseau and others should have come to regard it as «a curse instead of a blessing». No less influential than Voltaire, Rousseau was not a historian but only an eloquent advocate of certain historical hypotheses, beginning with his perverse arguments — in a discourse, given the same year as Turgot's, on the progress of the arts in relation to manners in which he emphasized not their advancement but their abuse. Rousseau's influence, partly good and partly bad, was reinforced by the Abbés Morelly and Mably, those champions of equality who had, Flint believed, «laid the foundation of the socialist theory of history»[62].

The eighteenth century produced other efforts to explain the larger patterns of history. One was that of Mably's brother, Condillac, who «represented universal progress as entirely dependent on the use made of language».[63] Other attempts for such large interpretations were based on hypotheses drawn from natural science, including Nicholas Boulanger («probably the first Frenchman influenced to any considerable extent by Vico», Flint speculated)[64], who based his conceptions on the universal Flood; Charles Dupuis, who offered an astronomical explanation of

60 *Philosophy of History*, 294.

61 *Philosophy of History*, 302.

62 *Philosophy of History*, 318. A thesis resumed, e. g., by Maxime Leroy, *Histoire des idées sociales en France*, I (Paris, 1946), 186.

63 *Philosophy of History*, 318.

64 A view no doubt derived from the comparison between Vico and Boulanger in Bonifazio Finetti, *Apologia del genere humano accusato d'essere stato una volta una bestia* (Venice, 1768), on which see Enrico De Mas, «Vico and Italian Thought», in *Giambattista Vico: An International Symposium*, ed. G. Tagliacozzo and H. White (Baltimore, 1969), 152-53.

mythology; and Volney, who, meditating on the revolutions of empires, hoped to substitute science for religion and who was «as decided a positivist as Comte himself, in all respects except in name»[65].

Flint ends his discussion of the eighteenth century with Condorcet, who remained, «amidst all the crimes and sufferings of the Revolution», one of the «sincerest and worthiest of its partisans». For him Progress outweighed Terror, as suggested in 1794 by his final profession of faith, his problematical belief in «perfectibility» and in the indefinite prolongation of human life — an error pointed out in the critique of C. A. Walckenaer (1798). Flint notes that between Turgot and Condorcet there were other celebrations of the idea of progress «of a somewhat kindred nature», including those of Isaac Iselin, J. D. Wegelin, Kant, J. G. Herder, and Joseph Priestley as well as his own countrymen, Adam Ferguson and Lord Kames; but in fact, Flint judged, Condorcet's only teacher was Turgot. Here, finally, Flint finds a comprehensive statement — albeit quite superficial, distressingly secularist, and implicitly socialist — of the idea and law of progress.

Neither the revolutionary nor the Napoleonic period was, with a few exceptions such as Daunou and Mme. de Staël, much favorable to the study of history, but the return of the monarchy changed this. «Consequently», Flint wrote, «when freedom returned with the Restoration, it soon appeared that there had been growing up diverse systems of opinion, all resting on, or at least involving, general theories of history»[66]. This was especially evident in philosophy, in which Victor Cousin's remarkably successful Eclecticism, which arose in reaction to the excesses of rationalism, «professed to be the outcome of all the philosophies of the past». Similar revisions could be seen in religious thought, especially as represented by Chateaubriand and other Catholic conservatives; in literature, which had renewed itself on the basis of nationalist and romanticism ideas; in politics, in which liberalism and constitutionalism was on the rise; and above all in historiography, which Augustin Thierry, Prosper de Barante, François Guizot, François Mignet, Adolphe Thiers, and Jules Michelet set on a new course.

VIII.

Coming finally to his own century, Flint divides historical science and historical philosophy into conventional schools: the Ultramontane and Liberal Catholic; the Socialistic; the Spiritualistic; the Democratic; the Naturalistic and Positivistic; the Democratic; and the Critical. Each of these schools, with its many members and fellow-travellers, receives extensive exposition and criticism on the route to Flint's own system, which, though ultimately unrealized, may be discerned in outline from what, according to his curious combination of eclectic and dogmatic methods, he sanctions and what he rejects.

65 *Philosophy of History*, 325.
66 *Philosophy of History*, 340.

The views of the Ultramontane, otherwise known as traditionalist or theocratic, school must be extricated from the theologico-political polemic of its chief representatives, who were De Maistre, Bonald, and (for a time) Lamennais. This party began with a passionate aversion to the eighteenth century and its «satanic» yet «providential» culmination, as De Maistre regarded it, in the Revolution, which for him was (we might say) the nineteenth-century counterpart of the holocaust[67]. De Maistre and Lamennais denounced the materialist turn that philosophy had taken since Descartes and Locke, and they looked above and beyond the human measure for an understanding of human experience. Society was natural, but as an organism, not a human creation such as a machine. Flint noted that this theory was identical with that of the Historical School and added that «De Maistre was the most notable French precursor of Savigny, the founder of that school»[68]. But these traditionalists were also proponents of absolutism and papal supremacy, and here Flint — like the French people in 1830 as well as his own Calvinist forebears — rejected their extravagant arguments as reconcilable neither with science nor with the Scriptures which they alleged.

Not all conservatives were both absolutist and ultramontane, and Flint note two authors who displayed just one of these proclivities. Under the Napoleonic regime Count Ferrand, an absolutist in politics but at the same time a critic of the papacy, wrote four-volume works both on the «Spirit of history», in the form of letters to his son, and on the «theory of revolutions», in which he denounced both Napoleon and the revolutionary and anti-religious heritage on which he built. On the other hand Ballanche was a theocrat but not an absolutist and, moreover, perhaps the first Frenchman before Michelet to have an insight into the thought of Vico. For Ballanche (a believer in metempsychosis) the basic pattern of history was produced by the conflict between patricians and plebeians and the sacred and unchanging tradition of Christian religion.

Among the writers in the Liberal Catholic party Flint pays special attention to the Abbé Gratry, who was another admirer of Vico and who aspired to construct on that basis a «new science of history». This «Christian Vico» had an optimistic and naively moralistic theory of progress by the exercise of free will and abstention from vice, and while Flint finds his ideas commonplace, he judged his sentiments at least to be commendable. In general Flint commended the spirit of Liberal Catholicism and its vision of history and lamented its later demise in the wake of «the disastrous pontificate of Pius IX»[69].

The Socialistic Schools were much more problematic and eventually led Flint to undertake a full-scale study in the last decade of the century. The contribution of Saint-Simon, building especially on Condorcet's ideas of progress and perfectibility, was in his historical insights, unrealized as they were, and especially in «assigning to the science of history a clearly defined place in the general system

67 *Philosophy of History*, 369.
68 *Philosophy of History*, 375.
69 *Philosophy of History*, 387.

of sciences» — and doing so in a more consistent way than his follower Comte. Too much might be made of his originality, for as Flint noted, referring to Fourier and Azais, «The social atmosphere seems to have been full of ideas of this kind when he wrote»[70]. Flint of course could not condole Saint-Simon's transfer of religious values to a future secular civilization; and he passed similar judgments on other members of this school, including Fourier, Buchez, Leroux, and Proudhon, whose doctrines, especially the idea of progress culminating in social equality, he expounded at some length.

IX.

In the 1890s Flint wrote a book on this subject based on lectures delivered to make socialism intelligible to an audience of workingmen. He traced the history of the term (from Pierre Leroux and Robert Owen), described the Social Question — wars between rich and poor, masters and servants, labor and capital — which had given birth to the doctrine; and he offered extended critiques of its chief theoreticians, including Marx, whose «unscientific» concept of labor value and the conclusions drawn from it he pronounced fallacious; labor alone produces nothing. As for socialist schemes of organization, «It is simply comical to hear Communism preached by revolutionists and anarchists»[71]. Every country had produced such, he remarked, and «all these countries supply the United States of America with it»[72]. Nor was the threat merely theoretical, for:

> If the workingmen of the large towns of the country were, as a body, to adopt the principles which have at certain periods swayed the minds of the workmen of Paris and Lyons [...], utter anarchy would be inevitable[73].

Not that Flint rejected the values of democracy, solidarity, and progress, but he took a more conventional and legalistic view of these principles.

> When we get, if we ever get, to manhood and womanhood suffrage, then, but only then, shall we be strictly a Democracy; and even then only in what may be called the lower sense of the term[74].

As for social solidarity, «Nationalism is a great and sacred fact», and Socialism could only detract from this ancient principle, as indeed from the family, democracy, morality, and, above all, religion. In the end Flint preferred Condorcet's to Marx's idea of human progress, though he still believed that it was part of the mission of the church.

70 *Philosophy of History*, 401.

71 *Socialism*, 41.

72 *Socialism*, 27.

73 *Anti-Theistic Theories* (Edinburgh, 1885, 3rd ed.), 36.

74 *Anti-Theistic Theories*, 205.

X.

The main rival of Socialism (to return to Flint's *Philosophy of History*) was the Eclectic and 'spiritualist' philosophy of Victor Cousin and his disciples, which indeed became virtually the official ideology of the July Monarchy. For Cousin as for Hegel, but in a more open fashion, history was the development of reflective intelligence, and its method of study was an eclectic combination of empiricism and idealism. It was Cousin and not (as Mill thought) Comte who saw «the necessity of connecting all our generalisations from history with the laws of human nature»[75]. Flint summarized and added his own criticisms to Cousin's Hegelian ideas, especially those concerning the role of great men as embodiments of, rather than contributors to the historical process. What Flint especially disliked in Cousin, as in Hegel, was the misplaced optimism leading to the view that civilization gains by every error and every war; nor did he agree with Cousin's disciple Jouffroy that wars were about to cease; for not only had there been subsequent civil wars in America, France, and Spain, but even at this time (the 1890s) the peoples of Europe were again preparing to fight.

Flint was more impressed by Cousin's colleague and follower, Théodore Simon Jouffroy, whose essay on «The Present State of Humanity» was «almost perfect. Jouffroy's philosophy of history was based on Cousinian distinctions between spontaneous and reflective thought, the latter reserved for the philosophers, whose mission was to comprehend the past and to prepare for the future; and between barbarism and civilization, the latter reserved for the Christian nations of France, England, and Germany. Jouffroy was wrong in thinking «that the whole of history is, in the last analysis, only the history of ideas». This was too optimistic: there were also emotions, which undermined intelligence. Nor did Flint agree with Jouffroy's judgments about France, England, and Germany; for Italy was almost on a par with these states, and others may well be on the rise[76].

Corresponding to Eclecticism in philosophy was «doctrinarianism» in politics. Flint was a particular admirer of Cousin's friend and co-beneficiary of the revolution of July 1830, François Guizot, for his efforts in exploring, along lines suggested by the leader of the German Historical School of Law, K. F. von Savigny, both the physiology and the physiognomy of history and «the truly scientific spirit and character of his method»[77]. Yet Flint thought Guizot deficient in his choice of France alone to exemplify the entire history of civilization and thought he would have done better to make comparisons with other European nations — as indeed Flint himself was planning to do. Guizot's major theme, the

[75] *Philosophy of History*, 458.

[76] *Philosophy of History*, 488: «The possibilities before the United States and Russia are so grand that no mortal has a right to deny that the time may come when the mightiest power by sea at present will be doomed to stand before the one, and the mightiest on land before the other, like Hector before Achilles, able only in presence of the stronger and more heaven-favoured foe to resolve, 'not inglorious at least shall I perish, but after doing some great thing that may be spoken of in ages to come'.

[77] *Philosophy of History*, 508.

idea of progress, was also taken more directly in two other works which Flint found worthy of comment, Javary's *Idea of Progress* (1851), which was the first good treatment of the subject, and Bouillier's *Morality and Progress*, which anticipated the notorious theories of Buckle. All of these, for Flint's taste, lamentably underestimated the spiritual dimension of progress. An exception to this criticism, he added, was Carrau (who also happened to be his own translator)[78].

The two great champions of the «democratic historical school» were Jules Michelet and Edgar Quinet, *protégés* of Cousin, whose careers were intertwined in so many ways[79]. Michelet's idea of history, drawing on Vico (whose work he translated), was «a generalisation of the history of Rome»; Quinet's, drawing on Herder (whose work he translated), was an elaboration of the concept of free will — the progress of the *Moi*. Both authors applied their original sources of inspiration to histories, grandly conceived, of France; and both contributed to the further reinforcement of the prevailing idea of progress, although their optimism, excessive for Flint's taste, was perhaps chastened by the experience of 1848.

Eclipsing the romantic views of Michelet and Quinet were the new doctrines of naturalism and positivism, which reproduced the sensationalist ideas of the eighteenth century. Here Flint pointed first to Charles Comte, whose idea of the physical development underlying history «was as great an advance on Montesquieu's had been on Bodin»[80]. More famous were the theories of Charles Comte's brother Auguste, who was likewise a beneficiary of eighteenth-century ideas. For the younger Comte history was only a part of a larger science, which was social physics or sociology, and once again it was the idea and 'law' of progress that haunted and dominated Comtean Positivism and that led Flint to extended commentary. Among the disciples of Comte, Flint placed not only Lafitte amd Littré but also Sainte-Beuve, Taine, and even Renan, whose approach to history, despite his ambitious claims, was less «scientific» than «intuitive».

Finally comes the critical school, headed by Cournot and Renouvier, whose aim, following the efforts of Reid and especially Kant, was to remedy the sorry condition in which philosophy was left ever since the destruction wrought by Hume on speculative thought. Cournot limited his philosophy to the modern period and joined it to a «faith in a self-perfecting development of humanity»; and while admiring Cournot's independence and sagacity, Flint rejected his secular line of argument, which overlooked the force of conscience and moral freedom[81]. More impressive to Flint was the work of Renouvier, much superior to that of Comte, especially his «analytical philosophy of history» (1864), whose emphasis on religion — and whose opposition to «all theories of physical and mechanical, fatalistic and predestinarian necessitarianism»[82] — suited Flint's

[78] *Philosophy of History*, 517.
[79] *Philosophy of History*, 530ff.
[80] *Philosophy of History*, 577.
[81] *Philosophy of History*, 654.
[82] *Philosophy of History*, 666.

own conception of the human past and its meaning. Never managing to finish this work, Flint did not even get around to setting down this conception in his own words, but it seems likely that the «criticist» doctrine which he attributed to Renouvier came closest to expressing his own projected, though never perfected, philosophy of history.

XI.

For his intentions and efforts, if not for the character of his achievements — Flint should be placed in the great tradition of Scottish philosophy from Hutcheson to McCosh, but he was waylaid by scholarly preoccupations arising from that «science of history» produced in the nineteenth century, and even in that mode, perhaps, his philosophical acume was deficient. As R. G. Collingwood put it, Flint's book was

> limited to a collection and discussion of views put forward by other writers, and although they are learned and painstaking works, they throw little light on the subject, for Flint never properly thought out his own point of view, and consequently his criticism of others is superficial and unsympathetic[83].

The criticism is just; but what Collingwood means, of course, is that Flint did not incorporate his judgments of other authors into his own philosophy of history; and some historians might conclude that (in contrast, for instance, to Collingwood's efforts to throw his own light on the subject) Flint's expositions of philosophers of history were all the more reliable for this reason (we do not turn to Collingwood for a *history* of German thought).

Moreover, Flint did have a large vision of the nature and history of thought; but it was very different from that of his Scottish antecedents and from Collingwood — being encyclopedic in an old-fashioned sense rather than philosophical in a modern academic and metaphysical sense. This vision appears most clearly in Flint's major publication on the old question of the classification of the sciences. Here he presented the sciences as «members of a magnificent system» set between the extremes of Positivism and Hegelian idealism, placed in a perspective going back to Plato, and yet oriented toward the demands of the future[84]. Flint traced such efforts from antiquity to modern times, including Varro, Cassiodorus, Isidore of Seville, Poliziano, Nizolio, Campanella, and of course Bacon, whose ideas he found best expressed in the encyclopedia of Johann Alsted. Approaching more recent times, however, this study, like the *Philosophy of History*, could not extricate itself from the historiography of the topic; and it remained, like Flint's own idea of intellectual progress, incomplete, weighted down by unmanageable bibliography and the realization that, as he wrote wearily,

[83] *The Idea of History* (Oxford, 1946), 142-43.

[84] *Philosophy as Scientia Scientiarum: A History of the Classification of the Sciences* (London, 1904), 3. The work was published in part in the *Presbyterian Review* (1885).

«There is no likelihood of there being fewer attempts at the classification of sciences in the present than in the past century»[85].

Flint had definite ideas about philosophy, too, and divided it into four parts: positive (the coordination of the sciences), critical (criticism of knowledge), metaphysical (theory of being and becoming), and practical (theory of final causes)[86]. For him of course philosophy was also tied to theology; and his theoretical efforts, devoted to theism and its enemies, placed him in the tradition of William Paley and Thomas Chalmers rather than of Hume and Hamilton. Yet this same tradition also inclined him toward historical scholarship, in which he hoped to find, if not wisdom itself, then at least evidence for the wisdom that he had received from his religious faith and a view of history that was in harmony with this faith.

In breadth and depth of erudition, if not in quality and relevance of philosophical thinking, Flint had few peers in the nineteenth century. One of the most distinguished of these was his close contemporary, Lord Acton — who knew, admired, and reviewed Flint's work and was equally devoted to the ideals of liberty and progress[87]. The difference was that Flint's professional obligations forced him to a literary production that was at least quantitatively superior to that of the equally devout and learned English Catholic scholar. Recognizing the «unchallenged superiority» of Flint's work, Acton invited him to write the final chapter for the projected twelve-volume *Cambridge Modern History*, but Flint neither wrote that chapter nor finished his own work on the assigned topic, which was of course the philosophy of history in Europe.

Nevertheless, it is clear in reading Flint's masterwork what shape this philosophy would take: it would tell the story of mankind as an endless struggle for liberty, of the workings of providence in this story, and of moral progress that represents its secular denouement. In these principles Acton saw the «master-key» to Flint's book[88]. It is unfortunate that this theodicean vision, like Acton's, remained a «madonna of the future» — a vision of the history of ideas not only as an offshoot of philosophy but, in an age of «science» and «criticism», its very incarnation. Enough, perhaps, that he, like Acton, should be granted an honorable place in the chronicles of historical scholarship, in particular in the field that is still, in some quarters, known as the history of ideas.

85 *Philosophy as Scientia Scientiarum*, 326-27.

86 Notebook 26 (Edinburgh U, MS 657), unpaginated.

87 *Essays in the Study and Writing of History*, ed. J. Rufus Fears (Indianapolis, 1985), II, 461-503.

88 *Essays in the Study and Writing of History*, II, 503.

X

THE SCIENCE OF ANTHROPOLOGY: AN ESSAY ON THE VERY OLD MARX

Marx's lifelong associations with anthropology are numerous and mutually illuminating. Historically, according to the commonest view, the rise of anthropology occurred in the middle years of the nineteenth century—and so of Marx's own life. At the time of his birth (1818) this field was still part of general philosophy; by the time of his death (1883) it had declared its independence as a separate discipline. What is more, the development of Marx's thought followed a similar trajectory from a philosophically "idealist" to a positive and "scientific" approach to man, as most of his contemporaries regarded this transformation. As a teen-age student at the University of Berlin, Marx took a course in "Anthropologie" with H. Steffans as part of his studies toward a law degree; and several of his early publications were directly or indirectly concerned with the sort of theoretical anthropology taught in conjunction with philosophy and jurisprudence.[1] His interests in the field continued in various ways throughout his life but emerged most prominently in his last years, when he began amassing notes on a quartet of modern anthropologists (Lewis Henry Morgan, Henry Sumner Maine, John Lubbock, and John Budd Phear), presumably in order to devote a more systematic work to anthropology in the context of his own social philosophy.[2] That work was never begun, though Engels continued some of these lines of investigation, and so the direction of Marx's thought is largely a matter of speculation. About the provenance and development of his anthropological thinking, however, we are much better informed; and it is to this question, the genesis of Marx's anthropological thought, that this paper is devoted.

I. *Marx and the Two Anthropological Traditions.*—Ideological controversies aside, the tendency which has done most to obstruct a historical understanding of Marx's thought has been to select an artificial or stereotyped perspective based on a superficial reconstruction of particular academic fields, especially philosophy, political thought, sociology, and economics.[3] The trouble is not that such views are incorrect but that

[1] *Index lectionum . . . in Universitate Friderica Guilelma* (Berlin, 1927), and see my earlier discussion, "The Metaphysics of Law: An Essay on the Very Young Marx," *American Historical Review*, **83** (1978), 350-67.

[2] *The Ethnological Notebooks of Karl Marx*, ed. Lawrence Krader (Assen, 1972), hereafter referred to as "*EN*"; and see below note 36.

[3] There is to my knowledge no satisfactory study of Marx's thought based on a comprehensive investigation of his learning; in any case this is no place for Marxian bibliography except as it bears on specific points.

they are inadequate. Marx cannot be appreciated in terms of twentieth-century textbook interpretations of the history of thought or of disparate branches thereof. More than most thinkers he was the product of a vast array of learning, not only modern knowledge and what we may sanction today as significant or "scientific" but also areas of pre-scientific and pre-Revolutionary erudition and speculation that we would hardly be aware of—except when we try to appreciate the perspective of omnivorous minds like Marx's. The point is that he struggled through and against, and tried to re-fashion or liberate himself from, an immense part of the western intellectual heritage—in some ways indeed recapitulated its development from the old regime to the age of Darwin—and if we hope to appreciate his accomplishment we must be aware of the extent and variety of his efforts.

Somewhat the same sort of criticism might be made about the history of anthropology itself, which likewise has been foreshortened and in a sense idealized, often resembling hagiography more than historiography. Anthropology, too, has a richer and certainly more ancient heritage than is suggested by myopic surveys such as the recent book by Marvin Harris.[4] In general, like other human sciences (most notably psychology and medicine but also law, politics, and perhaps political economy), anthropology has a dual heritage, one legitimate (so to speak) and the other illegitimate. The latter type, going back to the efforts of Herodotus and Pausanias, was empirically more solid but lacked academic credentials. The orthodox tradition is represented by "philosophical anthropology" understood in a general sense, which is to say a theory of human nature.[5] This tradition may be traced from the Greeks (especially the Sophists)

[4] *The Rise of Anthropological Theory* (New York, 1968). Standard surveys include Robert H. Lowie, *The History of Ethnological Theory* (New York, 1937), T. K. Penniman, *A Hundred Years of Anthropology* (New York, 1974), Annemarie de Waalmalefijt, *Images of Man* (New York, 1974), Fred W. Voget, *A History of Ethnology* (New York, 1975), Edward Evans-Pritchard, *A History of Anthropological Thought* (New York, 1981), and, most balanced and broadminded, Murray J. Leaf, *Mind, Man and Science* (New York, 1977); but none of these is of much use for present purposes. For the eighteenth- and nineteenth-century background see Georges Gusdorf, *Introduction aux sciences humaines* (Paris, 1974) and *Les Sciences humaines et la pensée occidentale*, VIII (Paris, 1978); also René Hubert, *Les Sciences sociales dans l'Encyclopédie* (Paris, 1923), and Michele Duchet, *Anthropologie et histoire au siècle des lumières* (Paris, 1971), as well as George W. Stocking, Jr., *Race, Culture and Evolution* (New York, 1968), esp. ch. 2.

[5] Notably Kant's *Anthropology from a Pragmatic Point of View*, trans. V. Dowell (Carbondale, Ill., 1978) and Hegel (work cited below, note 12). For this tradition the most recent studies are Michael Landmann, *De Hominis, Der Mensch im Spiegel seines Gedankens* (Munich, 1962), ix; also his *Philosophical Anthropology*, trans. D. Parent (Philadelphia, 1974); Eric Rothaker, *Einleitung in die Wissenschaften* (Tübingen, 1930) and *Probleme der Kulturanthropologie* (Bonn, 1965), and esp. *Neue Anthropologie*, 7 vols., ed. Hans Gadamer and Paul Vogler (Stuttgart, 1972-75), with volumes devoted to biological, social, cultural, psychological and philosophical anthropology. Why the sketchy and inadequate article in the *Dictionary of Philosophy* (VI, 159) says that "Modern philosophical anthropology: originated in the 1920s" is a mystery to me; M. J. Perry in his translation, Hegel's *Philosophy of Subjective Spirit* (Dordrecht, 1978), I, lxiii-v, lists 47 books on the subject in German, besides Hegel's, from 1800 to 1832.

through a Renaissance reflowering (when the term itself became current) through more formal expressions in German idealism, most notably Herder, Kant, Hegel, and the young Marx himself. By the eighteenth century empirical ethnology and theoretical anthropology overlapped, for instance in the *Encyclopédie*, but the distinction continued to hold well into the nineteenth century.

The "anthropology" with which Marx first became familiar was the old-fashioned theoretical (especially Hegelian) variety, which focussed on self-knowledge—the Subjective Spirit. In fact at Hegel's headquarters, the University of Berlin, the subject was taught in all the faculties—theology, medicine and law as well as philosophy—and the emphasis depended on the professional field which it served to introduce. For medicine "anthropology" meant a deterministic approach to the animal side of man; for theology, the soul with its attributes of free will and potential for grace; and for jurisprudence, a sort of mean between the two, conceiving of man as subject to natural laws yet capable also of moral choice.[6] In the faculty of jurisprudence "anthropology," though taught by a theologian in Marx's time (1836-38), served as a logical introduction to the art of judgment and legislation, on the assumption that an understanding of human nature was necessary to a theory of society and social control. This basic premise (though surely not this orthodox formulation) Marx retained throughout his lifelong search for a systematic science of society.

The academic starting point of Marx's long intellectual pilgrimage, then, was jurisprudence, and this self-proclaimed "science" represented his first philosophical as well as professional calling. At the University of Berlin he studied with the two giants of jurisprudence, the Hegelian Eduard Gans and Friederich Karl von Savigny, leader of the "historical school of law." Elsewhere I have tried to show that jurisprudence was crucial for the young Marx—that indeed his first intellectual crisis was worked out in the context of the conflict between Savigny's "realism" and Gans' "idealism," which Marx observed in the classroom in 1837 and which burst upon the public two years later over Savigny's famous thesis on the law of possession.[7] Marx was attracted by Savigny's emphasis on "positive" research and Gans' sensitivity to social justice, but he soon rejected the juridical "ideology" to which both were attached in favor of a more "scientific" approach to social problems. This break with legal orthodoxy was declared most unmistakably in a polemical article which

[6] Marx-Engels, *Collected Works* (New York, 1975), I, 703; hereafter referred to as "*CW*." For the theologican Schleiermacher, who also taught at Berlin, "anthropology" was located, and formed a sort of bridge, between *Ethik* and *Physik*, according to Dilthey's biography in his *Gesammelte Schriften*, XIV (Leipzig, 1970), 260.

[7] See Marx's famous letter to his father, 10-11 Nov. 1837, in *CW*, I, 10-21; and Max Lenz, *Geschichte der königlicher Friedrich-Wilhelms-Universität zu Berlin* (Halle, 1910), II, 834; also Manfred Riedel, "Eduard Gans als Schüler Hegels. Zur politischen Auslegung des Rechtsphilosophie," *Rivista di filosofia*, **68** (1977), 234-68, and my article (cited above, note 1). The work in question is Savigny, *Das Recht des Besitzes* (Berlin, 1865; 7th ed.).

also reveals most clearly the position of the young Marx on "anthropology." "The Philosophical Manifesto of the Historical School of Law" took as its central target not Savigny (recently appointed minister of justice) but Savigny's elder colleague Gustav Hugo.[8] The choice was appropriate as well as diplomatic, for Hugo's multi-volume treatise on civil law had indeed laid the philosophical foundations (and revealed the counterrevolutionary inclinations) of the *Historische Rechtsschule.* The particular object of Marx's wrath was the second volume of this work, provocatively entitled *Natural Law as a Philosophy of Positive Law.*[9] And the center of this target was the introductory section, which—representing the "metaphysical" underpinnings of the system—Hugo called "juristische Anthropologie."

II. *Gustav Hugo and "Juristic Anthropology"*—Hugo's "anthropology" was ancillary as well as philosophical. According to his assumptions, as to those of Savigny and Gans, jurisprudence encompassed a whole world of learning, theoretical and practical; and it still had ties with the grand tradition of legal systematizing going back (as Hugo and Savigny both traced it) through the early modern "Systematiker" and medieval scholastics to the great constructs of Romano-Byzantine jurisprudence.[10] In the eighteenth and nineteenth centuries these constructs, conventionally called juristic "systems" or "encyclopedias," continued to proliferate and indeed formed part of the basis of Marx's own introductory training.[11] Of these systems the most famous, in part because of the critical attention devoted to it by Marx, was that of Hugo, which contained a "juristic encyclopedia" and a history of civil law as well as the book on the philosophy of positive law.

[8] "The Philosophical Manifesto of the Historical School of Law," in *CW,* I, 203-10; and cf Christoph Schefold, *Die Rechtsphilosophie des jungen Marx von 1842* (Munich, 1970), and Hasso Jaeger, "Savigny et Marx," *Archives de philosophie du droit,* **12** (1967), 65-89. On Savigny the bibliography is enormous, but see the recent discussion in Peter Stein, *Legal Evolution* (Cambridge, 1980), and especially *Quaderni fiorentini per la storia del pensiero giuridico moderno,* **9** (1980), "Su Federico Carlo di Savigny."

[9] Gustav Hugo, *Lehrbuch des Naturrechts als einer Philosophie des positiven Rechts* (Berlin, 1809; 3rd ed.), hereafter "*LNR,*" which is volume 2 of his *Lehrbuch eines civilistischen Cursus* (43, on "juristische Anthropologie"). In general see F. Eichengrün, *Gustav Hugos Rechtslehre* (The Hague, 1935); A. Buschmann, *Ursprung und Grundlagen des geschichtlichen Rechtswissenschaft: Untersuchungen und Interpretationen zur Rechtslehre Gustav Hugo* (Krefeld, 1935); J. Blühdorn, "Naturrechtskritik und 'Philosophie des positiven Rechts,' zur Begründung des Jurisprudenz als positiven Fachtswissenschaft durch Gustav Hugo," *Tijdschrift voor Rechtsgeschiedenis,* **40** (1974), 3-17; and especially Giuliano Marini, *L'Opera di Gustav Hugo nella crisi del giurnaturalismo tedesco* (Milan, 1969). Hugo's terminology was consciously adopted by the author of a more famous book, John Austin, *Lectures on Jurisprudence, or the Philosophy of Positive Law* (London, 1851).

[10] *Das Recht des Besitzes,* 10, as well as *Geschichte des römischen Rechts,* 6 vols. (Heidelberg, 1815-31).

[11] Savigny, *System des heutigen römischen Rechts,* 6 vols. (Berlin, 1840-51); C. F. Mühlenbruch, *Doctrina Pandectarum* (Halle, 1830-31); and J. G. Heineccius, *Elementa juris civilis secundum ordinem Institutionem* (Marburg, 1727), and *Elementa juris civilis secundum ordinem Pandectarum* (Amsterdam, 1731).

The notion of "encyclopedia" is both the key to Hugo's social philosophy and the basis of the old tradition of anthropology from which Marx was trying to extricate himself. It was the descendant, of course, of the classical *encyclopaideia*, which consisted in many schemes of three sciences, namely, logic, physics, and ethics—with ethics itself being subdivided into the disciplines of politics, economics, and "ethics in the stricter sense," or moral philosophy.[12] It was to the last part of the encyclopedia that law belonged. Like any field with philosophical pretensions (here Hugo follows Kant as well as Aristotle) law had a theoretical (*reine*) as well as practical (*angewandte*) aspect; and the theory of law rested on the famous distinction of the classical jurist Ulpian, which equated it with "the knowledge of things divine and human (*divinarum atque humanarum rerum notitia*), or wisdom (*sapientia*).[13] This concept, celebrated and elaborated on for centuries, was taken by Hugo as the equivalent of "juristic anthropology," that is, a theory of human nature of use to both judges and legislators. According to Hugo, this theory of human nature stood in the same relation to law as metaphysics did to general philosophy, and so it provided the axiomatic and structural basis for a system of universal jurisprudence and, by extension, social philosophy. These were the claims which had first raised, and then dashed, Marx's hopes.

Hugo's work, overshadowed by that of Savigny and undermined by Marx's caustic critique, has not been fully appreciated, especially for Marx's "materialist" line of thought. Hugo was a product of the Göttingen tradition, which had turned more or less self-consciously away from speculative philosophy (à la Leibniz and Wolf) to "common sense," to "experience," and most conspicuously to the study of history.[14] What was a general inclination in Göttingen philologists, historians and other jurists became with Hugo a deliberate campaign against the hegemony of old-fashioned natural law philosophy, whether associated with enlightened despotism or revolutionary ideals. As an admirer of Montesquieu, a translator of Gibbon, and a critic of the Kantian school of jurisprudence (though not critical of Kant himself), Hugo was a pioneer in the assault not only on idealism, especially the Hegelian variety, but also on the whole "jusnaturalistic" syndrome referred to imprecisely as the "Philosophical School." In short, Hugo seemed opposed to the very same sort of idealist fallacy as the young Marx and indeed referred to it in virtually the same terms, the "metaphysics of law" (*Metaphysik der Rechtslehre*).[15]

[12] E. g., Heineccius, *Elementa Philosophiae*, in *Opera omnia* (Geneva, 1775), I. Hegel's own "Anthropologie" forms the second volume of his *Enzyklopädie der philosophischen Wissenschaften* (see above, note 6).

[13] *LNR*, 1, citing Digest I, 1, 1; and see my "Vera Philosophia: The Philosophical Significance of Renaissance Jurisprudence," *Journal of the History of Philosophy*, **14** (1976), 267-79.

[14] Essential for Background are Marini, *L'Opera di Gustav Hugo*, 94ff, and the chapters in Stintzing-Landsberg, *Geschichte der deutschen Rechtswissenschaft*, Abt. III, Halbbd. 2 (Munich, 1898) and 3 (Munich, 1910).

[15] Marini, *op cit.*, 167.

Hegel himself responded to this criticism, and after his death in 1831 Gans took over the defense, but Hugo had equally strong support among scholars like Savigny and Niebuhr and various literary figures, including Goethe.

Such were the beginnings of the "Historical School of Law," whose weaknesses were so sharply revealed, as its strengths were overlooked, by Marx. Yet the impetus of the Historical School toward "positive" and comparative studies were surely significant for Marx as a young law student, as it was (for instance, through the work of the brothers Grimm) for the infant field of ethnology.[16] What really irritated Marx were the political implications of a philosophical appeal to historical experience. Without a historical base, Hugo argued, law was "mere metaphysics" (*bloss Metaphysik*); and so he turned from the abstractions of natural law to the richer repository of positive law, including aspects of the "law of nations."[17] In general it was through a historical and comparative study of this international field, conventionally identified with universal history, that Hugo hoped to reconstruct, in a positive and historical fashion, a more valid and viable sort of "natural law." In this connection, too, Hugo presented a survey of the tradition, or at least antecedents, of such positive-natural law.[18] He admired few of them; even Montesquieu was "too little learned in the law." Among recent authors Hugo also recognized the party of the *philosophes*, the economists (*die Physiocraten oder Economisten*), various opponents of private property (*Gegner des PrivatEigenthums*) as well as better known English and German philosophers, notably Kant and Fichte; but none of them had caught the right balance between positive and rational science—between the real and the ideal.

Hugo's aim was to transcend and to supplant the old legal tradition, so long divided between antiquarians and rationalists. For Hugo jurisprudence had to be useful to the businessman (*GeschäfftsMann*) as well as to the scholar (*Gelehrter*), and he cited a contemporary jurist to the effect that "the law of nature was cited in the courts as unfrequently as the metaphysical laws of motion were used in the factories."[19] What is more, he generally opposed the imposition of the methods and standards of natural science upon the social, or in terms more appropriate to that age, the "moral sciences." In particular Hugo referred to the view of Hume that however inappropriate to "the speculative sciences of metaphysics, natural philosophy or astronomy," an appeal to "general opinion" was entirely justified "in all questions with regard to morals, as well as criticism." The immediately following reference to Kant suggested also that there was a kind of philosophical justification for this view,

[16] The only recent survey to appreciate the role of Savigny is Leaf (work cited above, note 4), ch. 5.

[17] *LNR*, 4.

[18] *LNR*, 22ff. Cf. P. H. Reill, *The German Enlightenment and the Rise of Historicism* (Berkeley, 1975), 71, and Landsberg, *op. cit.*, III, ch. 13.

[19] *LNR*, 29, 37.

namely, that a universalism of consensus was preferable to a universalism of rational consistency.

In any case it was to rouse the study of law from its academic torpor and to restore it to practical use that Hugo proposed to focus on "natural law" not in its abstract and rationalist sense but rather in its identification with undifferentiated and mutable physical reality. This contrast corresponded to the old distinction of medieval jurists between a "primary" and a "secondary" law of nature as well as that between positive and natural law;[20] but in the context of Hugo's own age it had a further implication: namely, the shift from a model based on physics (or metaphysics) to one based on biology. No doubt this was generally fashionable in the "romantic" climate of opinion of post- (and counter-) revolutionary (and Napoleonic) Europe; but Hugo took his justification from a more traditional source. Once again it was from Ulpian, one of the most controversial (some thought contradictory) formulas in all of civil law, namely, that natural law instead of being identified with reason was "that which nature teaches to all animals."[21] From it proceeds sexual union, Ulpian continued, and procreation, so that "all animals, and even wild beasts, appear to be acquainted with this law."

So it was that Hugo began his "juristic anthropology" with the presumption of man's animal nature (*Der Mensch als Thier*) and assumed that this animal nature is not only the source but also the basis of reason (*die Thierheit ist auch die Grundlage der Vernunft*). "Nothing in the intellect that had not previously been in the senses" (*Nihil est in intellectu, quod non fuerit prius in sensu*) was the Aristotelian (Thomistic) maxim that lent further support to this view; and Hugo's ultimate conclusion was that "juristically, man was nothing else than an animal" (*Das nun aber ein Mensch juristisch nichts Anderes sey, als ein Thier*).[22] On this insight there followed an analysis of the natural world according to the order of the old hierarchy, the "great chain of being," from inanimate to organic to human, and suggesting, with reference to Kant and Condorcet as well as to civil law, a principle of natural progress (*Fortschritt*) leading to higher forms of organization, not only racial but also social and political. Yet even with the breakthrough to consciousness and the crucial principle of freedom (*Freyheit*) men retain their natural roots, most notably through the patria (*Vaterland*), which leads back to the racial community (*MenschenRassen*) and the family. It was Hugo's belief—unfashionable even in our age—that a social philosophy and any system of laws had to accommodate the animal as well as the human, the subrational as well as the rational side of human nature.

Although language represented the most direct expression of reason and individual freedom, the indispensable condition for Hugo was the institution of private property. In other words the emergence of men

[20] Cf. Ennio Cortese, *La Norma giuridica*, I (Milan, 1964), 55.

[21] *LNR*, 38, citing Digest, I, 1, 2.

[22] *LNR*, 40ff. Cf. Saint Thomas, *De Trinitate*, I, 3.

from their animal past into conscious history was made possible by the establishment of private law, based upon a rational distinction between mine and thine (*Mein and Dein*; *meum et tuum*).[23] Hugo defended this institution of *PrivatEigenthum* from centuries of attack by idealists from Plato to Thomas More and from such utopians to more recent devotees of natural law in a non-positivistic sense. In historical terms private law was anterior to public law, that is, to political control (*Obrigkeit*); and in rational terms it was more important than any amount of political ordering. For Hugo the absence of private property was responsible for the creation of that menacing "nation without God and without law," the beggars, just as its equitable distribution was essential to the success of any constitutional arrangement (*Verfassung*). "Without private law," he wrote, "many believe that man would be reduced to a machine" (*Freilich glauben sehr Viele, ohne Privatrecht werde der Mensch zur Machine*) and his political organization to a despotism.[24] Without private property, he concluded, there could be no rationality, no morality, no justice and certainly no "philosophy of positive law."

To Marx, Hugo's historicist theses seemed more frivolous than the eighteenth-century natural law theories which they opposed. The historical school made a fetish of "sources" in the name not only of scholarship but also of an imaginary primitive state of nature that reduced man to an animal condition and philosophy to poetic fiction. In other words, Hugo reduced the rational to the "positive," which was identified with brute, irrational existence on the level of Pangloss's "Whatever is, is right." "With self-satisfied zeal," Marx continued, "he adduces arguments from everywhere to provide additional evidence that no rational necessity is inherent in the positive institutions, e.g., property, the state constitution, marriage, e.g., that they are even contrary to reason . . . ."[25] Here is the fallacious "positive" anthropology of the historical school. "*Everything existing* serves (Hugo) as an *authority*, every authority serves him as an argument. . . . The same levelling procedure is applied to *peoples.* According to Hugo, the Siamese, who consider it an eternal law of nature that his kind should have the mouths of chatterers sewn up and the mouth of a clumsy orator slit to the ears, is just as *positive* as the Englishman, who would consider it a political anomaly if his king were autocratically to impose even a penny tax." This was relativism reduced to the extreme of solipsism. "In one place, one thing is positive, in another something else; the one is as irrational as the other," as Marx summed it up. "*Hugo*, therefore, is the complete *sceptic.*"

In the name of history and anthropology, according to Marx, Hugo had not only betrayed science but had defaced the image of man himself. "The *sole distinguishing feature of man is his animal nature*" was Hugo's motto, and on this basis he perverted all human institutions and values, denying the attribute of freedom and implicitly even extolling slavery

[23] *LNR*, 93ff.
[24] *LNR*, 107.
[25] "Philosophical Manifesto," *CW*, I, 252.

under certain conditions.[26] "See *what kind* of schooling our *Young Germans* have received," Marx lamented. Worst of all, constitutional law was reduced to sheer power, to "animal law." It took little insight, Marx concluded, "to recognize behind all these fragrant phrases the dirty old idea of our enlightener of the *ancien régime*, and his dissolute frivolity behind all the extravagant unctuosity." Marx's dismissal of Hugo was psychologically complete, for in his elderly confrontation with a different sort of "anthropology," he could not even remember the name of the book on which he had cut his polemical teeth: "See Hugo's Naturrecht od ännlicher Titel," he reminded himself, "(hab ihn vergessen)."[27]

Underlying Marx's polemic was a broader concern with the foundations of human science, as became apparent two years later in his assault on the Hegelian philosophy of law. Having disposed of the corrupt "positive" approach of the Historical School, Marx turned his attention to the more sophisticated legitimation of the Prussian *status quo* represented by Hegelianism; having transcended Savigny's "realism," he tried to disentangle himself from the equally misguided "idealism" of Gans.[28] This he accomplished by the *German Ideology* of 1845-46, if not by the *Economic and Philosophic Manuscripts* of 1844, and at the same time began working on his own interpretation of human science through the application of new methods of analysis derived from political economy, a discipline he embraced after rejecting the law and after his encounter with Engels. This intellectual turning point, together with his revolutionary involvements set Marx on a single-minded course marked—at least as far as his attempts to build a systematic science of society are concerned—by the *Grundrisse*, the *Contribution to a Critique of Political Economy* and finally the unfinished monument, *Capital.*

III. *Beyond Das Kapital.* Or perhaps not so "finally." Marx's career has usually been discussed in the light of its central phases, especially his revolutionary activities and his economic theories; but another perspective is suggested by the more general philosophical and anthropological interests which he recurrently displayed. No one can doubt that Marx was committed first to the analysis and then to the destruction—or first the destruction and then the analysis of bourgeois society—and yet these interrelated projects by no means marked the boundaries of his curiosity. In the wake of the revolutions of 1848, when Marx withdrew into his second scholarly retirement, his interests expanded in various directions, not only into the past, especially into classical and medieval history, but also beyond the confines of western civilization, both in his journalism and in his "scientific" researches. Concern with "pre-Capitalist economic formations" and with the so-called "Asiatic mode of production" illustrates Marx's continually expanding horizons.[29]

[26] Hugo, *LNR*, 40; Marx, *CW*, I, 252.

[27] *EN*, 427.

[28] See my article cited above, note 1.

[29] Especially *Pre-Capitalist Economic Formations*, trans. J. Cohen (London, 1965). See a most interesting discussion in Marc Abeles, *Anthropologie et marxisme* (Brussels, 1976), 32ff.

In anthropological as well as other terms the pattern of Marx's thought developed from a theoretical to an empirical approach, more specifically from the deductive methods of the old jurisprudence to the inductive method implied by historical investigation, which Marx took as a prerequisite for economic analysis. In the first instance this transition was expressed as a change from idealism to "praxis," which in general meant "revolutionary practice." The implication for anthropology was suggested by Marx in the tenth of his "theses on Feuerbach."[30] "The standpoint of the old materialism is civil society; the standpoint of the new is human society, or associated humanity." After Marx's revolutionary hopes had been dampened by the events of 1848, he resumed once again his "positive" studies, this time in the British Museum; and his view of *praxis* became again more "scientific," which is to say historical and comparative, with particular reference to the earlier stages of western history, especially Roman and medieval.

The focus of Marx's antiquarian interests was the problem of the origins of private property, which was the center of attention in the years before the revolutions of 1848. The orthodox view, defended by jurists and historians alike, was that the emergence of property marked the beginning of consciousness, of liberty, and of civilization—in short of history in general. Historically, the Roman model was still standard; and at first Marx himself tended to follow the interpretations of Savigny's colleague B. G. Niebuhr, who pointed out that King Numa, and indeed all ancient lawgivers, had provided for property even before attending to religious matters.[31] For Marx this seemed to support both the idea of the material base's priority to the superstructure and (since Roman "public land" marked the distinction between patricians and plebeians) the assumption that history had begun with the class divisions created by property.

After the publication of *Das Kapital* (1867), however, Marx's views changed in one important respect owing to a new development in the controversy over the origins of private property, namely, the notion of "primitive communism," which since the late eighteenth century most scholars had regarded as subversive as well as retrospectively "utopian." But in the second quarter of the nineteenth century this idea received support from both "socialist" ideology and from historical scholarship, beginning with Jacob Grimm and Jules Michelet.[32] This Germanist thesis

[30] *CW*, V, 5.

[31] *Pre-Capitalist Economic Formations*, 74; and cf Niebuhr, *The History of Rome*, trans. J. Hare and C. Thirwall (Philadelphia, 1835), II, 97ff.

[32] Most notably in Michelet's *Origines du droit français* (Paris, 1838), ch. 2, following Jacob Grimm. Cf. F. Engels, "The Mark," in *The Peasant War in Germany* (Moscow, 1956), 161-81, and important discussion of the background by Paolo Grossi, "*Un Altro modo di possedere*" (Milan, 1977), trans. now by L. Cochrane as *An Alternative to Private Property* (Chicago, 1981); and Alfons Dopsch, *The Economic and Social Foundations of European Civilization*, trans. M. Beard and N. Marshall (New York, 1937), ch. 1.

was given classic expression in the investigations of Georg von Maurer into medieval village communities (*Markgenossenschaften*), and Marx happily incorporated these results into his own work, though objecting that Maurer neglected Celtic and other marginal societies whose early land laws were "entirely communistic."[33] By analogy with Darwinism, Marx posited a universal historical process beginning with a communal phase (not accepted by Darwin, however) and on this basis modified his revolutionary views.

The controversy over "primitive communism" and the origins of private property in general was enormously expanded from the 1860s, which happened also to be the formative period of modern anthropology. Within a very few years, in the wake of but not directly related to Darwin's *Origin of Species* (1859), appeared most of the founding classics of anthropology as a "scientific" discipline: Adolf Bastian's *Mankind in History* (1860), Maine's *Ancient Law* (1861), Bachofen's *Mother Right* (1861), McLennan's *Primitive Marriage* (1865), Tylor's *Early History of Mankind* (1865), Lubbock's *Origin of Civilisation* (1870), and Morgan's *Systems of Consanguinity* (1871) and *Ancient Society* (1877). Like Marx, several of these authors, especially Maine, McLennan, and Bachofen, had been trained in the law; Bachofen in particular, in an autobiographical fragment written for Savigny, hoped to draw from Roman experience the "one law" governing all human life and cultural evolution.[34] From this literature Marx seemed to take as much inspiration as, a quarter of a century before, he had from the classics of political economy. Above all he welcomed the support of Morgan, McLennan, and Bachofen for the notion of an original collective society linked to matriarchy or matrilinearity.

The appropriation of Morgan by Marx is a curious episode in intellectual history, especially since Morgan seemed to share with Hugo that fallacy, denounced by Marx, of man's strictly animal nature; but it was in keeping with the evolutionist vogue of the later nineteenth century, which made the "time ripe," as Engels puts it, for evolutionism as well as the "materialist conception of history" discovered independently by Marx and Morgan.[35] In any case, in the last decade or so of his life,

[33] Marx-Engels, *Selected Correspondence*, trans. D. Torr (New York, 1942), 235 (from Marx, 25 March 1868): "His books are exceptionally important. Not only primitive times but the whole later development of the free imperial cities, of the immunity of the landowners, of public authority and of the struggle between free peasantry and serfdom is given en entirely new form." And Marx adds, "Human history is like palaeontology."

[34] "My Life in Retrospect," in *Myth, Religion and Mother Right*, trans. R. Manheim (Princeton, 1967), 3.

[35] Marx and Engels, *Selected Correspondence*, 518. Carl Resek, *Lewis Henry Morgan, American Scholar* (Chicago, 1960), is a good brief biography, but there is no good study of Morgan's European connections. All the correspondence, including letters from Bachofen and Maine, and the best collection of Morganiana are in the Rush Rhees Library of the University of Rochester, from which certain letters and other materials have been published by I. N. Vinnikov, *Iz Arkiva L'iuisa Genri Morgana* (Moscow, 1935), with Russian translation.

Marx intensified his interests in pre- and extra-western societies and shifted his attention from political economy to a possibly even grander project based on the new discipline being created by British and American ethnologists. As he had prepared the ground for his economic theories by the critical notes embodied in his *Economic and Philosophic Manuscripts*,[36] so now he began his new onslaught on a larger province of the human sciences through notes on the positive investigations of early and primitive society by the founders of a scientific anthropology which was replacing the philosophic field that had predominated for centuries. Caught up in this interest he could not—perhaps he never intended to—finish his *Kapital*.

IV. *Marx and the "New Anthropology."* Marx's "ethnological notebooks," devoted to some of his last systematic reading in the rapidly expanding field of social science, consist of careful extracts and characterizations, together with additional references, comments and sometimes sharp polemic, of four books published in the last decade of his life. The prime target of these notes was the work of Henry Sumner Maine, whose interpretations Marx found malicious as well as misinformed. In the first place Maine misconstrued the nature of the primal social grouping by associating the family, specifically the Roman *gens*, with territory rather than blood. "Dies zeight," commented Marx in his inimitable and often comical Anglo-Latino-German, "wie wenig die Gens a fact observed by the identical Maine is."[37] This same ass (*Dieser asinus*) displayed the most ethnocentric conceptions of English institutions by trying, for example, to identify Roman property with English ownership: "Dieser lächerliche Bursche macht d. röm. Form d. absolute landed property zu 'English form of ownership,' " Marx wrote; "O Du Philister." On the other hand, Maine tried to project the English, perhaps the Victorian, family into prehistory; and here Marx cited Morgan in opposition: "Aber Herr Maine, dies only in Status of Upper Barbarism, far from being archaic." "Der comfortable Maine" gave himself away when he represented the "mass of influences" underlying culture as basically moral, and Marx returned to his ever-ready materialist thesis, concluding that "dies 'moral' zeigt wie wenig Maine von der Sache versteht; so weit diese influences (economical before everything else) 'moral' modus of existence besitzen, ist dies immer ein abgeleitenten, secondär modus u. nie das prius."

Marx rejected "D. Gans falsche Vorstellung des Maine"; but in his general indictment he included other "blockheaded Englishmen," among them "D. stubbige [Bishop William] Stubbs and [John] Austin," and "D. abominable (E.A.) *Freeman*," who tried to project class division (eorl/ceorl) back into pre-Conquest England.[38] The particular occasion for

[36] *CW*, III, 231-46, and *EN*, 287ff. Cf. Henry Sumner Maine, *Lectures on the Early History of Institutions* (New York, 1875). [37] *EN*, 294, 309. [38] *EN*, 315.

Marx's invective against "these self-righteous English canaille" was the never-ending Irish Question, but what bound them together in anthropological iniquity was an attitude which had provided Marx, at the very beginning of his career, with his most fundamental target; that is, respect for conventionally formulated legal tradition. The notorious formalism of Roman law, for example, Maine celebrated as a dramatization of the "origin of justice." "Dies scheint rather," observed Marx, "Dramatisation of how law disputes were becoming a source of fees profit to lawyers! u. dies nennt Herr Maine, als a lawyer, the 'Origins of Justice.' " And a bit later he noted, " 'Maine always mild when speaking of clergy and lawyers and higher class people generally.' " So Marx returned to his old assault on the peculiarly vicious (because uniquely effective) form of idealism that was the law of the old regime. Marx was commenting on modern as well as ancient jurisprudence when he denounced its superstitious formalism. "Diese excessive technicality of ancient law," he wrote in connection with Maine's praise of the Twelve Tables, "zeigt Jurisprudenz as feather of the same bird, als d. religiösen Formalitäten z. B. Auguris etc. od. d. Hokus Pokus des medicine man der savages."

On a number of grounds Marx questioned Maine's qualifications as anthropologist. Maine was complacent, ethnocentric, narrow in perspective, elitist—in a word, *bourgeois*. Unaware of the work either of Morgan or of J. J. Bachofen's *Mother Right*, Maine resorted parochially to Roman history and especially to the principle of paternal power (*patria potestas*) to argue the case for masculine succession. So it was among such "Aryan sub-races" as the Hindus, wrote Maine—to which Marx retorted, "The devil take this 'Aryan' cant."[39] For Marx this attitude merely reflected the sort of Anglo-Saxon prejudice which, for an example given by Maine himself, led "English blockheaded" judges to outlaw the power of Irish women to deal with their own property without their husband's consent. In such an ideological context, Marx comments, "Maine transports his 'patriarchal' family into the very beginning of things." More generally he stigmatized all primitive society (*Das ganze Primitive*) as "the despotism of groups over the members composing them." "O Du Pecksniff," Marx cried, digressing from his notes to show that true "despotism" was the product of modern individualism, "class interest" and authoritarian government, which had superseded ancient legal patterns. Marx rejected, too, Maine's defense of the pernicious view of "positive law" given currency by John Austin (another student of Savigny, who drew his conception from Hugo) as simple authoritarian command. Maine regarded Austin's work as "strictly scientific," but Marx dismissed it as childish (*Kinderische Trivialitäten*). In general Maine's arguments were not those of an anthropologist but of "either Jurist od. Ideolog."[40]

[39] *EN*, 324. Cf. Bachofen, *Das Mutterrecht*, partial translation by R. Manheim in *Myth, Religion and Mother Right*, 69-207.

[40] *EN*, 329.

Very different was Marx's attitude toward Lewis Henry Morgan's *Ancient Society*. What could a genteel Rochester lawyer have in common with a renegade German philosopher turned professional revolutionary? Marx admired Morgan not only for his massive foundation in "positive studies" but also for his emphasis on the technical and productive factors in social evolution. "Man works himself up" was one of Morgan's mottos and implied that material forces were no less significant in civilization than in more primitive stages of history.[41] In general Marx seems to have accepted Morgan's periodization of pre-history, or human evolution, that is, the three stages of "savagery" and three of "barbarism" underlying tooled and articulate civilization; and he singled out for emphasis one famous Morgan assumption: "The events of human progress embody themselves, independently of particular men, in a material record, which is crystallized in institutions, usages u. customs, u. preserved in inventions u. discoveries." What appealed to Marx above all was Morgan's insistence on the material base of culture, especially technology and the "arts of subsistence." In this way American practicality and Marxian *praxis*—American and historical materialism—reinforced one another, as did Marxist and Morganist idealistic hopes that society could somehow transcend this materialism. And indeed Morgan's work, through the efforts of Engels (drawing directly on Marx's notes), played a significant role in later Marxian tradition.[42]

More particularly Marx seized upon Morgan's fundamental insights into the emergence of the institution and idea of private property. Glossing Morgan's remarks on "the influence of property," Marx wrote, "It was the power [here crossing out Morgan's term "influence"] that brought the Aryan and Semitic nations out of barbarism into civilization."[43] The "passion for possession" accounted not only for basic social patterns but also for political organization. This had been the assumption of generations of jurists, including Savigny, whose treatise on "possession" was a major contribution to the early history of property, and of course Hugo; but in Morgan's work this insight, as Marx saw it, received empirical and so scientific confirmation. Beyond confirming old assumptions, Morgan also led Marx to a deeper understanding of the patterns of prehistory, and specifically to the notion of primitive communism—"communism in living," in Morgan's words [44]—antecedent to the stage of property and proprietary attitude of men toward their mates. Marx approved of the inference, made by Bachofen and McLennan as well as Morgan, of a primordial matriarchal organization, a society based on *Mutterrecht*, in which kinship was traced only through the maternal line and paternity was irrelevant even if known. Although such an arrangement implied a "promiscuity of intercourse" no more pleasing to Marx than to Morgan,

[41] *EN*, 224. Cf. Lewis Henry Morgan, *Ancient Society*, ed. Leslie A. White (Cambridge, Mass., 1964). [42] See below at note 48. [43] *EN*, 126; see above, note 8.
[44] *EN*, 115

it also meant that, contrary to the complacent views of bourgeois ethnologists like Maine, neither property nor male domination had any foundation in what philosophical anthropology had regarded as natural law.

The crux of Morgan's analysis as read by Marx was the emphasis he put on that "property-making organization," the monogamous family. "Systems of consanguinity sind dagegen passiv," Marx paraphrased; "recording the progress made by the family at long intervals apart, and only changing radically when the family has radically changed."[45] To this principle Marx added the further gloss, "Ebenso verhält es sich mit politischen, religiösen, juristischen, philosophischen Systemen überhaupt," and endorsed Fourier's view that the two basic factors of history were monogamy and private property." "Sie (Monogamie und Grund Privateigenthum) in Miniatur alle d. Antagonismen in sich, die sich später breit entwickeln in d. Gesellschft u. ihrem Staat."

In another respect Morgan's approach was in line with that of Marx, that is, using classical antiquity as an empirical base. From behind Greek customs, Morgan believed, "the savage peeped through"—or as Marx noted, "Dch d. Grecian gens guckt d. Wilde (Iroquois z. B.)." Yet again emphasis was on material factors, and Marx took to task such pedants ("Schulgelehrter Philistines") as George Grote, who assumed the similarity rested on some sort of agreement in mental forms. Grote's conclusion, that "The scheme and ideal . . . basis was the same in all," Marx repudiated: "Dear Sir, not ideal but carnal, Germanice fleischlich." The tie was not in religion but in material interest: "Das lumpige religiöse Element wd Haupsache bei gens, im Mass wie real cooperation u. common property alle werden; d. Weihrauchsduft, der übrig bleibt."[46] And likewise legal practices, had their roots in more immediate kinship patterns, such as the public justice of the phratry, which Marx took to be a form of vendetta (*Veränderte Form der Blutrache*). In these and other ways Marx brought his historical materialism to bear upon prehistory and anthropology.

For Marx the Roman experience remained a model of social and institutional development; and Morgan led him to renew his interest in civil law, this time centering on the clan, or *gens*, whose origins had been so hotly debated since Niebuhr's controversial interpretations. The question remained central to the pioneers of the new anthropology, too, most notably in Morgan's work on the Iroquois. Marx's own concern was to emphasize—in opposition to the consensus of classicists like Niebuhr, Thirwall, Mommsen, and Maine—the relatively late emergence of the monogamous bourgeois family. Following Morgan, Marx assumed rather that the emergence of civilization came only with the last three (of sixteen) stages of barbarism identified by the "rise of property," the monogamous

[45] *EN*, 112, 120.

[46] *EN*, 198.

family and finally the establishment of the "Aryan, Semitic and Uranian system of consanguinity and affinity."[47] In his earliest thoughts on the latter arising from his legal studies, Marx had tended to assume that the emergence of property, or more precisely the transformation of possession into property, marked the boundary line between the state of nature and civil society; and this carried over into his political writings and theories of class struggle. Late in life he affirmed this view again but tied it to its social embodiment, which was the family—and, issuing from the family, the *gens*. Here was the true starting point of history, which remained the "history of class struggle."

V. *The Revisionist Marx*. This was the trail which Marx left Engels to follow, but it is by no means clear that the follower maintained the same heading that the leader had been taking. Engels himself said it the year after Marx's death, in the preface to his *Origin of the Family, Private Property, and the State*: "My work can offer only a meager substitute for what my dear departed friend no longer had time to do."[48] However, Engels did try to elaborate Marxist doctrine by means of the broader perspective suggested by anthropology. Four years later he qualified the famous formula of the *Communist Manifesto*, that "The history of all hitherto existing society is 'the history of class struggle,' " by adding a footnote: "That is, all written history. In 1847, the pre-history of society prior to recorded history, was all but unknown."[49] Maurer, Haxhausen, and others showed "village communities . . . to have been the primitive form of society everywhere from India to Ireland," Engels continued: "The inner organization of this primitive Communistic society was laid bare, in its typical form, by Morgan's crowning discovery of the true nature of the gens and its relation to the tribe." In the light of this, Engels retraced the transition from primeval communities to stratified societies according to the forces of economic determinism and what a recent critic has called "dialectical naturalism."[50]

Engels' work followed closely Marx's ethnological notebooks, but there are, as usual, significant divergences in vision. Marx read and developed his views on anthropology from 1879 until his death in 1883; Engels took less than a year after that to publish a heavily reasoned, doctrinaire book based on Marx's notes. Engels seemed faithful to Marx's general line of criticism, but it is hard to believe that his positive achievement fulfilled what Marx envisaged in his efforts to transcend purely western experience. Like Marx, Engels denounced the legalism of writers like McLennan and Maine, and the idealism of writers like Lassalle and Bachofen.[51] It may be doubted, however, that Marx would have agreed that these men, as Engels complained, "did more harm by their theses than good by research," in view both of his devotion to "positive research"

[47] *EN*, index.

[48] Edited and translated by Eleanor Burke Leacock (New York, 1972), 71, Engels' preface to his first edition.

[49] Note added by Engels in 1888.

[50] See Norman Levine, *The Tragic Deception: Marx contra Engels* (Santa Barbara, 1975), 84, 157.

[51] *The Origin of the Family*, 75-84, preface to 4th edition.,

and of his appreciation of cultural as well as economic factors. "Marxism" aside, Marx's own thought is perhaps better understood as a road than as a static structure, a road which led toward, if it did not quite reach, the new field of anthropology.

Marx never wavered from his belief in progessive, natural and evolutionary (*naturwüchsig*) stages in history. This interpretation is often associated with the famous "four-stage" theory of Turgot and Adam Smith (hunting, pasturage, agriculture, and commerce), but it had a juridical form as well (the occupancy of land succeeding the hunting stage, the "civil" possession of land in the pastoral period, and then formal property beginning with agriculture and "industry").[52] Private property was the key—the beginning of "alienation" (in the economic and ideological sense which Marx bestowed upon this old legal term) and the end of community, the precipitant of the historical process. In his classic economic phase Marx divided this process into discrete "modes of production" (Asiatic, classical, feudal, and bourgeois), but he never really followed this typology.[53] Fascination with an original communal stage drew his interests farther back in time, and the impact of biological evolutionism further widened his horizons. Finally he turned to the model of Morgan, which introduced extra-economic and extra-western factors, cultural as well as technological.

What is most interesting about the very old Marx, however, is the way in which he seemed to be moving beyond a "materialist conception of history" that was exclusively economic and limited to class analysis. In the judgment of one of the great figures in the tradition of old-fashioned philosophical anthropology, Wilhelm Dilthey, the classical Marx of *Capital* had actually fallen back into crypto-Hegelian abstraction (an economic version of *Begriffsphilosophie*) with his notion of surplus value;[54] but his last concerns show that he had never departed from his insistence on "positive" research. Conceptually, too, Marx continued to look beyond the fictions of economic analysis. Implicit in his last notes, and explicit in the formulation made by Engels, was the aspiration of opening the door to larger categories, especially those of tribe, kinship, and sexuality;

[52] See Ronald Meek, *Smith, Marx and After* (London, 1977), 20ff; and, e.g., J. E. D. Bernardi, *Cours de droit civil français* (Paris, 1803), I, 236-42, "De la Propriété des choses, de sa nature et de son origine."

[53] Discussion in M. M. Bober, *Karl Marx's Interpretation of History* (Cambridge, 1927), 47ff, and William H. Shaw, *Marx's Theory of History* (Stanford, 1978), ch. 4. Neither Daniel Gandy, *Marx and History* (Austin, 1979), nor G. A. Cohen, *Karl Marx's Theory of History* (Princeton, 1980), are helpful for present purposes. On "AMP," Perry Anderson, *Lineages of the Absolutist State* (London, 1975), 462-549, is one who takes it very seriously, while Abeles, *Anthropologie et marxisme*, 43ff, questions its very existence and tries to explain the political context of the debate over the concept in the 1920s and 30s.

[54] *Gesammelte Schriften*, XVII (Leipzig, 1974), 186. On anthropology as "first science" see Michael Ermath, *Wilhelm Dilthey: The Critique of Historical Reason* (Chicago, 1978), 141ff.

and the result was to shift attention not only from bourgeois property to the longer-termed problem of the family but also from class struggle to that ultimate dialectic of mating and the family—precisely the direction which the new anthropology was itself taking.[55]

This interpretation is by no means to suggest a reversion to the idealism of the "very young Marx," but it is to infer a transcendence of the relatively narrow and parochial materialism of the middle (the "classical" and most easily vulgarized) Marx. From the beginning he had followed a path which brought him, according to a modern philosophical anthropologist, into "the ranks of those who, with Herder, developed the line of study that is now called cultural and historical anthropology."[56] His revulsion from idealism and discovery of the analytical potential of political economy led him into a self-consciously "scientific" (as well as revolutionary) phase culminating in his systematic critique of western capitalism. Finally, Marx was attracted to the pioneering researches of the first generation of social and cultural anthropologists, especially those of Morgan, whose Indian field work seemed to Marx to give his writings better authority than the more bookish speculations of Maine, McLennan, Bachofen, and others; and so he returned to the initial field of his youthful studies, though now, to be sure, in a positive, scientific, and truly universal form. Anthropology, representing the last phase of Marx's personal dialectical evolution, took him beyond Marxism as understood by most of his followers; and in this perspective it is hardly going too far to suggest that Marx was himself the first "revisionist." In any case, his hope was clearly to rise above the parochialism of western, bourgeois history. It is a pity that neither critics nor admirers have seen the fulfillment of the vision of the very old Marx.[57]

[55] The issues of original collectivism and matriarchy dominate the famous old collection edited by V. F. Calverton, *The Making of Man* (New York, 1931). Perhaps the most thoughtful discussion of more recent Marxist anthropology is the work of Maurice Godelier, especially *Perspectives in Marxist Anthropology*, trans. R. Brain (Cambridge, Eng., 1977).

[56] Michael Landmann, *Philosophische Anthropologie* (1st ed. 1955; 4th. edition, Berlin, 1976). Translated as *Philosophical Anthropology*.

[57] Mme Raya Dunayevskaya has been working on Marx's *Ethnological Notebooks* in connection with a proposed book on "Rosa Luxemburg, Women's Liberation and Marx's Philosophy of Revolution," a draft chapter of which appears in *News and Letters* (Jan.-Feb. 1979), 5-8, discussing also the discovery of the manuscript of the notebooks, reported in 1923, and the Russian translation published in 1941 (information which I owe to Ms. Suzanne Casey).

XI

"Second Nature": The Idea of Custom in European Law, Society, and Culture

For use almost can change the stamp of nature.

Hamlet, III, iv, 167

Altera Natura

"Custom is second nature" (*consuetudo altera natura*).[1] This has been a commonplace, though a debatable commonplace, at least since Aristotle. Primary Nature has been worshiped in many ways—has been matrified as well as deified—but Custom has enjoyed no such conceptual respect. While there have been countless historical and philosophical discussions of the "idea of nature," no serious effort has been made, so far as I know, to study the "idea of custom" in a comprehensive and critical fashion—nothing comparable, say, to R. G. Collingwood's *Idea of Nature* or to Robert Lenoble's *Idée de la nature*.[2] Yet as the virtual twin, or shadow, of nature, the idea of custom has run through the length and breadth, the height and depth, of Western thought and culture.

The contrast between nature and custom is evident in Western thought and linguistic usage going back to the pre-Socratics.[3] The story begins most explicitly with the crucial distinction between nature (*physis*) and law (*nomos,* in the sense of man-made rules), a duality that also invaded the fields of language, art, literature, and especially law.[4] Aristotle was the first to formulate the distinction between a primary and a second nature in philosophical terms. In his essay on memory, custom (*ethos*) seems to approach or take the place of nature, just as recalled experiences are gathered into general thoughts.[5] An analogous movement from the particular to the general can also be seen in the *Rhetoric*.[6] Here, defining pleasure as a movement of the soul to a natural state, Aristotle remarks that "that which has become habitual becomes as it were natural; for the distance between 'often' [*pollakis*] and 'always' [*aion*] is not great, and nature belongs to the idea of 'always,' custom to that of 'often.'" From the beginning the notion that repetition over time establishes a permanent pattern has been essential to the idea of custom.

"Custom" played a prominent role in ancient Roman rhetoric.[7] The term *consuetudo* was employed by both Cicero and Quintilian in the sense of a norm of the speech community as well as a form of human law.[8] Cicero contrasted everyday, customary life (*vitae consuetudo*) with the philosophical idealizations of Plato's *Republic*. These attitudes were preserved in the medieval *trivium* and various ways expanded by Renaissance humanists. Following the lead of Quintilian, Lorenzo Valla insisted on the primacy of custom (*consuetudo, usus,* or *consensus*) in language and denounced the technical jargon of scholasticism (in law and theology as well as philosophy) because it substituted a false "reason" for ordinary usage and "convention."[9] Language itself, according to Valla, was the product not of nature but of human custom (*hominum usus, qui verborum est autor,* and Quintilian's formula, *consuetudo vero certissima loquendi magistra*); and its principles were to be found not in formal philosophy but in the discipline of rhetoric in particular and the liberal and perhaps fine arts in general, especially since "art" itself was commonly distinguished from, or even regarded as a secondary and derivative form of, "nature."

In all of these contexts, over twenty-five centuries or more, one common theme has persisted, and that is the association of the idea and term "custom" and its semantic neighbors with law, rhetoric, grammar, and the European humanist tradition, and in modern times with philosophical and later empirical "anthropology." From the ancient Greek "custom is king" (*nomos basileus; despotes nomos*)[10] to Bagehot's "cake of custom" and modern ethnographic study of folkways and "norms," "custom" has usually signified forms of what Clifford Geertz has called "local knowledge" and internalist approaches to cultural understanding, often in contrast to the transcendent aspirations of theology, natural philosophy, and most mainstream social science.

It is hardly surprising that, philosophically, the idea of custom has commanded little respect—and the notion that it resembled nature was still less acceptable. Rather, for Cicero and Seneca, custom was contrary to nature, and Christian authors inclined to a similar opinion. Both Augustine and Jerome took the idea of "second nature" as a surrender to the corruption both of human nature and of human law and as further alienation from the divine; Clement of Alexandria spoke of "thrusting away custom as some deadly drug"; and Thomas Aquinas identified "second nature" with the bad habits (*malitia*) produced by the animal side of human nature.[11] Emblematic of this deep-seated prejudice was the reminder of Cyprian, often repeated (by Luther among others) and preserved in canon law, that Christ had represented himself not as the "custom" but rather as the "truth," referring to John 14:6, "Sed Dominus noster Christus veritatem se non consuetudinem cognominavit."[12]

Yet canon law, while drawing sustenance from patristic authority, increasingly had to come to terms with the limitations of the human condition and in effect with human history and customs, which indeed were conscripted into canonist service. Thus Gratian's *Decretum* opens with the fundamental proposition that "the human race is ruled in two ways, either by natural law or by unwritten customs"—either by nature or by second nature.[13] This has been a premise of Western social thought which not only antedated but also outlasted the medieval Christian formulation.

This brings us to the major premise in the story of "custom," which is that, between ancient Greco-Roman and modern anthropological conceptions, the major formulations have arisen within the world of Western jurisprudence—an intellectual and professional continuum that begins with the earliest stages of the Roman art of law and ends with the earliest stages of modern social science (which was itself in various ways endebted to the study of law).[14] From Gaius to Max Weber these theorists of custom and law—practitioners of "civil science" (*civilis scientia* or *civilis sapientia,* in the words of the Accursian Gloss)—form a "community of interpretation" which, ideological differences aside, has preserved a remarkable continuity of language, method, and conceptualization across many centuries and cultural frontiers. It is in large part out of this hermeneutical and honoratorial (judicial-scholastic-humanistic-scientific) tradition that the idea of custom has taken its modern shape, and this is the elusive target of the present study.

Custom and Law

"Custom" was not included among the classical sources of Roman law, except implicitly in the famous distinction between written and unwritten law (*ius scriptum, ius non scriptum*); but from the late third century jurists began to recognize custom—"local" and "long" or "longest" custom—in a more formal sense than mere "manners" (*mores*) or "usage" (*usus*) or even "prescription."[15] This conventional notion of custom as a product of popular and "tacit" consent (*consensus populi*) was developed in postclassical jurisprudence, found a permanent home in the Digest, became standard fare in university instruction, and thence passed into the mainstream of European legal, social, political, and cultural thought.

The standard definition of custom is attributed to the last of the classical jurists, Hermogenianus, writing in the fourth century: "But also those rules which have been established by ancient custom and observed, like a tacit agreement, are to be followed no less than the rules that are written."[16] Here in a nutshell, with certain other supporting texts, are the essential ingredients of the Western idea of custom, including those developed by the social and cultural sciences: the origins in social behavior, the popular and parochial base, the parity with law, and the element of time.

To this locus classicus, however, were added a large number of medieval and modern "extensions," produced by efforts to accommodate Roman ideas to European society. Beginning especially with Azo in civil law and Hostiensis in canon law, theories of *consuetudo* gave definition, intelligible form, relevance, and a kind of legitimacy to the feudal and urban institutions of late medieval Europe, and from there moved into various national traditions. The conceptual umbrella of *consuetudo* has given shelter to the massive materials gathered in the French *coutumiers,* in German *Gewohnheitsrecht,* and in the Spanish *usos* and *fueros,* as well as in the endless commentaries on all of these accumulations. English common law, according to Bracton, was wholly a product of *consuetudo,* and it illustrated marvelously the Aristotelian principle of pleasure, or "love" (quoted in this connection by Sir John Fortescue in the later fifteenth century), that "use becomes another nature" (*usus alteram facit naturam*)—and specifically that English use was altogether "natural" and "reasonable."[17]

In general, medieval discussions of custom were framed by the twin legal concepts of natural law (*ius naturale*) and the law of nations (*ius gentium*)—a legalistic version of the distinction between *physis* and *nomos*. Another way of stating this fundamental duality was to distinguish between a "primary law of nature" (*ius naturale primarium* or *primaevum*) based on reason and a "secondary law of nature" (*ius naturale secondarium*) based on convention and utility and equivalent to custom.[18] By definition, in any case, "custom" belonged to the realm neither of civil (that is, Roman) law nor of natural law but to the secondary realm of the "law of nations" (*ius gentium* or *ius naturale gentium*), including the societies of the New as well as the Old World; and it is in this fundamental legal sense that *consuetudo* expresses "second nature."

What jurists recognized as "customary," of course, was not random human behavior but more regular social patterns. At the very least, according to a medieval adage which simplified the Aristotelian formula, "Twice makes a custom."[19] Beyond this minimum requirement and despite scholastic complications, the European idea of custom preserved the attributes of its classical prototype—the contingent origin, the popular base, the temporal element, and especially the parity with written law.

Custom filled the gap left by the cessation of Carolingian legislation. Though its primary arena was the family, custom became increasingly identified with the usages of feudal society and, attached to the "fief," shifted from a personal to a territorial base. It was given its most concrete expression in the long-enduring institution of the cultivated field (*campagne*), which Gaston Roupnel called "the characteristic creation of the West . . . , the nature and spirit of its civilization."[20] In this and other forms European customs made their appearance in local settings and in terms of particular social predicaments for which evidence is scattered in randomly surviving charters, notarial acts, records of inferior jurisdictions, and occasionally oral tradition. As particular *coutumes* were gathered, by literate and lawyerly men, on a higher provincial level and became subject to legal interpretation, they helped to shape the idea of custom.

Over the centuries the idea of custom was commonly associated with various liberties (*libertates et consuetudines*), especially feudal but also provincial, municipal, and ecclesiastical.[21] At first, *consuetudo* reflected mainly the emergence of the feudal domain—seigneurial rights, jurisdiction, and especially taxes and servitudes, which had gained legitimacy in the course of time. All French customs, wrote an eighteenth-century commentator, were only "an expression of the authority of the lord of the fief." It was "custom" in this sense that, from the fourteenth century, was the principal target of peasant revolts. Yet, while capitularies and early charters speak of "new" and "old," of "good" and "bad," customs, *consuetudines* normally referred to accepted local usage. Lords and tenants argued over the application but seldom the meaning of "custom." Even in the peasant uprisings of the seventeenth century, for example, the rebel *croquants,* while protesting recent impositions, recognized the force not only of long-standing custom but also "new" customs sanctioned by a meeting of the three estates.[22]

More formally, the European idea of custom took shape as a reconceptualization of the old Roman idea of *consuetudo,* which gave local usages intelligibility and a certain borrowed legitimacy. The primary issue was always the relationship between custom and law (*jus*), and about this "the doctors disagreed," as indeed they have done ever since. A famous summary of this debate appears in a thirteenth-century collection entitled

Dissensiones Dominorum, in which the contradictions in the classical and postclassical texts are elaborated and exacerbated by modern "interpreters of ancient Roman law"—that is, pre-Accursian glossators.[23] "Some say that no custom, whether special or general, contrary to law abrogates or derogates from [civil] law. . . . They say that written law abrogates a custom contrary to law. . . . But others say that a custom which can be confirmed by express consent should be observed, for custom is nothing else than a tacit agreement, according to the Digest. Others say that a good but not a bad custom prevails over a law."

Here we can see the idea of custom situated at the very storm center of modern political and constitutional debates. Imperial, royal, and papal ideologists tended normally to argue that law, which was the exclusive monopoly of the sovereign, always superseded custom; but judicial doctrine inclined to the opposite view, which was that, according to the authoritative Accursian Gloss, "Custom abolishes law" (*Consuetudo vincit legem*), or in the words of Baldus, "Later custom annuls earlier law."[24] Politically, the suggestion was to place the *populus* above the *princeps* as a source of law, but the more practical purpose was to reinforce the professional judicial monopoly over legal interpretation.

Custom "represents the will of the people," Bartolus wrote (*consuetudo repraesentat mentem populi*); and so, ultimately, according to the common Aristotelian formula, the people were regarded as the "efficient cause of law" (*efficiens causa legis erat olim populus*).[25] Or as Bartolus alternatively put it, the four causes included "the natural cause, from [what was] frequently done or performed; the formal, from the consensus [of the people]; the efficient, from the time; and the final, from the rationale, the utility of the custom." In any case, the *populus* was the alpha and omega of *consuetudo.* But what was a "people"? The term and concept of *populus,* which had been transferred from ancient Rome to the Christian faith (*populus christianus* was a common expression of Augustine and Jerome), might be applied from communities ranging from an empire or nation to a village, a monastic community, a guild, or even smaller groups ("ten makes a people," was another medieval adage; *decem faciunt populum*); but it was normally defined by adherence to a particular "custom," whether general, provincial, local, or even familial.[26]

The most difficult question, debated for centuries by jurists and historians alike, was the origin of customary law. The first answer given by scholastic commentators was that custom emerged from social practice—"law arises from fact" (*lex ex facto oritur*) was the often-repeated formula.[27] Custom arose from usage and manners (*ab usu et moribus*), as Baldus put it.[28] For centuries this temporalized form of the commonplace distinction between de facto and de jure suggested the pattern of legal development, and it was reinforced by the Augustinian notion that human dominion, public as well as private, was based on force. Not only did law originate, humanly and historically, in custom but, by inference, right originated in might.

The element of time remained central to the idea of custom, and so was the notion of historical change. For if custom, representing a process in time, was continually being created, it was also and concomitantly becoming obsolete: *consuetudo* was ever counterbalanced by *desuetudo,* counterpart of the dual Aristotelian process of generation and corruption. In many ways, Odofredus observed, "custom today has changed" (*mutata est hodie consuetudo*).[29] In the sixteenth century Philippe Bugnyon devoted a whole treatise to laws which, "today" (*hodie*) had fallen "out of usage" (*ab usu longe recessit; hors d'usage*) through contradictions, confusion, and (in a modern sense) "abuse."[30]

Customs were tied to geographical as well as historical conditions. Technically, the rule was that "place determines act" (*locus regit actus,* or *formam actus*), but the more general premise was that both laws and judgments had to be in accord with the character and environment of a people. "The customs of a region must be followed," wrote Azo (*consuetudines regionis servandae sunt*); and local custom, according to the fourteenth-century *Somme Rurale* of Jean Bouteiller, was to be in accord with the "situation of a place" as determined by the local inhabitants.[31] Local customs should be followed, wrote Beaumanoir, "because we ought to remember what since childhood we have seen in use and judged in our province better than in others of which we do not know the customs and usages."[32] Such assumptions—that "local knowledge" had to be joined to high theory and general norms—furnished a sort of geohistorical base for philosophical and "scientific" as well as practical jurisprudence, and for less professional forms of social and cultural thought.

From Memory to Written Record

For historians as well as jurists, the essential question is how, concretely, custom was promoted from a social to a legal and even political level, how it came not only to "represent" but also to regulate the behavior of people. Here we confront a fundamental problem much discussed in recent years, which is the link between oral and scribal or literate culture.[33] How did custom pass from unrecorded, collective memory to authoritative written form? How, more technically, was *consuetudo* transformed into *jus consuetudinarium*? How, more specifically, did French *coutumes* become *droit civil,* German *Gewohnheit* become *allgemeines Recht,* and English customs become "common law"?

In theory, the answer came from simple social inquiry and judgment. As the English civilian John Cowell wrote, "It is enough for the profe of a custom by witness in the common lawe (as I have credibly heard), if two or more can agree, that they have heard their fathers say, that it was a custome all their time and that their fathers heard their fathers also say, that it was likewise a custome in their time."[34] This definition was equivalent to the "immemorial custom" celebrated by common lawyers like Cowell's nemesis Edward Coke and Matthew Hale (though it emphasized human testimony as well as judicial intuition), but it also held for continental customs, which were likewise authenticated transcriptions of popular memory.

The essential problem was one of "proof" or "approval," and it could be resolved in several ways. In primitive or preliterate societies no proof was called for; or rather the members of that society were themselves "living proof" of their customs. In more complex cultures a certain level of expertise was required, and in medieval Europe this meant first law-finders or lay "sayers of the law" (*sapientes, diseurs de droit, Gesetzsprecher*), who consulted their own memories or consciences, and then of more formally trained jurists, who claimed special expertise, or rather who received it from higher authority.[35]

From the twelfth century or earlier, "proof" implied the "redaction" of customs into written form, and to begin with this was a matter of private recording, exemplified by the *Libri Feudorum* assembled by Obertus de Orto and Girardus Niger, the anonymous *Establissements de Saint-Louis,* the *coutumes* of Beauvaisis by Philippe de Beaumanoir, the *Sachsenspiegel* by Eike von Repgow, the *Siete Partidas* of Alfonso the Wise, and perhaps the treatises of Glanvil and Bracton, which all gained authority only in retrospect. These collections represented not only a shift "from memory to written record" (in the words of M. T. Clanchy) but also the outcome of what Eugen Ehrlich called a "universalizing process," by which local customs were formulated and expanded geographically by judicial decisions and precedents.[36] This process was intensified by the introduction of more formal "Romano-canonical" procedures and by the teaching of civil and canon law in the universities.

Yet the institutions of popular approval were ostensibly retained. According to the fourteenth-century *Grand Coustumier de France* by Jacques d'Ableiges, custom was to be "proved by a meeting of ten men worthy of faith" (*prouvés en turbe par dix hommes dignes de foy*); and a little later Jean Bouteiller, in his *Somme rurale,* declared that custom was to be proved "by twelve of the wisest and oldest men of the place" (*douze hommes les plus sages et anciens du lieu*).[37] As Gilles Fortin wrote three centuries later of the *coutume* of Paris, "This customary law was for a long time observed without being written or engraved anywhere except on the hearts of the citizens who keep it; and if in doubt, the proof was not in books but in the assemblies [*turbes*] of those who knew the practice and ordinary usage"[38] (Fig. 4.1).

In France the development of custom from unwritten usages to learned doctrine, from fact to law, and from jurisprudence to legal philosophy, can be followed with some precision. The story begins in the thirteenth century when the central government began to take a serious interest in local customs, bound up as they were with the rival interests of feudal, seigneurial, and urban courts. By an ordinance of 1270 St. Louis instituted the device of the collective inquest (*inquisitio per turbam, enquête par turbe*), or rather adapted the old Carolingian inquest, designed originally to establish facts in criminal cases, to the authentication of local customs.[39] According to this ordinance, the royal commissioners (*enquêteurs*) convoked a certain number of sworn "wise men" representing the three estates, then proposed a series of customs for their consideration, and wrote down the customs mutually agreed upon.

This dramatic confrontation between king and people is a model of the aforesaid transition "from memory to written record." The assembled *turbiers* not only affirmed the existence—and more specifically the common and acknowledged "notoriety"—of each *coutume,* but they were also required to demonstrate the most minute "local knowledge." According to one thirteenth-century formulary, the members of the *turbe* were asked if they had ever "seen judgment by the said custom, and how many times, and by what judges, and between which persons, and at what time . . . and if all or the better part of the people agreed to introduce this custom."[40] Then, after unanimous agreement about the wording, the royal *enquêteurs* set the custom down in writing, leaving the delegates of the people to speak then or forever hold their peace. As for the organization of topics, sometimes the text followed Roman order, (persons, things, actions), sometimes feudal order (that is, beginning with "fief" or feudal jurisdiction and going on to questions of manorial rights, kinship, marriage, succession, and so forth).

In this process of "redaction" first the old "wise men" and later the

LA

COVSTVME

DE

PARIS,

CONFERE'E

AVEC LES AVTRES COVSTVMES DE FRANCE.

ET

EXPLIQVE'E PAR LES NOTES DE
Me CHARLES DV MOLIN *sur les mesmes Coustumes, les Arrests de la Cour, & diuerses autres Remarques.*

Ensemble vne recherche d'Autheurs, pour l'intelligence de la Coustume de Paris, & des autres Coustumes.

Commencée par M. G. FORTIN *Aduocat en Parlement,*

ET

Augmentée de plus des deux tiers par Me R. *aussi Aduocat en la Cour.*

AVEC VNE TABLE DES TITRES ET ARTICLES dans laquelle sont rapportez les Edicts, & Ordonnances de nos Roys, & tous les Arrests de la Cour de Parlement.

A PARIS,

Chez { IEAN GVIGNARD le fils, dans la grand'Salle, à l'Image S. Iean. *Et en la boutique de l'Angelier,* RENE' GVIGNARD, au premier pillier de la grand'Salle, au Sacrifice d'Abel. } au Palais,

M. DC. LXVI.

AVEC PRIVILEGE DV ROY.

Figure 4.1. Title page of a seventeenth-century edition of *La coustume de Paris* with the notes of Charles Dumoulin, as compiled in part by Giles Fortin. Source: Charles Dumoulin, *La coustume de Paris* (Paris, 1666). Courtesy of Princeton University Library.

lawyers played out, in the context of feudal relations and the institution of the royal inquest, the formation of a fundamental "social contract." Not only metaphorically but also in a technical legal sense, French customs were contractual ("sur le consentement des peuples des trois ordres," as Guy Coquille wrote in his sixteenth-century commentary on the *coutume* of Nivernais, "elles obligent *quasi ex contractu*").[41] In the eighteenth century another commentator celebrated the Bourbon *coutume* as "a public convention which one is obliged to execute and to observe in all good conscience."[42]

The introduction of writing changed the medium but not the spirit and intention of customary law, and indeed in the ritual of endorsement (*lecture et publication*), the reading retained parity with the process of writing and dissemination.[43] The formalism of the written word did not displace, it only reinforced the formalism of the spoken word. In oral procedure a man was still only as good as his word, and the words spoken by persons in a judicial proceeding could neither be changed nor withdrawn "under peril of their souls." So it was with French custom, for its recitation was almost a life-and-death matter to the subjects involved, concerning as it did their "liberties" and "honor," which was to say their property; and the texts of these usages were gone over with rabbinical care. In general custom was transformed into "customary law" (*droit coutumier*) "not in order to declare new law," as Pierre d'Angleberme put it, "but in order to preserve its memory" (*memoriae causa*).[44]

What complicates the idea of custom in social context is the fact that it cannot quite be fixed by legal formulation. In part this is because of the process of *desuetudo,* practical and theoretical obverse of *consuetudo,* in part because many customs, as Marc Bloch has shown in his extraordinary study of French rural history, have "no force apart from the wills of the inhabitants" and are preserved only in oral culture, where "human memory is the sole arbiter."[45] As Eusèbe Laurière observed in the seventeenth century, only "where the crops are showing" could customary law protect possession. In practice cultivated land was "subject to the law of nations and the common property of all." "How true it is," adds Bloch, "that all rural customs take their origin from an attitude of mind."

Redaction, of course, was intended to change all that. Endorsed by the crown in the famous ordinance of 1453, it was a process that clearly represented a political intrusion into the sphere of custom; and it was succeeded by a still more serious threat, which was the sixteenth-century movement to "reform" French customs. According to the official view, the ordinance of 1453 had created the authority "not only to publish the ancient customs but also to reform, to abrogate, and to adjust new articles and new customs, and to interpret and to revise them, with the advice of those in attendance, or the majority thereof."[46] This was the policy of Christofle de Thou, premier président of the parlement of Paris, leading figure in the reformation movement, and champion of legal uniformity.

Like redaction, "reformation" can be seen as a ceremonial reenactment of the original social compact, though admittedly under some duress. In conventional fashion, representatives of all three estates were in attendance, and especially those whose liberties, that is, interests, were at issue. The written record (*procès-verbal*) established by the royal officers was the very spirit of the custom (*l'âme de la coutume*); it began with a hierarchical listing of members of the nobles, churchmen, and bourgeois, and included an article-by-article account of the discussions of the unreformed custom—"in order to show how the redaction was conducted," wrote Simon Marion about the "first project" of the reformation of the Parisian custom, "and what disputes and difficulties were presented."[47] The fiction of popular approval was maintained by the view, which René Choppin expressed in his commentary on the *coutume* of Anjou, that the "new" custom, which was represented by some jurists as just "interpretation" of the old, went into force not with official publication but "from the moment when it was established in the assembly of estates, for the abolition or acceptance depends on the decision of the people."[48]

During the discussions objections were often raised that particular liberties were being neglected, or particular exemptions not recognized; and more than once complaints were lodged against de Thou for exceeding his authority.[49] In the reformation of the Parisian custom, for example, the bishop of Paris protested against infringement of the ancient liberties of St. Denis; and, speaking for the count, more recently duke, of Estampes, Marion argued that this *bailliage* was exempt because it "in no way recognized the custom of the *prévôté* of Paris." The social drama of "the reformation of customs" turned in reality on the struggle between local "liberties" and a larger conception of royal authority and national unity pursued by the lawyers of the last Valois.

In the long run the result was that political "approval" came to outweigh popular "consent" and the institutions through which it had been expressed. The seminal Ordinance of Montils-les-Tours of 1453 defined the procedures of royal visitation and redaction; but while the principle of consent by representatives of the three estates was preserved, this law also "prohibited any of the advocates of our realm from alleging or proposing other customs, usages and styles except those written down, agreed upon, and ordered."[50] Except in marginal cases where written rules were ambiguous or lacking, the *turbe,* too, became obsolete, and in 1667 it was officially abolished by an ordinance of Louis XIV. In matters of "proof," popular memory was established by written "certificates of usage" and "acts of notoriety"; and provincial custom was added to the canon of official legislation to be itself "interpreted."

Montesquieu summed up the process in this way: "These customs were preserved in the memories of old men, but insensibly laws or written customs were formed." Montesquieu was also aware of the political implications, for as he added, "Thus our customs were characterized in a threefold manner: they were committed to writing, they were made more general, and they received the stamp of royal authority." However imperfectly, "custom" was joined to royal jurisdiction—"private" to "public" law—as social base to governmental superstructure and so subjected, at least potentially, to official interpretation and control. In this way "custom" was given a political dimension lacking in the classical definition. Though still immune from legislative change, custom became, as Laurent Bouchel wrote in the early seventeenth century, "a civil law approved and received by the Estates of the province, under the authority of the king."[51]

The French School

If the idea of custom was given substance through judicial practice and political intrusion, it received theoretical form by academic jurists (Fig. 4.2). One of the best illustrations of the early modern idea of custom as an object of social and historical thinking is to be found in the commentaries on civil law by François Connan, published posthumously in 1553.[52] For Connan *ius civile* referred not merely to the particular tradition of Rome but more generally to the customs and laws of modern nations—to what Baldus had called the modern law of nations (*ius novissimum gentium*); and of course "custom," too, belonged to this modern law of nations. According to Connan, *consuetudo,* along with its darker sibling *desuetudo,* originated in the mores of particular peoples (*ius ex facto oritur*), those of the New as well as the Old World; was the product of willful human acts over a period of time; had the force of law (*pro lege*) and interpreted it (*consuetudo legem interpretatur*); and ceased to be valid—became *desuetudo*—

Figure 4.2. Scene at the Palais de Justice—a crier in the sixteenth century. Source: Henri Stein, *Le Palais de Justice et la Sainte-Chapelle* (Paris, 1912), facing p. 36. Courtesy of Princeton University Library.

not only through a natural process of "antiquation" but also through neglect and considerations of "equity," which for Connan was the true aim of "civil law."

Connan also spoke of custom as "second nature" (*altera natura*), but he did so in order to emphasize that *consuetudo* was indeed "other" than *natura*, and indeed marked a fundamental break with the natural world (*deflexit de via naturae*). In his view custom arose not from necessity or even instinct but rather from moral virtue and will (*virtutes hae non vocantur naturales, sed morales et voluntariae, quae non sunt naturae sed voluntatis*). Custom, in short, was the ruler of civil society, and could not be identified with natural instinct or with universal reason; nor could it be investigated and understood in such naturalistic and super- or subhuman terms. For Connan—invoking here Pindar's celebrated *nomos basileus*—this is exactly what the Greeks meant when they declared that custom or law was "king."

The study of law can be general and philosophical; the study of custom had to be carried on at least in part in an empirical, historical, and comparative way. In the sixteenth century Eguinarie Baron was the most prominent exemplar of this method.[53] In his own commentaries on "civil law" Baron declared the independence of French customs according to the old "pro lege" rule, that custom was the equivalent of law (*sola consuetudo, sine iudicio, pro Iure, id est Iure scripto servatur*), and, moreover, that judicial decisions had to follow accepted custom (*res iudicata non servatur sine consuetudine*). More generally, Baron tried to give local meaning to civil law by "accommodating it to the customs of the French and the royal laws" (*accommodata ad mores Galliarum et leges Regias* was his formula). Baron's work was in effect one of the first systematic efforts of comparative jurisprudence, a discipline which itself was conspicuously nourished by the idea of custom down to the time of Henry Sumner Maine.

The new methods of early modern French jurists reinforced another significant dimension of late medieval jurisprudence, which was the insistence on the practical rather than the theoretical character of law. If law originated in custom, it was given expression most fundamentally not by legislative "action" but by judicial decisions (*res judicatae*)—for these decisions, according to an old Roman maxim, were to be accepted as truth (*res iudicata pro veritate accipitur*), while judicial decisions were themselves not valid unless they were in conformity with custom (*res iudicata non servatur sine consuetudine*, in the words of Baron). What this signified for jurists like Ayrault, who compiled a new Digest based on *res judicatae*, was that the major part of law consisted in such judgments. The study and application of law and custom was a *prudentia* even more than a *scientia*—a *phronesis* even more than an *episteme* in currently fashionable terms—and based fundamentally not on theoretical rules but on "local" knowledge, which is to say knowledge not just of principle and its application but also of "people" and its environment, culture, and history.[54] In a manner of speaking it was the jurists who were the experts in the "second nature" of a people and in this sense in an early form of human science.

It is also clear that the idea of custom encouraged a historical interpretation of society and culture long before the historical schools of the nineteenth century. According to the formula cited by François Connan in the sixteenth century, "Manners should precede custom" (*mos praecedat consuetudinem*), just as custom itself preceded written law; and "written law confirms [custom] by the course of times" (*confirmat ab historia temporum*). In later ages this became a historiographical commonplace. As Jacques Godefroy put it in the seventeenth century, referring to the Roman as well as vernacular traditions, "If one thinks back to the origin of laws, one must recognize that customs preceded them, and indeed form the first part of positive law, though placed at the end."[55]

"Custom Is the Best Interpreter of Law"

In many respects *consuetudo* was absorbed by the culture of literacy and even transformed by it. Yet the break with oral culture was not complete. Invocation of "custom" was preserved not only in the oral pleading of lawyers but also, and more controversially, in the practice and theory of judicial discretion and "interpretation." The most generous view had been expressed by Odofredus in this way: "The power of custom is three-fold: it is the founder of law, the interpreter of law, and the abrogator of law" (*potestas consuetudinis est legum conditrix, est legum interpretatrix, est legum arrogatrix*).[56] This set of topoi was itself an extension of a late classical formula attributed to Paulus, that custom was the best interpreter of law (*optima enim est legum interpres consuetudo*), and it continued to be "extended" with abandon by modern jurists, theorists as well as practitioners. From the sixteenth century in particular there was a flood of treatises on interpretation, and *consuetudo* almost invariably figured as an aid to judicial interpretation, a supplement to "equity," and a limitation on political authority.[57] In this hermeneutical form, and in the growing rivalries between judiciary and legislature, the idea of custom persisted and even flourished into modern times, reinforcing the conception of custom as a fundamental category of judicial and social thought antecedent and superior to the law.

In France the idea of custom was given shape and substance in the context of a massive and continuous legal canon centering on the provincial *coutumiers*, some three hundred of them eventually, which were written aggregations of many more local collections that have largely disappeared from the horizons of historical research.[58] These surviving customals accumulated a vast amount of commentary, not only legal and practical but also historical, philosophical, and literary, including verse renditions of the *coutumes* of Normandy and Paris (as later the Napoleonic Code), composed in part for mnemonic purposes. The customs also produced an indigenous theory of interpretation (*ars hermeneutica*, as it was called from the seventeenth century). "In order not to be slaves, imitators, and worshippers of foreigners," wrote Coquille, "let us not involve the interpretation of our customs with the confusing rules of statutes" (referring to the opinions of the civilians of the Bartolist school).[59] According to Paul Challine's *Method for the Understanding of French Customs* of 1666, the *coutumes* had to be interpreted in their own terms (*se doivent expliquer par elles-mesmes*), should be abolished by nonusage, and, especially, should be related to "common law" (*droit commun*) and to social context.[60] When particular customs were defective, application might be made not only to royal ordinances and to "the reason of Roman law" but also to unwritten usages, neighboring customs, and "the general spirit of French custom," especially that of Paris.

From the time of Beaumanoir down to that of Marc Bloch it has been clear that French social customs need to be studied in particular geohistorical context. The test of local character was often the degree of "liberty" enjoyed by all the social orders, especially in contrast to the Roman tradition of tyranny and "paternal power" (*patria potestas; puissance paternelle*). "For in France it is liberty that is ancient," Coquille remarked, "and despotism that is modern."[61] In his province of Nivernais, for example, the old maxim of the feudal domination of land did not hold: not "nulle terre sans seigneur" but "nul seigneur sans titre." In Burgundy—in sharp contrast to Normandy—virtually all land without title was allodial. More generally, Le Roy Ladurie has pointed out the emergence of "anti-paternal" and "egalitarian" patterns of succession in Normandy and, from the new *coutume* published in 1510, in the Paris-Orléans area.[62] These features were emphasized and elaborated by later commentators, who tried to give legal and literary form to local traditions.

Increasingly, commentators tried to place their *coutumes* in historical perspective, employing for this purpose documents (including charters, the *procès-verbaux*, inscriptions, and monographic studies of feudal origins). In his commentary on the custom of Auxerre in the late seventeenth century, Edme Billon quoted Baldus to the effect that the original Gallic inhabitants, "though dominated by the Roman Empire and its constitutions, could not force themselves to follow them, and that this People (jealous of their liberties and regarding these laws as a servitude) formed in their own way particular customs in each province, which they guarded inviolably against the said constitutions made for everyone in general."[63] And the spirit of the original custom was presumably preserved throughout the processes of redaction, reformation, and interpretation.

The survival of some customs, at least in a general form, can be seen in the persistence of maxims, which reflected folk wisdom as well as legal experience. One of the most fundamental questions has been that of boundaries, which sometimes had a religious dimension (symbolized more famously by the Roman god Terminus) and which involved issues of time and locale. In French custom the setting of boundaries (*bornage*) was first a matter of private, then of feudal agreement. "All parties who require *bonnage* [sic] should have it," declared Beaumanoir, "and if they agree, they may set boundaries without legal process [*bonner sans justice*], but this is not the case in many seigneuries . . . , where [the custom is that] the tenant may not set boundaries without appealing to the lord."[64] The principle that was most widely recognized, however, was that "boundaries must be set under judicial authority" (*bornes se mettent par auctorité de justice*). This was the maxim that appeared in the medieval *coutumes* of Anjou and Maine, in Antoine Loisel's *Institutes coutumiers* in the early seventeenth century, and in the Civil Code of 1804. After the Revolution *bornage* could still be accomplished *amiablement* as well as *judiciairement*, but this implied a modern contractual agreement which could always be contested. By then, however, most boundary disputes were in fact settled in terms not of "property" but of "possession," which is to say in terms of the old customary law of *saisine* and under the jurisdiction of the newly instituted justices of the peace. Thus a customary rule was preserved over many centuries and legal and social transformations, accommodating popular will but inclining as usual toward expert legal judgment.

This exemplifies the life cycle of one particular usage. To illustrate the canon formation and deformation of a whole complex of customs, consider the long career of the *coutume* of Burgundy, which was a hybrid of Roman law and the old *Leges Burgundionum* established in the fifth century by King Gundobad "for the good and tranquillity of our people."[65] In the later Middle Ages the Burgundian customs emerged from conditions of what Marc Bloch characterized as "primitive communism," surviving at least in part until the seventeenth century. They preceded, and outlasted, both the old kingdom and the modern duchy of Burgundy; and they were applied and were interpreted over generations of social turmoil and hardship, including the disappearance of villages and last-ditch efforts to reaffirm seigneurial rights.

The Burgundian *coutume* was redacted in 1459 by Duke Philip the Good, responding to complaints and petitions from the three estates, which were assembled in Dijon in traditional fashion. The representatives were "interrogated concerning the fact of the customs," article by article, documentary sources were examined, and after corrections and many altercations, the text of the custom was established, following the arrangement of Roman law. In 1575 it was "reformed" according to the same inquisitional procedure and with the inevitable controversies between the estates and the royal commissioners. All of this was set down in the published *procès-verbal*—in order, as one witness put it, "to know how the redaction was conducted and what disputes and difficulties were presented."[66] A second reformation in the eighteenth century was judged to be unnecessary, though it was still "incomplete," as Professor Dunod admitted in 1756, and needed to be "a little more developed."

The *Coutumes générales de Bourgogne* was the first book published in Dijon (in 1490), and it was reissued at least seventy-five times down to the Revolution. Not to mention many manuscript sources, pre-redaction versions, and glosses, it was interpreted by at least eighteen jurists, from Barthélemy de Chasseneux (whose Latin commentary appeared in 1517 and was reprinted at least twenty times before the end of the seventeenth century) down to Jean Bouhier, president of the parlement of Burgundy (whose French commentary was published for the last time between 1787 and 1789). To complicate this scholastic and humanistic tradition further, Bouhier wrote a "history of the commentators on the custom of Burgundy," in which he upheld the Roman provenance and "spirit" of French customs against the rival "party" of customary law—and indeed the authority of Roman law as "common law" (*droit commun*) in Burgundy.[67]

In general the Burgundian custom was not only accommodated to civilian and canonist tradition but it was overlaid with scholastic apparatus, classical adornments, historical scholarship, comparisons with civil law and other customs, rational analysis according to the "enlightened" norms of modern natural law, and the debates over the proper way to unify French law. It was interpreted in terms of what might be regarded as rudimentary "rules of sociological method"—considerations of geography, the culture and "humors" of the people, historical tradition, social structure, and other aspects of "local knowledge" essential to the legal science of the old regime. In these and other ways the Burgundian custom enjoyed an extraordinary intellectual odyssey, especially under the leadership of the jurists, before disappearing, along with the other provincial customs, in the revolutionary maelstrom which took legal form on the famous night of 4 August—only to emerge again in the antiquarian labors of modern French scholars.

Custom and Codification

In Bouhier's time the major issue of the legal tradition was that of legal unification, or codification; and judicial opinion was sharply divided between two "parties"—that of Roman law, defended by Bouhier, and that of customary law, based on the Franco-Germanic interpretations of Parisian commentators and historians, who dreamed of a law "peculier to the French nation" (*peculier à la Nation françoise*).[68] The division is illustrated by the old anecdote, told by Coquille in the sixteenth century and repeated later by Bouhier, about the controversy between the "two great personnages of that time, who were successively presidents of the Parlement of Paris."[69] The first, "Pierre Lizet held that Roman law was our common law [*droit commun*] and accommodated to it as best he could our French law, which he thought invalid when contrary to Roman law." Contradicting this view, Christofle de Thou regarded French customs and laws as "our common law." This cultural dialectic was highlighted also by the competing reputations of the two greatest scholars of the day, the Romanizing Jacques Cujas and the Germanizing Charles Dumoulin.

The division between Germanists and Romanists continued into the eighteenth century and was duly noted by Montesquieu. Among the Germanic peoples, he wrote, everyone was "tried by the established customs of his own nation"; and the feudist tradition retained this principle of personality.[70] On the other hand, the foreign doctrines of Roman law were received only as "written reason" (*ratio scripta; raison écrite*)—and had no other claim to authority.

The idea of a racially pure French custom (*consuetudo Franciae* or *con-*

suetudo gallicana), applying at least to the territory between the Loire and the Rhine and distinguished both from Roman law and from the *coutumes* of other provinces, can be traced back to the thirteenth century; and by the sixteenth century it was firmly established in professional tradition.[71] In de Thou's time the best expression of the ideal of a national custom was that of the great feudist Charles Dumoulin, who commented on all of the French *coutumes* as well as the *stilus* of the parlement of Paris and monuments of French law. Dumoulin rejected the authority of Roman law in favor of the native feudal law of France; and indeed it was his program, which he expressed as "the concord and union of the customs of France," that in effect served as the theoretical basis for the reformation of French customs led by Dumoulin's colleague de Thou.[72] For Dumoulin the *coutume* of Paris was dominant in France (*caput huius regni etiam Gallicae et Belgicae consuetudines*), and this thesis was defended by many of his followers down to the Revolution—and, indeed, in legal as well as scholarly terms, long afterwards. In the next generation, Louis Le Caron, himself a commentator on the Parisian custom as well as an editor of the *Grand Coustumier de France,* celebrated a generalized "French law" (*Droit françois*) based on the custom of Paris.[73] So, a century later, did Dumoulin's disciple and biographer Julien Brodeau, who argued that Paris was not only "the ordinary residence of the kings and their court" but also "the center of the state" (*le centre de l'Estat*).[74] And a century after that François Bourjon was celebrating the "common law" of France as "the exact explication of [Parisian] custom."[75]

The scholarly investigation of French legal tradition, beginning especially with Dumoulin, reinforced this royalist thesis through imaginative as well as historical reconstruction. In his *Institutes coustumières* Antoine Loisel sought the heritage of native French law and folk wisdom in a variety of medieval sources, literary and proverbial as well as legal; and his work, like Dumoulin's, had a considerable following (Fig. 4.3).[76] One successor was François de Launay, whose commentary on Loisel's work emphasized the extreme antiquity of this heritage. "Charlemagne himself did not distinguish laws from customs," Launay wrote; and, further, "It is certain that the ancient custom of which we hear in the capitularies was a general rule for the whole kingdom, a law universally observed in all of France."[77] In the eighteenth century Pierre Groseley went on to claim that French customs could be traced back "to the ancient inhabitants of Frankish Gaul."[78]

What these juridico-historical scholars were seeking was nothing less

Figure 4.3. Antoine Loisel (1536–1617), from a wax bust. Source: Ernest Charvet, *Les dernières années d'Antoine Loisel* (Beauvais, 1880). Courtesy of Princeton University Library.

than the "common law" or "spirit of the law" of France—an imaginative legal fiction akin to the "immemorial custom" imagined by Edward Coke. In civil law the "spirit" of law (*mens legum, esprit des lois*) referred to its true meaning or its "reason" (*ratio legis*); and so jurists like Domat and Montesquieu employed the phrase. Groseley, a friend of Montesquieu, was careful to distinguish his researches into the "spirit" of French law (*l'esprit particulier de nostre Droit coutumier actuel* was his phrase) from the project of his more distinguished colleague. For Groseley the "spirit" of the law resided not in nature in the sense of universal reason but rather in the "second nature" of the French people—in Challine's words, "the general spirit of all the customs of France" (*l'esprit général de toutes les Coutumes de France*).[79] According to Claude de Ferrière, writing in the later seventeenth century, French custom "was formed by nature and reason" and it was generally opposed to the abstract "reason" supposedly possessed by Roman law. "People are most naturally inclined to follow what conforms most closely with their state and their manners and what concerns their common interest," he continued; and further, "the common inclinations of peoples come from the diversity of social orders and environments and may be called 'civil reason' [*la raison civile*], which is the foundation of customs and laws."[80]

Just a few years before the Revolution, P. G. Michaux celebrated custom as a reflection of the ancient state of things—"social laws" (*loix sociales*, or *loix fondamentales*) as distinguished from the "political" and "administrative" creations of Roman law and modern legislators. "Customs were not the work of the French monarchy and . . . not the work of the Roman domination," Michaux argued. On the contrary, "customs are the true monuments of the nations of Europe . . . and the creation of these nations as a body" (*le propre ouvrage de ces nations en corps*). As for the French people, he concluded, "We emerged into a social and political order . . . not as imagined by Pufendorf and other [social-contract] theorists but rather as revealed in our customs."[81] One can hardly imagine a less fashionable position to take in 1783.

Natural Law

It was over the life cycle of a legal genre—the texts and critical commentaries on *droit coutumier*—that the modern idea of custom took its form and content. There was, however, another school of legal thought and practice which gave further definition to the old regime conception of custom (and further impetus to the codification movement, which was aimed in effect at superseding custom). What Gierke called the "antique-modern" doctrines of natural law revived the old distinction between "primary" and "secondary natural law," and, of course, it was to this second, derivative class that custom was consigned.

"There are two kinds of law used in all nations of the world," wrote Jean Domat in the later seventeenth century. "One is natural law and the other the laws proper to each nation, such as customs authorized by long usage."[82] Thus Domat paraphrased and "naturalized" the famous observation of Gaius, that "all peoples observe in part their own special law and in part a law common to all men"; and he accommodated not only a universal law based on reason but also a localized custom based in effect on the accidents of history and on human will. As God created nature or indeed was Himself nature (*Deus, id est Natura* was the medieval formula)—so man created a "second nature," which was custom.

Natural law of course dominated the social thought of the Enlightenment, especially that of "jusnaturalists" like Leibniz, Pufendorf, and Domat, who hoped to bring reason and "natural order" to the wilderness of European customs. One of Domat's contemporaries, Louis Boullenois, had gone so far as to propose a sort of Cartesian jurisprudence that would dispense with conventional scholarship and practical judgment and, in his words, deliver itself over to "meditation."[83] In practice this meant isolating and ordering the economic interests of men in a rational way that amounted to the juridical equivalent of Physiocracy. By thus joining the "passions and the interests"—in effect, by isolating and ordering the economic nature of men—Boullenois hoped "to lead French customs to unanimity" and so "to reduce a great kingdom to the same law."

The same impulse to rationalism can be seen in practical jurisprudence. French jurists like François Bourjon and Pierre de Merville tried to reduce the customs of Paris, Normandy, and others to natural "principles" or "maxims"; and P. C. L. Gin, following Domat, published a "reasoned analysis" of French law by comparing Roman law with the *coutume* of Paris (a work which, from the first edition of 1782, evolved directly and with little change of substance into his commentary on the Napoleonic Code in 1803).[84] Montesquieu made his own contribution by piecing together a "theory of feudal laws" and disengaging the tradition of customary law from the errors of Romanist interpretation.[85]

French custom itself also tended to incorporate notions which legal theorists attributed, belatedly, to "jusnaturalism." Principles of self-defense (the formula *vi vim repellere*) and especially the "natural liberty" of men were not discoveries of modern philosophy but rather part of the legacy of customary law as the "common law of France," which also had access to principles of natural law. As Nicolas Bohier had written of the *coutumier* of Bourges, for example, "This custom shows by natural law that all men are born free."[86] And as François Bourjon wrote over two centuries later, the principle that "every person is free if there is no contrary law or judgment" is part of the "common law of France and the custom of Paris."[87]

The French Revolution was a paradigmatic battleground for the clash between the ideals of natural law and the inertial forces of custom—which by then seemed not an expression but the very antithesis of the *Volonté Générale*. On the question of codification in particular, philosophes, Jacobins, and Bonapartists seemed united in their common devotion to natural law, to legislative solutions for social problems, and to the idea that pure reason would prevail. "Do you want new laws?" Voltaire had asked: "Burn yours and make new ones." Such indeed was the apparent result of the Revolution. The major target of the provincial uprisings of July 1789, beyond the chateaux and feudal titles, was "custom" and all that it stood for. Subsequent revolutionary legislation put an end not only to the feudal and corporate society of the old regime (as well as many of its written records) but also to the provincial customs accumulated over the centuries. In the spirit of the provincial *cahiers* and the extraordinary "sacrifices" made by the French nobility on the famous night of 4 August, the National Assembly "entirely destroyed the feudal regime" (the *complexum feudale* is the phrase of Dumoulin quoted in the assembly sessions of 4 September) and with it the accumulated customs, local and general, of many centuries.[88]

The next step was a "new judicial order," and one of the first items on the agenda was the construction of a code, although this was accomplished only after a decade of war, political extremism, social upheaval, and the legal confusion of *le droit intermédiaire*. As J. J. R. Cambacérès declared in his first "project" of 1793, the aims were first to destroy existing laws and customs and then, by a "perfect legislation," "to establish forever the empire of liberty and the destiny of France."[89] In the preliminary discussions of the code, which were the modern and authoritarian counterpart to the *procès-verbaux* of the old customs, the citizen redactors (and sometimes the first consul himself) denounced the old customs, paradoxically, as derogations from the national will. Still more dangerous was the attendant notion of judicial "interpretation," warned one of the Bonapartist redactors, for this old form of corruption represented a loophole through which all the abuses of the old regime would return.[90]

These fears were not imaginary, for in fact much of the substance of the Civil Code was drawn from old regime customs, especially that of Paris, and the attendant jurisprudence. The institution of private property itself, though theoretically following the "absolute" definition drawn from civil law, was in fact based on the old customary distinction, preserved in the Burgundian as well as Parisian *coutume,* between feudal and usufructuary domain (*domaine direct* and *domaine utile*).[91] Not surprisingly, since the "Committee on Feudalism" was headed by Merlin de Douai, a distinguished jurist and editor of a massive *Répertoire de jurisprudence* appearing almost continuously between 1784 and 1830. Conservative attitudes also infected the Committee of Redaction, on which Cambacérès was opposed by J. E. M. Portalis, who celebrated custom as "the wisdom of our fathers which formed our national character" (*la sagesse de nos pères, qui ont formé le caractère national*), and he did not scruple to cite Dumoulin and other feudists in this connection. Regarding the Civil Code as a "bridge between the old and the new law," Portalis argued that "we should preserve what we do not have to destroy."[92]

Moreover, if the Revolution aroused the codifiers, it also awakened the People, who were the source of custom and law and who, infused with a new "bourgeois" spirit, continued themselves in their actions to "interpret"—to modify, extend, and abrogate—the legislation which Jacobins and Bonapartists had imposed on the French nation. They continued, that is to say, to produce their own customs according to changing needs and pressures; and as always the jurists followed—when they did not guide—this new spirit by producing a corresponding jurisprudence and social philosophy and by contributing to what Philippe Sagnac called a "return to custom."[93]

Over succeeding generations the highly abstract law assembled in the Napoleonic Code was in many ways applied and interpreted in the light of customary law and the habits and mentality of the old legal profession (which Napoleon was shortly to restore). During the restoration the credit of the idea of custom—and the idea that "custom is the best interpreter of law"—continued to rise. In the interpretations of conservative jurists, in the theories of the Historical School of Law, and in Romantic historiography, the canon of customary law was given new life, along with many of its premises, prejudices, and (in some cases) political inclinations. In short, like Talleyrand, French customs also "survived"; they survived through social habits and persisting mentalities as well as judicial decisions and legal and historical reconstructions.[94]

Custom and Social Science

The idea of custom was present at the birth of modern social science, first as a threat and then as a central problem in the understanding of social structure and change. "Social science" was associated in particular with the great enterprise of codification designed to complete Napoleon's neo-Roman imperial edifice. The fashionable term "Science sociale" was used precisely in this connection not only by latter-day philosophes and Ideologues, whom Napoleon despised, but also by the redactors of his code. In a *Discours sur la science sociale* delivered at the Institut National in 1798, Cambacérès had celebrated legislation, political economy, and moral philosophy, and their common goal, which was nothing less than the "perfecting of social relations" and the fulfilling of "civilization."[95] In effect French "social science" arose as an expression of a kind of internal imperialism in which customs would be subjected to the Bonapartist effort of social engineering.

In another discourse presented to the institute at this time, A. L. Jussieu was even more specific about the connections between *la science sociale* and the understanding of customs and laws.[96] "Social science studies the various colonies emerging from the Roman Republic," Jussieu declared;

> it examines elsewhere the customary laws and codes of the ancients, the laws favoring marriage, the perhaps too limited rights of mothers over children, the negotiations of the Athenian people to form and especially to abolish their laws; and it always seeks lessons for this generation in the experience of earlier centuries. It concentrates especially on the early period of the French monarchy; it reflects on national sovereignty, the liberty of suffrages and individual liberty, on moral elements, the nature and effects of public opinion, on the way to shape public spirit and to determine the level of prosperity of modern peoples.

The fundamental problem of this new conception of social science was first and best expressed in the exchanges between Cambacérès and Portalis—reflecting and often invoking the spirits of Rousseau and Montesquieu, respectively. Portalis rejected Cambacérès's plan to "perfect everything" and to "foresee everything." "How can one control the action of time?" asked Portalis.[97] "How oppose the course of events or the imperceptible force of manners? How know and calculate what experience alone can reveal to us?" In the context of the new "social science," in other words, the old contest between custom and law, debated so often by the doctors of law, was once more recapitulated, this time in connection with the methodology of modern social science.

This was the issue taken up in a more scholarly fashion by another post-revolutionary product, the Historical School of Law, which had branches in France as well as Germany. Savigny, the leading figure of this school, took the French debates over the Code Napoléon as the point of departure and the principal source of documentation for his famous manifesto "On the Vocation of this Age for Legislation and Jurisprudence."[98] To the notion of a perfect society created by modern legislation, the Historical School opposed the model of customary law, along with its natural accumulation of jurisprudence. The old notion that custom reflects the spirit of the people was revived by Romantic scholars—Herder's and Savigny's *Volksgeist* being the equivalent of Bartolus's *mens populi* and the feudists' *esprit du droit coutumier,* the "spirit of a people" as determined by learned jurists. For Savigny, custom was scientific not through its efforts of legislation but rather through its understanding of the continuing force of custom—"first," in Savigny's words, "as part of the aggregate experience of a community, and second [as] a distinct branch of knowledge in the hands of the jurists." For Savigny, too, "custom" located the battle between the legislative and judicial forces—and the local knowledge essential to the understanding of custom was the mark of the scientific expert.

The Philosophical School of Law, deriving its strength from Hegel, engaged Savigny's Historical School in mortal combat; but despite methodological differences, there was remarkable agreement about the source, if not the role, of custom: it was the product of nature and of human "spirit" and will. "The basis of right is, in general, mind [*das Geistige*]," declared Hegel; "its precise place and point of origin in the will [*der Wille*]. The will is free, so that freedom is both the substance of right and its goal, while the system of right [*Rechtssystem,* that is, system of law] is the realm of freedom made actual, the world of mind [*Geist*] brought forth out of itself like a second nature [*eine zweite Natur*]."[99] Characteristically (though at the same time quite in keeping with the old legal tradition), Hegel reconciled primary and secondary nature by historicizing them.

The founding fathers of modern social science, especially anthropology and sociology, carried on the assumptions and attitudes developed by the old jurisprudence and its epigones in the Historical and Philosophical schools. The exception was France, where Comte's positivist model of "Sociology" superseded Savigny's and Hegel's small followings. In England the key figure was Henry Sumner Maine, who took comparative jurisprudence as the high road to social understanding. In legal terms his work was hardly as influential as that of the arch-codifier Bentham or John Austin, whose *bête noire* was the idea of popular custom (which he dismissed as "only a moral rule until enforced by the tribunals"); but then law and social science long remained estranged in England.[100] In Germany Ferdinand Tönnies—reacting to the naturalist approach of Hobbes—proclaimed custom to be the most direct expression of the *Volksgeist*. "Custom is social will itself," he wrote "distilled from habit, usage, and practice."[101] And in support of his position he summed up the view of Savigny, that "law grows in a manner which common usage terms customary law [*Gewohnheitsrecht*], that is to say, it originates in customs and popular beliefs first, in jurisprudence next; everywhere, then, by forces quietly doing their work, and nowhere by the arbitrary fiat of a legislator."

When Albion Small, one of the founders of sociology in the United States, wrote the history of his discipline, he too found it necessary to take as his point of departure the debate over custom and codification which Savigny had publicized a century before. Small was quite aware of the contributions of legal science to social science, and in particular to the ethnographic and anthropological conceptions of "custom" and the collective behavior of so-called primitive peoples in general.[102] In this transmuted, modernized form, "custom" retained many of its former traits, including its popular character, its cultural specificity and historicity, and its estrangement from nature. "Custom," according to the *Encyclopedia of the Social Sciences,* applies "to the totality of behavior patterns which are carried by tradition and lodged in the group. It is not properly applicable to those aspects of communal activity which are obviously determined by biological considerations."[103]

In this entry Edward Sapir recognized, at least in a general way, the heritage of the term "custom" as "a common sense concept which has served as the matrix for the development of the more refined and technical and anthropological concept of culture." In the new, ostentatiously more "scientific" *International Encyclopedia of the Social Sciences,* this article has been replaced by one on "norms" (which, with unconscious irony and historical innocence, remarks that the old *Encyclopedia* "did not even mention the term 'norms.'"[104] Here the question of origins is posed, but in purely abstract, behavioralist, causal, and explanatory terms; and while custom is acknowledged "tacitly to be supported by social approval," in general the term (and by implication the older literature on the subject) has been consigned to the antiquarian, and so presumably irrelevant, stages of social science. And no doubt the old questions posed by Portalis, Savigny, and indeed Albion Small (who was virtually disowned by his successors in the Chicago school) have been deposited in the same dust bin by the new—legislative as well as "scientific"—experts.

Custom in Perspective

This is only a part of the story of "custom," for as I have suggested there are also literary, psychological, religious, and especially philosophical dimensions that invite exploration. By definition, of course, "custom" fell short of perfection. In the early modern period it was denounced by religious doctrinaires like Luther and Calvin, for whom it was a "public pestilence." More secular-minded persons, however, tried to come to terms with the idea of custom and even, like Montaigne, came to identify it, in effect, with the human condition. "After at first rejecting custom," Jean Starobinski has concluded, "Montaigne for want of anything better ultimately reconciled himself to it: since the present is the only place in which men can dwell, it is unwise to shake its foundation."[105] For Montaigne custom was indeed second nature (*l'accoutumance est une seconde Nature*) and, in his rendering of Pindar, "empress and queen of the world"—"another powerful and imperious mistress," as Pierre Charron put it, or in the words of Bacon, "the principal magistrate of man's life."[106]

Renaissance moral thought, drawing on classical and Christian sources, displayed a striking ambivalence toward the idea of custom. Though born in nature, custom went its own way and became the most oppressive of tyrants. "Who would believe how great and imperious is the authority of custom?" Charron asked. "Those who call it another nature have not gone far enough, for it does more than this; it struggles against nature."[107] For Montaigne's friend and soul mate Etienne de la Boétie, it was custom above all that subjugated man to tradition and undermined his natural freedom. "Custom," he concluded, "is the first cause of voluntary servitude" (*la premiere raison de la servitude volontaire, c'est la coustume*).[108] Pascal, beset by religious anxieties as well as concern for the human condition, carried the argument another step. Custom is not only second nature, he concluded, but a "second nature that destroys the former"; and "as custom is a second nature, so nature itself is only a first custom."[109] This humanizing critique of philosophy was brought to its logical and epistemological extreme by Hume, for whom "custom" replaced the imputation of natural "causes" through reason, whose natural sovereignty he came, on the most conventional grounds, to reject. "Custom then," he concluded, alluding again to the Pindarean formula, "is the great guide of human life"—and, indeed, by extension, of philosophy.[110]

But the efforts of philosophers, rhetoricians, and jurists have not succeeded in preserving the conceptual status of the idea of custom. From the seventeenth century custom was more thoroughly eclipsed than ever by nature, and the science thereof; and political considerations contributed further to its decline. For custom was undeniably fashioned at least as much by social experience as by the discourse of the learned, as much by the moved and the shaken as by the movers and the shakers.

"Custom," then, the concept as well as the term, seems to have returned to its hiding places in ordinary language, and it is for the most part left to historians to reconstruct its extraordinary adventures as companion and rival of primary nature. Following the fortunes of "second nature" gives us access to various levels of Western historical experience. It leads us, for example, into the prehistorical and metahistorical labyrinth of Western languages, into the technical recesses of the Western legal tradition, into the little explored area of preliterate culture, into the upper layers of social history and the lower reaches of political theory, into the transcultural career of an enduring intellectual and professional canon, into the ideological context of revolutionary action and counterrevolutionary reaction, and into the prehistory of the modern sciences of society, culture, and politics. It also reminds us that these disciplines, as well as the study of history broadly conceived, have a richer heritage than the prevalence of "scientific" styles of research and rhetoric might suggest; but I leave the moral of this story for another occasion.

Notes

1. Azo, *In Ius civile summa* (Lyon, 1564), 233 v: "Dicitur consuetudo, quasi communis assuetudo: et alias dicitur consuetudo, et in alia significatione, altera natura," one of many statements of this conventional view. Cf. Walter Ullmann, *The Medieval Idea of Law as Represented by Lucas de Penna* (London, 1946), 62; also, more generally, Hans Kelsen, *Society and Nature* (Chicago, 1943).

2. The exception is Gerhardt Funke, *Gewohnheit* (Bonn, 1958), and his entry

in the *Geschichtliche Grundbegriffe,* ed. O. Brunner et al. (Stuttgart, 1972–); also *Historisches Wörterbuch der Philosophie,* although these treat the psychological rather than the social aspect of custom (i.e., "habit").

3. Charles H. Kahn, *The Art and Thought of Heraclitus: An Edition of the Fragments with Translation and Commentary* (Cambridge, 1979), 260–61, 335, on fragment #119, "character is fate" (*ethos anthropoi daimon*).

4. See, e.g., W. K. C. Guthrie, *A History of Greek Philosophy,* III (Cambridge, 1969), 55ff.; Felix Heinemann, *Nomos und Physis* (Basel, 1945); Martin Ostwald, *Nomos and the Beginnings of Athenian Democracy* (Oxford, 1969); Clarence J. Glocken, *Traces on the Rhodian Shore: Nature and Culture in Western Thought from Ancient Times to the End of the Eighteenth Century* (Berkeley, 1967), 116.

5. *On the Soul,* tr. W. S. Hett (Cambridge, Mass., 1975), "On Memory and Recollection," 304; cf. Richard Sorabji, *Aristotle on Memory* (London, 1972), 56. Though dealing with psychology, these classical texts were also extended to "custom" in a social and collective sense.

6. *Rhetoric,* tr. J. Freese (Cambridge, Mass., 1967), 1370a5.

7. I refrain from reproducing all the references, but besides modern dictionaries, see H. Estienne, *Thesaurus linguae graecae* and *Thesaurus linguae latinae; Suidae lexicon;* Thomas Cooper, *Thesaurus linguae Romanae et Britannicae;* DuCange; and lexicons of jurisprudence (e.g., Calvinus, Ragueau) and of philosophy (Chauvin).

8. For example, Cicero, *De Finibus,* V, 74; Quintilian, *Inst. orat.,* I, 1. Also cf. Varro, *De Lingua latina,* VIII, 27; Aulus Gellius, *Noctes atticae* XII, 13, 29; and Sextus Empiricus, *Outlines of Pyrrhonism,* I, 146, tr. in J. Annas and J. Barnes, *The Modes of Skepticism* (Cambridge, 1985).

9. *In eundem Poggium libellus primus,* "Praefatio," in *Opera omnia,* ed. E. Garin (Turin, 1962), I, 386. See Lawrence Manley, *Convention 1500–1750* (Cambridge, Mass., 1980), 90ff.; Salvatore Camporeale, *Lorenzo Valla. Umanesimo e teologia* (Florence, 1972); Sarah Stever Gravelle, "The Latin-Vernacular Question and Humanism: Theory of Language and Culture," *Journal of the History of Ideas* 49 (1988), 367–86.

10. Pindar, *Nemean Odes,* IV, 10; Herodotus, *History,* VII, 104; and see Marcello Gigante, *NOMOS BASILEUS* (Naples, 1956).

11. Augustine, *Contra Julianum Pelagium* (*Patrologia Latina,* XLIV, 816), and *Doctrina christiana,* II, 19–27; Jerome, *Epistolae,* XCVIII, 3; Clement, *Exhortation to the Greeks,* x; Thomas, *Summa Theologiae,* Ia, 63, 5; II, i, Q. 95–97. On "second" and other grades of natural law in theologians as well as jurists, see Reginaldo Pizzorini, *Il Diritto naturale dalle origini a S. Tommaso d'Aquino* (Rome, 1978), 203.

12. *Epistolae,* lxxiv (Gratian, *Decretum* I, D. VIII, ii, c. 5); also Tertullian, *De Virginibus celandis,* c. 1; and cf. Gerhard Ladner, *The Idea of Reform* (Cambridge, Mass., 1959), 137.

13. *Etymologiae,* V, 2, cited by Gratian, *Decretum,* I, d. 1. In general, Hostiensis, *In primum librum Decretalium commentaria,* 1, "Quid est consuetudo. . . . Usus rationabilis competente tempore confirmatus"; Rufinus, *Summa Decretalium,* D. 1, "Mores autem isti partim sunt redacti in scriptis et vocantur ius constitutum; partim absque scripto utentium placito reservantur, et dicitur simpliciter consuetudo."

See also *Corpus juris canonici, per regulas naturali ordine digestas* (Cologne, 1738), I, 79ff., offering twelve definitions of *consuetudo;* René Wehrle, *De la Coutume dans le droit canonique* (Paris, 1928), 40ff.; and the article in *Dictionnaire du droit canonique.*

14. The best guide to the massive literature on the European legal tradition is Helmut Coing, ed., *Handbuch der Quellen und Literatur der neueren europäischen Privatrechtsgeschichte* (Munich, 1976–); also, the recent surveys (especially Franz Wieacker and Adriano Cavanna); and cf. my various essays in *History, Law and the Human Sciences* (London, 1984). A recent book of major importance is L. Waelkens, *La Théorie de la coutume chez Jacques de Révigny* (Leiden, 1984), with edition of various manuscript texts.

15. Digest, I, 1, 6 (Ulpianus), "Hoc igitur ius [civile] nostrum constat aut ex scripto aut sine scripto, ut apud Graecos: *ton nomon oi men eggraphoi oi de agraphoi*"; and I, 3, 32.2 (Julianus), "Inveterata consuetudo pro lege non immerito custoditur, et hoc est ius quod dicitur moribus constitutum." On customary law in general see Siegfried Brie, *Die Lehre vom Gewohnheitsrecht* (Breslau, 1899), Francesco Calasso, *Medio evo del diritto,* I (Milan, 1954), Auguste Lebrun, *La Coutume* (Paris, 1932), Eugen Ehrlich, *Fundamental Principles of the Sociology of Law,* tr. W. Moll (Cambridge, Mass., 1936), 436ff., Filippo Gallo, *Interpretazione e formazione consuetudinaria del diritto* (Turin, 1971); Paul Ourliac, *Etudes d'histoire du droit médiéval* (Paris, 1979), I; and R. W. and A. J. Carlyle, *A History of Medieval Political Thought in the West* (New York, 1903–36), II, 50–67; III, 41–51; IV, 45–50; VI, 17–25, 150–53.

16. Digest, I, 3, 35 (Hermogenianus), "et ea, quae longa consuetudine comprobata si per annos plurimos observata, velut tacita conventio non minus quam ea quae scripta sui servantur"; Code, VIII, 52 ("Quae sit longa consuetudo"), 2, "Consuetudinis ususque longaevi non vilis auctoritas est, verum non usque adeo sui valitura momento, ut aut rationem vincat aut legem"; and in general Burkhard Schmiedel, *Consuetudo im klassischen und nachklassischen römischen Recht* (Graz, 1966).

17. Bracton, I, 1, 2, "Cum autem fere in omnibus regionibus utatur legibus et iure scripto sola Anglia usa est in suis finibus iure non scripto et consuetudine. In ea quidem ex non scripto venit, quod usus comprobavit." Fortescue, *De Laudibus Legum Anglie,* ed. S. B. Chrimes (Cambridge, 1949), 5. I omit here the various "customs" produced by guilds and monastic communities.

18. See, e.g., François Connan, *Commentariorum juris civilis libri X* (Paris, 1553), fol. 18v, and Hugues Doneau, *Opera omnia* (Lucca, 1762), I, 48; cf. Ennio Cortese, *La Norma giuridica* (Milan, 1962–64), I, 55–56, and Gierke, *Natural Law and the Theory of Society, 1500–1800,* tr. Ernest Barker (Cambridge, 1934), 38, with many later references; also the critical discussion in Samuel Rachel, *Dissertations on the Law of Nature and of Nations* [1676], tr. J. P. Bate (Washington, 1916), 23.

19. Pierre de Fontaines, *Le Conseil à un ami,* ed. A. J. Marnier (Paris, 1846), 492.

20. *Histoire de la campagne française* (Paris, 1932), 20; also Kassius Hallinger, "Consuetudo, Begriff, Formen, Forschungsgeschichte, Inhalt," *Untersuchungen zu Kloster und Schrift,* ed. Max Planck Institut für Geschichte (Göttingen, 1980), 140–66; *Revue historique du droit français et étranger* [hereafter *RHDFE*] 65 (1987); and *Droit: Revue française de théorie juridique* 3 (1986), various articles.

21. See, e.g., Isambert et al., eds., *Recueil général des anciennes lois françaises,* IX (Tours, 1458), 390, confirming the Norman custom. Cf. the essential work of François Olivier-Martin, *Histoire de la Coutume de la Prévôté et Vicomté de Paris* (Paris, 1922), I, 25ff.; Robert Besmier, *La Coutume de Normandie* (Paris, 1935); Olivier Guillot, "Consuetudines, Consuetudo: Quelques remarques sur l'apparition de certains termes dans les sources françaises des premiers temps capétiens (à l'exception du Midi)," *Mémoires de la Société pour l'histoire du droit et des institutions des anciens pays bourguignons, comtois et romands* [hereafter *MSHDB*], XL (1983), 21–48; K. J. Hollyman, *Le Développement du vocabulaire féodal en France pendant le haut moyen age* (Paris, 1957), and Robert Latouche, *The Birth of Western Economy,* tr. E. Wilkinson (New York, 1961). Cf. René de la Bigotière, *Commentaires sur la Coutume de Bretagne* (2d ed.; Rennes, 1702), "avertissement."

22. Roland Mousnier, *Fureurs paysannes* (Paris, 1967), 71.

23. *Dissensiones Dominorum sive Controversiae veterum iuris romani interpretum qui glossatores vocantur,* ed. G. Haenel (Leipzig, 1834), 151–52 (#46); cf. John P. Dawson, *The Oracles of the Law* (Ann Arbor, 1968), 129–30. For a later summary, see Pietro Tommasi (+1508), *De Consuetudine,* in *Tractatus Universi Juris* (Venice, 1584), fols. 381r–90v.

24. Accursius, Gloss ad D. I, 3, 32, "Consuetudo vincit legem, sicut una lex vincit aliam"; and Baldus, *In primam veteris [Digesti] partem Commentarius* (Orléans, 1574), fols. 20r and 21r. The locus classicus is *Digest,* I, 3, 33 (Ulpian), "Diuturna consuetudo pro iure et lege in his qui non ex scripto descendunt observari solet." Cf. Odofredus, *Lectura super Digesto veteri* (Lyon, 1550), fol. 14v, "Consuetudo inveterata servatur pro lege, nam consuetudo est jus non scriptum"; *Lex Salica,* prologue; *Leges Visigothorum,* V, xii, and virtually the same wording in a capitulary of Charlemagne (cited by Calasso, *Medio Evo,* 196), "Longa consuetudo, quae utilitatibus publicis non impedit, pro lege servabitur [servetur]"; and *Petri Exceptiones,* iv, 3, "Et enim, ut in Digestis loquitur, longi temporis usu approbata, non habet minorem authoritaten quam lex scripta." François Connan, *Commentarii,* fol. 40v, "Inveterata enim consuetudo pro lege non immerito observatur"; and Pierre d'Angleberme, *Commentarius in Aurelianas consuetudines* (Paris, 1517 [1509]), fol. clxxxvi, "Hoc ius *agraphon* Graeci vocant, id est non scriptum, quas patrias leges (inquit Plato) cognomento vocitant. Sunt enim diuturni mores utentium animis comprobati, et pro legibus observati."

25. *Commentarii,* fol. 17v; also *Super Digesto veteri* (n.p., 1535), fol. 21r (ad D. I, 3, 32), "consuetudinis sunt quattuor cause, [viz.] naturalis, ut frequens factum sive actus, formalis ut consensus, efficiens ut tempus, finalis ut ratio, ut utilitas consuetudinis"; and see now Joseph Canning, *The Political Thought of Baldus de Ubaldis* (Cambridge, 1987). Cf. Jean Coras, *In titulum Pandectarum de Iustitia et Iure* (Lyon, 1568), 247; and Andrea de Isernia, *In Usus feudorum commentaria* (Frankfurt, 1598), 4; A. London Fell, *Origins of Legislative Sovereignty and the Legislative State* (1984—), on Coras and the "four causes"; and cf. Hermann Kantorowicz, *Studies in the Glossators of the Roman Law* (Cambridge, 1938), 37.

26. Jeremy Duquesnay Adams, *The* Populus *of Augustine and Jerome* (New Haven, 1971); and cf. George Boas, *Vox Populi* (Baltimore, 1969). A. Esmein, "Decem faciunt populum," *Mélanges P. F. Girard* (Paris, 1913), I, 457–73, citing, among other sources, the *coutumes* of Brittany, Bourges, and Nivernais.

27. Antoine Favre, *Jurisprudentiae Papinianae Scientiae* (Lyon, 1667), 12, "ex facto enim, ut vulgo aiunt, ius oritur" (Code II, 4, 15), and Ulrich Zasius, *Operum omnium* (Lyon, 1550), IV, col. 16, and III, col. 101; and see Luigi Prosdocimi, "Ex facto ius oritur," *Studi senesi*, LXVI–VII (1954–55), 808–19, and Cortese, *La Norma giuridica*, II, 150.

28. Baldus, *Commentaria*, fol. 20r, and cf. Bartolus, *Omnia opera* (Venice, 1590), col. 18r, "Dicit Pet. usus et mores sonant factum, ex quo descendunt consuetudo. . . . Consuetudo quando declaret legem, quando illam corroborat, quando illam imitatur, quando tollit, et quando per legem tollatur." And see Walter Ullmann, "Bartolus on Customary Law," *Jurisprudence in the Middle Ages* (London, 1980).

29. Odofredus, *Lectura super Codice* (Lyon, 1552), fol. 3r; cf. Connan, *Commentarii*, fol. 42r (see below, at n. 52), and François Le Douaren, *In primam partem Pandectarum . . . enarratio*, in *Opera omnia* (Lucca, 1765), I, 14, "quia non sufficit usus populi, nisi longus, et inveteratus sit."

30. *Traicté des lois abrogées et enusitées en toutes les cours du royaume* (Lyon, 1563). Cf. François Connan, *Commentarii*, fol. 42r, "Antiquitatur autem lex non solum quae nimia vetustate consenescit, sed et quae recens et nuper nata aut non observatur, aut sane non ad longum tempus."

31. Azo, *Summa* (Venice, 1561), col. 123; and *Somme rurale* (Paris, 1603), 5: "Coustume locale selon les anciens est un establissement tenu et gardé au pays et par les anciens sages à ce d'accord et enfermez estre et demeurer ainsi selon la situation du lieu, où ce est fait tel: et par si long temps que a coustume prescrite et confermée peut et doit suffire."

32. Philippe de Beaumanoir, *Coutumes de Beauvaisis*, ed. A. Salmon (Paris, 1899), 3 ("C'est li prologues"); and cf. 5, "Et bien i pert a ce que les coustumes sont si diverses que l'en ne pourroit pas trouver ou roiaume de France deus chasteleries qui de tous cas usassent d'une meisme coustume."

33. Especially Jack Goody, *The Logic of Writing and the Organization of Society* (Cambridge, 1986), Brian Stock, *The Implications of Literacy, Written Language and Models of Interpretation in the Eleventh and Twelfth Centuries* (Princeton, 1983), and Jan Vansina, *Oral Tradition* (Chicago, 1965); and more specifically Th. Buhler-Reimann, "La Ritualisation comme moyen de maintenir vivante une coutume orale," *MSHDB* 49 (1983), 103–10, Louis Ligeron and Michel Petitjean, "La Coutume en rites: Quelques exemples de symbolisme juridique," *MSHDB* 40 (1983), 283–93, and Paul Guilhiermoz, "La Persistance du caractère oral dans la procédure civile française," *Nouvelle revue de droit française et étranger* 13 (1889), 21–65.

34. *The Interpreter, Digested into the Method of the Civil or Imperiall Institutions* (Cambridge, 1607). And cf. M. T. Clanchy, *From Memory to Written Record: England 1066–1307* (London, 1979).

35. Beaumanoir, *Coutumes de Beauvaisis*, I, 346 (683): "Coustume si est approuvee par l'une des .II. voies, dont l'une des voies si est quant ele est generaus par toute le contée et maintenue de si lonc tans comme il puet souvenir a homme sans debat. . . . Et l'autre voie que l'en doit connoistre et tenir pour coustume si est quant debas en a esté et l'une des parties se vout aidier de coustune et fu aprouvee par jugement si comme il est avenu mout de fois en parties d'oirs et en autres

quereles." In general see *La Preuve, Recueils de la Société Jean Bodin pour l'histoire comparative des institutions* (Brussels, 1963–65), esp. vol. II.

36. Clanchy, op. cit.; Ehrlich, *Fundamental Principles of the Sociology of Law*, tr. W. Moll (Cambridge, Mass., 1936); and cf. J. P. Dawson, *A History of Lay Judges* (Cambridge, Mass., 1960). The most authoritative source for feudal custom was the *Libri Feudorum;* on which E. M. Meijers, "Les glossateurs et le droit féodal," in *Etudes d'histoire du droit,* ed. R. Feenstra and H. Fischer (Leiden, 1956–66), III, 261–70, the still valuable work of Savigny's student E. A. Laspeyres, *Libri Feudorum* (Berlin, 1830), and D. R. Kelley "De Origine Feudorum: The Beginnings of a Historical Problem," in *History, Law, and the Human Sciences*. Many commentaries on the *Libri Feudorum* are collected in *Tractatus Universi Juris,* X (1).

37. Jacques d'Ableiges, *Le Grand Coutumier de France,* ed. Louis Le Caron (Paris, 1598), 102, "Coutume est un raisonable establissement non escript, nécessaire et profitable pour aucun humain besoign, et pour le commun profit, mis au pays, et par le peuple gardé et approuvé, notoirement par le cours de 40 ans"; and Bouteiller, *Somme rurale,* 6 (see above, n. 31); also *Las Siete Partidas,* ed. G. Lopez (Paris, 1851), 24, "costumbre es derecho o fuero que non es scripto, el qual han usado los homes, luengo tiempo, ayudandose del en las cosas et en razones sobre que lo usaron." And cf. Georges Duby, *The Three Orders: Feudal Society Imagined,* tr. A. Goldhammer (Chicago, 1980).

38. *Conference de la Coustume de Paris, avec les autres coustumes de France* (Paris, 1605), "Epitre."

39. Hippolyte Pissard, *Essai sur la connaissance et la preuve des coutumes* (Paris, 1910), Yvonne Bongert, *Recherches sur les cours laïques du Xe au XIIIe siècle* (Paris, 1949), Piero Craveri, *Ricerche sulla formazione del diritto consuetudinario in Francia (sec. XIII–XVI)* (Varesi, 1969); J. P. Dawson, *Oracles of the Law,* Henri Beaune, *Introduction à l'étude historique du Droit coutumier français* (Paris, 1880), and Henri Klimrath's pioneering *Travaux sur l'histoire du droit français,* ed. L. Warnkoenig (Paris, 1843).

40. Document (Echevinage de Rheims, 1253) cited by Aubépin, "De l'Influence de Dumoulin sur la législation française," *Revue critique de législation et de jurisprudence* 6 (1855), 77.

41. Coquille, *Commentaires sur les coustumes de Nivernois,* in *Les Oeuvres* (Paris, 1646), 2.

42. *Coutumes générales et locales . . . de Bourbonnais,* ed. M. A. des Pommiers (Paris, 1732), iii, "La Coutume étant un contrat et une convention publique, on est obligé de l'exécuter et observer, meme en conscience."

43. Heinrich Brunner, *Wort und Form im altfranzösischen Process* (Vienna, 1868), 661.

44. *Commentarius in Aurelianas [Orleans] consuetudines,* fol. clxxxvi v: "ut consuetudo in scripturam redigatur: potest redigi memoriae causa, non ut novum ius dicatur, nam scriptura non inventa est: sed ad probandum."

45. *French Rural History,* tr. J. Sondheimer (Berkeley, 1966), 46, 70, 59. "And so," Bloch concludes his learned but romantic essay, which strives to reach beyond written sources, "the past continues to dominate the present."

46. René Filhol, *Le Premier Président Christofle de Thou et la réformation des*

coutumes (Paris, 1937), 115, and J. P. Dawson, "The Codification of the French Customs," *Michigan Law Review* 38 (1940), 765–800.

47. Bibliothèque Nationale MS Fr. 5281, "Premier project de la nouvelle Coustume de Paris," fol. 1v; and cf. MS Fr. 5282, "Second project," and MS Fr. 5254, Marion's "Observations." In 1580 Marion was spokesman for the nobility, Antoine for the clergy, two lesser known lawyers for the third estate.

48. *Commentaires sur la Coustume d'Aniou* (Paris, 1662), 3.

49. *Procès-verbal,* published by Louis Le Caron, *Nouveaux commentaires sur la Coustume de . . . Paris* (Paris, 1613), 234r.

50. Isambert, IX, 253. In its legal development the idea of custom was distinguished from simple "usage," curial "style," and statutory forms. See Barthélemy de Chasseneux, *Consuetudines ducatus Burgundiae* (Frankfurt, 1574), col. 1–3, "Primo quaeritur, quid sit consuetudo. . . . Et dicitur consuetudo a con, quod est simul et suetudo usus: quasi communis usus. . . . Et differt consuetudo ab usu, stylo et statuto: nam ab usu differt tanquam causa, a suo effectu: quia consuetudo per usus inducitur: et usus proprie dicit factum, consuetudo ius. . . . A Stylo differt, quia stylus proprie dicitur circa illa quae tangunt modum ordinandi acta, et sententias et aliae quae scribuntur stylo quo scribitur. consensu introducitur: consuetudo vero tacito. . . . Sed tamen finaliter concludit, quod consuetudo potest esse scripta." Cf. Pissard, *Essai,* 167.

51. *De l'Esprit des Lois,* Bk. XXVII, ch. 45. Laurent Bouchel, *Les coustumes générales des bailliages de Senlis* (Paris, 1631), 1, "Coutume" is a "loy civile approuvée et reçue par les Estats du pais, sous l'authorité du Roy." Cf. Jean Viguier, commentary on *Les Coustumes du pais et duché d'Angoumois* (Paris, 1650), 2.

52. *Commentarii Iuris Civilis Libri X* (Paris, 1553), I, x (fol. 39v–44v, passim), fol. 41r, "Quae consuetudo tantum gerit naturae similitudinem, ut altera natura esse videatur, cum tamen non sit. Idcirco virtutes hae non vocantur naturales, sed morales, et voluntariae, quia non sint naturae, sed voluntatis, a qua nascuntur, et natae perficiuntur. . . . Eadem ratione factum arbitror, ut populorum mores appellantur ea, quae ipsis tacito assensu quodam, nullo certo authore communis vitae consuetudo attulisset. . . . Morem, inquit [Vergil, iii, 5], praecessisse dicit, quem secutus est cultus moris, id est consuetudo. . . . Consuetudo ususque longaevi non levis authoritas est, verum non usque adeo sui valitura momento, ut aut rationem vincat, aut legem. . . . At vero civitates, corpora etiam et collegia civitatum, quin et eiusdem quasi gentis et agnationis populi sibi consuetudinis authores sunt. . . . At desuetudo, ut volunt, nil aliud est quam consuetudo contraria, antecedenti consuetudine vel legi, quod si ita est, ut consuetudo, sic et desuetudo non sola patientia vel negligentia inducetur, sed contrariis factis et rebus . . . ," etc.

53. *Opera omnia,* ed. F. Baudouin (Paris, 1562), 67 (on Digest 1, 1, 3): "Consuetudo absoluta et inveterata, et longa, et diuturna, et Ius moribus vel consuetudine introductum, et mos maiorum, et interpretatio prudentium, a Iureconsultis in iis rebus, quae non ex scripto descendunt, et observantur, dici solet. Est autem consuetudo, communis usus iubens quae facienda sunt, et prohibens contraria: non dico verbis, sed rebus ipsis, atque factis. . . . Sicut enim leges scriptae firmantur consuetudine utentium, ita consuetudo iudicatis rebus firmatur, ut cum longa consuetudo, quasi civium conventio, nos teneat, tum maxime si secundum morem ali-

quando etiam iudicatum sit. Nam et sola consuetudo sine iudicio, pro Iure, id est, Iure scripto servatur: res iudicata non servatur sine consuetudine nisi perpetuo similiter iudicatum sit." And cf. Kelley, "Civil Science in the Renaissance: Jurisprudence in the French Manner," in *History, Law and the Human Sciences.*

54. *Rerum ab omni antiquitate iudicatarum Pandectae* [1573] (Geneva, 1677), on Digest 50, 17, 207; Baron, loc. cit., and Connan, *Commentarii,* fol. 43r, "Consuetudo legem interpretatur"; "Res iudicatae consuetudinem confirmant."

55. Jacques Godefroy, *Commentaires sur la coustume réformée du pays et duché de Normandie* (Rouen, 1626), 1: "Si on veut retrograder à l'origine, on sera contrainct de reconnoistre que les Coustumes ont précédé, et partant font la première partie du droict positif, quoy qu'on les mette les derniers." Cf. Connan, *Commentarii,* fol. 40r.

56. *Lectura super Digesto veteri* (Lyon, 1550), fol. 14v; cf. Azo, *In Ius civile summa,* 233v, "Et quidem videtur quod consuetudo sit conditrix legis, et abrogatrix, et interpretatrix," and many other references, all following Digest, I, 3, 37 (Paulus), "Si de interpretatione legis quaeritur, in primis inspiciendum est, quod iure civitatis retro in eiusmodi casibus usa fuisset: optima enim est legum interpres."

57. More on this question in D. R. Kelley, "Civil Science in the Renaissance: The Problem of Interpretation" (above, n. 14), with further references.

58. References here are minimal; in general see André Gouron and Odile Terrin, *Bibliographie des coutumes de France* (Geneva, 1975), and Jean Caswell and Ivan Sipkov, *The Coutumes of France in the Library of Congress* (Washington, D.C., 1977); also C. A. Bourdot de Richebourg, *Nouveau coutumier général,* 4 vols. (Paris, 1724), and Charles Berroyer and Eusèbe de Laurière, *Bibliothèque des Coutumes* (Paris, 1699). And see Olivier-Martin, *La Coutume de Paris,* Paul Viollet, "Les Coutumes de Normandie," *Histoire littéraire de France,* XXXIII (Paris, 1906), 41–190, and [Garnier], *La Coutume de Paris, mise en vers* (Paris, 1768). The major repository of research on French customs is *RHDFE,* published from 1855 to the present.

59. *Commentaires,* 1, "Et noue afin de ne nous rendre serfs imitateurs et admirateurs des estrangers, ferons bien de n'infrasquer et embrouiller l'intelligence de nos coustumes selon les reigles perplexes des statuts"—for which the civilian rules of "interpretation" were much more rigorous.

60. *Méthode générale pour l'intelligence des coustumes de France* (Paris, 1666), *règle* no. 1. Cf. *Coutume de la prévosté et vicomté de Paris, commentée par Julien Brodeau* (Paris, 1669), and Choppin, *Commentaires sur la Coustume d'Aniou,* which also discuss problems of method and interpretation. The massive literature on "interpretation" (especially the work of Woldemar Engelmann, Vincenzo Piano Mortari, and Enno Cortese) is limited almost entirely to Roman and canon law.

61. *La Coutume de Nivernais,* ed. A. Dupin (Paris, 1864), 57.

62. *The French Peasantry 1450–1660,* tr. A. Sheridan (Berkeley, 1987), 136; and Jean Yver, "Les caractères originaux du groupe des coutumes de l'Ouest de la France," *RHDFE* 30 (1952), 18–79.

63. *Coutume du Comté et Bailliage d'Auxerre* (Paris, 1693), preface: "Balde, et plusieurs autres Docteurs disent que, quoique les Gaulois, soumis à la domination de l'Empire Romain et ses Constitutions; ils ne pouvoient cependant s'assujeter à les suivre, et que ce Peuple (jaloux qu'il estoit de conserver sa liberté, prenant lesdites loix pour une servitude) se fit à la fantaisie des Coutumes particulières en

chaque Province, qu'il garda inviolablement contra lesdites Constitutions qui estoient faites pour tous en general."

64. *Coutumes de Beauvaisis,* I, 436 (851): "Toutes gens qui requierent bonnage le doivent avoir et bien pueent les parties, s'eles s'acordent, bonner sans justice, mes que ce ne soit en divers seignourages ou il ait pluseurs seigneurs; car en devise de pluseurs seigneurs li tenant ne pueent bonner sans les seigneurs apeler," adding "et pour ce se convient il garder en chascune vile selone la coustume." See also Loisel, *Institutes coustumières* (Paris, 1607), 46 (241), and Henri Roland and Laurent Boyer, *Locutions latines et adages du droit français contemporain* (Lyon, 1978), I, 118.

65. *Leges Burgundiorum,* in *Monumenta Germaniae Historica, Leges,* ed. L. R. Salis (Hannover, 1892), 29.

66. Bourdot de Richebourg, II (ii), 1169ff. In general see Guillot (see n. 21) Emile Champeau, "Coutumes de Bourgogne et coutumes du duché de Bourgogne," *MSHDB* 2 (1935), 47–76, and E. Champeau, ed., *Les Ordonnances des ducs de Bourgogne* (Paris, 1908); Josette Metman and Michel Petitjean, "Le Coutumier bourguignon glosé," *MSHDB* 40 (1983), 103–110; Petitjean, "La Coutume de Bourgogne. Des coutumiers officieux à la coutume officielle," *MSHDB* 42 (1985), 13–20; J. Bart, "Coutume et droit romain dans la doctrine bouguignonne du XVIIIe siècle," *MSHDB* 28 (1967), 141–72, and "Les tentatives de réformation de la coutume du duché de Bourgogne," *MSHDB* 42 (1985), 91–100; A. B. Poulalier, *Essai sur l'histoire de la dévolution héréditaire dans les successions ab intestat en Bourgogne* (Dijon, 1912); Pierre Bodineau, "Les rédacteurs 'inconnus' de la coutume de Bourgogne de 1459," *MSHDB* 40 (1953), 111–25; P. de Saint-Jacob, *Les Paysans de la Bourgogne du Nord au dernier siècle de l'ancien régime* (Paris, 1960), and Marcel Bouchard, *De l'Humanisme à l'Encyclopédie: L'Esprit public en Bourgogne sous l'ancien régime* (Paris, 1930). And cf. F. I. Dunod de Charnage, *Observations sur les titres des droits de justice, des fiefs, des cens, des gens mariés et des successions de la coutume du Comté de Bourgogne* (Besançon, 1756), "avertissement."

67. Bouhier, *Oeuvres de jurisprudence* (Paris, 1787), I, 353, "Observations sur la coutume du duché de Bourgogne"; *Histoire des commentateurs de la Coutume du duché de Bourgogne* (Dijon, 1742); and J. Bart, "Les préoccupations du président Bouhier pendant les dernières années de sa vie," *MSHDB* 28 (1967), 141–72. Bouhier (*Oeuvres de jurisprudence,* I, 190–200) also published the local usages of Dijon, which had been set down from oral testimony ("Il est coutume de Dijon que," etc.).

68. Bouhier, *Oeuvres de jurisprudence,* 359. See A. J. Arnaud, *Les Origines doctrinales du code civil français* (Paris, 1969), G. Tarello, *Le Ideologie della codificazione nel secolo XVIII* (Genoa, 1971), and *Storia della cultura giuridica moderna,* I, *Assolutismo e codificazione del diritto* (Bologna, 1976), and J. Q. C. Mackrell, *The Attack on Feudalism in Eighteenth-Century France* (London, 1973).

69. Bouhier, op. cit., 396, and Coquille, *Les Oeuvres,* 2.

70. *De l'Esprit des lois,* bk. XXVIII.

71. Olivier-Martin, *Coutume de Paris,* I, 25ff.

72. *Oratio de concordia et unione consuetudinum Franciae* (Paris, 1546), and *Pars prima commentariorum in Consuetudines Parisienses* (Paris, 1539); and see Kelley, "Charles Dumoulin and the Gallican View of History," *Traditio* 22 (1966), 347–402.

73. See Kelley, "Louis Le Caron Philosophe," in *History, Law and the Human Sciences.*

74. *Commentaire,* 3. On academic aspects of this controversy, beginning with Louis XIV's founding of chairs in French customary law to rival the old professorships in civil law, see Alfred de Curzon, *L'Enseignement du droit français dans les universités de France aux XVIIe et XVIIIe siècles* (Paris, 1920), and Christiane Chêne, *L'Enseignement du droit français en pays du droit écrit (1679–1793)* (Paris, 1982).

75. *Le Droit commun de la France et la coutume de Paris réduits en principes* (Paris, 1747), 1; and see Renée Martinage, *Bourjon et le Code Civil* (Paris, 1971).

76. See above, n. 64; also Michel Reulos, *Etude sur l'esprit, les sources et la méthode des Institutes coutumières d'Antoine Loisel* (Paris, 1935). Cf. Klaus Luig, "Institutionen-Lehrbücher des nationalen Rechts im 17. und 18. Jahrhunderts," *Ius Commune,* III (1970), 64–97.

77. *Commentaire sur les Institutes Coutumières de Mr. Antoine Loisel* (Paris, 1688), xxxiii. "il y avoit une ancienne Coutume en France; car Charlemagne luimeme n'auroit pas distingué les Loix d'avec les Coutumes. . . . Or il est certain que l'ancienne Coutume dont entendent ces Capitulaires estoit une règle générale de tout le Royaume, une Loi universellement observée dans toute la France."

78. *Recherches pour servir à l'histoire du droit françois* (Paris, 1752), 122ff., and see Kelley, "Ancient Verses on New Ideas," *History and Theory* 26 (1987), 319–38.

79. *Méthode,* 134, citing Loisel (whose *Institutes coustumières* he edited in 1656).

80. *Nouvelles Institutions coutumières* (Paris, 1692), t. 1, "Du Droit coutumier en général coutume ou usage n'est autre chose qu'un Droit non écrit, qui s'est introduit par un tacite consentement du Souverain et du Peuple, pour avoir esté observé pendant un temps considérable"; and t. 5, "Les inclinations communes des peuples viennent de la diversité du gouvernement et des climats; nous les pouvons appeller la raison civile, qui doit estre le fondement des Coustumes et des Loix."

81. *Les Coutumes considérées comme loix de la nation dans son origine et dans son état actuel* (Paris, 1783), 30, 97.

82. *Les Loix civiles dans leur ordre naturel* (Luxembourg, 1702), preface: "Pour les loix de ces deux sortes de matières [public and private], il y en a de deux sortes dont on a l'usage dans toutes les Nations du monde. L'une est de celles qui sont de Droit naturel, et l'autre est des Loix propres à chacque Nation, telles que sont les Coutumes qu'un long usage a autorisées." And cf. Vico, *Diritto universale,* ed. P. Cristofolini (Florence, 1974), 93 (I, 91), "'Ius naturae prius' et 'posterius' interpretum eadem quae 'prima natura' et 'naturae consequentia' stoicorum."

83. *Dissertations sur des questions qui naissent de la contrariété des loix et des coutumes* (Paris, 1732).

84. D. R. Kelley, *Historians and the Law in Postrevolutionary France* (Princeton, 1984), and the literature there cited.

85. *De l'Esprit des lois,* bk. XXX. Cf. Antoine Le Conte, *Methodus de Feudis,* printed with G. Fornerius, *De Feudis tractatus* (Hanover, 1599), and Hervé, *Théorie des matières féodales et censuelles* (Paris, 1785), 1, "le système féodal," and 386, "la Doctrine féodale."

86. *Consuetudines Bituricenses* [Bourges] (Paris, 1543), fol. 1: "Haec consuetudo comprobatur iure naturali quo omnes homines nascuntur liberi"; and cf. *Les Notes de Maistre Charles Dumoulin sur les coutumes de France* (Paris, 1715), 29.

87. *Le droit commun de France et la Coutume de Paris* (Paris, 1742), ch. 1; Argou, *Institutions du droit françois* (Paris, 1771), 5 (all born free except for "nègres" in the French colonies); Jean d'Arrerac, *Pandectes ou Digestes du droict romain et françois* (Bordeaux, 1601), 67, "Ceste loi permet de repousser la force et l'injure par une contraire force." Cf. Q. Skinner, *Foundations of Modern Political Thought* (Cambridge, 1979), I.

88. *Archives Parlementaires* (Paris, 1862), VIII, 574. See also Marcel Garaud, *La Révolution et la propriété foncière* (Paris, 1959), and Xavier Martin, "L'Unité du droit français à la veille de 1789: une aspiration modérée?" *Il Pensiero politico* 19 (1986), 319–28.

89. P. A. Fenet, ed., *Recueil complet des travaux préparatoires du Code Civil* (Paris, 1927), I, 1; and see François Papillard, *Cambacérès* (Paris, 1961).

90. Fenet, *Recueil*, II, 169.

91. E. Meynial, "Notes sur la formation de la théorie du domaine divisé (domaine direct et domaine utile) du XIIe au XIVe siècles dans les romanistes," *Mélanges Fitting* (Montpellier, 1908), II, 409–61.

92. F. Portalis, ed., *Discours, rapports et travaux inédits* (Paris, 1844), I, 19, 90ff. Cf. II, 263, citing Dumoulin on the first title of the Parisian custom, "Et illae consuetudines erant jus peculiare et commune Francorum et Gallorum."

93. *La Législation civile de la révolution française* (Paris, 1898), 387; also Edmond Seligman, *La Justice en France pendant la révolution (1789–1792)* (Paris, 1901), A. Mater, *L'Histoire juridique de la révolution* (Besançon, 1919), P. P. Viard, *Histoire générale du droit privé français (1789–1830)* (Paris, 1931), and D. R. Kelley and Bonnie Smith, "What Was Property? Legal Dimensions of the Social Question in France (1789–1848)," *Proceedings of the American Philosophical Society* 128 (1984), 200–230, with further references.

94. See Soboul, "Persistence of 'Feudalism' in the Rural Society of Nineteenth-Century France," *Rural Society in France*, ed. R. Forster and O. Ranum (Baltimore, 1977), and Valette, *De la Durée persistante de l'ensemble du droit civil français pendant et depuis la révolution de 1789* (Paris, 1872).

95. Fenet, *Recueil*, I, 11. On Cambacérès's famous address see Georges Gusdorf, *Les Sciences humaines et la pensée occidentale*, IX, *La Conscience révolutionnaire. Les Idéologues* (Paris, 1978), 746, and especially Sergio Moravia, *Il Pensiero degli Idéologues. Scienze e filosofia in Francia (1780–1815)* (Florence, 1974), 746. This is an aspect not discussed by Keith Baker, "The Early History of the Term 'Social Science,'" *Annals of Science* 20 (1964), 211–26, or by B. W. Head, *Ideology and Social Science* (The Hague, 1985), 109ff.

96. *Discours. Corps Législatif. Conseil des Cinq-cents.* (Paris, An 7; BN Le.43.3603), 3: "La science sociale étudie l'organisation des colonies diverses émanées de la République Romaine; elle examine ailleurs les droits coutumiers, les codes des anciens, les lois favorables à l'union conjugale, les droits peut-être trop restreints des mères sur les enfans, le marché mesuré du peuple athénien pour former et surtout pour abroger ses lois, et toujours elle cherche à tirer l'expérience des siècles précédens des leçons pour la génération actuelle."

97. Fenet, *Recueil*, I, 469; and see Arnaud, *Les Juristes face à la société du XIXe siècle à nos jours* (Paris, 1975), 31.

98. *Vom Beruf unsrer Zeit für Gesetzgebung und Rechtswissenschaft* (Heidel-

berg, 1814), 28, with an appendix publishing some of the preliminary discussions, pro and con, of the French courts concerning the Civil Code; and *System des heutigen römischen Rechts* (Berlin, 1940), I, 116; also "Su Federico Carlo di Savigny," *Quaderni fiorentini per la storia del pensiero giuridico moderno* 9 (1980), and Peter Stein, *Legal Evolution: The Story of an Idea* (Cambridge, 1980). On custom the major work from the Historical School is G. F. Puchta, *Gewohnheitsrecht* (Erlangen, 1828). Of Savigny's and Puchta's discussion of *Volksrecht*, Georges Gurvitch observed (*L'Idée du droit social* [Paris, 1932], 476), "C'est précisément le dernier fondement de la réhabilitation de la coutume par l'école historique."

99. *Philosophy of Right*, tr. T. M. Knox (Oxford, 1942), 20. Knox's rendering of "Recht" exclusively as "right" tends to individualize and desocialize Hegel's usage and obscure its connections with the tradition of law.

100. Maine, *Ancient Law* (London, 1861), 7ff., and Austin, *Lectures on Jurisprudence* (London, 1873), II, 553.

101. *Custom: An Essay on Social Codes*, tr. A. Borenstein (New York, 1961), 131, citing Savigny; *Community and Association*, tr. C. Loomis (London, 1955), 240, and *On Social Ideas and Ideologies*, tr. E. Jacoby (New York, 1974), 129, on the historical school. See also Paolo Grossi, *"Un altro modo di possedere"* (Milan, 1977), on the debates over "primitive communism," which cut across the frontiers between law and early social science, and Henri Lévy-Bruhl, "Rapports du droit et de la sociologie," *Archives de philosophie du droit* III–IV (1937), 21–25.

102. *Origins of Sociology* (Chicago, 1924). Later surveys of the history of anthropology and sociology make little of this legal connection. See Ernst Becker, *The Lost Science of Man* (New York, 1971), and D. R. Kelley, "The Prehistory of Sociology," in *History, Law and the Human Sciences.*

103. *Encyclopedia of the Social Sciences*, ed. Edwin Seligman (New York, 1930–35).

104. *International Encyclopedia of the Social Sciences*, ed. David L. Sills (New York, 1968–79).

105. *Montaigne in Movement*, tr. A. Goldhammer (Chicago, 1958), 293.

106. *Les Essais*, I, xxiii, "De la Coustume et de ne pas changer aisement une loi reçüe"; see also III, x. Bacon, *Essays*, xxxix, "Of Custom and Education," devising his own provenance for the Aristotelian topos: "[Machiavelli's] rule holdeth still, that nature, nor the engagement of words, are not so forcible as custom." Charron, *De la Sagesse*, ed. A. Duval (Paris, 1820), II, 191.

107. Ibid., 201.

108. *De la Servitude volontaire*, ed. Malcolm Smith (Geneva, 1987), 51.

109. *Pensées*, nos. 325, 440, 426, 93, 144.

110. *An Enquiry Concerning Human Understanding*, III, vi; and cf. *A Treatise of Human Nature*, II, iii: "It is that principle alone which renders our experience useful to us, and makes us expect, for the future, a similar train of events with those which have appeared in the past."

XII

Civil science in the Renaissance: the problem of interpretation

'Interpretation', like its modern descendant 'Criticism', has often come under attack by champions of authorship and authority. From Petrarch to Susan Sontag, authors have taken stands 'against interpretation as a way of protecting the creative process from scholastic instrusions and distortions – and even, as in current 'deconstructionist' criticism, from usurpation of the authorial role.[1] Both sides are certainly aware that the struggle is in part political (even on that lowest level of interpretation, which is translation: 'traduttore, tradittore'); for it centres on the meaning, hence control of the social effects, of the work in question.

This time-honoured war between authors and critics has a striking (and much more political) counterpart in the field of law, which has paralleled (and often overlapped) Western literary history. From Justinian, who gave shape to the European legal tradition, to Napoleon, who reshaped it for the modern world, 'authorities' and 'interpreters' have been at odds, if not sword's point; for here the prize is the political and social control embodied in the law and in the attendant authority to define and to apply it – in effect sovereign power.[2] *Cuius interpretatio, eius legislatio.* Both of these emperors,

[1] *Against Interpretation and other Essays* (New York, 1967), and cf. Jonathan Culler, *The Pursuit of Signs* (Ithaca, 1981).

[2] G. G. Archi, 'Interpretatio iuris – interpretatio legis – interpretatio legum', *Zeitschrift der Savigny-Stiftung für Rechtsgeschichte, Römische Abteilung*, C (1970), 1–49; F. Pringsheim, 'Justinian's prohibition of commentaries to the Digest', *Gesammelte Abhandlungen*, II (Heidelberg, 1961), 85–106; J. Charmont and A. Chausse, 'Les interprètes du code civil', in *Le Code civil 1804–1904, livre du centenaire* (Paris, 1904), II, pp. 131–72; Helmut Coing, *Die juristischen Auslegungsmethoden und die Lehren der allgemeinen Hermeneutik* (Cologne, 1959); *Archives de Philosophie du Droit*, XVII (1972), 'L'interprétation dans le droit'; Ronald Dworkin, 'Law as interpretation', in *The Politics of Interpretation*, ed. W. Mitchell (Chicago, 1983), pp. 249–70; and D. R. Kelley, 'Hermes, Clio, Themis: historical interpretation and legal hermeneutics', in *History, Law and the Human Sciences* (London, 1984), with further bibliography.

therefore, strictly forbade any 'interpretation' at all. Their efforts were in vain, of course; and the logomachy still goes on – critics versus authors, interpreters versus legislators, judiciary versus executive, perhaps even practitioners of civil disobedience versus government. What Justinian called 'the vain discourse of posterity', Napoleon the 'murder' of his code, Mark Twain the leavings of 'the most degraded trade' and Harold Bloom a 'map of misreading', has progressively obscured the Word that Was in the Beginning. It has also, of course, called for further 'interpretation'.

'Civil science' is the name given by medieval jurists to Roman jurisprudence in the posthumous form it assumed after the twelfth-century revival of ancient learning. Although bound to ancient legal 'authority', European civil science – *sanctissima civilis scientia*, as Sebastian Brant called it – was in fact the product of what jurists as well as philosophers and theologians came to call 'hermeneutics' (*ars hermeneutica* is the phrase used by Leibniz in his youthful essay on jurisprudence),[3] which was to say the theory and practice of 'interpretation'. How this came about was explained by Johannes Oldendorp in his *Interpretatio privilegii duplicis* of 1543, a commentary on the Emperor Frederick Barbarossa's constitution *Habita* of 1159, which bestowed the right of interpreting civil law on authorised *doctores legum*.[4] The 'double grounds' for this privilege were pedagogical utility and religious propriety; that is, the need to make ancient ideas intelligible to beginning students and to reconcile them with Christian truth. Thus, from being a punishable crime (*pena falsitatis*), interpretation was transformed into a major rubric of medieval and modern jurisprudence, spawning not only endless justifications of interpretation but also a new methodological and philosophical genre devoted to legal hermeneutics.

The chief source of inspiration came from the classical texts of civil law itself, especially from that fragmentary monument, the Digest, which was a highly edited and poorly organised anthology of over a millennium of ancient jurisprudence. For interpretation the *loci classici* were the first three titles of Book I (on the theory of law, the origin of law and the chief sources of law) and titles sixteen and seventeen of the last, the fiftieth, book (on the meaning of words and on the various rules of law).[5] The motto of legal interpretation – the

[3] See below at note 53.

[4] *Interpretatio privilegii duplicis, quod Friderichus primus, omnium Imperii ordinum consensu, summa aequitatis ratione motus, concessit bonarum literarum studiosis* (n. p., 1543); cf. *MGH, Constitutiones*, I. 249. Baldus, *Super Digesto veteri commentarii* (n. p., 1535), fol. 3r.

[5] *Digest* (ed. Mommsen-Krueger), I and L, 16–17; and see the invaluable Fritz Schulz, *History of Roman Legal Science* (Oxford, 1953).

license for judges and bane of legislators for centuries – was the formula of Celsus, preserved in title three of Book I, that 'understanding laws means knowing not merely their words but their force and effect' (*vim et potestas*). This meant above all the 'will' (*voluntas*) of the prince, though necessarily as construed by the magistrate.

The oldest school of medieval civilians was that of the glossators, whose work was summed up in Accursius's great *Glossa ordinaria*, assembled around 1265, covering all the major texts of civil law, including the Digest, Institutes and Code, together with a collection of medieval imperial law called the *Consuetudines feudorum*.[6] Traditionally, *glossa* meant explanation of a single word; and for the most part the glossators avoided going beyond the literal meaning of terms and so violating Justinian's ban on interpretation, although they were in fact capable of textual emendation on an elementary level. They were also aware of the role of judicial opinion; and in a legendary debate the glossator Azo, opposing his colleague Lothair and offending the Emperor Henry VI, commented that the *imperium* itself (the so-called *merum imperium*) might be exercised not only by the emperor but also by magistrates.[7] To this extent the loophole of 'interpretation' – and the conflict of judiciary and legislature – was already opened by the thirteenth century.

This loophole (and the attendant conflict) became wider in the work of their successors, the post-glossators, or commentators, who no longer pretended to stick to the absolute letter of the law, and who introduced a variety of philosophical and literary devices in order to accommodate – the more technical term was to 'extend' – the ancient legal canon to modern conditions and demands.[8] In fact these scholastic jurists, called 'Bartolists' after their most famous (and authoritative) representative, departed so far from textual tradition that, by the fifteenth century, a humanist reaction had set in, calling for a return to the sources. In trying to reconstruct the 'historical sense' of texts legal humanists were not only following classical precedent but also anticipating the modern debate over

[6] The best bibliographical guide to the extraordinarily rich and diversified literature on European legal science is Helmut Coing (ed.), *Handbuch der Quellen und Literatur der neueren Europäischen Privatrechtsgeschichte*, I and II (Munich, 1973–5); also Walter Ullmann, *Law and Politics in the Middle Ages* (Ithaca, 1975).

[7] M. P. Gilmore, *Argument from Roman Law in Political Thought 1200–1600* (Cambridge, Mass., 1941).

[8] On the problem of interpretation, see especially Ennio Cortese, *La norma giuridica* (Milan, 1962–4), and Vicenzo Piano Mortari, 'Il problema dell "interpretatio iuris" nei commentatori', *Annali di storia del diritto*, I (1958), 29–109. There is a vast literature on individual authors.

'intentionality'; for they were literally trying to read the 'mind' or 'intention' of the original author, which was assumed to coincide with the 'meaning' of the law (*mens*, *voluntas* or *sententia* were terms applied indifferently to both).[9] This literal- or literary-minded sort of 'criticism' was marginal, however, to the main thrust of professional jurisprudence, which continued to be towards 'extensive' interpretation.

The tendency towards *extensio interpretiva* began with the 'ultramontane' (especially the French) commentators of the later thirteenth century, most notably Jacques de Révigny and Pierre Belleperche, who were deeply suspicious of the Italian Gloss and could not in any event accept the absolute authority of 'the emperor's law' for the French monarchy. So they became committed to the search not merely for legislative intention (*mens legum*) but rather for the underlying, or overarching, 'reason' and justice in a particular law. 'Not the intention of the law-giver but the rationale of the law' (*nec ex mente sed ex ratione*) was Jacques' formula, and Pierre went even further in the direction of judicial discretion (*nec ex mente sed ex interpretatione*).[10]

The fashion set by these 'moderns', as they were called, was followed in Italy (whose relations with the Emperor were also ambivalent at best). The pioneering figure was Dante's friend Cino da Pistoia, who had studied with the French commentators. Taking as his motto 'all novelty is pleasing' (*omnia nova placent*), Cino claimed the right to a contrary opinion even though (as he put it) all the doctors disagreed.[11] His disciples Bartolus and Baldus, champions of the Italian city-states so neglected by the emperors, extended his fondness for novelty into an elaborate theory of interpretation, with 'reason' gaining precedence over 'authority' in many ways, especially political. Their *extensiones*, naturally, were designed to benefit not the French monarch but the Italian *civitas*, which belonged to the modern law of nations (*novissimum ius gentium*) and which, like any corporation, could give itself a head. 'The city [*civitas*]

[9] W. K. Wimsatt, *The Verbal Icon* (Louisville, 1954), p. 37. The confusion between the meaning of a text and that of an author is illustrated by a passage in a famous eighteenth-century work by C. H. Wolff, *Principes du droit de la nature et des gens*, trans. M. Formey (Amsterdam, 1968), p. 321: 'Interpréter, c'est déterminer le sens qu'on a voulu attacher à certains signes. On appelle ce sens, l'*esprit* de celui qui a parlé, ou fourni ces signes. Ainsi l'*Interprétation*, c'est la découverte, ou du moins l'exposition quelconque de l'esprit indiqué par certaines paroles, ou par certains signes.'

[10] Révigny, *Lectura super Codice* (Paris, n. d.), on *Code*, I.14.5; Belleperche, *In libros Institutionum . . . commentarii* (n. p., n. d.), on *Institutes*, I.1.3; and see E. Meijers, *Etudes d'histoire du droit*, III (Leiden, 1966).

[11] *In Codicem . . . doctissima Commentaria* (Frankfurt, 1578), fol. lr.

is itself the prince' is Bartolus's famous formula of civic independence, whose spirit 'civic humanists' might share even while deploring the implied anachronism. This attitude of Bartolus, Baldus and others, transcending particular political crises of the Renaissance, reflects an attitude which I like to call 'civil humanism'.

In general, Bartolus and his colleagues preferred the most straightforward sort of interpretation, which rested on 'propriety' (*proprietas*, which is basically, according to Quintilian, calling things by their right names). After this they might resort to etymology, or 'allusion', which of course referred to the philosophical or speculative, not the historical variety, but even then only if it did not contradict the definition. Bartolus admitted degrees of 'latitude' in interpretation and the use of analogy (*similia ad similium*); but the major devices were furnished by the requirements of reason and equity.[12] Following the lead of Cino and his French masters, Bartolus tended to identify rationality (*ratio*) not only with intention (*mens*) but also with liberal interpretation (*extensio*). Beyond that he could also invoke 'natural law' and the 'law of nations', which was itself based, as Gaius had said, on 'natural reason'. The utility of these appeals may be appreciated by noting that the 'rules of law' declared both 'actions' and 'peoples' to be subjected finally not to civil law but, as Baldus had said, to the law of nations.[13]

'Civil science' was reshaped by humanism in several ways from the later fifteenth century. First and most conspicuous was the application of philological and historical methods of criticism to the texts (including Greek passages) of Roman law.[14] The attendant conflict between the *mores italicus* and *gallicus* – in effect legal scholasticism versus legal humanism – created more heat than light, since practitioners of the science of law, no less than those of the science of theology, had no intention of submitting to the authority of the lower arts, including the 'historical sense' required by grammar and the 'eloquence' which rhetoric sometimes seemed to prize above

[12] Bartolus, *In primam [Digesti] veteri partem Commentaria* (Turin, 1574), fol. 16rff. and (on the 'rules of law') 248rff.; Baldus, *Super Digesto veteri*, fol. 4v. And see Norbert Horn, *Aequitas in den Lehren des Baldus* (Cologne, 1968).

[13] Commenting on *Digest*, I.1.1, Baldus makes the point in the form of a syllogism: 'Populi sunt de iure gentium, ergo regimen populi est de iure gentium. Sed regimen non potest esse sine legibus et statutis, ergo eo ipso quod populus habet esse, habet per consequens regimen in suo esse, sicut omne animal regitur a suo proprio spiritu et anima.' See also Cino da Pistoia, *Super Codice et Digesto veteri lectura* (Lyon, 1547), fol. 4r, and Baldus, *Super Digesto veteri*, fol. 10r; and C. Karsten, *Die Lehre von Vertrag bei den italienischen Juristen des Mittelalters* (Rostok, 1882).

[14] See now Hans Troje, *Graeca leguntur* (Cologne, 1971), and D. R. Kelley, 'Civil science in the Renaissance: jurisprudence Italian style', in *History, Law and the Human Sciences*.

justice. Humanists could claim indeed to be more faithful to the 'intention' of the original law-giver (and thus to respect Justinian's ban), but old-fashioned jurists rejected this with their own claims to serve the higher aims of the law.

In the end the influence of humanism on legal interpretation was significant but, in conceptual terms, marginal. Within the professional tradition the consequences may best be seen in Andrea Alciato's great commentary of 1520 on the Digest title *De verborum significatione*. Going beyond Bartolism, yet rejecting the literary excesses of mere 'grammarians' like Valla, Alciato distinguished four modes of interpretation, beginning with the literal, which was to say linguistic, 'propriety' tied ideally to the will and intention of the author, though in case of doubt recourse might also be had to definition or etymology.[15] The second type of interpretation was improper (*improprietas* was the term), though this did not necessarily mean error, since it might rest on a convention or 'fiction' which did not produce misunderstanding (such as the use of foreign terms). Third was interpretation according to common usage (*ex usu*), which was permissible, though undesirable, given the tendency of vulgar language to degenerate into 'abuse'. 'What is common usage today', Alciato remarked, 'cannot be presumed to have been so formerly.' Last of all came *extensio*, and here Alciato discussed a wide range of means and conditions and ways of pushing interpretation beyond propriety and custom. Besides the conventional extensions made through analogy, through the application of rules (*regulariter*) and through invocation of natural law and 'equity' (*epieikeia*), Alciato devoted one whole book to literary extensions, that is to say, proverbs (supplementing the 'adages' of Alciato's older friend, Erasmus), figures and tropes, from metaphor to irony. Technically, of course, these were 'improper' but they were essential since the law, like the Bible as interpreted by Erasmus, was 'literature' as well as 'science'.

Another area in which civil science and humanism overlapped was the art of rhetoric, which became the basis for the so-called 'new logic' associated with Rudolph Agricola, Philip Melanchthon and especially Peter Ramus (though in fact the apparatus of Aristotelian dialectic was never wholly rejected or replaced). The convergence

[15] *De verborum significatione* (Lyon, 1536); and see Hans Troje, 'Alciats Methode der Kommentierung des "Corpus iuris civilis" ', in A. Buck & O. Herding (eds.), *Der Kommentar in der Renaissance* (Godesberg, 1975); and Guido Kisch, *Erasmus und die Jurisprudenz seiner Zeit* (Basel, 1960).

between 'topical' logic and legal interpretation in the fifteenth century produced a new genre devoted to the theory and practice of *extensio* of authoritative legal text. In a stream of monographs from Nicolas Everardus's *Topica legalia* (1516) to Leibniz's *Nova methodus iurisprudentiae* (1667) and beyond, jurists sought a proper 'method' of law through rational reorganisation. In treatises by Oldendorp, Bartolommeo Cepolo, Costantino Rogerio, Pietro Andrea Gammaro, Claudius Cantiuncula, Johannes Apel, Matteo Gribaldi and Christopher Hegendorph, legal hermeneutics came into its own.[16] In the context of the general sixteenth-century pursuit of a true 'Method', these champions of *interpretatio extensiva* continued the search for the 'inner meaning', or inherent 'reason' of laws.[17] But the goal of interpretation always remained the common good; and as Oldendorp warned, legal error not only undermined justice, it also produced social and political corruption (*error corrumpit politicis ordines et introducit confusionem poenitendam*).[18]

As the method of civil science was developed by treatises devoted to legal 'method' and the theory of 'extension', so its vocabulary was fixed by another new genre. This was the tradition of juridical lexicography, which was basically an 'extension' of the Digest title *De verborum significatione*, and which, like the parallel works of Valla and Erasmus, treated not merely the individual words (*paroles*), according to the Sausurrean distinction, but also the common language (*langue*) of juridical discourse. As Barnabé Brisson wrote in his great dictionary, 'Since the meaning of texts is obscure, we must have recourse to the proper usage [*proprietas*] of the word, and what and whom is referred to, and we must explain and extract the sense

[16] The major collections are in Nicolas Reusner, *Cynosura juris* (Speier, 1588), and *Variorum opuscula ad cultiorem jurisprudentiam adsequendam pertinentia* (Pisa, 1769); and see also Piano Mortari, *Ricerche sulla teoria dell'interpretazione del diritto nel secolo XVI* (Milan, 1956), and *Diritto, logica, metodo nel secolo XVI* (Naples, 1978); Cesare Vasoli, 'La dialettica umanistica e la metodologia giuridica nel secolo XVI', in *La formazione storica del diritto moderno in Europa* (Florence, 1977), I, pp. 237–79; Gerhard Otte, *Dialektik und Jurisprudenz* (Frankfurt, 1971); Theodor Vieweg, *Topik und Jurisprudenz* (Munich, 1975); Aldo Mazzacane, *Scienza, logica e ideologia nella giurisprudenza tedesca del sec. XVI* (Milan, 1971); Georges Kalinowski, 'La Logique et son histoire', *Archives de Philosophie du Droit*, XXVII (1982), 275–89; and Norbert Bobbio, *L'analogia nella logica del diritto* (Turin, 1938), as well as various works by Guido Kisch, Rodolph Stintzing, *Geschichte der deutschen Rechtswissenschaft*, I (Munich, 1880), and the old classic of C. H. Eckhardt, *Hermeneutica Iuris* (Pisa, 1750).

[17] Stephanus Fredericus, *De interpretatione legum*, in *Tractatus universi juris* (Venice, 1584), I, fol. 210r., quotes the famous preference of St Paul for the life-giving spirit over the deadening letter. Various more or less elementary rules or 'canons' of interpretation are given by Hegendorph, *Epitomi tyrocinii iuris civilis* (in Spiegel, *Lexicon*), and Oldendorp, *De copia verborum et rerum in iure civili* (Lyon, 1543).

[18] *De duplici verborum, et rerum significatione* (Venice, 1557), fol. 7r.

of what they say.'[19] It is significant that this lexicographical development occurred just during the heroic age of modern philology and the emergence of 'Criticism' in a modern sense, which had the effect of reinforcing ties with ancient legal science.

Roman law has commonly been identified with authoritarian attitudes, but there is obviously more to it than the gross formulas of absolutism. In order to find its deeper 'meaning', we must look behind the political rhetoric and into the structure, conceptualisations and terminology of 'civil science'. From the beginning and perhaps prehistorically, civil law has been fundamentally anthropocentric, presuming and unfolding from the thinking – or at least the wilful and responsible – subject. 'All our law', as Gaius put it, 'has to do with persons, things and actions.'[20] This ancient legal trichotomy seems to correspond directly with the general structure of Indo-European languages (subject, object, verb) and to presume a condition of (self-) consciousness, which in these terms distinguishes 'personality' from 'reality' through 'action'. *Personalitas, realitas, actio* – these are the rudimentary categories of psychology and speech as well as social custom and law, the connection being established by predication in some sense, which is to say human judgement. Absolutely central is the factor of will (*voluntas*), which defines the individual in civil society (as in discourse) and which also reflects the relationship between the law and the law-maker.

In this connection it is interesting to pursue a bit further the interaction of language and law in the social arena defined by the Gaian triad. Law is basically a product of 'action' in the sense not only that politically it was expressed in 'acts of law' expressing sovereign will, but also that particular law in the first instance was created by individual appeals for justice (*legis actiones* was the technical phrase).[21] Civil science seems to contain a rudimentary sort of 'action theory' whose field seems to correspond, in terms of structural linguistics, to language (*langue*) as individual acts to words (*paroles*). For interpreters of the law, words were in a sense socialised

[19] *De verborum significatione* (Halle, 1743), preface. And see Jacob Spiegel, *Lexicon juris civilis* (Basel, 1539); Oldendorp, *De copia verborum et rerum in iure civili* (Lyon, 1546); Hotman, *Novus commentarius de verbis iuris* (Basel, 1563); and P. C. Brederode, *Thesaurus dictionum et sententiarum ex Bartoli a Saxoferrato operibus* (Frankfurt, 1660); also Guido Kisch, 'Juridical lexicography and the reception of Roman law', *Forschungen zur Rechts- und Sozialgeschichte des Mittelalters* (Sigmaringen, 1980).

[20] *Digest*, I.5.3; and see D. R. Kelley, 'Gaius Noster: substructures of Western social thought', in *History, Law and the Human Sciences*, and the literature there cited.

[21] It was proverbial that, as Claude de Seyssel wrote, *Speculum Feudorum* (Basel, 1566), p. 4, civil science 'non in speculatione sed in actione consistit'. In general, see Riccardo Orestano, *Azione, diritto soggettivo, persone giuridiche* (Bologna, 1978).

– or actions verbalised? – and the two were assumed to be translatable.[22] What is more, practising jurists had to judge reality as well as legal principle (*de facto* as well as *de iure*) conditions, and so – long anticipating the development of the seventeenth century – were tied to the logic of probability. These considerations underline the special meaning of the title which the civil scientist gained in the Renaissance: he was *Iuris Interpres*, critic both of words and things, judge both of persons and actions, and pretender still to the ancient monopoly of 'true philosophy'.[23]

Could the jurist then usurp the function of the legislator? A very good question, said Bonifacius Amerbach.[24] The official answer was, of course, no. As Alberico de Rosate repeated in the fourteenth century, 'the author of a law should be its interpreter' (*legis auctor debet esse interpres*).[25] And yet if the judge was obliged to construe statutes *strici iuris*, he nonetheless also had to apply them and resolve problems. Here the premise – one might better say the fiction – of the identity of the word and the spirit of a law was most useful, since 'propriety' in principle pertained only to the latter. If there could be no exception to the law, remarked Bartolus, there might well be to its words, and he spoke even of 'irrational statutes'. In any case, considerations of justice and that most pliable concept of equity (Aristotelian *epieikeia*) could never be ignored, and like Bartolus, Alberico admitted the necessity of 'extensive' interpretation in criminal cases. 'The statutes demand decapitation of murderers, but are madmen or infants decapitated?' he asked. 'Certainly not,' because of their age or because, in the case of *furiosi*, their condition is punishment enough.

Probably the most obvious judicial limitation on, or even alternative to, legislative sovereignty was the other major source of law, arising from the will not of the prince but of the people. This refers

[22] Conceptually, the intersection of ideas of language and of action comes in the notion of custom, especially in the mutual pattern of change and process of obsolescence (*desuetudo*), which is reflected in the medieval (and indeed Justinian) formula 'Hodie'. Odofredus, *Lecutra super Codice* (Lyon, 1552), fol. 3r, 'mutata est hodie consuetudo' and 'leges per desuetudine possunt tolli'; and Placentinus, *Summa Codicis* (Mainz, 1536), p. 17, 'hodie nec populus Romanus nec Senatus'. See also Emilio Albertario, 'Hodie', *Studi di diritto romano*, VI (Milan, 1953), 125–42.

[23] Developed further in my 'Homo politicus: the perfect jurist as Rennaissance man', forthcoming in *The Journal of the Warburg and Courtauld Institutes.*

[24] *Defensio interpretum iuris*, in Guido Kisch, *Humanismus und Jurisprudenz* (Basel, 1955), p. 82.

[25] In *Tractatus de statutis, diversorum autorum et j. c. in Europa praestantissimorum* (Frankfurt, 1608), p. 10; relevant works by Baldus and others are also collected in this anthology.

not only to the belief that, according to the legendary *lex regia*, the Roman Populus was the original source of sovereignty (*maiestas*) but more importantly to the medieval interpretation that a people never lost its right to make laws for itself, notably in its customs, which indeed 'represented' its spirit or mind. 'Consuetudo', as Bartolus put it, 'repraesentat mentem populi.'[26] The mighty force of custom had been recognised in classical jurisprudence, which regarded it (in a famous formula of Paulus) as 'the best interpreter of law' (*optima enim est legum interpres consuetudo*). Medieval civil science went further and attributed to custom the power to make and even abrogate law: 'Consuetudo', wrote Azo, 'conditrix legis, abrogatrix et interpretatrix.'[27] Part of its force arose from the fact that custom was born of 'natural reason', according to Gaius, and was, in the more famous Aristotelian formula, a kind of 'second nature' (*altera natura*). In any case, *consuetudo* brought popular culture into the tradition of legal interpretation.

Guardians of the ancient legal canon, civil scientists were also masters of social and political thought; and it is fascinating to see them giving shape and meaning to their world through linguistic and hermeneutical virtuosity. On many levels their vocation was to 'civil'-ise: they thought and judged 'civilly' (*civiliter* meant 'according to the *ius civile*', as *regulariter* meant 'according to the *regulae antiqui iuris*' and *communaliter* meant 'according to consensus').[28] They were agents of 'civility' (*civilitas* being equivalent to sociability and even 'civilisation'). Like the humanists but earlier and more professionally, 'civilian' jurists sought to bring the urbanity of the *civitas* and the activism of the *civis* to late medieval society. Drawing upon Greek political philosophy as well as Roman legal science, they were led in many ways to 'think big' – to extend their horizons and to distinguish larger social and political patterns, assessing the nature and behaviour of collectivities and institutions as well as individuals. They developed – that is, they inherited and 'extended' – a massive vocabulary and conceptual apparatus designed to comprehend the

[26] *Commentaria*, fol. 16r; and Ullmann, 'De Bartoli sententia: concilium repraesentat mentem populi', in *Bartolo da Sassoferrato* (Milan, 1962), II, pp. 707–33.

[27] Azo, *Summa Codicis* (Venice, 1566), on Code, 8.52, and Odofredus, *Lectura super Codice* (Lyon, 1552); cf. Accursius on *Digest*, I.3.37; and Walter Ullmann, *The Medieval Idea of Law as Represented by Lucas de Penna* (London, 1946), p. 62. See also the extended commentaries of François Connan, *Commentarii juris civilis* (Paris, 1553), fol. 43r, and Conrad Lagus, *Methodus iuris utriusque traditio* (Lyon, 1566), p. 18.

[28] Alciato, *De verborum significatione*, p. 20, defining 'interpretatio civiliter' as 'secundum ius interpretari'. 'Homo natura civile est' was William of Moerbeke's rendering of Aristotle's 'political animal' (*zoon politikon*); see pp. 46–7 above.

wide range of social groupings and political forces that agitated the city and countryside of Europe.

Through the conceptual efforts of jurists, then, social groups were literally personified (accommodated, that is, to the first Gaian rubric of *personalitas*); and the world was peopled by corporate entities, *personae fictae*, endowed with personalities, hence with liberties, status and responsibilities before the law.[29] Thus was created an extended family of socialising and communalising concepts and terms drawn from antiquity and given modern form. Legal 'bodies' (*corpus* being the most general term) materialised, were described, defended and manipulated by jurists – and sometimes were criticised by juridical nominalists who could not accept the paradox (variant of the 'holist fallacy') that a group could be composed of individuals and yet be itself an individual without parts. Such was the meaning, for example, of the term *universitas*, which had Ciceronian and Augustinian connotations. Jurists separated such corporate concepts from the more general rubrics of genus and species and distinguished them from each other – *societas* being ordinarily a secular organisation formed for a particular purpose, for example, while a *collegium* signified nothing more than the accident of living together. There were of course many classes of such corporate entities, ecclesiastical, municipal, academic and artisanal; and many intricate permutations and combinations. The history of corporatism, still dominated by the spirit if not interpretations of Otto Gierke, has been usefully extended in several recent works, most notably those of Pierre Michaud-Quantin and Anthony Black, but invites further exploration.[30]

If civil science possessed a language of sociability, it developed also a 'language of power', emanating from the arena of 'public law' and largely neglected by feudal custom and virtually inarticulate in feudal monarchy (except in such para-legal devices as 'distraint'). Political forms, too, had to be constructed, or accounted for, and of course legitimised; and in this connection a large variety of political entities and forces were identified and analysed. Many of the political questions of the Renaissance had been disputed for generations by jurists, 'ultramontanes' as well as 'citramontanes', canonists as well as civilians; but new methods and historical context gave these issues new meaning and in some cases new urgency in times of civic,

[29] P. W. Duff, *Personality in Roman Private Law* (Cambridge, 1938), and Grossi (ed.), *Quaderni fiorentini* (1983), on the topic of juridical personality.

[30] Michaud-Quantin, *Universitas, expression du mouvement communitaire dans le moyen âge latin* (Paris, 1970), and *Etudes sur le vocabulaire philosophique du moyen âge* (Paris, 1970); and Black, *Guilds and Civil Society* (Ithaca, 1984).

national and international crisis from the fifteenth century. At the same time the legal profession itself, extending its influence from the academy to the forum, had become massively and inextricably entangled in the political as well as social and economic activities of European states, and had come to establish a certain monopoly over (at least official) political discourse. The political realm, too, experienced what a legal historian has called 'the triumph of the professionals'.[31]

How did the 'civil scientists' discuss political questions within the conventions of their 'antique–modern' discourse? In the first place we should notice the fundamental, though not always articulated assumption of the primacy of written culture, in the sense not only that 'written law' (*ius scriptum*, virtually identified with the *ius civile*) was prior to custom but that custom (even while continuing to be defined as *ius non scriptum*) was assimilated into written culture. Typography magnified the difference between scribal and oral culture, and the 'authority of the written word' became proverbial.[32] Long identified with the art of oratory in terms of education and purpose, lawyers distinguished themselves by becoming the masters and (in many respects) the slaves of print culture, along with its proliferation of records and litigation, which were the subjects of endless celebrations or laments. Modern political thought, or 'public law', was in many ways a creature of the modern world of 'publicity'.

The central assumption of medieval and modern civilians was always the status of their discipline as a 'science' (*scientia*) because it treated matters in terms of cause and effect.[33] The basic hermeneutical premise of Bartolism was that 'knowing was understanding through causes', and indeed there were no grounds for discourse at all without a 'cause' in the technically legal sense; for according to a much discussed maxim, all consequences cease when the cause ceases (*cessante causa, cessat effectus*).[34] *Causa* was an extraordinarily

[31] John P. Dawson, *A History of Lay Judges* (Cambridge, Mass., 1960), p. 69.

[32] This is one of the few facets of the problem not treated by Elizabeth Eisenstein in her widely discussed book on printing as an agent of historical change. More generally, see the provocative work of Brian Stock, *The Influence of Literacy* (Princeton, 1983).

[33] Jean Coras, *De iure civili in artem redigendo*, in *Tractatus universi juris*, I, fol. 62v, poses the classic question whether jurisprudence is *ars* or *scientia*.

[34] Baldus, *Super Digesto veteri*, fol. 4r, and Coras, *De iuris arte libellus* (Paris, 1560). On the concept of 'cause', see André Tiraqueau in *Tractatus varii* (Lyon, 1574); see also Cortese, *La norma giuridica*, index, and A. London Fell, *Origins of Legislative Sovereignty and the Legislative State* (1984); and in general, Robert MacIver, *Social Causation* (Boston, 1942), and Quentin Skinner, '"Social meaning" and the explanation of social action', in Patrick Gardiner (ed.), *The Philosophy of History* (New York, 1974), pp. 106–26.

complex and often confusing term, possessing connotations not only social, in the sense of a position to be defended or grounds for judgement ('just cause'), but also natural, and specifically Aristotelian. According to the famous fourfold scheme of Aristotle, the people, or in recent times the prince, represented the 'efficient cause'; the texts of the laws the 'material cause'; the extension of law from individuals to society in general the 'formal cause'; and justice or public utility the 'final cause'. All legislative and judicial activity was carried on within this teleological framework.

In the discussion of political questions, the professional 'duplicity' of civil scientists – the habit and requirement of *duplex interpretatio* – was reflected in various conceptual polarities, which have been analysed by Pietro Costa from the standpoint of structural semantics, of the vocabulary of political thought.[35] *Imperium* and *iurisdictio*, *potestas* and *auctoritas*, *princeps* and *populus*: these are a few of the dualities which inform the arguments of medieval and Renaissance jurists in their various political engagements, not including the recurrent controversies between secular and ecclesiastical institutions. They are not the 'ascending' and 'descending' themes inferred by Walter Ullmann, nor the confrontation between *rex* and *iudex*, nor the opposition of rulership and constitutionalism, nor yet that between absolute and ordinary power (recently surveyed by Francis Oakley).[36] They are rather manifestations of conflicting appeals to 'power' and socialised conceptions of 'legitimacy'. The tension between these political and legal lines of thought are preserved in the modern concept of 'sovereignty' and attendant notions of resistance. Nor have legal or political philosophers been able to reconcile or to transcend them.

In this connection a word needs to be said about 'civic humanism' (a phrase which might have been rendered 'bourgeois humanism' if someone other than Hans Baron had established the English equivalent of the original *Burgerhumanismus*). Civic humanism has been a topic of much debate and no little exaggeration in recent years, partly because scholars have allowed humanist rhetoric to drown out, and in important ways to discredit, the comparatively pedestrian work of more professional scholars. Political posturing and propagandising by humanists as well as their more conspicuous participation in contemporary issues have in many ways overshadowed the contributions of jurists to social and political thought. Yet as historians used to notice, civil scientists like Bartolus and

[35] *Iurisdictio: semantica del potere politico nella pubblicistica medievale (1100–1400)* (Milan, 1969).

[36] *Omnipotence, Covenant and Order* (Ithaca, 1984).

Baldus possessed not only technical legal expertise but also the values and goals of a new *civiltà*, including a commitment to the ideals of citizenship and the *vita activa*, a favourable attitude towards republican 'liberty', and even towards resistance to tyranny, although the arguments remained decorously, rigorously and classically legal.[37] Like late scholastic theology (as defended by Heiko Oberman), scholastic jurisprudence from the fifteenth century enjoyed not a 'waning' but a 'harvest time', reaped in political terms by city-states and national monarchies as well as by empire and church.

Some of the most crucial problems of interpretation occurred in the confrontations and conflicts between rival national traditions, since Roman law was technically the 'emperor's law' and to this extent unwelcome in the realms of kingdoms which 'recognised no superior in temporal things', according to the adaptable canonist formula. The issue arose in commentaries on the title in the Code, 'Cunctos populos', which suggested that the emperor was 'lord' of the whole world (*dominus mundi*).[38] This was rejected by French, Spanish, English and some Italian jurists, who invoked another popular formula, that their king was 'emperor in his kingdom' (*rex imperator in regno suo*). French legists used this principle during the rivalry between Francis I and Charles of Spain in the imperial election campaign in 1519, as in effect did Thomas Cromwell, defending Henry VIII's statutory break with Rome.[39] In general the French king had, from the thirteenth century (if not, arguably, from Carolingian times), accumulated his own 'regalian rights', which were interpreted by royal legists partly in terms of, partly in opposition to, civil law, and which furnished the material for a larger theory of 'sovereignty' (*maiestas*), expressed most famously in the *Republic* of Jean Bodin.

[37] See, e.g., *L'opera di Baldo* (Perugia, 1901); also Peter Riesenberg, 'Civism and Roman law in fourteenth-century society', *Explorations in Economic History*, VIII (1969–70), 237–54, and J. P. Canning, 'A fourteenth-century contribution to the theory of citizenship: political man and the problem of created citizenship in the thought of Baldus de Ubaldis', *Authority and Power*, ed. Brian Tierney and Peter Linehan (Cambridge, 1980), pp. 197–212, and his forthcoming book on Baldus, as well as the old work of C. N. S. Woolf on Bartolus (Cambridge, 1913). Reference here is to Hans Baron's *Crisis of the Early Italian Renaissance* and the massive literature it has inspired, and to Oberman, *The Harvest of Medieval Theology* (Cambridge, Mass., 1963).

[38] Belleperche, *In aliquot Cod. leges* (Frankfurt, 1571), p. 8, a passage which, according to Baldus, Bartolus published as his own (see *Dictionnaire de biographie française*); also Alberico de Rosate, *Super Codice* (Lyon, 1545), fol. 7r, and Giason del Maino, *In primam Codicem partem Commentaria* (Venice, 1579), fol. 2v.

[39] In the famous opening lines of the Act of Appeals, 1533; the formula also adorns the *Siete Partidas*.

The fundamental dilemma of civil science was surviving and adapting itself to a large variety of expanding and jostling national traditions; and it is in this connection that we encounter one of the central problems of 'interpretation'. I refer to translation in the literal sense of expressing in civilian terms the various local, provincial and national customs of Europe. In a very basic sense this entailed the comparative study of law, for example, in the interpretation of municipal statutes in Italy and in the enterprises of certain national jurists setting out variously (depending on their immediate purpose) to establish analogies, common denominators or contrasts between civil law and native customs or legislation. Although commentators on French *coutumes* from the time of Beaumanoir had at least inadvertently had to Romanise (later to de-Romanise) provincial customs, the pioneer of comparative law was the first of Alciato's French disciples, Eguinaire Baron, who composed a series of 'bipartite commentaries' on the texts of Roman law in order to suggest the corresponding French institutions (*roy* and *princeps*, *Parlement* and *Senatus*, *Chancelier* and *Praetor*, *interpretatio* and *practiquer les lois*, and so on).[40] This was the sort of 'interpretation' carried on by Etienne Pasquier's *Interprétation des Institutes de Justinian* (which began as a translation but ended as a critical, comparative commentary) and, in England, by William Fulbeke's *Parallele or Conference of the Civil Law, the Canon Law, and the Common Law of this Realm of England.* And other examples could be cited for Germany, Italy and Spain.

In the context of what Piano Mortari has called 'juridical nationalism', such comparisons commonly became invidious. Protestant jurists in particular deplored the supposed rigidity and absolutist character of Romanism. In France the model was the 'anti-Tribonianist' critique of François Hotman, who came to believe that the influence of Roman law was irrelevant, if not pernicious, and more generally that law, like language, should be in agreement with the character and 'humours' of a people. The English counterpart was the professional chauvinism of common lawyers like John Fortescue and Edward Coke. 'Upon the text of the civil laws', declared Coke, 'there be so many glosses and interpretations, and again upon these so many Commentaries, and all these written by Doctors of equal degree and authority, and therein so many diversities of opinions, as they rather do increase than resolve doubts and

[40] See D. R. Kelley, 'Civil science in the Renaissance: jurisprudence in the French manner', and 'History, English law and the Renaissance', in *History, Law and the Human Sciences.*

uncertainties, and the professors of that noble Science say, That it is like a Sea full of waves.'[41]

By contrast, common law, regarded since Bracton as a species of custom, affected to stand apart from interpretation. So it was, too, with English statutes which had to be kept and observed, according to a fourteenth-century statute roll, 'without addition or fraude, by covin, evasion, art or contrivance, "ou par interprétation des paroles" '.[42] Not *ius dare* but *ius dicere* was the way Bacon aphorised it. The practical result, however, was often to give authorial voice to the judge: (not *rex* but, in Coke's rephrasing) *iudex est lex loquens*; and Coke indeed claimed to speak for the true meaning not only of the statutes, the yearbooks and the law reports but also for the 'immemorial custom' of England – and this even as he took a classic stand 'against interpretation'.[43]

In various ways civil science in the Renaissance began to drift away from its ancient moorings. Increasingly, jurists worked within the confines not of the *ius civile* (the *ius proprium* of ancient Rome) but rather of the 'law of nations' (the *ius gentium*, or *ius naturale gentium*) which accommodated 'peoples' and 'actions' never envisaged by Caesar or Justinian or even by Irnerius and Accursius. Concerning the 'status of men', for example, there were various changes brought by modern times, wrote Alberico de Rosate, which were not treated by ancient law.[44] The 'law of nations' also involved questions of international commerce and especially war, which itself stemmed ultimately from disagreement about words – 'from those possessive pronouns "mine" and "thine" ', as Alberico de Rosate wrote (*ab istis pronomibus meum et tuum*).[45] This was the so-called 'secondary law of nations', which was produced not (as the primary form) by 'right reason', according to Hugues Doneau, but by 'necessity' (which proverbially 'knew no law') and indeed the actions – the history – of peoples since the beginning of civil society.[46] With these issues we enter the (legally) uncharted realm of 'public utility': as Pierre Ayrault wrote, 'in republics one has sometimes to consider not only

[41] *The Second Part of the Institute of the Laws of England* (London, 1671), proem.

[42] T. F. T. Plucknett, *Statutes and their Interpretation in the First Half of the Fourteenth Century* (Cambridge, 1922), p. 49; cf. Bacon, 'On judicature'.

[43] See J. G. A. Pocock's *Ancient Constitution and the Feudal Law* (new edition forthcoming).

[44] *Commentarii super Digesto veteri* (Lyon, 1545), fol. 44v: 'secundum moderna tempora varii sunt status hominis de quibus hoc titulo [I.3] non tractatur . . . quia status hominis sub perpetuo motu consistit'.

[45] *Ibid.*, fol. 14v; and cf. Walter Ullmann, *The Medieval Idea of Law*, p. 47.

[46] *Opera omnia* (Lucca, 1762), I, p. 48.

what is just in itself but also what is needed for the state'.[47] We leave the realm of juridical discourse for contingencies of social actions and reasoning of state.

So it was that civil scientists came often to work under the rubric not of law but rather of 'custom', and this offered new resources for the process of interpretation, since *consuetudo* marked the intersection between fact and law (might and right, as some would infer). It marked, too, the entry into the forum of oral culture and social memory. 'It is enough for the profe of a custom (as I have credibly heard)', wrote John Cowell, 'if two or more can depose that they heard their father say, that it was a custome all their time and that their fathers heard their fathers also say, that it was likewise a custome in their time.'[48]

In France the actual writing down or redaction of a custom required the agreement of the local estates, after which 'interpretation' had the same restrictions as for 'written' (that is, civil) law. Yet this by no means stemmed the flow of interpretations. Pasquier's friend Antoine Loisel, also a member of the French school, turned his attention from Roman law to native customs and tried to find the 'spirit' of such customary law not only in medieval legal texts but also in literature, proverbs and oral tradition. Loisel's *Institutes coutumières* was in effect a pioneering treatise on the anthropology of law, later recognised as an anticipation of the work of the nineteenth-century historical school of law.[49] Politically, the implication of such works was to suggest the priority of judicial 'interpretation' – in effect as an act of popular mind-reading – to the Romano-Byzantine model of legislation, hence to the primacy of princely 'will'. This was another attempt by critics, in a way, to gain parity with authorial initiative by asserting the popular as the truly authorial 'will' – and themselves, of course, as its spokesmen.

Not only the practice but also the theory of interpretation – legal hermeneutics – was introduced into European customary law. In France, Paul Challine published in 1666 a quasi-Cartesian 'method for the interpretation of the customs of France'. While forbidding the addition of words and demanding that customs be construed in their own terms (*se doivent expliquer par elles-mêmes*), Challine requires the interpreter to determine the 'motive or intention' of the law; he

[47] *De l'Ordre et instruction judiciaire, dont les anciens Grecs et Romains ont usé en accusations publiques. Conferé a l'usage de nòstre France* (Paris, 1576), fol. 22.

[48] *The Interpreter* (London, 1607).

[49] Michel Reulos, *Etude sur l'esprit, les sources et la méthode des Institutes coutumières d'Antoine Loisel* (Paris, 1935).

allows laws to be overridden by non-usage; and he provides for supplementing them, when 'defective', by a variety of devices, including recourse to royal ordinances, nearby customs, what he calls 'the general spirit of French custom' (expressed best in the *coutume* of Paris) and finally what he calls 'the reason of Roman law' (that is, whatever French lawyers may find useful).[50] What started as a loophole in civil law has obviously become a great portal of critical and creative interpretation.

But the greatest portal of them all, short of the executive justice of the Queen of Hearts, was 'natural law', whose spirit was conveyed by the texts of civil law and magnified by the new philosophy of the seventeenth century that put all, at least all convention, in doubt.[51] Of course the language and ideas of the *ius naturale* were embedded in civil science. It was commonplace in customary as well as civil and canon law, for example, that 'by nature all men are free', as Nicholas Bohier quoted from the *coutume* of Bourges.[52] But not until the age of what Gierke called 'antique–modern' political thought were such abstract notions taken seriously as a way of reforming jurisprudence. As Leibniz hoped to find a 'new method of jurisprudence' appropriate to this sort of naturalism, so Jean Domat tried to reformulate civil law in purely 'natural' terms; Hobbes affirmed the superiority of 'natural reason' to the 'artificial' and obscurantist variety practised by Coke, invoking the old hermeneutical rule which subordinated what he called the 'Grammatical construction of the letter' to the 'Intention' of a law – by which he meant, of course, its rationality as determined by the Philosopher (if not the Sovereign).[53]

There is no doubt that the first aim of 'jusnaturalism' was to take still another stand 'against interpretation'; and in the eighteenth century political absolutism and the codification movement reinforced such pretensions, as indeed did invocations of 'natural

[50] *Methode générale pour l'intelligence des coutumes de France* (Paris, 1666).

[51] The classic work of Otto Gierke, *Natural Law and the Theory of Society*, trans. Ernest Barker (Cambridge, 1934) has never been superseded; but see Georges Gurvitch, *L'Idée du droit social* (Paris, 1932), and Otto Wilhelm Krause, *Naturrechtlicher des sechszehnten Jahrhunderts* (Frankfurt, 1982).

[52] *Consuetudines Biturcensis* (Paris, 1543), fol. lr: 'Haec consuetudo comprobetur iure naturali quod omnes homines nascuntur liberi'; and cf. Coras, *In titulum Pandectarum de justitia et jure* (Lyon, 1568), p. 299. See *Digest*, I.5.

[53] Leibniz, *Nova methodus discendae docendaeque jurisprudentiae* (Frankfurt, 1667); Domat, *Les Loix civiles dans leur ordre naturel* (Luxemburg, 1702); and Hobbes, *A Dialogue between a Philosopher and a Student of the Common Laws of England* (1661), ed. J. Cropsey (Chicago, 1971), p. 97. And cf. Peter Stein, *Regulae Iuris, From Juristic Rules to Legal Maxims* (Edinburgh, 1966).

liberty' and 'absolute property'.[54] Yet in practice the appeal to naked reason – to a 'natural law' that is metahistorical and metalinguistic as well as metatextual – was an invitation to the most 'extensive' of all interpretation. For purposes of interpretation, the *ius naturale* was more flexible even than *consuetudo*, to the extent at least that it tended to liberate judgements from legal convention, and to transform the ancient legal maxims into juridical counterparts of Descartes' 'clear and distinct ideas'; and in this sense it fundamentally changed the style of modern political and social thought.

But this vision of 'perfect jurisprudence' could remain intact only on the level of theory, and in fact civil science was never successfully 'naturalised'. It could not escape what has been called 'the horizon-structure of experience', that is, its anthropocentric orientation; nor could it avoid practical involvements; and despite claims to treat human matters in terms of 'cause and effect', the idea of *causa* was permeated with questions of value and motive. Far from being an exercise in pure reason, jurisprudence involves a certain kind of 'prejudging' (*praeiudicium* being one of the conventional topics of civil science, according to Cantiuncula's analysis).[55] This is not 'prejudice' in the 'prejudiced' (that is, prejorative) Enlightenment sense, however, but rather in the hermeneutical sense of what Gadamer, and Heidegger before him, called the 'fore-structure of knowledge', which is one of the conditions of 'social meaning' and indeed communication. And as Gadamer has also pointed out, *praeiudicium* originally (and 'civilly') referred not to a false judgement but rather to a legal precedent or provisional verdict before a final judgement – on the basis of that 'experience of tradition' essential to human science.

Nor, despite resemblances between what jurists called 'inductive interpretation' and empiricism, can jurisprudence be assimilated to Baconian natural science. 'Since laws vary', wrote Gammaro in his

[54] E. Meynial, 'Notes sur la formation du domain divisé (domain direct et domain utile) du XII au XIVe siècle dans les romanistes', *Mélanges Fitting* (Montpellier, 1908), II, pp. 409–61 and Paolo Grossi, *Le situazioni reali nell'esperanza giuridica medievale* (Padua, 1968).

[55] Cantiuncula, *Topica legalia* (Basel, 1545). Cf. Gadamer, *Truth and Method*, trans. G. Barden and J. Cumming (New York, 1975), pp. 238, 289; and see Gunther Buck, 'The structure of hermeneutical experience and the problem of tradition', *New Literary History*, X (1978), 31–47. The commonest criticism of Gadamer, especially by Jurgen Habermas, is the neglect of the social dimension; but this is conspicuously not true of legal hermeneutics; and Gadamer agrees that philosophical attention to this connection might further deflect such criticisms.

treatise on *extensio*, 'the interpretation of law is obviously bound to contingencies.'[56] As Ian Hacking has recently pointed out, jurisprudence rests not on pure reason but rather on a 'logic for contingencies'. This could only mean probable judgement, which (as Claudius Cantiuncula admitted in his pioneering treatise of 1520) was all that argument from precedent (*praeiudicium*) permitted. And this was precisely the position taken by Leibniz, one of the founders of the logic of probability, in his discussion of the old theory of legal interpretation (*ars hermeneutica* he called it). In the long as well as the short run, then, *civilis scientia* remained a human not a hard science – part of the 'moral' rather than the 'natural' world, as Hotman wrote, or according to the ancient and currently fashionable distinction, a form of *phronesis* not *episteme*.[57] For legal (as for social) judgement, pure logic must be subordinate to practical reason, rational consistency to human values (good or bad), explanation to interpretation, and universal to 'local knowledge'.

An extraordinary illustration of the vitality of Renaissance civil science appears in the work of Giambattista Vico, the first version of whose 'new science' was expressed in terms of Roman law. Beginning with the humanist *ars interpretationis*, with all of its emphasis on historical context and avoidance of anachronism, Vico went on to devise ways of 'divining' antiquity and interpreting primitive culture, especially through ingenious extensions of the old technique of etymology. Out of custom came civilised law, according to Vico, and out of the pre-historical principles of lordship, liberty and self-defense came all the civil institutions of the modern age, including the concept of sovereignty (*summum imperium*).[58] Like Bodin, Vico expanded his horizons from civil law to the law – and the historical 'world' – of nations. Among the several faces of Vico's final 'new science' we find not only a 'natural law of nations' but a 'philosophy of authority', in effect Vico's way of realising the old claim of civil science to be, as he repeated, *vera philosophia*.

But the old-fashioned wisdom of civil science was in many ways out of step with the intellectual fashions of the Enlightenment,

[56] *Topica legalia*, p. 7: 'Sed legis interpretatio est de contingentibus, quia leges variantur'; and cf. *De extensionibus*, in *Tractatus universi juris*, XVIII, fol. 248v: 'Interpretatio iuris non est scientia.' See also Pierre Ayrault, *Rerum ab omni antiquitate iudicarum Pandectae* (Geneva, 1677). In general, see Hacking, *The Emergence of Probability* (Cambridge, 1975), p. 86; Alessandro Giuliani, 'The influence of rhetoric on the law of evidence and pleading', *The Juridical Review*, LXII (1969), 216–51; Lawrence Manley, *Convention 1500–1750* (Cambridge, Mass., 1980); Richard J. Bernstein, *Beyond Objectivism and Relativism* (Philadelphia, 1984).

[57] *Jurisconsultus* (Basel, 1559), p. 11.

[58] See D. R. Kelley, 'Vico's road', in *History, Law and the Human Sciences*.

which was anything but a great age of interpretation. Then legislative reform and the great movement for codification overshadowed judicial remedies. Voltaire's famous advice to burn old laws and make new ones was taken seriously even by jurists, and the Revolution called up visions of a society without legal machinery. 'No more courts!' cried the former advocate Adrien Duport, addressing the committee for judicial reform at a high point of populist enthusiasm. 'No more judges!'[59] At one point Napoleon himself expressed the hope that lawyers could be done away with; and of course he tried to prohibit any tinkering with, or academic criticism of, his great 'Code of the French People', as it was originally called.[60] His hopes were dashed in the most massive way. Within a generation the Civil Code recapitulated the same evolutionary pattern – cautiously literal glosses, increasingly 'extensive' commentaries and freewheeling revisions – that it took the civil law almost five centuries to pass through.

In fact the early nineteenth century saw an extraordinary revival of hermeneutics not only in theology and philosophy but also in jurisprudence. Paralleling the famous work of Schleiermacher and Ast were the theories of legal interpretation hammered out by champions of the rival philosophical and historical schools, centreing in particular on the famous debate between Thibaut and Savigny, and in the wake of that the much more destructive criticism of renegade jurists like Marx and Proudhon (for whom civil law and its modern incarnation, the Code Napoléon, represented the soon-to-be-superseded Old Testament of social thought).[61]

In the past century the legal tradition has produced a variety of schools of interpretation – positivist, formalist, sociological, not to speak of fascist, communist and other more or less blatantly political varieties – and through the work of Hans Georg Gadamer and Emilio Betti legal interpretation has contributed to the recent upsurge of philosophical hermeneutics, in which the metalegal structure of civil science is preserved. In particular Gadamer has pointed out that the category of 'thing' as well as that of 'person' must, to be meaningful, be interpreted in a social sense.[62] In other words, *res* must be

[59] *Archives parlementaires*, XII, 570.

[60] Cf. Cocczius, *Code Fréderic, ou corps de droit pour les états de sa majesté le Roi de Prusse*, tr. from German (1751), xviii: 'Et afin que les Particuliers n'ayent pas occasion d'en corrumpre les Loix par les Interprétations données de leur propre autorité, le Roi a défendu sous sévères peines de faire des Commentaires, soit sur tout le Droit du Pays, soit sur quelqu'une de ses parties. Par la même raison il a défendu aux Professeurs qui instruisent la jeunesse . . .' etc.

[61] D. R. Kelley, *Historians and the Law in Postrevolutionary France* (Princeton, 1984).

[62] *Truth and Method*, p. 289, and *Philosophical Hermeneutics*, trans. D. Linge (Berkeley, 1976), pp. 69–81.

understood not according to the old Cartesian duality (*res extensa, res cogitans*) or to the Kantian *Ding an sich*, but rather as the *res* of civil law, which represents an extension as well as an object of consciousness, desire and sociability (or belligerence) – which is to say, of personality, action and politics.

In any case, criticism and critical theory, interpretation and the theory of interpretation, are all alive and well; and the struggle for the authority to give, preserve, correct, control and extend meaning goes on in law as in literature and philosophy. The old formula traditionally applied to the king seems much more appropriate for the process of criticism – which indeed 'never dies'. Authors and legislators to the contrary notwithstanding, 'the problem of interpretation' is still with us – though some critics will probably disagree.

XIII

JURISCONSULTUS PERFECTUS: THE LAWYER AS RENAISSANCE MAN*

LAWYERS have always had a bad press. Cicero (who should have known) spoke of them as mean and mercenary. Peter the Chanter in the twelfth century denounced their mendacity and treachery.[1] Martin Luther repeated the old proverb, 'Juristen bose Christen'.[2] In the Renaissance the lawyer became a major target of criticism, a stock figure of satire. In the poetry of Guy Coquillart he is Reginald Grab-all (*Regnaud Prens-tout*) or Edward of the well-oiled palm (*Oudard de la main garnie*).[3] In the prose of Rabelais, François Hotman and Noel Du Fail he is a *chicanous*, or *chicanous du merde*.[4] In the polemic of Henry Cornelius Agrippa he is a professional liar and the vainest of all vain pretenders to learning.[5] In an English comedy of the Stuart period he becomes Benjamin Gripe, who changes his name only when he changes his sour and pettifogging ways.[6] 'Ambition, error, ignorance, envy, fraud, and treason'—these were some of the occupational vices that another French poet, Scévole de Saint-Marthe, warned his son against.[7]

Could a lawyer ply his trade without payment, asked a sixteenth-century textbook?[8] Of course not. Could he defend bad causes?[9] Quite possibly; and to many lay observers, such seemed to be his main occupation. In short the lawyer was a sort of Machiavelli of private life, who pandered to, and of course profited from, people's lowest instincts and interests. Reformers, revolutionaries, and reactionaries alike took up the old theme that the world would be far better off without their legal services. As Dick the Butcher suggested to the rebel Jack Cade, 'The first thing we do, let's kill all the lawyers'.[10]

Yet this is obviously not the whole picture. For the Renaissance in particular it represents only one half—the devil's half—of a diptych which reflects the extremes of good and evil. The dignity of lawyers, like that of humanity in general, had a

* This article grew out of lectures given in 1985 at the Folger Shakespeare Library in February and at the Warburg Institute in March, and I dedicate it to the memory of Charles Schmitt.

1 John Baldwin, 'Critics of the Legal Profession: Peter the Chanter and his Circle', *Proceedings of the Second International Congress of Medieval Canon Law*, Rome 1965, pp. 249–59.

2 *Table Talk*, tr. T. Tappert, in *Luther's Works*, LIV, Philadelphia 1967; and see R. Stintzing, *Das Sprichwort 'Juristen bose Christen'*, Bonn 1875, and C. Kenny, 'Bonus Jurista, Malus Christa', *Law Quarterly Review*, XIX, 1903, pp. 326ff.

3 J.-V. Alter, *Les Origines de la satire anti-bourgeoise en France*, Geneva 1966, pp. 166ff.

4 F. Hotman, *Antitribonian*, Paris 1603, pp. 70, 106; François Rabelais, *Pantagruel*, IV, 12; N. Du Fail, *Contes et discours d'Eutrapel*, in *Œuvres facétieuses*, Paris 1874, p. 263. Cf. R. Marichal, 'Rabelais et la réforme de la justice', *Bibliothèque d'humanisme et renaissance*, XIV, 1952, pp. 176–92, and E. Nardi, *Rabelais e il diritto romano*, Milan 1962.

5 Agrippa, *De Incertitudine et vanitate scientiarum declamatio invectiva*, ch. 91, n.p. 1531.

6 *The Honest Lawyer*, by 'S. S.', London 1616; *Short Title Catalogue* 21519.

7 *Opera latina et gallica*, Paris 1629, p. 112:

> Nostre temps desdaignant telle simplicité,
> Comme estant mieux appris et mieux exercité,
> Au bien d'elles reçoit pour guides de la vie,
> L'ambition, l'erreur, l'ignorance, l'enuie,
> Les fraudes, les trahisons et sur tout donne lieu
> Au damnable mespris de la crainte de Dieu.

8 Caspar Manzius, *Tractatus Advocatis, Procuratoribus, Defensoribus, Syndicis etc.*, Ingolstadt 1659, p. 20.

9 R. Delachenal, *Histoire des avocats au Parlement de Paris 1300–1600*, Paris 1885, p. 296.

10 William Shakespeare, *II Henry VI*, iv, 2.

glorious as well as a miserable aspect. Francesco Petrarca, law-school drop-out and despiser of the academic study of law, nevertheless placed the ancient jurisconsults among the founding fathers of the humanities.[11] In classical tradition the jurist had been regarded as a 'priest of the laws' (*sacerdos legum*), the very archetype of the wise man; and Renaissance jurists restored this claim along with the study of Roman law.[12] In early modern times the jurists' self-image came to resemble Erasmus's man of faith and erudition or even the heaven-storming chameleon featured in Pico's 'Oration on the Dignity of Man' rather than the low-minded mercenary of popular opinion and literary cliché. The legal profession, too, was exalted. With rhetorical self-indulgence modern jurists began to take up the ancient formula that jurisprudence was *vera philosophia*, true philosophy, and they did not scruple to claim precedence for it over all other disciplines.[13] 'Not content with the glory of being identified with the highest philosophy', wrote Leibniz in 1667, 'jurisprudence is driven to occupy alone the throne of wisdom'.[14]

It so happened that the idealized aspect of the old science of law (*legitima scientia* was the professional formula) was reaching a high point at precisely the time when the new science was emerging as a dominant intellectual force. Leibniz himself was torn between conventional jurisprudence and natural philosophy as the basis for an understanding of man and his world, and his youthful essay on a *New Method of Jurisprudence* offers a way of access into this curious world of pre-scientific thought. For in order to gain a clear view of the Renaissance jurist at his best, we shall have to make him out across the great conceptual divide created by the seventeenth-century revolution of science; and this requires a certain effort of imaginative understanding and reconstruction of a kind of learning which not longer appeals to—since it no longer directly serves—our modern world.

The ruling topos in the idealization of legal science was the 'perfect jurist' (*jurisconsultus perfectus*). Before the 'scientific revolution' the jurist was the very model of the secular intellectual—the 'man of science' who yet held justice above truth, the disinterested observer who was yet committed to the common good, the Platonic philosopher returned to the cave of human conflict. Consider Leibniz's own conception of the 'perfect jurist' (*idea jurisconsulti perfecti* is his phrase).[15] For background Leibniz sketched a brief history of western jurisprudence culminating in the work of the great French scholars the previous century. In particular Leibniz invoked the names of five jurists who had inclined toward the reformed religion as well as the 'reformed jurisprudence': Hotman; his colleagues Hugues Doneau and

[11] M. P. Gilmore, 'The Lawyers and the Church in the Italian Renaissance', *Humanists and Jurists*, Cambridge Mass. 1963.

[12] '... ab aliis sacerdotes ab aliis philosophi sunt appellati, quod philosophiae potentissimam partem ...', in Valla's encyclopedia, *De Expetendis et fugiendis rebus opus*, Venice 1501; but the formula was repeated and discussed in virtually every commentary on Justinian's *Digest.*

[13] Ibid.; and cf. D. R. Kelley, 'Vera Philosophia: the Philosophical Significance of Renaissance Jurisprudence', in *History, Law and the Human Sciences* (hereafter *History etc.)*, London 1984; and cf. William J. Bouwsma, 'Lawyers and Early Modern Culture', *American Historical Review*, LXXVIII, 1973, pp. 303–27.

[14] G. W. Leibniz, *Nova Methodus discendae docendaeque jurisprudentiae*, Frankfurt 1667, p. 233; see also Fritz Sturm, *Das römische Recht in der Sicht von Gottfried Wilhelm Leibniz*, Tübingen 1968, as well as Hans-Peter Schneider, *Justitia Universalis*, Frankfurt 1967.

[15] *Nova Methodus* (as in n. 14), pp. 293, 315.

François Le Douaren; Calvin's former schoolmate François Connan; and Jean Coras, a major legal philosopher, though better known as the judge in the notorious case of Martin Guerre.[16] Leibniz also referred to Valentinus Forster, a younger German alumnus of the French school, whose hagiographical history of civil law down to these contemporary French masters he drew upon.[17]

In his search for a new method Leibniz gave pride of place to universal 'natural law', but he also recognized the value of human 'positive law' as formulated in Roman jurisprudence. This more concrete and conventional legal wisdom he referred to as the *ars hermeneutica*, or hermeneutics.[18] In other words, a generation after Galileo's assertion of the mathematical nature of philosophy and on the verge of making his own contributions to this new natural science, Leibniz was still celebrating human law as a form of wisdom and indeed, in the ancient formula mentioned earlier, as 'true philosophy'. For Leibniz as for medieval jurists civil law was still in a way the embodiment of reason, and indeed was often called 'written reason' (*ratio scripta*) to indicate its superiority to all other legal traditions. This suggests some of the force still retained by jurisprudence after the rise of the 'new science' and the presumed eclipse of scholastic and Renaissance learning.

What was this *jurisconsultus perfectus* celebrated by Leibniz? As the label for a literary genre it was a little less, as a rhetorical topos a little more, than a century old; but as a professional ideal it went back to Roman antiquity, perhaps as far back as Appius Claudius (mid-fifth century B.C.), one of the decemvirs who made a fabled trip to Athens for philosophical counsel, or even further.[19] In the seventeenth century Arthur Duck quoted François Baudouin as 'thanking Providence that Joseph was raised up in Egypt, Daniel in Babylon, Pericles in Athens, and Papinian in Rome to save civil society and the honour of Justice'.[20] Such figures—heroes before Agamemnon—suggested that the toga might sometimes outshine the sword as a social ideal.

In the Renaissance the 'perfect jurist' had to be a 'good Christian' as well as a 'good man'; but the most conspicuous model was classical, and in particular those republican *honoratiores* beginning with Scaevola, who had in effect founded the art of legal interpretation and formed, as Max Weber argued, a kind of ideal type linking the ancient art of law with the modern sciences of society.[21] The intermediary stages were occupied by the law professors created by the Emperor Justinian and their students (known as 'new Justinians'),[22] and later by the medieval glossators and practitioners of 'civil science' (*civilis scientia* being the conventional term for academic jurisprudence).[23] The perfect jurist was thus the product of the medieval university and, more particularly, the descendant of Master Irnerius of Bologna, who (so the story goes) single-handedly raised the study of law from a

16 See Natalie Z. Davis, *The Return of Martin Guerre*, Cambridge 1983.

17 *Historia iuris Romani*, Helmstadt 1610; see below, n. 30.

18 *Nova Methodus* (as in n. 14), p. 338.

19 The major collection of treatises on the topic is Nicolas Reusner, *ΧΕΙΡΑΓΩΓΙΑ, sive Cynosura iuris*, Speier 1588 (henceforth Reusner); and see below, n. 42.

20 *De l'usage et de l'autorité du droit civil dans les états des princes chrétiens*, Paris 1689, p. 52.

21 *Economy and Society*, tr. E. Shils and M. Rheinstein, New York 1968, II, pp. 792–802; and see Paul Koschaker, *Europa und das römische Recht*, Munich 1958.

22 Justinian, constitution *Omnem*, prefacing *Digest*.

23 See my three essays on 'Civil Science in the Renaissance', one on Italian and another on French legal and social thought, in *History etc.* (as in n. 13), and a third, subtitled 'The Problem of Interpretation', in Anthony Pagden (ed.), *The Languages of Political Theory in Early Modern Europe*, Cambridge 1987, pp. 57–78.

lowly art to a methodical and professional science which came to be signalled, guaranteed and advertised by an academic degree on the doctor's level. By the thirteenth century, in the words of a contemporary poet,

> Civil law rode richly
> And canon law proudly
> Before all the other arts.[24]

By the sixteenth century some jurists did not hesitate to claim that civil law, not theology (and certainly not medicine), was the true 'queen of sciences'.

What made these 'doctors of law' so pre-eminent? Their rise to academic glory had begun with Justinian's teachers of law. These *antecessores* had been so called, explained Accursius (in one of his many inventive but erroneous etymologies), because they 'anteceded' all others in learning and virtue.[25] Beyond these qualities their medieval successors added a claim to true 'nobility' (*nobilitas ... propter magnam scientiam* is the phrase of Baldus) and indeed, added Pierre Rebuffi, to immortality (*non solum scientia tribuit nobilitatem, sed etiam immortalitatem*).[26] The earliest of the European 'doctors of law', all four of them students of Master Irnerius in the twelfth century, have been (self-)memorialized in another contemporary verse:

> Bulgarus has the golden mouth,
> Martinus in lore ranks high,
> Hugo the very spirit of laws,
> And lastly Jacob, who am I.[27]

(Notice, for future reference, Hugo's epithet, *mens legum*—spirit, mind, or meaning of the laws—a technical term later adapted as the designation for the professional aim and ideal of the 'perfect jurist'.)[28] From these 'four doctors' down to his own day, remarked one sixteenth-century jurist, more law books were produced than in the millennium before Justinian.

After the 'glossators' of the thirteenth century came the more philosophical-minded 'commentators'. These masters of the so-called 'Italian method' found their eponymous hero in the most authoritative of all jurists, Bartolus of Sassoferrato, who became the basis of a still more potent mythology and academic '-ism'. 'Nemo jurista nisi Bartolista' was a proverb in the sixteenth century, and even today it is said that a Spaniard, to boast of his preparation and readiness, might say that he 'has his Bartolus' (*tiene son bartol*).[29] From here the semi-legendary procession of jurists is described in another Latin jingle, this one attributed to Andrea Alciato and adorning the major anthology of treatises devoted to the 'perfect jurisconsult':

[24] Henri d'Andeli, *The Battle of the Seven Arts*, tr. L. Paetow, Berkeley 1914, p. 43:
> La Loi chevaucha richement
> Et Decret orguilleusement
> Sor trestoutes les autres ars.

[25] Accursius, *Digestum vetus*, Paris 1576, *ad titulum*.

[26] Baldus, *Super Digesto veteri*, n.p. 1535, fol. 3r, and Rebuffi, *De Privilegiis scholasticorum Tractatus varii*, Lyons 1581, p. 500. Cf. Andrea Alciato, *Emblemata*, Padua 1626, no. 6, 'Ex literarum studiis immortalitatem acquiri'.

[27] Charles Homer Haskins, *The Renaissance of the Twelfth Century*, Cambridge 1927, p. 201:
> Bulgarus os aureum, Martinus copia legum,
> Mens legum est Ugo, Jacobus id quod ego.

[28] See below, p. 94.

[29] Pierre Legendre, 'La France et Bartole', *Bartolo da Sassoferrato, Studi e documenti per il VI centenario*, Milan 1962, I, p. 135, and Bruno Paradisi in the same volume. Cf. Etienne Pasquier, *Les Recherches de la France*, VIII, xiv, in *Œuvres*, edn Amsterdam 1723, I, p. 787; and Guido Kisch, *Gestalten und Probleme aus Humanismus und Renaissance*, Berlin 1969.

In law first place to Bartolus goes;
Baldus in court pre-eminence shows;
Third Paolo Castro, teacher of note;
Then Alexander's decisions we quote,
Followed by Giason del Maino's light,
And others we cite for books if not right.[30]

This takes us down to the French school of the sixteenth century, founded by this same Alciato, who added the eloquence and erudition of humanism to the professional training of civil science. His students (the *Alciatei*, as one critic called them) have been memorialized in another piece of punning Latin doggerel:

Among the 'François' of law, the leading lights are four:
Of interpreters François Duaren is first in legal lore;
Then François Connan, counsellor whom we esteem;
Third, François Baudouin, Hellenist supreme;
And François Hotman in words the leader of all, some say;
Followed by Baron, Doneau, Dumoulin, Gribaldi, Budé ...[31]

The approach espoused by these masters of the 'French method' was taken up as well by German, Dutch, English and Spanish jurists; and it persisted well into the eighteenth (in a diluted form even into the twentieth) century. The 'perfect jurist' was thus the product and beneficiary of a rich heritage of history, legend and eponymous heroes (or villains), linking classical and modern times and celebrated reverently in Renaissance history, philosophy, literature and, in a large variety of iconographic forms, art.

'Bartolism' has often been derided as a particularly virulent form of scholasticism, particularly by rhetoricians like Lorenzo Valla and members of the French school; but from a less partisan standpoint it appears as a central and shaping feature of Renaissance culture, most especially in political terms. For Bartolus and Baldus displayed not only technical legal expertise in 'both laws' but also the values and aspirations of a new *civilità*, a new political culture based on a commitment to the ideals of citizenship and the 'active life'.[32] As Ernst Kantorowicz pointed out, they also expressed a sort of 'craving after worldly fame' which was more often attributed to the Italian humanists. Referring to the Accursian gloss, 'the dead live

[30] Reusner (as in n. 19), appendix:
In iure primos comparatius caeteris
Partes habebit BARTOLUS,
Decisiones obfrequentes, actio
BALDUM forensis sustinet.
Non negligens maxime est tyronibus
CASTRENSIS explanatio
Opinionem tutius symplegadas
Superabis ALEXANDRO duce:
Ordines IASON atque lucis nomine
Videndum est properantibus.
His si qui alios addiderit interpres,
Onerat, quam honorat, verius.

[31] Ibid.:
Franciscos celebrat consultos Gallia Iuris
Quatuor, et sacri lumina magna fori.
Primus in his claris studiis Duaerenus et arte;
Interpres legum maxime herde fuit.
Alter honore potens Connanus, et ubere censu,
Consilio Francus rexit, et ore forum.
Tertius ingenii Balduinum acumine praestans,
Crecropio nutrit pectora plena sale.
Iure medens quartus latrae facundia lingua,
Tu bonus es studiis dux Hotomanne meis.
At non his cedunt Cuiacius ore ... etc.

[32] See *L'Opera di Baldo*, Perugia 1901, especially the contribution of Iulio Tarducci (pp. 409–66), and Peter Riesenberg, 'Civism and Roman Law in Fourteenth-Century Italian Society', *Explorations in Economic History*, VII, 1969–70, pp. 237–54.

through glory', Kantorowicz commented that 'perhaps this path, too, was first trodden by the jurists'.[33] In recent years there has been much talk of 'civic humanism', especially in the wake of the seminal work by Hans Baron, but very little attention to the contributions of Renaissance jurists like Bartolus and Baldus, who in many ways fit this pattern, since they too championed civic responsibility, republican liberty, and even active resistance to tyranny.

The difference is that their ideological outlook, which might be distinguished as 'civil humanism', was largely independent both of the political 'crisis' described by Baron and of the 'Machiavellian moment' defined by John Pocock; but this hardly justifies the neglect of this perhaps broader and no less enduring tradition. In any case this professional cast of mind was another part (as Machiavellism in either of its guises was not) of the legacy of the 'perfect jurist'.[34] There is another and more direct connection between Renaissance culture and the juridical ideal type still recognized by Leibniz. Significantly, it seems to me, Bartolism emerged at the same time and under the same conditions as the social ideal of the *uomo universale*, the Renaissance man. In this period, from the fourteenth to the seventeenth century, historians have identified a variety of idealizations of manhood (only marginally, alas, of womanhood) which, aspiring to virtuosity as well as to universality, seemed to supersede, or at least to overshadow, sainthood and knighthood.[35]

The most prominent role in the Renaissance theatre of life was surely that of the Prince, especially because of Machiavelli's sensationalist caricature, which came to life on the Elizabethan stage (among other places); but there were other striking incarnations, such as the perfect Courtier, the perfect Diplomat or Orator, the Counsellor, the Historian, the Critic, perhaps the Baconian Man of Science, and even the Compleat Angler (likewise a synthesis of contemplation and effective action, or at least good intentions). It was in this cast of characters that the Perfect Jurist first appeared. On the one hand he had to be an encyclopedic scholar, since jurisprudence included (as one sixteenth-century lawyer wrote) 'the history of human acts, a knowledge of physics or medicine, mathematics and other matters treated by the liberal arts'.[36] On the other hand he claimed to be the fulfilment of that ultimate social type, the 'political man' (*homo politicus*, in the phrase used by Baldus and other commentators), the model of 'civic' as well as 'civil humanism'.[37] He represented the last stage of evolution of that 'political animal' classified by Aristotle and invoked by Renaissance jurists (*animal civile* or *sociale*). 'Furthermore', declared a sixteenth-century scholar, 'truth is to be found in our jurisprudence no less than in philosophy'.[38]

[33] E. Kantorowicz, *The King's Two Bodies*, Princeton 1957, p. 277.

[34] In general the centre of discussion has shifted from Hans Baron, *The Crisis of the Early Italian Renaissance*, Princeton 1966, to J. G. A. Pocock, *The Machiavellian Moment*, Princeton 1976, and a variety of commentators and critics; see also *idem*, 'The Machiavellian Moment Revisited', *Journal of Modern History*, LIII, 1981.

[35] For special versions of Jacob Burckhardt's concept see Lester K. Born, introduction to Erasmus, *Education of a Christian Prince*, New York 1936; Allan H. Gilbert, *Machiavelli's Prince and its Forerunners*, Durham N. C. 1938; Garrett Mattingly, *Renaissance Diplomacy*, New York 1955, ch. 1; D. R. Kelley, 'History as a Calling: The Case of La Popelinière', in *Renaissance Studies in Honor of Hans Baron*, ed. A. Molho and J. Tedeschi, Florence 1971, pp. 773–89; and M. E. Prior, 'Bacon's Man of Science', *Journal of the History of Ideas*, XV, 1954, pp. 348–70.

[36] Antoine Favre, *De Jurisprudentiae Papinianae Scientia ad ordinem institutionum imperialium efformata*, Lyons 1607, preface.

[37] See below, n. 55. 'Homo natura civile animal est' is William of Moerbeke's translation of Aristotle's phrase.

[38] Favre (as in n. 36), p. 10.

This common professional view was reinforced by the growing attraction between the study of law and the newly revived philosophy of Plato—not the private, poetic, occultist Platonism of Ficino but the political Platonism of the *Republic*, which, like Roman legal science, taught that philosophy, founded on the search for justice, was the very foundation of public life and the education of the 'political man'. Even in monarchies like France, England and the Empire, however, the ideal was not the 'philosopher-king'; it was rather the 'philosopher-jurist'. It was the culture of Renaissance humanism, in fact, that completed the formation of the original *jurisconsultus perfectus*. Not only did the 'new jurisprudence' of the French school take humanism as its starting point but it also claimed the law itself as a member of the humanities, and most especially as a branch of moral philosophy. This was the view taken by the French jurist Barthélemy de Chasseneux in his *Catalogue of the Glories of the World*, which was a set of fascinating and encyclopedic, if pedantic and legalistic, variations on the theme of hierarchy. Chasseneux rehearsed the old claims that civil law was a full-fledged 'science' because it proceeded through 'causes' and 'reasons', but he also insisted that the study of law deserved a place in the charmed circle of the liberal arts. Among the worldly 'glories' celebrated by Chasseneux in 1529 the most prominent was this master of two cultures, the *doctor legum*, produced by the convergence between the office of the jurist and the Renaissance ideal of manhood, which Chasseneux illustrated with reference to Pico's 'Oration' as well as the usual freight of legal allegations.[39] Set at the very centre of creation, man nonetheless had the ability to scale the heights of learning and virtue. At birth, Chasseneux wrote, the soul was but a *tabula rasa*, and yet he was 'perfectible' (*perfectibilis*) through science, which brought true 'nobility' and placed man not a little below but actually a little above the angels (who were unfortunately innocent of the 'true philosophy' of jurisprudence). In pursuit of human perfection, he concluded, one could do no better than ascend the ladder of learning through the liberal arts to the heights of civil science, certified and exalted by the degree of doctor of laws. And of these doctors of law, Chasseneux continued, who was the fairest of all? Who stood highest on the ladder of legal learning? Modesty forbade his naming names, but in this part of his book, which amounted to a kind of 'mirror for lawyers', he set down several criteria for interested parties to keep in mind. Of all those holding the LL.D. degree, Chasseneux declared, those are to be preferred who, among other things, 'actively teach', 'who have the higher salary', 'who compile or write books', 'who have seniority', 'who are graduated from the larger, more famous and better regarded university', and 'who have the most degrees' as well as other unnamed honours.[40] Here, then, at the head of the academic procession, decked out in hat, gown and insignia, walks the epitome of the life contemplative and active, the ultimate Renaissance person—the *jurisconsultus summa cum laude.*

[39] *Catalogus gloriae mundi*, Paris 1529, x, 2. And cf. x, 9, 'Tamen etiam scientia seu professio iuris dicitur ars liberalis, aut studium liberale', referring to *Digest*, I, i, 1, on 'vera philosophia', and adding, 'Et in toto corpore iuris vera theologia invenitur et docetur'.

[40] Ibid., x, 25.

In order to narrow still further the focus on 'perfect jurisprudence' we must consider another remarkable phenomenon of modern history, a phenomenon which touches on natural as well as civil science. This is the international and interdisciplinary pursuit of a valid 'method' of study.[41] Probably the most famous pre-Baconian and pre-Cartesian discussion of 'method' was that of Peter Ramus (also mentioned by Leibniz, though disapprovingly), which had a particularly important impact on law. Beyond the vast literature of Ramism there was also a flood of treatises on the best way of learning, teaching and practising law (*methodus, modus, ratio* and *institutio* are a few of the key terms). Out of this methodological pandemonium emerged a new protrepic genre which prescribed the education of the perfect jurist, the handbook for lawyers which, in various languages, might be identified as *Speculum jurisconsultorum, Juristenspiegel, Lunette des avocats, Mirror of Lawyers*, and in general guides to the office of a good advocate or judge. In the sixteenth and seventeenth centuries such treatises are almost beyond numbering. Before 1600 well over a hundred were published, most notably from Nicolas Everardi's *Loci argumentorum legales* of 1516 and Claudius Cantiuncula's *Topica Legalia* of 1520 down at least to C. H. Eckhardt's *Hermeneutica juris* of 1770 (and 1802) and including English as well as Italian, German, French, Spanish, and Dutch entries.[42]

The earliest of these treatises were little more than student guides, exhorting would-be lawyers to methodical study. 'Avoid drunkenness' (*caveat a crapula et ebrietate*), advised Giovanni Battista Caccialupi in the 1460s; choose a teacher carefully, obey him, read the proper books, and learn the best methods of allegation and disputation; for this has always been the way to form a 'new Justinian'.[43] Over a century later Alberico Gentili, regius professor of civil law at Oxford, was giving much the same advice—and warning young men against the pedantry of those literary virtuosi he referred to scornfully as 'the new sect of Alciato' and against the methodological eccentricities of the 'larvae' of Peter Ramus. 'What is a good judge?' Cantiuncula had asked—and answered, nothing more than 'a good man, trained in speaking the law and determining equity, and called to this office by public authority'.[44] Even Jean de Coras, though fully abreast of the 'new learning', placed experience after erudition and integrity in the list of qualifications for a good and perfect judge (*Petit discours des parties et office d'un bon et entier iuge*).[45] In Honoratus

[41] See especially Theodor Vieweg, *Topik und Jurisprudenz*, Munich 1974; Cesare Vasoli, 'La Dialettica umanistica e la metodologia giuridica nel secolo XVI', in *La Formazione storica del diritto moderno in Europa*, I, Florence 1977; Aldo Mazzacane, *Scienza, logica e ideologia nella giurisprudenza tedesca del sec. XVI*, Milan 1971; and various articles by Hans Troje, e.g. in *Tijdschrift voor Rechtsgeschiedenis*, XXXVIII, 1970, pp. 519–63, and in *Der Kommentar in der Renaissance*, ed. A. Buck and O. Herding, Godeberg 1975, pp. 47–61, and 'Wissenschaft und System in der Jurisprudenz des 16. Jahrhunderts', in *Philosophie und Rechtswissenschaft*, ed. J. Bluhdorn and J. Ritter, Frankfurt 1969; also Friedrich Ebrard, 'Über Methoden, Systeme, Dogmen in der Geschichte des Privatrechts', *Zeitschrift für schweizerisches Recht*, LXVIII, 1948, pp. 95–136; George Kalinowski, 'La Logique juridique et son histoire', *Archives de la philosophie du droit*, XXVII, 1982, pp. 275–89; and in general C. Vasoli, *La Dialettica e la retorica dell'umanesimo*, Milan 1968, and Neal Ward Gilbert, *Renaissance Concepts of Method*, New York 1960.

[42] See Helmut Coing (ed.), *Handbuch der Quellen und Literatur der neueren europäischen Privatrechtsgeschichte*, II, Munich 1977, essential for bibliography and commentary, and especially the section on humanism by Troje (as in n. 41), pp. 724–54.

[43] Gazalupis, *Modus studiendi in utroque iure*, in Sebastian Brant, *Titulorum omnium iuris ... expositiones*, Lyons 1578, p. 434.

[44] *De Officio iudicis libri duo*, Basle 1543, II.

[45] J. de Coras, *Petit discours des parties et office d'un bon et entier iuge*, Lyons 1596. Cf. *De Iuris arte*, Lyon 1560, his commentaries on *Digest*, I, 1, and in general A. London

Draco's versification of the basic textbook of civil law (*Institutiones imperiales in carmen contractae*) the 'office of a judge' was, for mnemonic as well as aesthetic purposes, represented in a jingling poetic form, thus joining Themis, goddess of justice, with the muses in a way hardly imagined by legal humanists.[46] The best and certainly most amusing illustration of the conservative image of the professional lawyer was offered by Alberico Gentili in 1582. With the kind of anti-intellectualism that only intellectuals can summon up, Gentili (whose own children were brought up to be trilingual) denied the value of history and philology and completely rejected the programme of Baudouin and Bodin for combining these with the law. Even Baron and Le Douaren he dismissed as 'scholars rather than jurists' (*sapientes potius quam jurisconsulti*). The old medieval 'doctors of law' were more useful than all the modern 'encyclopedists', Gentili insisted. Modern lawyers had neither time nor use for the erudition of a Varro—or a Cujas. After all, he wrote, 'We can't all do everything' (*non omnia possumus omnes—man kann nicht alles*), and he saw nothing at all wrong with skipping certain passages of the *Digest* with the old motto of philistinism, 'It's all Greek to me' (*Graecum est, non potest legere*).[47] Under the influence of humanism, however, the standards of legal education were raised to a higher and sometimes grandiose level. In the classical anthology of treatises on legal method published by Nicolas Reusner in 1588, two essays were devoted specifically to the 'perfect jurisconsult'.[48] One was an anonymous treatise which dealt mainly with what we might call the 'higher criticism' of the legal canon, based on the resources of modern philology. The other one, by Johann Freigius, discussed the idea of the perfect or polished jurist (*idea jurisconsulti perfecti*, the same phrase that Leibniz would use almost a century later). Freigius's work also contains a fold-out diagram, setting forth in the dichotomies of Ramist logic all of the qualities necessary for the perfect jurist, who is here also styled *homo politicus*.[49] Such a person, endowed with both humanist culture and technical expertise, ought to possess fortune as well as learning, will as well as intellect, and a grasp of law as well as the other arts and sciences; and yet Freigius's emphasis, like that of Chasseneux, is always on the second, more universal attainments.

This portrait is in effect that of the philosopher-magistrate, and it would be copied, redrawn, and touched up by many hands over the next century and more, including those of Antoine Favre in 1607 and of Leibniz sixty years after that—both of them, like Freigius and Ramus, advertising a 'new method' which the perfect jurist ought to employ. In this idealization of the jurist—that 'truth is in our jurisprudence no less than in philosophy'—we can detect a certain Platonic influence. In the seventeenth century John Doderidge's *Lawyer's Light*, for example, was aimed at those who, as he put it, 'covet to contemplate with their inward eye the express and perfect Image of an English lawyer ...'[50] Among the necessary qualities,

Fell, *The Origins of Legislative Sovereignty*, Königstein 1983.

46 *Elementa iuris civilis seu Institutiones imperiales in Carmen contractae*, Lyons 1551.

47 *De Iuris interpretibus*, London 1582, fol. 44. Cf. G. Astuti, *Mos italicus e mos gallicus nei dialoghi 'de iuris interpretibus' di Alberico Gentili*, Bologna 1937, and Diego Panizza, *Alberico Gentile, giurista ideologo nell'Inghilterra elisabettiana*, Padua 1981.

48 Reusner (as in n. 19), 'Pars altera', ('De Jurisconsulto perfecto, et de optimo iuris interpretandi'), no. 21; also no. 36, and see the discussion by H. Troje, *Graeca Leguntur*, Cologne 1971.

49 Favre (as in n. 36), preface 1607, 'De perfecto Iureconsulto', and adding, 'Bonum Iurisconsultum haereticum esse nullomodo posse'.

50 J. Doderidge, *The English Lawyer*, London 1631; repr. Amsterdam 1973, p. 1.

Doderidge listed power of memory, eloquence ('neither outworn nor new-fangled' language, he warned) and knowledge of learned jurisprudence, including the continental methodizers like Freigius and Hotman as well as Aristotle, his categories and his four causes, and humanists like Budé, Alciato and Cujas. Within this Latinate and Platonizing enclosure Doderidge hoped to confine the irregular growth of English land law and to enhance somewhat the uncouth image of the common lawyer. Louis Le Caron, an alumnus of the French school and author of a *Digest of French Law,* also invoked the philosophy of Plato when he identified the task of the jurist with the 'office of the philosopher', since it involved the search for and dispensation of justice in accordance with the Idea of the Good, which Le Caron equated rather simplistically with 'public utility'. The true 'mark of sovereignty' was not legislative power, he argued, but rather *haute justice,* and the delegation of this authority, equivalent to the *merum imperium,* to magistrates Le Caron found philosophically as well as politically sound—'very *politique* and in accordance with the view of our Plato'.[51] This was an essential ingredient of that harmonic justice (*eunomia*) which Plato had also envisioned for his Republic.

French legists have normally been associated with absolutism, and yet some of them were hardly less enthusiastic than English common lawyers for judicial power. Contemporaneously with Edward Coke, for example, Etienne Pasquier and his old colleague Antoine Loisel discussed, almost nostalgically, the authority formerly enjoyed by Roman jurists (the *responsa prudentium* which had the force of law down to the time of Justinian); and Pasquier praised the judiciary (*les cours souverains*) as a major source of French law equal in value to the royal ordinances.[52] Loisel endorsed this view by composing, in dialogue form, a history of the French legists from the 'lawyers of the last Capetians' down to the time of Pasquier—after whom, indeed, he named his book.[53] This was another way of celebrating the role, and the role-models, of the perfect jurist. In many ways, however, vernacular jurists—English common lawyers as well as French 'feudists'—were suspicious of efforts to civilize, that is, to classicize and in effect to Romanize, native legal traditions. Consequently the *jurisconsultus perfectus,* in its classic form, remained largely within the tradition of Latin learning, of what German jurists called the *usus modernus Pandectarum,* and on the last stretches of what Ernst Curtius has romantically called 'the crumbling Roman road from the antique to the modern world'.[54]

In general the idea of the perfect jurist was a modern reincarnation of the ancient jurisconsult, formed by a synthesis of the old civil law Italian style and the newer jurisprudence in the French manner. Both schools were devoted to the ancient legal canon, and both were devoted to a model of the 'political man' (*homo politicus*) that transcended Aristotle's 'political animal'.[55] They were thinking not

51 *Pandectes ou Digestes du droict françois,* Paris 1587, I, p. 3; and see D. R. Kelley, 'Louis Le Caron Philosophe', in *History etc.* (as in n. 13).

52 *Interprétation des Institutes de Justinian,* ed. M. le duc Pasquier, Paris 1847; *Les Lettres,* Paris 1619, XIX, letters 8–14; and *Divers opuscules,* Paris 1652, pp. 95ff.

53 *Pasquier, ou Dialogue des avocats du Parlement de Paris,* ed. A. Dupin, Paris 1844.

54 *European Literature and the Latin Middle Ages,* tr. W. Trask, New York 1953, p. 19.

55 J. P. Canning, 'A Fourteenth-Century Contribution to the Theory of Citizenship: Political Man and the Problem of Created Citizenship in the Thought of Baldus de Ubaldo', in *Authority and Power,* ed. B. Tierney and P. Laneham, Cambridge 1980, p. 200, and now *The Political Thought of Baldus de Ubaldis,* Cambridge 1987; also Nicolai Rubinstein, 'The Meaning of the Term "Politicus" in Early Modern Europe', in Pagden (as in n. 23), pp. 41–56.

merely of man as 'by nature political' but of the jurist as the expert 'interpreter of law'. Not only in the Latin of Baldus and others in the fourteenth century, but also in sixteenth-century French and English, the 'politique' or 'politicus' was the civil scientist, the paragon of learning and judgement who was the true overseer, arbiter and critic of society and of what by the sixteenth century was already being called 'political science'. It is interesting and relevant to notice that, in the context of the religious and civil strife of the later sixteenth century, this notion of the 'political man' was acquiring very different overtones. In the wake of the massacres of St Bartholomew in particular, the 'politique', or sometimes 'politician', was identified not with the man of law and justice but with the man of unscrupulous ambition—in a word (which was indeed coined as a synonym at just this time, the 1570s) with the 'Machiavellian' or 'Machiavellist'.[56] In a treatise devoted to the doctrine of 'reason of state' Bogislaus Philipp von Chemnitz included among these 'new and especially Italian politiques' (*noviores politici praecipue Italici*) not only Niccolò Machiavelli but also the civil lawyers of the Empire.[57] These are altogether appropriate reminders of the other side of the lawyers' diptych, the darker and devilish image, now further blackened by the association of the proverbial 'bad Christian' with the newer myth of 'Old Nick', as Machiavelli became in English literature and folklore.

The perfect jurist seldom dirtied his hands with politics, but on one central issue he had to take a stand. This was the age-old, politically charged but never satisfactorily resolved question of interpretation—not only the legal dimension of the 'hermeneutical art' treated by Leibniz (which sounds theoretical and harmless enough) but also the question of judicial discretion, authority and even independence. Though forbidden by Justinian, the privilege of *interpretatio* had been restored by his medieval successors, especially Frederick Barbarossa, and granted to the 'doctor of law', alias the *interpres juris*.[58] From being a punishable crime, then, 'interpretation' became an essential and celebrated rubric of civil law; and for centuries the debate has raged between two schools of thought—literal versus liberal construction, or, in medieval and Renaissance terms, 'restrictive' versus 'extensive' interpretation. In general the 'perfect jurist' was master of *interpretatio extensiva*, which is to say revealer (paraphrasing St Paul) not of the deadening letter but of the life-giving 'spirit' of the laws.[59]

Here again we encounter the crucial term applied honorifically by Jacobus to his colleague Hugo and referring more generally to the final interpretive aim of both ancients and moderns. This notion of *mens legum*, the 'spirit of the laws', or *ratio legum*, the 'reason of laws', was also what Leibniz had in mind in his own 'new method' of jurisprudence; and it was pursued even more 'extensively' (as jurists

[56] D. R. Kelley, *The Beginning of Ideology*, Cambridge 1981, pp. 203ff.; and 'Murd'rous Machiavel in France', in *History etc.* (as in n. 13).

[57] *Dissertationes de Ratione Status in Imperio nostro Romano-Germanico*, n.p. 1640, preface.

[58] Johann Oldendorp, *Interpretatio privilegii duplicis, quod Friderichus primus ... concessit bonarum literarum studiosis*, n.p. 1543.

[59] See Vincenzo Piano Mortari, *Richerce sulla interpretazione del diritto nel secolo XVI*, Milan 1956, and his various essays collected in *Diritto, Logica, Metodo nel secolo XVI*, Naples 1978; also and above all Ennio Cortese, *La Norma giuridica*, Milan 1962–64, esp. II, pp. 295–362.

would say) by legal philosophers like Domat, Vico, Montesquieu and perhaps even Hegel, continuing through the tradition of which Max Weber spoke.[60] How can one call up this 'spirit' of the law? Like other contemporary scholars seeking the holy grail of 'method', the advocates of 'perfect jurisprudence' concentrated their efforts first on the rehabilitation of logic, usually in conjunction with rhetoric. Though often vilified, Aristotelianism continued to be important in legal methodology, especially in establishing the connection between law and politics. The key was Aristotle's famous system of four causes, which had been used in this connection ever since the time of the early commentators. Jean Coras explained this application: 'The efficient cause of law, formerly the people, is now the prince', he wrote. 'The formal cause is the extension of the laws from the individuals to society in general ...; the material cause is the interactions among citizens ...; and the final cause is public utility and tranquillity, as expressed in the law [Coras means the Twelve Tables], that "the good of the people must be the supreme law".'[61] In this way Coras legitimized law in terms of its human sources, its demographic coverage, social context and political goals; and so he gave philosophical status and authority to the accumulated texts of legal tradition. In this way, too, Coras raised to a high conceptual and political eminence the guardians of this legal tradition and of the 'spirit of the laws'.

The primary goal of the perfect jurist was always 'interpretation of laws', and such indeed was the subtitle of Vincent Placcius's treatise of 1662, *De Jurisconsulto Perfecto.*[62] Like the classical (though not the Byzantine) jurisconsults, European civilians had to render 'responses' and 'decisions', and on this elementary level their judgements were incontrovertible. Just as an error could never be alleged in the law (as Baldus had repeated), so it was a rule of law that judicial decisions were to be identified with truth itself (*res judicatae sunt veritas*).[63] On the basis of the rubric *res judicatae* ('the first and perhaps only part of law') Pierre Ayrault, another alumnus of the French school, built a novel sort of empirical Digest—a 'Pandects' of legal positivism—which elevated individual judgements, and implicitly the judge, to a law-making as well as a law-finding function. 'For what is a constitution but something taken from many judgements and opinions ...?' he asked, reinforcing in a practical way the Platonic position of Le Caron.[64] 'Experience is the true master' (*usus ille docendi magister*, a formula derived from classical rhetoric), he added, urging that 'in those things which pertain to a particular art, one should have recourse to the experts' (*recurri ad peritos in iis quae ad artem eorum pertinent*).[65]

Modern jurists were faced with the task of organizing their post- and extra-Roman experience, and this produced a flood of treatises on proper scientific, which in general was to say pedagogical, 'method'. Valentinus Forster's handbook on the 'Interpreter', for example, was actually a treatise on the art of interpretation, which summarized the four major kinds of construction—common, extensive,

[60] D. R. Kelley, 'The Prehistory of Sociology: Montesquieu, Vico and the Legal Tradition', in *History etc.* (as in n. 13).

[61] *In titulum Pandectarum de Iustitia et Iure*, Lyons 1568, p. 247.

[62] *De Iurisconsulto perfecto, sive Interpretatione legum in genere*, Hamburg 1693.

[63] *Digest*, L, 17, p. 207, cited, e. g., by R. J. Pothier, *Pandectes de Justinien mises dans un nouvel ordre*, Paris 1823, p. 480.

[64] *Rerum ab omni antiquitate iudicarum Pandectae*, Geneva 1616.

[65] Ibid., p. 84. Cf. Quintilian, *Institutio oratoriae*, I, 1; Pliny, *Historia naturalis*, XXVI, 6; Horace, *Ars poetica*, 71.

restrictive and declarative—as well as the formal 'rules of law'.[66] Forster also discussed the question of equity, 'ethico-political law' and, in opposition to Gentili, the value of history in the interpretation and application of laws. The problem confronted by Forster and many other jurists in this age of methodizing was this: in order to reach perfection jurists had to grasp in a logical way the structure as well as the substance of the law. By analogy with Aristotle's 'natural' categories jurists devised 'legal' ones (*transcendentia legalia, topica legalia,* as they were termed) and produced handbooks of specifically 'legal' dialectic and rhetoric.[67] Jurists of course had their own 'rules' (the *regulae antiqui juris* of the Digest) and their own standards of and ways of arriving at judgement— including 'prejudice' (precedent), 'analogy', and (in a special sense) 'etymology'.[68] In the next century this distinction would lend itself to a veritable war of two methods (if not two cultures), but before the revolution of natural science the civil scientist had already defined his proper sphere as something possibly including, but certainly going beyond, the categories of the natural world. In the sixteenth century a new methodology emerged which held out the prospect of a reform of various branches of knowledge, including the tangled and overgrown old legal tradition.

This was the so-called 'new logic' devised by Rudolph Agricola, Philip Melanchthon, and especially Peter Ramus, as a way of giving concreteness, utility and humanity to the study of dialectic. From the 1540s Ramist method had an extraordinary impact on the study of law. Students were attracted not only by the elaborate, often pretentious schema of Ramus but also by its anti-Aristotelian thrust and, at least implicitly, by its associations with Protestant doctrine.[69] What Ramism offered was a way of ordering material that was not abstractly logical but rather concretely rhetorical—'topical' in a literary and utilitarian sense. It was accommodated to memory rather than reason, to persuasion rather than disputation, and to convention rather than nature. Because of its authoritarian and in a sense anthropological character, Ramism seemed especially well suited to jurisprudence, and above all to the task of modernizing civil law, bringing it into line with humanist learning, and conscripting it into the service of various national states.

A number of later sixteenth-century jurists, including Freigius and Johann Althusius, flirted with this new doctrine and thereby stirred the fires of debate over scientific 'method'. Like many other avant-garde, or at least trendy, intellectual movements before and since, Ramism provoked hostile reactions, especially from professional philosophers and jurists. The height of Parisian fashion, Ramus was, for the later sixteenth century, the successor of Abelard, the ultimate corrupter of youth. One English critic, Abraham Fraunce, sounded the alarm against this upstart theorist and his 'harebrayne' disciples who 'prate of Method that never knew order'.[70] Away with Ramus's bifurcations and back to Aristotle's four causes, Fraunce advised in his *Lawiers Logike* of 1588; forget all those invented 'topics' and get down to the facts, down to cases—which is to say, down to the substance of English law. Fraunce illustrated this substance, amusingly enough, with reference not only to

66 *Interpres seu de interpretatione juris*, Wittenberg 1613.

67 Matteo Gribaldi, *De Methodo ac ratione studiendi libri tres*, Lyons 1541, p. 165.

68 Cantiuncula, *Topica legalia*, Basle 1545; and cf. Guido Kisch, *Claudius Cantiuncula*, Basle 1970.

69 Classic discussion in R. Stintzing, *Geschichte der deutschen Rechtswissenschaft*, I, Munich 1880, but see n. 41.

70 A. Fraunce, *The Lawiers Logike*, London 1588, dedication to the lawyers of Gray's Inn.

Plowden's Reports but also to the *Shepherd's Calendar.* In both of these sources—in Collyn's love-sick 'weale and woe' as well as in recorded law suits—one could study the concrete 'causes' of human behaviour. Intellectually and institutionally, English lawyers had more restricted horizons than their continental colleagues and had managed for the most part to avoid contamination from the civil law (except in such subsidiary jurisdictions as chancery and the prerogative courts). For most common lawyers it was enough to have a practical grasp of the texts and trade secrets of their professional guild. William Noy's book *The Compleat Lawyer,* for example, was little more than a catechism of the law of tenures and estates—which, he taught, represented the very beginning of civilization.[71]

Humanists were contemptuous of this insularity and what Henry Spelman deplored as the 'barbarous dialectic' and 'uncouth method' preserved in the Inns of Court.[72] Common lawyers like Fraunce, however, rose to the defence of their nativist and vernacularist cause, arguing that English law, even in the form of that hodge-podge called law-French, was 'sufficiently elegant because it is fully significant'. In these terms it was possible for the English to offer their own portrait of the ideal jurist. One such likeness was drawn by Edward Hake at the end of the sixteenth century. Referring to the English notion of 'equity', Hake remarked that if the king had 'two bodies', the judge had two knowledges, one private and the other judicial; and the latter was the true source of his pre-eminence. Invoking the authority of Melanchthon, Hake went on to identify 'equity' (*epieikeia*) with that same 'spirit of the law' celebrated by the ancient lawyers in contrast to the 'quercks and quidditityes strained from the trewe sense of the law' by later commentators.[73]

For the English, of course, this 'spirit' was to be taken 'owt of the grounds and fountaines' of common law. In the end the English were able to lay claim to perfect jurisprudence by a stratagem, as neat as it was narrow-minded, which simply identified common law with natural law in the sense of the instinctual wisdom of the English people as expressed in its customs. Such was the position taken by Edward Coke and William Dugdale in their efforts to defend their professional monopoly. When Dugdale declared that English law was 'no other than pure and tried reason', he was referring not to the universal reason of Cicero or Bartolus but rather to the empirically tested validity of common law, which had been formed ultimately not by legislation or logic (except perhaps in retrospect) but rather by the intuitions and interpretations of English jurists drawn from a legacy of 'immemorial custom'.[74] In his assertion of judicial authority, of the ability of judges literally to read the 'mind' of the people (who made custom) and the kings (who made statute), Coke went so far as to appropriate a claim formerly reserved for the crown. Not the king's will but the king's judges represented the 'voice of the law'—not *rex* but *judex* was *lex loquens.* Coke did not have to search for the 'perfect jurist', in other words; he had already found this ideal, and it was—himself.

Continental jurists of the seventeenth century took a much less complacent attitude towards legal reason and perfection. One of the most striking things about

[71] W. Noy, *The Compleat Lawyer,* London 1670.

[72] Spelman to his mother (1598), cited in Wilfred R. Prest, *The Inns of Court,* Totowa N. J. 1973, p. 142; cf. Fraunce (as in n. 70), preface.

[73] E. Hake, *Epieikeia,* ed. D. C. Yale, New Haven 1953, p. 34.

[74] W. Dugdale, *Origines Judiciales,* London 1671, III.

civil science in this age was the impulse, going beyond Aristotle and Ramus, towards a philosophical and political system. This was actually an extension of the old professional search for the 'spirit of the laws'. In a sense this modern *esprit de système* was also inherent in the classical tradition, which from at least the time of Cicero had tried to order the social world according to a fundamental trichotomy, consisting of the categories of 'person', 'thing' and 'action'—that is, first and centrally, the free (normally male, adult) *persona*; second, and peripherally to *personalitas*, the 'real' world (*realitas* in the sense not only of *res*, physical things, but also of property and 'real estate'); and finally *actio*, that is, both the interactions of persons competing for possession and the 'actions at law' required to keep, recover or transmit such possessions.

One example of such a system based on the old civilian trichotomy was the encyclopedic work of Grégoire de Toulouse, author of another of the 'methods of law' as well as of an ideal 'Republic'.[75] In his *Syntagma juris universi* Grégoire changed the order, and indeed laid claim to a 'new method' based on nature, by taking up (as God Himself had done) 'things' before 'persons', and by completing his triadic recapitulation of the universe with human actions. Grégoire's 'republic' was not only man- and law-centred; it was in the most fundamental—and consciously anti-Machiavellian and anti-Bodinian—way lawyer-centred. (It might be noted that this secular trinity also corresponds, in a general way, to the still more fundamental anthropocentric categories of Indo-European languages—namely, subject, object, verb; but I refrain here from pursuing further the fascinating subject of what I think of as the metaphysical foundations of social and legal thought, except to suggest one of the ways in which 'perfect jurisprudence' claimed, in modern terms, to constitute wisdom and 'true philosophy'.)[76]

From this brief suggestion of the meta-legal basis of civil science (and the philosophical basis of perfect jurisprudence) it should be apparent that the legal tradition was in many ways at odds with new fashions in natural science. In the long struggle between nature and culture, in other words, the 'perfect jurist' inclined very conspicuously toward the latter—like Charles Lamb perhaps, preferring the man-made hubbub of the city to the tedium and threats of nature. As Hotman wrote in his *Jurisconsult* of 1559, civil law belonged not to 'natural' but to 'moral' (or, as we should say 'social') philosophy.[77] Or as Antoine Favre put it a half-century later in his own portrait of the 'perfect jurist', jurisprudence was the product not fundamentally of physical and quantitative considerations (*non ex sensu solo, ut mathematicis et physicis*, are his words) but rather of a kind of reasoning that is proper only to mankind (*sed ex ratiocinatione: quae cum solius hominis propria sit*).[78] Professional interpreters of the law could hardly expect to remain on the level of pure reason,

[75] Grégoire de Toulouse, *Syntagma iuris universi*, Frankfurt 1591, and *De Republica*, Lyons 1609; cf *De Iuris arte*, Lyons 1580; also Claude Collot, *L'École doctrinale de droit public de Pont-à-Mousson*, Paris 1965, and Luigi Gambino, *Il De Republica di Pierre Grégoire*, Milan 1975.

[76] D. R. Kelley, 'Gaius Noster: Substructures of Western Social Thought', in *History etc.* (as in n. 13).

[77] F. Hotman, *Jurisconsultus, sive de optimo genere iuris interpretandi*, Basle 1559, XI; also in Reusner (as in n. 19).

[78] A. Favre (as in n. 36), *De Jurisprudentia*, 'Lectori meo'.

called upon as they were to make practical judgements about concrete cases. 'For generalities', as Coke remarked, 'never bring anything to a conclusion'.[79] For good or ill, law was at bottom a form of prudence or practical reason (*phronesis*, the Greeks named it), bound irremediably to what Clifford Geertz has called 'local knowledge'; and the 'perfect jurist' could never forget this fact of professional life.

What about the connection between jurisprudence and more purely empirical science? Ostensibly, the procedure of the jurist seems analogous to inductive reasoning, and indeed *interpretatio inductiva* was a recognized form of legal judgement.[80] And of course Bacon himself, trained in the law and a master of rhetoric, celebrated the positive value of English customs above abstract formulas. 'Law originates in fact' (*lex ex facto oritur*) was a civilian maxim often quoted by the English, and so was the acknowledgement that law arose most directly out of particular judicial decisions ('things judged', *res judicatae* in the civilian terms discussed earlier).[81] The analogy between law and empirical science should not be pushed too far. In fact legal 'induction', so-called, was much closer to Aristotelian rhetoric than to Baconian method. Like the Baconian Man of Science, the Perfect Jurist appealed to practical 'experience', but it was to historical experience, or to a legacy of 'precedents', very different from scientific data as commonly understood. Although Bacon's procedure may owe something to his legal training and was tied to 'history' and 'memory', 'legal empiricism' should really be associated not with pure reason, it seems to me, but with the 'logic of probability', which (as Ian Hacking has recently argued) arose just at this time, the mid-seventeenth century.[82] By that time, however, there had long been a connection between judicial logic and probability (which formed, indeed, one of the *topoi* of sixteenth-century legal method).[83]

The best example is once again the work of Leibniz, for whom 'the whole of judicial procedure is just a kind of logic applied to questions of law'. And of this kind of logic, we should again notice, the master was none other than the Perfect Jurist. Yet, inspired by enthusiasm for the new science, many jurists began to claim a more rational and in this sense 'natural' status for their legal tradition. Joining the contemporary 'quest for certainty', they reached out beyond—or tried fundamentally to transform—their own tradition; and increasingly they turned from authority to logical, geometrical and even mathematical models of interpretation. From Coras to Leibniz, emphasizing the analogy between law and geometry was a common way of bringing civil law into line with the values, or rather value-free claims, of natural science. They looked with new eyes on those ancient legal 'rules' which had been glossed conventionally for centuries ('Liberty is a thing beyond price' is one of these *regulae antiqui juris*; 'slavery is death') and indeed proceeded to promote them from their original level of Roman common sense to that of universal

[79] *Les Reports de Edward Coke*, London 1600–15, VII, preface.

[80] Alberico de Rosate, *Tractatus de statutis*, Frankfurt 1608, VIII.

[81] Cortese (as in n. 59), II, p. 150; Luigi Prosdocimi, '"Ius vetus" accursiano e "Ius novum" postaccursiano', *Atti del Convegno internazionale di studi accursiani*, Milan 1968, III, p. 950; and D. R. Kelley, 'Clio and the Lawyers', n. 61, in *History etc.* (as in n. 13).

[82] *The Emergence of Probability*, Cambridge 1975, p. 86; and cf. A. Giuliani, 'The Influence of Rhetoric on the Law of Pleading', *The Juridical Review*, LXII, 1969, pp. 216–51.

[83] Cantiuncula (as in n. 68), VII.

propositions, natural principles and quasi-geometrical 'axioms'.[84] In his effort to arrange 'civil laws in their natural order', Jean Domat placed 'rules of law' at the very beginning of his treatise and virtually identified them with the 'clear and distinct ideas' of Descartes.[85] Domat's colleague Louis Boullenois was even more unabashedly Cartesian in his method. 'I have put aside all that I have read in our [legal] authors', he wrote, 'and I have delivered myself over to meditation'—though, like Descartes and Domat, he then went on to smuggle into his modern social philosophy a large measure of ancient legal convention.[86]

Thomas Hobbes even tried to bring rationality to English law. In his *Dialogue between a Philosopher and a Student of the Common Laws*, Hobbes assailed the 'artificial' and 'dogmatic' reason practised by Coke and affected to reduce it to a 'natural' or 'mathematical' reason that alone promised certitude.[87] For an ordinary pleader 'mere Rhetorick' might suffice, but the office of the perfect jurist demanded a more philosophical view. In this connection Hobbes borrowed the old legal maxim rejecting what he called 'the Grammatical construction of the Letter' in favour of the 'Intention' of the legislator, by which of course he meant its 'reason' in a modern philosophical sense. It hardly needs saying that this 'reason' was to be determined by the sovereign; for Hobbes's naturalism, or jusnaturalism, was placed ultimately in the service of the national state—the 'leviathan'. This was the juridical climate of opinion in which Leibniz created his portrait of the *jurisconsultus perfectus*. Returning to the old Bartolist insistence on law as a hard science, Leibniz gave it a modern twist by associating it with the new philosophy, invoking the names of Galileo, Hobbes, and the 'incomparable' Lord Verulam.[88] Yet his main purpose was still pedagogical. In effect he was still trying to simplify learning along the lines set by Valla, Ramus, and (in the law) Freigius and Althusius. He praised those 'restorers of jurisprudence', Le Douaren, Cujas, Hotman and Doneau, for cutting various 'Gordian knots' of jurisprudence, and contributed to the enterprise himself by rejecting the conventional three-fold division of legal categories, arguing that 'actions' could be classified simply under 'persons' or 'things'. For Leibniz the office of the jurist was threefold: 'historical' (but in the Baconian, in effect unhistorical, sense of learning the substance of the law), 'exegetical' (interpreting the 'real' as well as the 'textual' significance of the law), and 'polemical' (applying the law to particular cases).[89] In carrying out this charge the 'perfect jurist' should avoid all 'philological curiosities and equivocations', all historical, etymological, or philosophical questions, all uncertain or obsolete laws, which might cause confusion

[84] See Peter Stein, *Regulae Juris, From Juristic Rules to Legal Maxims*, Edinburgh 1966.

[85] J. Domat, *Les Lois civiles dans leur ordre naturel*, Luxemburg 1702, I, p. 6. And see Franco Todescan, 'Domat et les sources du droit', *Archives de philosophie du droit*, XXVII, 1980, pp. 55–66, and Giovanni Tarello, 'Sistemazione e ideologia nelle "loix civiles" di Jean Domat', *Materiali per una storia della cultura giuridica*, II, Bologna 1972, pp. 125–65.

[86] L. Boullenois, *Dissertations sur des questions qui naissent de la contrarieté des loix et des coutumes*, Paris 1732, p. xiv.

[87] Ed. J. Cropsey, Chicago 1971, p. 57 etc.

[88] *Nova Methodus* (as in n. 14), p. 329.

[89] Ibid., p. 293: '... *Historicam*, originem, autores, mutationes, abrogationesque Legum enarrantem; *Exegeticam*, ipsos Libros Authenticos [of Justinian] interpretantem; ... *Polemicam* seu controversiariam, casus in Legibus indecisos ex ratione et similitudine definientem'.

and detract from the ideals of ease and simplicity.[90] Instead he should concentrate on reducing the law to logical 'elements', that is, definitions and precepts.

Galileo had made a famous remark about the 'great book of nature', that it could be read only in geometrical and mathematical terms, and for Leibniz this was no less true of human judgement. By analogy with the 'natural theology' of Raimond de Sebonde, Leibniz distinguished a 'natural jurisprudence' likewise free of revelation and authority.[91] Only by reducing all things human and cultural to the common denominator of *Natura* could jurisprudence reach its goal of becoming 'true philosophy'; only by renouncing the role of 'historians' or 'memory-experts' (Galileo's contemptuous epithets) and by turning to the new philosophy could a student of the laws fulfil the ideal of the *jurisconsultus perfectus.* Leibniz hoped to put an end to the classical aim of 'reducing law to an art' and assert its status as a true, and a new, 'science'. In his *New Method of Jurisprudence*, in other words, he had really come not to praise but rather to bury the old values and purposes of humanist learning; and it is hardly going too far to say that the 'perfect jurist' was done in by natural law as Leibniz understood it. The demise of the old ideal was hastened by the political assumptions of the Enlightenment, which prized naturalistic social theory, administrative action and neo-Byzantine 'codification' above judicial 'interpretation', legal remedies and and 'local knowledge'.[92]

Except in the work of a few anti-Cartesian eccentrics like Vico, who rejected the fashionable sort of 'natural law' in social as well as philosophical terms, the Renaissance model of the perfect jurist seemed obsolescent and superseded, or at least overshadowed, by an imperious 'science of legislation', which found expression in an international codification movement, in a variety of revolutionary laws culminating in the Napoleonic Code. Not perfect jurisprudence but perfect legislation was the ideal of Bonapartism, as it had been of Jacobinism; the Emperor would himself be the last Renaissance man. For Napoleon, as for Justinian, the worst fate would be for lawyers and professors to begin the process of 'interpreting' his legislative masterpiece. So indeed, and inevitably, it happened; and Napoleon's Code went through very much the same schools of interpretation—from literal-minded exegesis, to legal 'extension', to philosophical reform—as Justinian's collection had done after its twelfth-century revival.

During the Restoration, and in the company of what has been called the 'conquering Bourgeoisie', the legal profession made a stunning professional revival.[93] What is significant here is that so, in a sense, did the neo-classical image of the ideal jurist. The 'legends' of the great Renaissance scholars, especially Cujas and Dumoulin, were restored; and French law students were told by their teachers that they, too, were 'priests of the law', and that their discipline was the ultimate 'science' of society. But such professional chauvinism sounded rather hollow in an age of

[90] Ibid., pp. 307–8: 'Ommitantur vero curiositates Philologicae, Synonymiae ... Ommitantur denique, quae non tam sunt Quaestiones Juridicae, quam vel Historicae ...; vel Philologicae ...; vel Philosophicae ... Omissis igitur his omnibus nempe (1.) incertis, (2.) abrogatis, (3.) Manifestis, (4.) alienis, mira erit hujus Elementorum Libelli brevitas facilitasque'.

[91] Ibid., p. 294; and see *Dialogue concerning the Two Chief World Systems*, tr. S. Drake, Berkeley 1953, p. 113.

[92] G. Tarello, *Storia della cultura giuridica moderna*, I, Bologna 1976. Cf. D. R. Kelley, 'Vico's Road: From Philology to Jurisprudence and Back', in *History etc.* (as in n. 13); and see now B. A. Haddock, *Vico's Political Thought*, Swansea 1986.

[93] D. R. Kelley, *Historians and the Law in Post-revolutionary France*, Princeton 1984.

industrial expansion, class conflict and threatening, if not continuous, Revolution. Never again, it seems to me, were the lawyers able to assert their former intellectual, moral, social and especially political and constitutional pretensions. Never again could they make a serious claim to a monopoly over human science in a general sense. Never again could civil law ride 'richly ... before all the other arts', or jurisprudence 'occupy alone the throne of wisdom'. The 'true philosophy' of law sustained by Renaissance humanism was eclipsed by naturalistic, or scientistic, models of social science underlying nineteenth-century doctrines of Positivism, Marxism, and the new disciplines of economics and sociology, which were founded on materialist premises, quantitative methods, and universalist aspirations and which did not need licensed custodians of outmoded lore to further their aims. Nor has this attitude toward history changed markedly in much of contemporary jurisprudence or, for that matter, social science.

It may be a bit melodramatic to describe this, as Harold Berman has recently done, as 'the breakdown of the Western legal tradition'.[94] Virtually every age sees itself, and most professions see themselves, in a state of 'crisis', and the law has certainly had its ups and downs. There never was a 'perfect jurisconsult', of course, but then there never was a 'Renaissance man' either (nor even, if we believe certain older historians, a Renaissance). What there was, and what is significant to recall, was a noble dream of human wisdom, which drew its inspiration from a broad view—an anthropo-, nomo-, and logo-centric view—of culture and the human condition and which sought to establish a science of humanity in its own terms. In the longest perspective these reflections on the 'perfect jurist' represent not only an aspect of Renaissance culture and a chapter in the early history of social thought but also an introduction to the story of what Ernest Becker has called 'the lost science of man'—which has seen methods of studying human behaviour as narrow and technical as that professionalized study of law lamented by Renaissance humanists.[95] Historically, the old tradition of jurisprudence, understood in its broadest and most human terms, is as good a place as any to begin looking for this lost science. Like the Renaissance itself it represents a heritage worth examining and points, I like to think, to a road which may be worth exploring—even if it does not lead to 'perfection'.

[94] H. Berman, *Law and Revolution*, Cambridge Mass. 1983.

[95] E. Becker, *The Lost Science of Man*, New York 1971.

XIV

Men of Law and the French Revolution

The French Revolution marked both the end of an old legal tradition and the beginning of a new social ideal that nevertheless invoked ancient values and terminology. "Here is how I define the Revolution," wrote Jules Michelet: "the coming of Law, the resurrection of Right, the reaction of Justice."[1] None of the generation of 1789 better understood this ideal than the lawyers who moved into public life in the spring of that year—those men of law who were left over from that carefully ranked and privileged corporation which was disappearing along with the rest of the "society of orders." Institutionally cut off from the past (their "Order" having been abolished in September 1790), the former *avocats* were nonetheless equipped professionally to deal with the future, especially in times of social turmoil and political maneuvering, at least in an ad hoc way. By education and training they were prepared to understand social and constitutional issues, and always to take the lead in argument and persuasion.[2] From what better vantage point can we assess the French Revolution as a social process which began, for many of its participants as well as many later historians, with a quest for justice, social as well as political?

1 *La Révolution française*, introduction. Bibliographical and historiographical references will be limited to those bearing on this fairly specialized topic; unless otherwise noted, place of publication is always Paris.

2 See above all Michael Fitzsimmons, *The Parisian Order of Barristers and the French Revolution* (Cambridge, Mass., 1987), and the important new collection, *La Révolution et l'ordre juridique privé: Rationalité ou scandale?* Actes du colloque d'Orléans, 11–13 septembre 1986 (1988). For background on the lawyers see also J. P. Royer, *La Société judiciaire depuis le XVIIIe siécle* (1979); Lenard Berlanstein, "Lawyers in Prerevolutionary France," in *Lawyers in Early Modern Europe*, ed. W. Prest (New York, 1980); Isser Wolloch "The Fall and Resurrection of the French Civil Bar, 1789–1820s," *French Historical Studies* 15 (1987), 241–62; Francis Delbeke, *L'Action politique et sociale des avocats au XVIIIe siécle* (Louvain, 1927); A. J. Arnaud, *Les Juristes face à la société du XIX siècle à nos jours* (1975); R. Marie, *Le Recruitement de la magistrature pendant la periode révolutionnaire* (Rennes, 1909); A. Bardoux, *Les Légistes, leur influence sur la société française* (1877); Gaudry, *Histoire du barreau de Paris* (1864); V. Jeanvrot, *La Magistrature* (1882); and J. Bourdon, *La Magistrature sous le Consulat et l'Empire* (Rodez, 1942).

Legal history has been out of fashion for at least two generations in revolutionary studies, but there are significant advantages deriving from the materials and attitudes of this old scholarly tradition.[3] In general legal sources, especially jurisprudence and discussion of judicial organization and reform, represent a compressed, if distorted version of historical experience and aspiration; and they suggest a level of social and political thinking which is at once more immediate and less fanciful, more practical and less interested, more concrete and personal, than that of conventional political philosophy or polemic, from which our interpretations of revolutionary ideology and experience are largely derived.

My main concern here is with the long-term impact of revolutionary efforts (from the 1780s to the 1830s), with the continuities rather than with the ups, downs, and reversals of politics and war; and so I attend not to the great movers and shakers, not to the mass of the moved and the shaken, but rather to an intermediate range of social and intellectual agents. This middle-range activity is well represented by the professional (and para-professional) group defined, in the democratic fashion of the 1790s, as "men of law"—there were of course no women—who were involved in the everyday operations of judicial and social institutions, or the devising of new ones, under whatever political structures happened to prevail at the moment in the tumultuous last decade of the eighteenth century.

What the Revolution offered these *hommes de loi* was an extraordinary laboratory for political and social experiment—experiment based in part on Enlightenment theories but was carried out in a social ferment which had ostensibly wiped away the institutional heritage of many centuries. More than the great orators of the revolutionary assemblies or the famous statesmen who rose and fell across the political spectrum of that age, the lawyers were the real experts of the systematic approach to the understanding and regulation of collective human behavior. If they had suffered a decline as political theorists (as William Church argued),[4] they enjoyed a remarkable rise to prominence in the context of what they themselves were first to call "la science sociale," and this is the main subject of this inquiry.

[3] On French legal history in general, Jacques Godechot, *Les Institutions de la Révolution et l'Empire* (1968; 2nd ed.); Philippe Sagnac, *La Législation de la révolution française (1789–1792), Essai d'histoire sociale* (1898); P. P. Viard, *Histoire générale du droit privé français (1789–1830,* (1931); E. Seligman, *La Justice en France pendant la révolution (1789–1792)* (1901); A. Mater, *L'Histoire juridique de la révolution* (Besançon, 1919); Hiver, *Histoire critique des institutions judiciares de la France de 1789 à 1848 (1848)*; Louis La Ferrière, *Histoire des principes, des institutions et des lois pendant la révolution française* (1851–52); and C. A. L. Rasenack, *Gesetz und Verordnung in Frankreich seit 1789* (Berlin, 1967).

[4] "The Decline of French Jurists as Political Theorists, 1660–1789," *French Historical Studies* 5 (1967), 1–40.

The fundamental dilemma of political and social thought has never been better expressed than by one of the most distinguished of these men of law, Citizen (later Count) Portalis, one of the reactors of the Civil Code of 1804:

> How can we control the action of time? How resist the course of events or the imperceptible force of custom? How know and calculate in advance what experience alone can reveal to us? Can foresight ever be extended to objects which thought itself cannot yet grasp?[5]

Portalis's even more distinguished colleague Cambacérès (playing Second to Napoleon's First Consul) certainly thought so, and said as much in the civil legislation on which he had been working since the first years of the Revolution. His hope not only to "reform everything" but also to "foresee everything" defined a basic issue dividing lawyers over three centuries of attempts at legal reform and unification.

After 1789 the spirits of Montesquieu and Rousseau—the "spirit of the law" and the voice of the "social"—contended with one another in the debates of the men of law in the revolutionary assemblies. On the one hand was the principle of the "division of powers," in which the judiciary guarded against legislative tyranny; on the other hand the insistence on the "general will" exercised by political virtuosi (and of course most conspicuously by Napoleon). Such were the terms in which lawyers began to construct what Cambacérès himself designated "social science."[6] On the level not only of high politics but also of social behavior, then, it was the lawyers above all who gave theoretical and practical expression to the experience of revolution.

At the beginning of 1789 the legal profession, replica and guarantor of the old society of orders, was full of inertia—full of itself, that is to say, and of its traditions and privileges. In December of the previous year the President of the Parlement of Paris complained of the literary and social "effervescence" and "ideas of innovation" threatening his "sovereign court" as well as the crown itself.[7] Jurists on the heights of their career ladders, both lawyers and magistrates, tended to be suspicious of change. The proud Order of Advocates luxuriated in an antiquity and a pedigree almost as impressive as its mother institution, the Parlement of Paris, which, with its provincial extensions, formed a "mystical body" devoted to royal justice and an intellectual and a

5 F. A. Fenet, *Recueil complet des travaux préparatoires du Code Civil* (1827), I, 469; and see L. Schimséwitsch, *Portalis et son temps* (1936).

6 *Discours sur la science social* (1789), and cf. Jussieu, *Discours* (to Corps Législatif and Conseil des Cinq-cents [An 7 1799]; BN Le433606). See also Georges Gusdorf, *Les Sciences humaines*, VIII (1978), 401; Sergio Moravia, *Il Pensiero degli idéologues: scienza e filosofia in Francia (1780–1815)* (Florence, 1974), 746; and B. W. Head, *Ideology and Social Science: Destutt de Tracy and French Liberalism* (The Hague, 1985), 109.

7 Flammermont, *Remonstrances du Parlement de Paris au XVIIIe siècle* (1898), III, 795. Legal Pamphlets in Bibliothèque Nationale, shelf-mark "Lb39".

professional elite based on a monopoly of "legal science" as taught in the faculties of law and as practiced in the royal, municipal, and seigneurial courts. Professors of civil law quarrelled with the more recently licensed professors of French customary law, but never about the preeminence of their common profession.[8] Along with a powerful *esprit de corps* and a sense of tradition going back, at least mythologically, to classical antiquity as well as to the "lawyers of the last Capetians", these jurists had accumulated privileges which made them, no less traditionally, the target of intense social criticism, satire, and abuse. "Duplicity," venality, and corruption were only a few of the charges which spoiled the lawyers' self-image as caretakers of the Constitution and "priests of the law." The *cahiers de doléance* of 1789 were filled with such complaints about the old judicial order.[9]

Yet—two-faced as usual—the legal profession had always been in the forefront of social change, playing a central role in the formulation of these cahiers and in a sense beginning the revolutionary process, through the so-called "judicial uprising" (*émeute judiciaire*) of 1788, when the Parlement defied the king and was sent, in the official phrase, "on permanent vacation."[10] This was the last political gasp of the Parlement, as the king's act of suppression was carried out by the last *lit de justice* of the French monarchy. To Tocqueville this affair demonstrated "how the Parlement with the aid of its precedents overturned the monarchy." In any case the parlementaire mentality persisted into the revolution, especially in the form of concern for "liberties" and the "French constitution," and it would make an even more prominent come-back under Napoleon and the Restoration.

In some ways the Estates General offered a more attractive forum for ambitious lawyers than either the *barreau* or the Parlement; for with the transformation of the Estates into a "National Constituent Assembly," they had the chance to become legislators as well as judges and advocates. They flourished in the last years of the monarchy. Over half of the deputies to the Estates were "advocates" by education if not occupation, and 70 of them were officially inscribed in the Order of Advocates for 1789.[11] That their ideological

[8] Christian Chêne, *L'Enseignement du droit de français en pays de droit écrit (1679–1789)* (Geneva, 1982).

[9] [Bergasse], *Cahiers du tiers-état* (1 Jan. 1789); *Extraits des Cahiers de Etats Generaux. Sur la Réformation de la Justice* (n.d.; BN Lf2351), citing the cahiers of 1560 and later; see also R. Aubin, *L'Organisation judiciaire d'après les cahiers de 1789* (1928), E. Champion, *Le France d'après les cahiers de 1789* (1897), Guy Chassinand-Nogaret, *The French Nobility in the Eighteenth Century*, tr. W. Doyle (Cambridge, Eng., 1987), on the cahiers of the nobility, and Phillip Dawson, "The Bourgeoisie de Robe in 1789," *French Historical Studies* 4 (1965), 1–21; also D. R. Kelley, "Lord Deliver Us from Justice," *Yale Journal of Law and the Humanities* 5 (1993), 159–68.

[10] Flammermont, III, 735; cf. Tocqueville, *L'Ancien régime et la révolution*, ed. A. Jardin (1953), II, 53 (from unfinished fragments), and Jacqueline Lafon, "La Fin du Parlement de Paris," *Etudes d'histoire du droit parisien* (1970), 229–46.

[11] See *Almanach national* (1789).

importance far outweighed their impressive numbers is shown by the flood of "brochures" and journals, official and unofficial. "Discourses," "Reports," and, endlessly, "Opinions" (a legal genre democratized in the context of revolutionary journalism and polemic) competed for the attention of literate and engaged Parisians and the provincials swept into politics from the spring of '89; and the tide continued to rise over the next decades. There was a pandemonium of professional (and para-professional) ideas about how to build a new social system and attain liberty and equality, if not fraternity, and to fulfill the ideal of nationality.

The members of what used to be regarded as the "fourth estate" ranged from the most radical, beginning with Robespierre, to the most conservative, such as Nicolas Bergasse, who resigned in protest from the National Assembly and lived to defend the interests of his fellow emigres and royalists a generation later. Three were victims of the Terror (Le Chapelier and, on the same day, Thouret and Epremesnil); but most had extensive life spans; and many of them, together with colleagues who rose to prominence in the 1790s, continued to maneuver and to opinionate over several decades—and, with Talleyrand, to "survive."[12]

What enhanced the position of lawyers at the end of the old regime was the emergence of a new political culture, which is most clearly defined in transformations of vocabulary and forms of discourse, perhaps even more than in the substantive issues being debated.[13] Revolutionaries acquired their own code and keywords, inflating some and devaluing others in their pursuit of particular causes. "Innovation" was the order of the day: "Do you want good laws?" Voltaire had asked; "then burn yours and make new ones"; and this is just what the men of law on the left proposed to do. "Destruction" was thus often a more favorable term than "reformation," "prediction" more than "prudence." "Antiquity," "honor," "custom," and "tempered" government were regarded as almost dirty words, such as the term "advocate" itself, which suggested champions of particular "interests" of the old regime and which would be officially banned. Everybody spoke of "liberty," "property," the "social," the "constitution," and especially "revolution" but more often than not—as Edmund

[12] The major guide is A. Martin and G. Walter, *Catalogue de l'histoire de la révolution française*, 5 vols. (1941–50), listing over 50,000 items and some 2000 *hommes de loi*. For activities of the licensed avocats Fitzsimmon's *The Parisian Order of Barristers* is invaluable, but it does not cover all the writing and teaching of "men of law."

[13] Keith Baker, *Inventing the French Revolution* (Cambridge, 1990); cf. Janis Langins, "Words and Institutions during the French Revolution: the case of Revolutionary Scientific and Technical Education," in *The Social History of Language*, ed. Peter Burke and Roy Porter (Cambridge, 1987), 136–60, and Jacques Guilhaumou, "Qu est-ce fair parler la loi?" in *La Révolution et l'ordre juridique*, I, 127; William Sewell, *Work and Revolution in France* (Cambridge, 1980); and the old study of Jean Belin, *La Loqique d'une idée-force: l'idée d'utilité sociale et la révolution française (1789–1792)*, and his supplementary thesis, *Les Démarches de la pensée sociale* (1939).

Burke showed in his *Reflections on the Revolution in France*—in opposed senses. Thus Bergasse agreed that there should be an "absolute revolution" (*révolution absolue*) but he meant this in a gradual, a planetary rather than a political sense.[14] So the "carnival of words" continued, and with it the social and political influence of the men of law.

Behind this logomachy was not only a grim reality but also an unprecedented opportunity, for lawyers, to construct a "new judicial order." From late August 1789 to late August 1790 members of the Committee for the Constitution (including Talleyrand as well as working members like Sieyès, Duport, Le Chapelier, and Thouret) confronted the question crucial to the principles of the Declaration of the Rights of Man and the New Constitution, just off the press, concerning "the organization of judicial power," and in this context the most basic questions of judicial control and national goals. Some lawyers succombed to what Mona Ozouf has called the "don-Quichottisme du Comité de la Constitution," but they were always drawn back to practical questions by their more conservative colleagues. In these debates, in any case, began one of the seminal ages of social science (as the lawyers believed and began to proclaim) and indeed of social engineering (as we may infer), which culminated in 1804 with the publication of the "Civil Code of the French People," soon to be called the Code Napoléon.

The opening statement on judicial reorganization was made by Nicolas Bergasse on 17 August 1789. "Judicial power" (*pouvoir judiciaire*) was superior to all other public powers, he declared, recalling the terrible *lettres de cachet*.[15] In his youth Bergasse had admired Turgot and had enjoyed an afternoon's conversation with the elderly Rousseau—who avoided discussing Bergasse's work but who predicted the political storms to come. Bergasse had also written and

14 *Archives parlementaires*, VIII, 440ff. For convenience I refer to this collection (which is fuller than the contemporary *Moniteur*), although most of the research was done in the original pamphlets, mostly listed in Marin and Walter under the author or title (in case of anonymous publications) with the BN shelf mark. See also F. A. Aulard, *Les Orateurs de L'Assemblée Constituante* (1882), and G. Guatherot, *L'Assemblée Constituante, Le Philosophisme en action* (1914), as well as A. Lameth, *Histoire de l'Assemblée Constituante* (1828–29), and individual biographies. Bernardi published an "Essai sur les révolutions du droit français" in 1785; see also J. M. Goulemot, "Le Mot Révolution et la formation du concept de Révolution politique (fin XVII siècle)," *Annales historiques de la révolution française* 39 (1967), 417–44.

15 *Discours sur les crimes et les tribunaux de Haute traison* (1790; BN Le29138–75A); see also Etienne Lamy, *Un défenseur des principes traditionels sous la Révolution, Nicolas Bergasse* (1920), and Jean Egret, *La Révolution des notables, Mounier et les monarchiens 1789* (1959). Bergasse's position was by no means as conservative as that of others, some of whom wanted no changes at all and who rejected ever Bergasse's modest proposals; e.g. Louis-René Chauveau, *Sur l'organisation du pouvoir judiciaire* (Dec. 1789). In a "tragi-politi-comique" drama published in 1790 (*La Journée des dupes*) Bergasse complained of "ces avocats, dont la horde obscurcit l'assemblée [nationale], se croyant autant de potentats."

dedicated to Voltaire an idealistic work on "the humanity of the judge," in which he attacked all forms of social and political "prejudice"; and he carried some of this idealism over into the Committee on the Constitution. He hoped that justice would express the "national will" and be free and non-venal, and he supported the notion that the people should have a say in the selection of their judges. However, he also praised the old magistracy, argued for royal control over judicial appointments, and reproached what he called "dissociability" and the contempt for experience associated with Rousseau. Bergasse's plan for reform, following the English model recommended by Montesquieu, was "loudly applauded," according to the *Archives parlementaires*, and commended in the *Moniteur* and *Mercure*. Yet the Assembly rejected his proposal. "The moment was not favorable to moderation," Bergasse admitted ruefully, and along with his colleague Mounier he soon resigned.

Over the next seven months other plans were submitted and discussed. The "code" assembled by Sieyès, no jurist, was also discarded. That of Thouret, which kept faith with the *cahiers* by emphasizing both the "rights of man" and the "separation of powers," was looked on more favorably. Most radical of all was the proposal of Adrien Duport, whose searching if somewhat utopian views helped to define the terms of the debates over "judicial power" in the new social order. In his enthusiasm Duport went so far as to suggest that revolutionary justice might dispense altogether with the legal profession which he had himself served so faithfully. "No more judges!" he cried. "No more courts!"[16] Duport made the beau geste of bestowing the income of his parlementary office on the state; and he argued that achieving justice was a purely logical process, a syllogism in which the facts formed the minor premise, the pertinent law the major, and the judgment the conclusion. In a democratic regime laws were not professional secrets understood only by privileged experts, not mysteries of the "priests of the laws," but "social conventions" that could be understood or applied by any fellow citizen (*concitoyen*).[17]

Duport's ideas went too far, of course—even Robespierre put in a kind word for the lawyers—but they were in keeping with one of the most extraordinary acts of 1790, the suppression of the Order of Advocates. After September of that year there were no longer *juges*, *avocats*, *procureurs*, and other kinds of *gens de robe*—nor indeed would there be any more of the "accursed robes," as Duport's friend Chabroud called them.[18] There would be only defrocked *hommes de loi* who would speak for the judicial aspect of the "general will."

16 *Archives parlementaires*, XII, 570: "Point de juges! Point de tribunaux!"; and see G. Michin, *Essai sur l'histoire du parti feuillant, Adrien Duport* (1924).

17 *Principes et plan sur l'etablissement de l'ordre judiciaire* (1790; BN Le^{29}.536); *Archives parlementaires*, XII, 570); cf. the "Opinion" (30 March 1790) by Charles Chabroud; also G. Michin, *Essai sur l'histoire du parti feuillant, Adrien Duport* (1924), and Fournel, *Histoire du barreau*, 79.

18 *Archives parlementaires*, esp. XII, 574, 408ff; and see Fitzsimmons, *The Parisian Order of Barristers*, 33ff.

Protests had been made by lawyers against the suppression of the Parlement—by Cazalès, for example, by the Parlement of Toulouse, and (secretly) by the Parlement of Paris—but threats of treason charges (*lèse nation*) ended such protests, as the elections produced replacements for the old magistracy.

As J. P. Fournel lamented, the degradation of the Order took place in the presence of its most distinguished members, including the *bâtonnier* Tronchet and probably Fournel himself, who added bitterly, "Ma carrière est terminée."[19] It is a curious and never satisfactorily explained circumstance that none of the over one hundred men of law in the Assembly objected publicly to the abolition of their corporation. One reason was that the parlementary spirit—the esprit de corps repeatedly denounced by critics of the old regime—lived on; and the "former advocates" (*ci-devant avocats* being the official phrase) did not expect to have, and in fact did not generally have, much trouble in finding a place in the "new judicial order."

What was the place of this order in the brave new world of the Constitutional Monarchy? In a discourse of 24 May 1790 J. G. Thouret praised judicial power as having unparalleled "influence on the happiness of individuals, the progress of public spirit, and on the stability of the new constitution." Yet questions remained; and in the first journal of the new men of law, the *Gazette de nouveaux tribunaux*, featuring Thouret's discourse as its editorial statement, a qualification was registered.[20] No doubt it was essential "to obey the general will," he wrote, "but patriotism has its doubts, and the Committee on the Constitution will consider these in the following articles." The major questions were reduced to ten and submitted by Bertrand Barère to the Assembly for deliberation:[21] should there be juries *à l'Anglais* for civil and criminal justice? Should the courts be sedentary or ambulatory? Should there be degrees of jurisdiction, i.e., courts of appeal and revisions of judgment? Should judges have life tenure? Should they be chosen by the people or by the king? And should a committee be appointed to discuss these and other questions?

Under the influence of *Anglomanie*, a fashion since Voltaire's day, the *jurés* and the *juges de paix* would form the lowest level of the new order.[22] Invoking the name of Burke, Duport defended this as a healthy "restitution" of Frankish

[19] *Histoire des avocats au parlement* (1813), II, 544.

[20] *Gazette des nouveaux tribunaux*, I (1791), reprinting as its editorial statement Therout's discourse (24 May 1790): "Le pouvoir judiciaire est celui des pouvoirs public, dont l'exercice habituel aura le plus d'influence sur le bonheur des particuliers, sur les progrès de l'sprit, sur le maintien de par l'ordre politique, et sur la stabilité de la constitution."

[21] *Archives parlementaires*, XII, 489; and cf. Barère, *Montesquieu peint d'après ses ouvrages* (Suisse, an V [1797]).

[22] *Histoire du barreau de Paris dans le cours de la révolution* (1816), 104; and see Richard M. Andrews, "The Justices of the Peace of Revolutionary Paris," in Douglas Johnson (ed.), *French Society and the Revolution* (Cambridge, Eng., 1976), 167–216.

custom and other "liberties" of Germanic provenance. More conservative jurists were contemptuous of this importation. Fournel later scoffed that in the countryside this office had been familiar for centuries under feudal terminology (*châtelains*, *syndics*, *procureurs*, *fiscaux*, etc.). This most unrepentant of former advocates recognized "three kinds of revolutionaries: the tricksters, the tricked, and the trumpeters" (*les trompeurs, les trompés et les trompettes*), and by 1790 the latter seemed to prevail. Anyway, the office of justice of the peace, open to any male citizen over 30, expressed the committee's desire for popular justice, and it was adopted by the Assembly.

On a higher level the democratic character of the new judiciary was encouraged by the provision for popular election. One immediate endorsement came from Jeremy Bentham, who saw "unpopularity" as the only alternative.[23] Related to this was the age-old question of life-tenure (*l'inamovabilté*) of judges. A reading of Rousseau suggested that magistrates should be directly responsible to, hence dismissible by, the General Will, while students of Montesquieu argued that "irremovability" was needed as a protections against legislative or executive tyranny. The men of law were bound to root out the private interests of the old magistracy; yet many had fond memories of its accomplishments as a counterbalance to monarchy. In the end they decided on a tenure of six years as a symbol, but the movement for complete *inamovabilité* was never abandoned.

As for the possibility of legal appeal and revision of judgment, some men of law objected because it implied imperfection in revolution legislation. If law was identified with reason, how could one anticipate disagreements among reasonable men? The answer, according to one lawyer, was that appeal signified merely review and so reinforced the rationality of the judicial process. The crucial step was taken of establishing higher courts called *tribunaux de cassation*, each possessing six judges and an alternate, to give final expression to "judicial power" in the new order.[24] All male citizens over 30 were eligible, but not surprisingly lawyers predominated in the elections. In Paris all 42 of the judges elected were *hommes de loi*, 29 of them "former advocates" and 4 judges, not counting those with judicial experience in the provinces—now organized as "departments."

It would be difficult and not especially rewarding to follow all the twistings and turnings of the *droit intermédiaire* through the upheavals of the First French Republic, especially in times of Jacobin extremism. The self-righteous

23 *Archives parlementaires*, XV, 370; and cf. Bentham, *Draught of a new plan for the organisation of the Judicial establishment in France* (n.p., 21 Dec. 1789).

24 From 1796 this court issued its own *Bulletin*; see J. Crépon, *Cour de Cassation, origines, organisation, attributions* (1892).

radicalism of the Jacobin view of law is captured (if caricatured) well in a verse quoted by a lawyer who had lived through the period:[25]

When God to the lawless Hebrews spake,
When He His wisest laws did make,
He spoke His words not from the Plain
But from, on high, the great Mountain,
[refrain:] The great Mountain.

This was legislative hubris with a vengeance, but it was a not an attitude which many practicing lawyers could share, at least until the advent of Napoleon as law-maker.

During the period of "intermediary law," the "new judicial order" was subjected to further reforms and innovations (as well as disruptions by the extraordinary jurisdictions of the Terror), although professional journals such as the *Gazette des nouveaux tribunaux* tried to collect a settled and settling jurisprudence out of revolutionary practice.[26] Few members of the Order of Advocates participated in the "revolutionary justice" of 1794 (just 5 of 54 elected judges), though many resumed their careers in 1795 and later. Some men of law moved into retreat (e.g., Fournel and Tronchet) or into exile (Bergasse and Duport), while others were (as Fournel put it) "tués révolutionnairement" (Thouret and Le Chapelier as well as Robespierre and Barnave); but many more stayed, survived, and even rose to high office (Cambacérès and, after a time in exile, Portalis). Throughout this period the legal profession was accommodated if not wholly recognized, but its role was severely reduced by the innovations of civil (citizens') and political justice. Lawyerly skills were obviated on the one hand by the encouragement of voluntary and forced arbitration (*arbitrage*) and the untrained justices of the peace, and on the other hand by the fetish of legislative remedy and suspicion of uncontrolled, interpretive "jurisprudence."

Yet the break was not complete, and some elements of legal continuity can be seen. A certain level of professionalism was ensured by the preservation, in the Constitutions of 1793, 1795, and 1797, of the Tribunal of Cassation; by 1804 this (renamed) *Cour de Cassation* and other "courts of the first instance" restored much of the old undemocratic hierarchy of jurisdictions, in which

25 Berriat-Saint-Prix, *La Justice révolutionnaire* (1870), 70:
Quand Dieu fit entendre sa voix,
A l'Hebreu rebelle et volage;
Quand l'Eternelle dicta des lois,
Qui devait le rendre plus sage;
Pour prononcer de tels arrets,
Il ne s'est par mis en campagne,
Mais il a donné ses decrets
Du Haut de la Montagne (bis).

26 Fitzsimmons, *The Parisian Order of Barristers*, 61, n. 72, 70, n. 11, and 277–78.

judicial expertise was again required and rewarded. Despite the dissolution of the law faculties in 1795, the teaching of law, too, was continued on at least an elementary level in the *écoles centrales* established the next year—e.g., by J. P. Proudhon in Besançon, by Henrion de Pansey in the Haute-Garonne, by Berthelet in Garde, and by Perreau in the central school of the Panthéon. Under the Consulate the founding of the *Académie de Législation* (in which Bernardi taught) and the *Université de Jurisprudence* reflected still more serious efforts to encourage the professional and even historical and theoretical study of law, though to be sure in post-revolutionary terms.[27]

Jurisprudence, although it was suspect in the wake of revolutionary legislation, could never be completely neglected. At first it was limited largely to interpretation of laws made since 1790 and attended to by old-fashioned jurists. A prime example is the royalist Auguste-Charles Guichard, who assembled a series of codes on practical aspects of the *droit intermédiaire*, especially property, confiscation, succession, justices of the peace, and the Tribunal of Cassation.[28] This author of *Le Code des juges de paix* (1795), according to the editorial blurb, "is a man who since the beginning of the revolution has never stopped preaching the observation of law, the respect for property and individual liberty . . . , who is the openly declared enemy of the destroyers [*disorganisateurs*], intriguers, and rascals, and has not escaped the rule of these monsters [of the Terror] who have usurped supreme power."[29] Fortunately, this statement goes on, "the miraculous fall of these tyrants" has encouraged "the return to order and justice." For Guichard justice meant jurisprudence, and three years later his "code and memorial" of the Tribunal of Cassation was advertized as a collection of judicial "decisions, whose authority is as great as that of the laws themselves."

The problem for the jurists of that generation, however, was that "the laws themselves" were still unstable, unsystematic, and subject to shifts in the political climate—*lois de circonstance*—and the "general will" required a more formal and comprehensive expression of its socio-juridical base. Henrion de Pansey, an old regime legal scholar who became a baron of the Empire and who would end

27 Jean Imbert, "L'Enseignement du droit dans les ècoles centrales sous la révolution," *La Révolution et l'ordre judiciaire*, 248–65; and Hugues Richard, *Bénigne Poncet, le professeur de législation a l'école central de la* Cote d'Or (Dijon, 1977); cf. H. B. Gibault, *De l'Enseignement dans ses rapports avec l'ordre politique* (n.d.).

28 *Code des Juges de Paix* (An II "avis de l'éditeur," and *Code et mémorial du Tribunal de Cassation* (An VI [1798]); also *Code des confiscations et sequestres* (An III [1795]), denouncing "populicide"; and cf. *Journal typographique et bibliographique*, ed. P. Roux (An VI [1797–98]). From 1798 there was a category of "jurisprudence" as well as "législation" in the *Journal général de la littérature de France* (an VI).

29 A few years later Guichard defended Joseph Arena, a conspirator in a plot to assassinate Napoleon.

his life as a Restoration judge, put it this way: "It is not enough to constitute a government; it is equally necessary to organize society."[30]

This was the condition underlying that question so fundamental to the "new judicial order—namely, codification. Since the late middle ages the ideal of legal unification had been discussed; but not until the feudal regime had been "entirely abolished" and the old laws had been in effect and in a few cases actually (in Voltaire's image) "burned" could this goal be realized. As Merlin de Douai observed in his collection of "intermediary jurisprudence" of 1801, the voice of France had been calling out for a "new edifice" of law for over a decade.[31] "There will be made a code of civil laws common to the whole kingdom," declared the Assembly in September 1791; and two years later Cambacérès presented the first "project" for codification. It was a time of Jacobin euphoria and an apparent awakening of the national will, expressed just two weeks before in the famous *levée en masse*. "The age so devoutly wished for has finally arrived to fix forever the empire of liberty and the destinies of France," proclaimed Cambacérès.[32] He dedicated two further projects to this "grand edifice of legislation," and Jacqueminot a fourth, before a government commission came up with the plan which evolved into the Civil Code of 1804.

The Civil Code was created in an imperial rather than a revolutionary spirit. In the wake of the excesses of Jacobinism, legislative virtuosity, and especially the Terror, the *esprit philosophique* was increasingly overshadowed by the *esprit juridique*, as Sagnac remarked;[33] and this renewed appreciation for legal science encouraged the delicate work of codification which Napoleon, as First Consul, inaugurated in 1800. On the committee of four jurists assigned to the task of "civil legislation" were Portalis, recently returned from exile in Germany and appointed to the Conseil d'Etat the next year; Tronchet, former advocate (and in 1789 *bâtonnier*) of the Order, counsel for Louis XVI at his trial, and first president of the Court of Cassation; Bigot de Préaumeneu, also a former member of the Order, a judge in 1790, and a prisoner under the Convention before reemerging to enjoy Bonapartist favor; and Jacques Maleville, another member of the monarchist party (with Portalis and Tronchet), judge on the Tribunal of Cassation in 1791, and secretary of the committee.[34] To these names might be

[30] *Oeuvres juridiques*, ed. Rozet (1834), 191; and see J. H. M. Salmon, "Constitutions, Old and New: Henrion de Pansey before and after the Revolution", *Historical Journal*, 38 (1995), 907–31.

[31] *Recueil alphabétique des questions de droit* (an IX [1801]), "avertissement."

[32] F. Papillard, *Cambacérès* (1961). See Fenet, I, 1; also I, 11, "En détruisant les lois et les coutumes existants, il fallait leur substituer une législation parfaite, qui ne laissât plus de doutes à resoudre, ni difficultés à craindre." According to Gaudry (*Histoire du barreau*, II, 494), Cambacérès agreed with Napoleon to "couper la langue de tout avocat qui lui aurait déplu."

[33] *La Législation civile*, 396.

[34] Lydie Schimséwitsch, *Portalis et son temps*. See Portalis, *De l'usage et de l'Abus de l'Esprit philosophique durant le dix-huitième siecle* (1827); Fenet, I, 467, etc.; François Villaret, *Le bâtonnier Tronchet et la naissance d'un droit nouveau* (extr. *La Vie judiciaire*); and Jean

added those of J. M. Locré, another former advocate and from 1800 secretary to the Conseil d'Etat, whose *procès verbaux* were the basis of important works on the "spirit" of the new French codes, and Merlin de Douai, former member of the Committee on Feudalism *procureur-général* of the Tribunal of Cassation, member of the Conseil d'Etat, and compiler of collections of revolutionary (and pre-revolutionary) jurisprudence, who did not attend the meetings of the committee on codification but who, as Napoleon remarked, was certainly there "in spirit."[35]

The process of codification (begun 11 August 1800, published 21 March 1804) was another "carnival of words," but in this case more legalistic than ideological. Over the previous decade the "men of law" had created many new laws, and abolished old ones, but now they enjoyed the unique opportunity of legislating on a large scale. In general the procedure was for the committee members to present arguments for the respective titles and then for select respondents—the Tribunal of Cassation, "tribunes" from the twenty-eight appeal courts, and finally spokesmen for the Conseil d'Etat, itself composed mainly of lawyers—to present positions pro or con. In this way the texts of the Code were worried over and hammered out. The First Consul himself (who had once dreamed of a society without lawyers) attended over half—57 of 100—of the sessions, supplying blunt, practical, self-serving, and transparently imperialistic comments.[36]

In official rhetoric and public imagination the Civil Code was represented as a derivation of pure reason and "natural law." For *Le Peuple*, for example, "the truth is one and indivisible, and so should be its law." In fact it was not a statement of theory but rather, as Sagnac put it, a work of transaction. What is more, the mentality of the men of law acted to preserve and to renew the force of legal tradition; for the doctrinal origins of the Code can be traced back not only to old regime jurisprudence, notably to the work of Jean Domat and R.-J. Pothier (accounting for over half the 2281 articles), but also to Roman law, which had furnished Napoleon's primary model, especially in matters of property and the partriarchal family. "The Revolution has made possible a new creation," wrote the earliest commentator, Riffé, in 1803; and the Code was indeed surrounded by the official rhetoric of rationalism and natural law. Yet, in view both of the form and ideological intent of Napoleon's legislative work, it is

Latour, *Jacques de Maleville (1741–1824) l'homme politique et le jurisconsulte* (Bordeaux, 1929).

35 Louis Gruffy, *La Vie et oeuvre juridique de Merlin de Douai* (1934).

36 Fenet, III-VI; *CODE CIVIL des François, Avec les Discours qui ont éte prononcés par les Orateurs du Gouvernement, nommé par le PREMIER CONSUL pour exposer, devant le Corps Législatif, le motif les Lois dont le Code est Composé (an XIII)* (1804); J. Maleville, *Analyse raisonnée de la discussion du Code Civil* (1805); Locré, *Esprit du Code Napoleon, tiré de la discussion* (1805); and see also A. J. Arnaud, *Les Origines doctrinales du code civil français* (1969); R. Batiza, *Domat, Pothier and the Code* (n. p., 1973); and *Le Code Civil, 1804–1904, Livre du Centenaire*, 2 vols. (1904).

hard to disagree with Riffé's further acknowledgement, that "This code is founded mainly on Roman law."[37]

After the coup of 18 Brumaire the Roman analogy was increasingly plain, for the next day Napoleon inaugurated his legislative designs, and a month later a *senatusconsultum* established both a "senate" and a "tribunate" as well as his own "consular" office. In these early months of ostentatious republicanism Napoleon fumed at an anonymous pamphlet entitled "Caesar, Cromwell, Napoléon"; but an adviser remarked that there was nothing to criticize except the timing. A better parallel however, was the imperial author of the *Corpus Civilis*; for Napoleon truly fancied himself to be the new Justinian, with his "citizen-redactors" recapitulating the roles of Tribonian and his colleagues who assembled the texts of Romano-Byzantine law. The story is told that during the first months of Revolution, while confined to his quarters in Auxonne, Napoleon had spent twenty-four hours in a room with only Justinian's Digest for company, and his recollection of the work had amazed his colleagues during debates.[38] Justinian, too, had achieved mighty conquests, abolished the republican constitution of the Consulate (as Napoleon would soon do), and claimed a popular mandate—the Rousseauist General Will being the counterpart of the legendary *lex regia* by which the Roman *princeps* claimed his authority. The imperialist formula "What pleases the prince has the force of law" was cited regularly by Bonapartist as well as Byzantine jurists.[39]

Like Justinian, too, Napoleon provided for a pedagogical and professional foundation for his legislative creation—to produce Bonapartist jurists like the "Justinian's freshmen" (*novi Justiniani*, as the Byzantine law students were called). Neither the *Académie de Législation* (first called the "Institute of Jurisprudence and Political Economy") nor the *Université de Jurisprudence*, founded respectively in 1800 and 1801, really accomplished this, although various associated publications began to collect materials for a new jurisprudence and to represent it as a "science" no less essential than legislation—"the first of all the sciences . . . because it linked man at once to heaven and to earth."[40] To replace these institutions of the *droit intermédiaire* the law school of Paris finally opened in 1806 and began a distinguished tradition of academic jurisprudence, including C. E. Delvincourt, a former advocate installed as first professor of the "Code Napoléon," and J. F. Berthelot, professor of Roman law (as he had been before the Revolution).[41] In 1806 there were some 2000 students enrolled in the

37 Riffé-Caubray, *Les Pandectes françaises* (1803); and on property, *Code civil*, arts. 544–45.

38 Louis Madelin, *Histoire du Consulat et de l'Empire*, VI (1939), 186ff.

39 *Digest* I.4.1: "Quod principi placuit legis habet vigorem."

40 *Journal de Jurisprudence* (publié par l'Académie de Législation, n.d.), 5f; cf. *Procès-verbal de la séance d'ouverture de l'école de droit de Paris, le Mardi 5 Frimaire au 2me année de L'Empire et du règne du NAPOLEON* (n. d.), 14, and Rondonneau, *Napoléon le grand, considéré comme législateur* (1808).

41 Delvincourt, *Institutes du droit civil français* (1808), and Berthelot, *Apologie du droit*

twelve new French law schools, the first of a new generation of professional jurists who, encouraged by the restoration of the Order of Advocates in 1810, would begin applying the Code to a modernizing society.

Another striking parallel between the French and Byzantine emperors was the determination that their codifications should, in Justinian's words, "be valid for all times." Yet it was precisely the creations of the systems of legal education that created the "vain discord of posterity" dreaded by Justinian and witnessed by Napoleon. What one historian has called the "renaissance of legal studies under the Consulate" acted not only to do but also to undo the Emperor's will.[42] What came out of the pandora's box opened up by Napoleon's new lawyers, practical as well as academic jurists, was that most fearful of all juridical concepts—"interpretation." Justinian had explicitly banned the practice; and common juridical wisdom, repeated by Robespierre among others, was that the interpretation of the law belonged exclusively to the power that had originally made it. Thus A. S. G. Coffinières, in his collection of Napoleonic jurisprudence (based on decisions of the Conseil d'Etat and the Court of Cassation) repeated the old Romanist adage that the power of interpretation was the power of legislation (*ejus est legem interpretari, cujus est legem condere*)—adding that today (1809) such power belonged exclusively to *Sa Majesté*.[43]

During the deliberations over the Code, Bonapartist jurists had professed shock at even hearing the term mentioned during discussions of article 5 of the Code. Through the loophole of "interpretation" all the abuses of the old regime would return, worried one magistrate, and "the empire of [feudal] custom would be reborn."[44] This warning was prophetic, for in the wake of codification neo-feudal constructions indeed resurfaced both through judicial decisions (publicized in the collections of jurisprudence of Merlin and others) and through those academic commentaries which, as Baron Locré lamented, "kill the law".[45]

In the long run neither the Emperor's will nor the legal fundamentalism of Jacobins and Bonapartists could withstand the encroachments of social reality or the process of legal interpretation required to accommodate the law to the shifting contours of that reality. And without such license to interpret, asked

romain ou de la raison écrite (n.d.), responding to criticism by Garat; cf. Perreau's course of 1799, in *Elémens de législation naturelle* (1834, 2nd ed.).

42 H. Hayem, "La Renaissance des études juridiques en France sous le Consulat," *Nouvelle revue historique du droit français et étranger*, 29 (1905), a volume containing other useful studies.

43 *Le Code Napoléon expliqué par les décisions suprèmes de la cour de cassation et du conseil d'état* (1809).

44 Fenet, VI, 169 (Maillir-Garat); and in general see J. Bonnecase, *La Pensée juridique française* (Bordeaux, 1933), and E. Gaudemet, *L'interprétation du Code Civil en France depuis 1804* (Geneva, 1935), 13.

45 Locré, *Esprit*, 1: "On a dit, avec raison, de ces commentateurs qu'ils tuent la loi."

readers of Montesquieu, how could there be "judicial power" comparable to the legislative power of the state? "There were judges before there were laws," argued one defender of interpretation—and, implicitly, of the old magistrature which had so effectively preserved this principle.

In 1810 Henrion de Pansey published a defense of "judicial authority" (including *inamovabilité*), associating it with the old legal tradition, (which he had celebrated in his first book forty years before on the legendary sixteenth-century jurist Charles Dumoulin, hero of the codification movement) and the "fundamental laws" of the old "tempered monarchy," and citing the sixteenth-century Chancellor de l'Hôpital that "the prince should never meddle with the exercise of judicial authority."[46]

Notions of judicial discretion were reinforced by more theoretical liberties taken by academic jurists with the text of the law. Succeeding the "cult of 1804" was a series of schools of interpretation which (virtually recapitulating the history of Roman law in its European afterlife) moved still further from the intention of the original legislator in the effort to accommodate the law to the social and economic conditions of the nineteenth century. Such interpretations, academic and judicial, entailed, at least surreptitiously, a return to the old legal traditions and old regime attitudes and practices, especially with regard to ideas about the role of the judiciary, about the stabilizing function of the family, and about that fundamental and problematic expression of the human condition, "absolute" (but not absolute) private property. In various ways there was, as Sagnac put it, "a return to custom."[47]

In the wake of revolution and empire, in other words, feudalism and corporatism raised their heads, or at least lurked beneath the surface of the jurisprudence generated by the Code; and the justification was still that time-honored formula preserved in Justinian's Digest, that "Custom is the best interpreter of the law."[48] Moreover, Napoleon's magistracy was a continuation of the judicial establishment of the old regime, not only through preservation of the old esprit which haunted the corridors of the Palais (home of the Court of Cassation as it had been of the Parlement, and adorned with portraits of old regime jurists) but also through the careers of particular lawyers, judicial Talleyrands who also "survived" and carried over into the Restoration many elements of the old legal mentality.

They had survived, of course, by serving, in lawyerly fashion, many masters and clients—and many values. In the 1790s the *hommes de loi* had learned the language of Jacobinism, and a decade later they adopted as easily the new

46 *De l'authorité judiciaire*, in *Oeuvres juridiques*, and cf. Fenet, VI, 151.

47 *La Législation civile*, 187, and see Valette, *De la Durée persistante de l'ensemble du droit civil pendant et depuis la révolution* (1872).

48 *Digest*, I, 3, 37: "Consuetudo optima legum interpres"; and see my "The Idea of Custom in European Law, Society, and Culture," *The Transmission of Culture in Early Modern Europe*, ed. A. Grafton and A. Blair (Philadelphia, 1990), 131–72.

imperial style. Prudently, the faculty of law cheered as loudly for Napoleon on his return in 1814 as they had, and would, for Louis XVIII on his first, and second, restorations.[49] After such formalities, of course, men of law went about their business, which had to do above all with property and succession questions in the wake of political disruption, and so, in a legalistic way, with reshaping the new post-revolutionary world, or in some cases to restore the old pre-revolutionary one—all, needless to say, in the language of Restoration society.

The "men of law" who survived (and sometimes even profitted from) the Revolution helped to carry on or to create several conduits of old regime learning, attitudes, habits, and values, which went beyond the historical curiosity of scholars like Augustin Thierry or resentment of victims like Fournel. As one advocate wrote in 1814, "The glory of the bar is like a beautiful tree whose branches seem from a distance to touch the ground."[50] In academic and professional terms the old legal tradition, with roots in the old regime and contacts with the people, was given renewed vitality, and its members tried not only to reestablish their position as legal experts and arbiters but also to represent their discipline as the essential "social science" of the Restoration period. In 1810 Cotelle, professor of French law under Napoleon, took up the baton of the old Order of Advocates dropped by Tronchet in 1789 and, along with this symbol, some of the projects of the order. In 1822 Cotelle's successor Billecocq revived the "conferences" held in the Library of the Advocates (also restored, although the books had been dispersed during the Revolution) as a way of reinforcing the old esprit de corps—both by instructing young advocates and by strengthening ties between lawyers and judges.[51]

Upon the restoration of the Bourbon dynasty—"in the nineteenth year of the reign of Louis XVIII"—the lawyers were ready to adapt to the new Charter and the language of neo-royalism and constitutional monarchy. A.-A.-P. Dupin (the very first graduate of Napoleon's law school) addressed his colleagues (25 June 1814) to remind them that the purpose of this document was "to seek [its] principles in the French character and in the venerable monuments of the past." "Why has the ancient judiciary been so highly regarded and the tribunals of the Revolution so little?" Dupin went on to ask.[52] The answer was that the

[49] G. Colmet Daage, *L'École de droit de Paris en 1814, 1815 et 1816* (1887); cf. A. J. Tonneau, *Un jurisconsulte de transition*, Charles Toullier (Rennes, 1962), 171; and see especially Werner Giesselman, *Die brumairische Elite: Kontinuität und Wandel der französischen Führungsschicht zwischen Ancien Regime und Julimonarchie* (Stuttgart, 1976).

[50] Gibault, *Guide de l'avocat* (1814).

[51] Billecocq, *Discours prononcé pour la réprise des conférences de la Bibliothèque des avocats* (mardi 12 nov. 1822), invoking "nos sages dévanciers."

[52] Dupin, *Les Magistrats d'autrefois de la révolution (25 juin 1814)*; and cf. *Mémoires* (1855). There is still no adequate biography of this juridical Guizot; and the same goes for many of these jurists—Bernardi, Gin, Bergasse, Guichard, and others.

old jurists had judged according to conscience, and he himself spent much of his later scholarly efforts (over almost sixty years) championing and publishing the work of his predecessors going back especially to the golden age of French legal science in the sixteenth century, represented especially by Antoine Loisel's *Pasquier, ou dialogue des avocats* (1602), which was a landmark and a centerpiece in the canon of the French legal profession and in the defense of "judicial power."[53]

From the standpoint of intellectual history the story of the men of law in France from old regime to Restoration can be seen as a grand struggle for the control of words. After 1789 they had to learn, in political terms, first the new language of natural rights and "general will," then that of republican and imperial government, and finally that of constitutional monarchy.[54] The dissolution of the old Order of Advocates was accompanied by efforts to expunge its symbols and language. In order to erase the memory of the past an emperor of China had tried to burn all books, wrote J. E. D. Bernardi; the Revolution went one better by rendering the old books of authority not only obsolete but unintelligible.[55]

Yet the men of law kept much of the old lingo, and Portalis and his colleagues in particular spoke the same language as Dumoulin and Pothier. Discussing the rights of ownership, Henrion de Pansey apologized for using the word *seigneur*, adding that he had no desire to revive the old "feudal idiom";[56] but in fact, like Toullier and other conservative colleagues, Henrion did continue to exploit old feudal "opinions" and customary practices; and of course Dupin's scholarly labors were intended to resurrect the language and life of his colleagues across several centuries of professional activity (and across the caesura created by the Revolution) and to reconcile them with the legacy of revolution.

Like the Bourbons, then, the men of law of the older generation seemed to have forgotten nothing, but unlike that unlucky family, they had learned a great deal. Had they, however, learned enough? In the Restoration the legal profession found new life and a new relationship with politics and the new propertied, ruling elite, with whom the "fortunes" (favorite word of magistrates and bourgeois) of the lawyers was closely bound up. Over a generation of noisy

53 Reprinted in Dupin's famous handbook for lawyers, *Profession d'avocat*, 2 vols. (1832), first edition (by Camus) 1770; and cf. Henri Bordier, *Le Archives de la France* (1855), 2–15; also D. R. Kelley, "Ancient Verses on New Ideas: Legal Tradition and the French Historical School," *History and Theory* 3 (1987), 319–38.

54 P. L. C. Gin, for one, had taken up the old theme of linguistic virtuosity in *De l'Eloquence du Barreau* (1803; lst ed. 1767), remarking (3) that "le nouveau barreau s'élève sur les ruines de l'ancien."

55 *De l'Origine et des progrés de la législation française* (1816), introduction, remarking that "le fil de nos traditions nationales sera totalement rompu"; and (iii) on "property."

56 *Oeuvres judiciaires*, 327: "On ne suppose pas l'intention de faire revivre l'idiome féodale."

political experience lawyers had learned the uses of the word, and concept, "revolution"; and they would put it to good use in the constitutional transformation of 1830, sometimes referred to, because of its aftermath as well as inception, as the "revolution of the advocates."

Dupin, in the discourse he gave in 1829 when he became *bâtonnier* of the Order of Advocates, celebrated the old legal tradition, quoting Montesquieu's famous aphorism, to "illuminate the laws by history and history by the laws".[57] Read Bodin, he advised his younger colleagues, read Coquille, Loyseau, and especially Dumoulin; and you will "march with the power of five centuries of precedents." Dupin cited again the final words of Loisel's *Pasquier*, demanding that they "conserve for our Order the rank and honor which our ancestors have acquired by their merits and works in order to pass them on to our successors." This was the basis of Dupin's idea of "revolution," and the premises he maintained as an active supporter of the Orleanist party and participant in the "three glorious" July days the following summer. Less than a month later he dedicated the new edition of his *Profession d'Avocat* (1830) to Louis-Philippe (on whose *Conseil privé* he had served "for many years") and thanked him for receiving the deputation from the Order of Advocates after the July Revolution and for giving his support.[58] Like Loisel, Dupin addressed his book to the advocates of his time as a "as a work of family, of community," which brought the wisdom and the prejudices of the centuries to the July Monarchy.

No more than the July Monarchy itself, however, were jurists like Dupin, for all their learning, able to come to terms with new economic and social realities, especially the class divisions and other dislocations of an industrializing society in which Labor was coming to count as much as Property. The new forms of "social science"—political economy and then sociology—attacked such questions directly, while the old jurisprudence was still burdened with its ancient heritage, forms, and values, and of course its commitment to prevailing political structures. In retrospect the Revolution of 1848 transformed the legal tradition more fundamentally than the Revolution of 1789 had done, and the contending ideologies of liberalism and socialism made old-fashioned jurisprudence increasingly irrelevant to—or rather rendered it powerless before—a politics preoccupied by the Social Question and the specter of Revolution.[59]

After 1848, then, the old legal tradition was apparently dead, and its claims to be a science of society were largely discredited. With the experience, the process, and the historical interpretation of Revolution, however, its connections were profound and immediate; and historians of the revolutionary period and its various aftermaths cannot afford to neglect the insights offered by the

57 *Profession d'avocat*, 5.

58 *Profession d'avocat*, 2 vols. (1832), iii, 721.

59 See, e.g., Gaston Morin, *La Révolte des faits contre le Code* (1920) and *La Révolte du droit contre le Code* (1945).

"men of law" in their struggles to grasp and to exercise control over history. We may pretend, with the help of modern social sciences, to achieve on a grand scale that old hermeneutical dream, to know the past better than it knew itself; but this will not exhaust the processes of historical understanding and the many layers of historical experience; and in these terms the Revolution remains—and changes—with us.

INDEX